Modern Southeast Asia Series

Stephen F. Maxner, General Editor

Jerry Daniels, the Hmong, and the CIA

HOG'S EXIT

Gayle L. Morrison

Texas Tech University Press

This book is typeset in Minion Pro. The paper used in this book meets the minimum requirements of ANSI/NISO Z39.48-1992 (R1997). ∞

Designed by Barbara Werden
Maps by Gayle L. Morrison

Library of Congress Control Number: 2013936485
ISBN (cloth): 978-0-89672-791-5
ISBN (paper): 978-0-89672-792-2
ISBN (e-book): 978-0-89672-793-9

Printed in the United States of America
13 14 15 16 17 18 19 20 21 / 9 8 7 6 5 4 3 2 1

Texas Tech University Press | Box 41037 | Lubbock, Texas 79409-1037 USA
800.832.4042 | ttup@ttu.edu | www.ttupress.org

In loving memory
Timothy G. Eldridge (1956–2009)
Smokejumper [MSO '82]

"You are the dream of love I dreamt about forever."
|| Puccini's *La Bohème* ||

One ‖ Bangkok: late April–May 6, 1982

Two ‖ Missoula: May 2–8, 1982

Three ‖ Missoula: May 8–10, 1982

Four ‖ After the Burial: May 11, 1982–2012

Maps

HMONG refugees started to arrive in the United States from the "secret war" in Laos not long after the Vietnam War ended in 1975. In 1978 I started working in Hmong refugee resettlement at Lao Family Community (LFC) in Santa Ana, California. At that time there was almost a complete lack of information about the Hmong from Laos. I wanted to know more about the history of the people I was working with, so I started taping oral history interviews with my Hmong coworkers. In those early interviews, I sometimes heard guarded mention of a man with the unlikely name of "Mr. Hog." This "Hog" fellow was an American who supposedly worked for the Central Intelligence Agency and had stuck by the Hmong through the difficult war years. I was skeptical about this story. Then I heard he was working with the Hmong who were in refugee camps in Thailand, and I learned his real name was Jerry Daniels.

In 1982 I was still at LFC when the Hmong world around me was badly jolted by the news of the untimely death of Mr. Hog. Hmong leaders headed to Montana to attend his funeral; later I heard it was a three-day traditional Hmong ceremony. The unusual circumstances of a traditional Hmong funeral ceremony being organized and implemented to honor an American CIA case officer was something I didn't forget.

My oral history interviews with Hmong coworkers continued and then expanded to include the Hmong community at large. Over time I heard more about Jerry "Hog" Daniels, but it was 1997 before I took serious action and started to focus on recording oral histories that eventually would capture both the process of the traditional Hmong funeral ceremony and the layers of events and emotions surrounding the life and death of Daniels. This Preface includes a brief look at some of the methodological, cultural, and historical considerations that went into my research and writing.

Good oral history research is a slow process, time- and labor-intensive. For ten years I steadily uncovered a network of people who knew Jerry "Hog" Daniels. In addition to the Hmong, there were family members, coworkers, and a multitude of good friends who spanned continents and decades. In the end I audiotaped and transcribed interviews with almost 100 of these folks, more than 80 percent of whom had attended either the memorial service for Daniels in Bangkok or his funeral in Montana. Those interviewed were roughly 70 percent American, 30 percent Hmong (born in Laos and now living in the United States), along with three Thai nationals. My objective was to document in detail their firsthand experiences of Daniels as told in each person's unique voice. Initial interviews provided the foundation of individual accounts; subsequent interviews (multiple meetings with each person) allowed participants time to reflect between interviews and gave me the opportunity to probe for deeper memories and speculations. Eventually I intertwined narrative pieces

pulled from individual memoirs to produce a dynamic picture of the simple life pleasures that Daniels relished as well as the reality of responsibilities of the life he led.

In order to create an accurate sense of the traditional Hmong funeral ceremony, I
spent more than a year attending many Hmong funerals and interviewing numerous
experienced and knowledgeable Hmong funeral practitioners. This exposure produced a composite text that is narrated by a single unnamed voice. The Hmong funeral as described in this book is consistent with most Hmong family/clan spirit
beliefs [*peb cov dab quas*]. The details of how the ceremony was modified for the
funeral for Jerry Daniels came from his Hmong funeral organizers.

Because this work is oral history, I have chosen not to use [*sic*] to mark where an
error appears in an interview or letter; I feel that is unnecessary. However, a brief
review of my choices regarding Hmong name order, Southeast Asian place names,
and Hmong language will assist the reader's entry into the world of *Hog's Exit*. Those
who are not familiar with Hmong name order should be alerted that while most of
the Hmong personal names are westernized (given name first followed by family/
clan name), traditional Hmong name order is family/clan name first followed by
given name. In *Hog's Exit* a person may be referred to either way. For example, Cha
Moua uses the westernized name order (Cha Moua) when referring to himself; others who refer to him often use the traditional Hmong name order (Moua Cha). In
addition, most adult men acquire another name component, often building on a
childhood name (*shown here in italics*), as in Cher *Cha* Moua or Tong *Su* Vang. These
"adult names" are well known in the Hmong world, where a man might use all varia-
tions of his name depending on the context. Regarding place names in Laos and
Thailand, with one major exception (Long Cheng rather than Long Tieng) I have
used the war-years spellings; the reader should be advised that some of these spellings have changed on more recent maps. For Hmong words, White Hmong Roman-
ized Popular Alphabet (RPA) spelling appears throughout. Readers will also benefit
from knowing that each chapter begins with summary of that chapter's contents.

"Hmong" and "Meo" are terms that refer to a tribal people who live in the high
rugged mountains of Laos, Vietnam, Thailand, and China. Both terms appear in
Hog's Exit. While "Meo" would have been in common use during much of the time
that Daniels spent in Laos and Thailand, modern Hmong perceive it as a denigrating
term. Since Hmong people in the United States are called (and call themselves)
"Hmong," most of the speakers I interviewed preferred to use the term "Hmong"
even if they would have used "Meo" at the time the story took place.

I have one final thought to share on the overall structure of this book. If *Hog's Exit*
were to be presented in a form as lean as haiku, it would be limited to the four Fragments. The first three Fragments set the stage and function as a prologue. The fourth
one functions as an epilogue. The rest of the book expands the remarkable story that
is only suggested in the imagery of the Fragments.

WOULD like to extend a warm and sincere thank-you to everyone I interviewed over the ten years it took to research and write this book. A very special thanks goes to Roger Wax-eng Thao, Hmong culture and funeral expert, who worked extensively with me so that I might better understand the complex Hmong funeral rituals. Another very special thanks goes to the entire Daniels family, especially Kent "Dan" Daniels, for multiple interviews, and unlimited access to photos, letters, audiocassette tapes, and memorabilia, as well as unflagging enthusiasm for this project. This book couldn't have been done without the support of the Daniels family.

A special thanks goes to the Missoula Smokejumpers, especially Tim Eldridge [MSO '82]. As a seasoned and knowledgeable smokejumper, Tim cheerfully answered hundreds of questions and was the reader for the technical and historical accuracy of the smokejumper sections. His native-son love for Montana was insightful and inspiring. Additional thanks goes to the National Smokejumper Association, in particular Chuck Sheley [CJ '59], Bill Fogarty [MSO '57], and Chris Sorensen.

Friends who graciously hosted me in my travels were Nai V. and Pheng Moua of Fresno, California; Laura Leonelli of Sacramento, California; Sally Peterson of Raleigh-Durham, North Carolina; and Nancy and Toby Scott of Helmville, Montana. Thank you all for your generous hospitality.

For assistance with photographs, thanks goes to Dan Gamelin, Paul C. Jurney, Peter F. Morrison, John Willheim, and all those I interviewed who dug through their basements, attics, garages, and closets to locate old photos. Additional thanks goes to the K. Ross Toole Archives at the University of Montana–Missoula for access to photo archives, Missoula Technology and Development Center, Region One office of the U.S. Forest Service, and the Air America Archives at University of Texas–Dallas. Special thanks goes to Peter F. Morrison for technical assistance on creating appropriate maps.

Others who have earned my appreciation are MacAlan Thompson, who consistently supplied prompt and accurate answers to questions about arcane information; Anne Frank, former librarian at the Southeast Asia collection, University of California–Irvine, who located numerous elusive articles and books; Gail Hanowell and all of the reference librarians at the Missoula Public Library; Bao V. and Mouasu Bliaya for "who's who" information regarding the Missoula Hmong, 1968–74; Larry Woodson and Susan Smith Finn for providing letters and photos; Mrs. Norma Hughes and her mother, Leone Oxford, who at ninety-nine years old located her 1982 diary in order to confirm the date of the spirit-release ceremony for Jerry Daniels; Sutayut Tam Osornprasop and Khun Xuwicha Hiranprueck for answering questions about Thai culture, language, and history; Jacques Lemoine for permission to quote extensively from his lovely book, *Showing the Way*; Gina Froelich for technical consulting in several of her multiple areas of expertise; Roger Warner for providing introductions, editing suggestions, and much encouragement; manuscript readers at various points: Tim Eldridge, AvaDale Johnson, Donna Kennedy, and Deirdre McNamer; miscellaneous assistance from Arthur J. Dommen, Fred Donner [MSO '59], Karen Harper, and Elizabeth Kirton; and Robert Beckley [RAC '83], Robert Hubble [MSO '91], Suzy Marzalek, and Suzy Moser—friends who helped more than they realize. To all of these people and to anyone I inadvertently left out, I thank you.

June 11, 1941: Jerrold Barker Daniels is the fourth son born to Ronald L. "Bob" and Louise Daniels in Palo Alto, California. The Daniels family moves to Montana when Jerry is ten years old.

1959: Jerry Daniels graduates from Missoula County High School in Missoula, Montana. From 1958–60 he is a smokejumper for the U.S. Forest Service. In fall 1960 Daniels enrolls as a freshman at the University of Montana in Missoula.

1961: John F. Kennedy takes office as U.S. president. Bill Lair, a paramilitary officer working for the Central Intelligence Agency (CIA), makes covert contact in Laos with anticommunist leader Lieutenant Colonel Vang Pao of the Royal Lao Army (FAR); Lair is the founder and architect of paramilitary operations in northern Laos ["Project Momentum"]. Shortly thereafter Jerry Daniels is hired to work as a cargo kicker for Air America, a CIA proprietary airline contracted to drop arms and supplies to Vang Pao's tribal soldiers in Laos. In Marana, Arizona, Gar Thorsrud establishes Intermountain Aviation, a fledgling CIA proprietary.

1962: Geneva Accords affirm Laos is a neutral state, prohibiting foreign military intervention. All but a few American military and CIA personnel are withdrawn from Laos. North Vietnam ignores the agreement and a substantial number of communist North Vietnamese Army (NVA) troops remain there.

1962: After air dropping cargo over Laos and Tibet, Daniels returns to the United States to work for Intermountain Aviation. In May and June Daniels participates in CIA's "Operation Coldfeet," a Skyhook operation contracted to Intermountain. In northern Laos, CIA constructs a secret airstrip in the remote Long Cheng valley.

November 1963: Lyndon B. Johnson assumes the office of U.S. president after the assassination of President John F. Kennedy.

1960–64: Daniels and other former smokejumpers work alternately for Air America as cargo kickers over Laos, and for Intermountain Aviation in Arizona. Between fall 1960 and summer 1964 Daniels completes eight quarters of college at the University of Montana.

1964: In August Congress passes the Gulf of Tonkin Resolution, which effectively declares war on North Vietnam. In December the air war in northern Laos begins with "Operation Barrel Roll." CIA's "secret war" in Laos is under the direct control of William Sullivan, U.S. ambassador to Laos. The most important military headquarters in Laos is at Long Cheng in Military Region 2, the stronghold of Hmong leader General Vang Pao. Daniels quits Intermountain and attends winter quarter at the University of Montana.

1965: In March, "Rolling Thunder" air strikes begin in North Vietnam. In October, the CIA's Far East chief Bill Colby visits Long Cheng. In December, Daniels returns to Laos as an air operations "Customer" assigned to Lima Site 36, Na Khang, in Military Region 2. He remains there until April 1968.

1966: In February there is a major attack on Na Khang by communist troops; Daniels and all defenders are forced to evacuate for several months. In June Richard Helms is sworn in as Director, CIA. The Joint Chiefs of Staff implement "Project 404," assigning 117 American military advisors and five Department of Defense civilians to Laos. In October, U.S. Air Force pilots volunteer for the classified "Steve Canyon" program, flying small 0–1 light spotter airplanes in Laos; these pilots are called Ravens.

1967: In January there is a second major attack on Na Khang; this time the site is successfully defended. The American air war in Laos and North Vietnam expands.

1968: There are 110,000 communist troops in Laos—both Pathet Lao and North Vietnamese Army. Vang Pao's Hmong Special Guerrilla Unit (SGU) army takes heavy casualties. In March the top-secret American radar bombing installation on Phou Pha Thi in northern Laos is overrun by North Vietnamese troops; twelve of the nineteen Americans on the mountain are dead or declared missing. Loss of this site is a major factor in President Johnson declaring a bombing halt over North Vietnam. Also in March, the My Lai massacre in South Vietnam shocks Americans, increasing antiwar sentiment and prompting student strikes in the United States. In April, Daniels takes an extended leave of absence from Laos to return to the University of Montana.

1969: In January, Richard M. Nixon takes office as U.S. president. Daniels graduates from the University of Montana in June. In July, NASA's Apollo 11 is the first U.S. manned moon landing. Half a million "hippies" converge at the Woodstock Festival in late summer. Daniels attends his father's funeral in Montana in December.

1970: The first USAF B-52 bombings in Laos are against the 67,000 North Vietnamese troops there. Daniels is in Virginia for CIA Junior Officer Training. In March, Daniels returns to Laos. On May 4, four people are killed and nine injured by the Ohio National Guard when students at Kent State University protest Nixon's invasion of Cambodia.

1970–73: Daniels works at Long Cheng as CIA's chief of operations and case officer/advisor for General Vang Pao and the Hmong SGU troops.

1973: Ceasefire peace agreements are signed in Paris regarding Vietnam and Laos. The U.S. Agency for International Development (USAID) and CIA develop postwar reconstruction projects in Laos in anticipation of a negotiated and orderly U.S. departure from Southeast Asia.

1974: In February the kidnapping of heiress Patty Hearst produces a media frenzy. In April a new coalition government is formed in Laos. In June all U.S. military personnel and Air America aircraft leave the country. Daniels remains at Long Cheng implementing postwar development projects. President Richard M. Nixon resigns in August after the Watergate scandal; Gerald Ford assumes the office of U.S. president.

1975: In late April a massive U.S. helicopter evacuation takes place in Saigon as South Vietnam is suddenly taken over by communist forces. In May, Daniels organizes the evacuation of General Vang Pao and 2,500 Hmong officers and family members from Long Cheng, Laos, to neighboring Thailand. Daniels works in Thailand with Hmong refugees who fled Laos. In December the coalition government in Laos is replaced by a communist government.

1976: In August, Daniels leaves Thailand and visits Pakistan, Kenya, and Tanzania before arriving in the United States eight days later. He receives a Letter of Commendation from Secretary of State Henry Kissinger for his work in the refugee program. He returns to work in Thailand for the U.S. State Department Refugee Program as chief ethnic affairs officer (EAO) for highland Lao refugees.

1977: Jimmy Carter takes office as U.S. president.

1980: Daniels receives the Superior Honor Award from the Department of State for his work in the refugee program in Thailand, 1979–80. In November, Daniels travels to Nepal for his "Everest safari."

1981: Ronald Reagan takes office as U.S. president. In April/May, Daniels makes his last home-leave visit to the United States. An anticommunist Hmong military resistance in Laos and Thailand strengthens in response to continued harsh treatment of civilians by the communist Lao government. In November the United States claims that there is clear evidence that the USSR is using chemical weapons in Southeast Asia, especially against the Hmong in Laos; the USSR denies the charges.

May 1, 1982: The U.S. Embassy in Bangkok, Thailand, reports that Jerrold B. Daniels, a U.S. government employee, was found dead in his apartment.

May 4, 1982: A Buddhist ceremony is held for Daniels at Wat Mongkut in Bangkok, Thailand. Preparations begin for shipping the body of Jerry Daniels to Montana.

May 8–10, 1982: Jerrold "Hog" Daniels is mourned in a three-day traditional Hmong funeral ceremony in Missoula, Montana. He is buried in the Missoula Cemetery, May 10, 1982.

HOG'S EXIT

MISSOULA, Montana, sits astride the Clark Fork River, 100 miles west of the Continental Divide on the forested side of the northern Rockies. Ringed by gentle hills covered with sage and prairie grasses with rugged mountains beyond, in summer Missoula is the picturesque hub of five valleys and a coveted destination for world-class trout fishing. Known as the Garden City of Montana, in winter this lively university town is energized—not bound—by ice and snow.

Missoula is the hometown of Jerry "Hog" Daniels—a town where long winters and an egalitarian spirit bring together laborers, professionals, college students, and business owners to share the many local saloons. Take a seat at one of the older drinking establishments, mention the name of "Jerry Daniels" to patrons of a certain age, and over a pint of beer the men who knew him may talk to you about his quirky humor, physical endurance, and intelligence. The women will smile and tell you about those blue, blue eyes and his exceptional good looks. Both will say he was a true Montanan: independent, honest, hard-working with a lot of grit. And when he wasn't working, he hated to waste his time with sobriety.

Like many boys in rural America in the 1950s, young Jerry Daniels spent much of his time tromping through woods and fields with a fishing pole and rifle. At seventeen, his natural inclination for outdoor adventure and physical challenge led him to become a smokejumper, the elite firefighters who parachute from airplanes into remote terrain to fight fire. His work ethic and good nature caught the eye of his supervisor. Daniels was barely nineteen years old when his name was put on a short list that was "sent east." The year was 1960.

Next door to Vietnam, a clandestine side of the Vietnam War was just getting started in the small land-locked Kingdom of Laos. The U.S. Central Intelligence Agency (CIA) was surreptitiously trolling for energetic young men with the very skill set that the smokejumpers had: physical stamina, a can-do spirit, knowledge of parachutes, and the survival skills of a good woodsman. The cream of the crop were quietly invited to go to war in Southeast Asia against communist forces in Laos. They would perform their duties secretly, working for the CIA on the Lao side of the border, in direct support of U.S. foreign policy in Vietnam. An overseas adventure appealed to Daniels; he and several of his smokejumper friends signed on.

In Laos Daniels met one of the local hilltribe people, the Hmong. They were short, stocky, and tough, and their simple lifestyle and blunt speech suited him. Within a few years these hilltribesmen were transformed into an army of Special Guerrilla Unit (SGU) soldiers. They were led by the charismatic and fiercely anticommunist General Vang Pao. Years later, working his way up through the ranks, Jerry "Hog" Daniels would become Vang Pao's CIA advisor.

In 1962 the U.S. government publicly recognized Laos as a "neutral" country, outside the boundaries of the incipient war in Vietnam. In reality, Laos became a second theater of war that grew from modest and deniable CIA support for self-defense by local villagers into fierce fighting between anticommunist and procommunist troops. Vang Pao's anticommunist SGU irregulars were trained, armed, and supported entirely by the Central Intelligence Agency. The pro-communist Pathet Lao troops and North Vietnamese Army (NVA) troops were backed by North Vietnam. For fifteen hard years, the Hmong warriors and their families carried the heaviest burden of America's secret war in Laos.

Hog Daniels lived with the Hmong at Long Cheng, the highly classified CIA-Hmong operations air base in remote northeastern Laos. There he earned the respect and confidence of both General Vang Pao and the Hmong guerrilla troops. In 1975, shortly after South Vietnam abruptly fell to communist forces, the United States was hastily pulling out of Laos as well, without much of a backward glance. By mid-May, Hog Daniels was the only American still on the ground at Long Cheng. At great personal risk he set up and accomplished an air evacuation that moved General Vang Pao and 2,500 of the CIA's beleaguered Hmong allies to Thailand. He would not abandon the people he had worked with for so long.

When Laos was lost to communist forces and pro-U.S. Hmong fled across the river border to escape the new regime, Daniels stayed and worked for six years in the refugee camps in Thailand, continuing to be a pivotal agent in U.S.-Hmong history. As an experienced and highly knowledgeable CIA man on loan to the State Department, he was the very best at sorting out bona fide refugees from Laos. By now, half of his life had been spent in Southeast Asia—fighting enemy troops, dealing with government bureaucracies, and enjoying an occasional release in the casual bars and indulgent sex markets of the cities. At five feet ten inches and 160 pounds, he was still trim and active with only a hint of softening around those blue eyes and along the jawline.

At forty-one years old, Daniels knew he had done about all he could do for the Hmong refugees in Thailand. With increasing intent his thoughts turned to home: the tall timber; the trout that grow big in the deep cold water of Flathead Lake; the geese, grouse, and antelope that live in the dull shimmer of eastern Montana's vast wheat fields. He had land to develop, good friends to reconnect with, beers to drink, and deer to slay. It was almost time to go.

In April 1982 the report of the sudden death of Daniels in Bangkok devastated his family and shocked his friends, Americans and Hmong alike. The U.S. Embassy in Bangkok promptly determined his death to be accidental, yet concealed all critical evidence from its investigation and permanently sealed his casket before shipping it home. Questions about his death went unanswered, immediately fueling dark suspicions about what really happened to Daniels. Why all the mystery? Was there a cover-up?

While the Daniels family was numb with grief, the Hmong who had worked with Daniels stepped forward to organize his funeral. He had been a bridge from their homeland of Laos to the refugee camps in Thailand to resettlement in the United States. Now they would be a bridge for him. In a three-day ceremony held in Missoula, timeless Hmong rituals instructed the soul of Jerry Daniels on a spirit journey that took him past ghosts and demons, and across harsh landscapes to rejoin the ancestors. While Hmong friends stayed at the funeral home to attend to his soul, American friends gathered in downtown saloons to swap stories about his remarkable and colorful life.

Ultimately, the funeral of Jerry "Hog" Daniels provides a window into what was most important to the two distinct cultures in which Daniels lived: the Hmong desire to ritually ensure safe passage of the deceased—letting him go forward to his next life—and the American desire to keep the departed close and alive through memories and storytelling. Both cultures honored a man they deeply loved, a man whose reputation had made him a living legend. And both questioned his mysterious death: What was the truth inside the sealed casket?

GREGG ELOVICH

(e-mail sent to author, 1999)

Howdy:

I'm looking for information on a CIA officer assigned as an advisor to General Vang Pao during the war in Laos. I've heard the wildest stories about Jerry, including that his death in postwar Thailand was faked to cover his return to Laos as a godlike freedom fighter. Some believe that Jerry didn't die in Bangkok. This belief is based on a rumor that Jerry's coffin was too small to hold a man of his stature, that it was never opened to verify that Jerry's body was in it, and that Jerry is alive wandering the hills of Laos seeking revenge. I even had one Hmong acquaintance claim that he had seen Jerry in Texas a few years back.

My interest? There are close to 50,000 Hmong people here in Fresno, California, so I've had the opportunity to brush shoulders with Jerry's helicopter pilot, his body guards, and numerous other associates and acquaintances. The folks I know kept saying, "Jerry told me to do such and such." I thought "Jerry" was just some term of endearment for any American, but then one day this guy brings in a portfolio of photos of him and his companions. Among them was this picture of an American and General Vang Pao. My interpreter took one look at the picture, got all excited and said: *THAT'S JERRY!* And so many other people have spontaneously identified the American as Jerry Daniels, I'm convinced that he did exist as an individual.

I find the myth equal to the reality in that it's the only wide recognition that he's likely to get. Still, I'd like to know more about Jerry Daniels as he really was. Any help you can give me would be most appreciated.

Adios,

Gregg

THOMAS J. "T. J." THOMPSON

A lot of times I go to places and sit down in the bar just to get away. I don't have many guys to drink with anymore, so I don't drink that much now, but I *did*. Probably one of my last real flings was when we put Jerry in the ground. After I came back from that deal, my buddy Toby didn't drink for eleven months and I didn't drink for about four. Anyway, I get to listenin' to those punks sittin' around the bar . . . chewin' tobacco and showin' off their tattoos. Then I get to thinkin' about Hog and Clean and Bag, Kayak and Bamboo, Digger and Ringo. That whole group that was there in Laos. It was like destiny brought us all together during that extremely busy, critical phase. It was an amazing and special chemistry that made a lot of difference.

People who lived in Laos with Jerry, like Clean, they got to know him pretty well. But there's a lot about the way Jerry thought that people overlooked or didn't understand. See, Jerry and I started runnin' around together when we were young in the late '50s and early '60s. We were fightin' fire together in Montana, California, different places. Then we worked together in Arizona and overseas, too. We were young together, we did things together. So you sort of get into each other's heads and understand what and how the other one's thinkin' before they get too old and get inhibited.

Well, anyway, I sit in the bar and I just keep quiet. Because if I told those punks 5 to 10 percent of what we did they'd say I was 90 percent full of bull.

SHUR V. VANGYI

In May 1982 I was living in California. I dreamed that Jerry came to see me and he said, "Long time, no see! I'm coming back home now. I hope you will come and visit me in Missoula. I no longer want to stay in Thailand. In three days I'll be home. I have to adjust to the time difference and jet lag from Thailand to the U.S., but three days will be enough. Then you come visit me in Missoula." That's what he said to me in my dream.

When I woke up, that dream bothered me, you know? For Hmong, when you dream like that, if you are not expecting someone to show up but you see him or her coming tomorrow or the next day, that can be a bad dream, like a bad omen, or it can be real.

I called General Vang Pao. I said to VP, "I had a bad dream. Suddenly Jerry says he's coming home. What do you think?" He said, "Well, maybe he's coming home for real. Don't worry about it." But I still had a bad feeling. If Jerry comes home, who will help the Hmong refugees in Thailand? Three days later I heard that he was dead.

One

BANGKOK

Late April–May 6, 1982

Discovery

TWO State Department cables regarding the death of Jerrold B. Daniels in Bangkok, Thailand; initial reaction from a coworker in Bangkok; diagram of the apartment of Jerry Daniels; reactions from family and friends in Missoula, Montana; reactions from Hmong friends in the United States and American friends in Washington, DC, and Virginia; questions about the odd circumstances of death, including blood oxygen levels; body to be shipped to Montana.

DEPARTMENT OF STATE cable from U.S. Ambassador John Gunther Dean, May 1, 1982

FR AMEMBASSY BANGKOK

TO SECSTATE WASHDC NIACT[1] IMMEDIATE 7733

LIMITED OFFICIAL USE BANGKOK 24254

SUBJECT: UNIDENTIFIED BODY FOUND IN USG EMPLOYEE QUARTERS

1. BODY OF MALE WAS DISCOVERED IN APARTMENT LEASED BY USG EMPLOYEE JERROLD B. DANIELS, AT APPROXIMATELY 1200 HRS LOCAL MAY 1, 1982.

2. BECAUSE OF ADVANCED STATE OF DECOMPOSITION, POLICE HAVE NOT BEEN ABLE TO IDENTIFY DECEASED. EMBASSY IS TRYING TO LOCATE JERROLD B. DANIELS AND ASSISTING POLICE IN IDENTIFYING REMAINS.

3. THERE HAS BEEN PRESS INTEREST AND SPECULATION THAT BODY MAY BE DANIELS. SUGGEST NOK [NEXT OF KIN] NOT BE REPEAT NOT BE NOTIFIED UNTIL POSITIVE IDENTIFICATION OF DECEASED.

4. EMBASSY WILL KEEP DEPARTMENT ADVISED. DEAN

MACALAN THOMPSON, former USAID Laos Refugee Relief Program; former Refugee Program, U.S. Embassy, Bangkok, Thailand

Oh, yes, the old Hog stories still abound.

Jerry Daniels died in his apartment in Bangkok at the end of April 1982, not quite naturally, but not, to the best of my belief, in some "murderous plot." I've never seen the official State Department report or other official reports of death, but what basically happened is that he died of carbon monoxide poisoning.

Do you remember all those years reading in the local papers—the *Bangkok Post*, the *World*, and the *Nation*—about *farangs*, foreigners, dying because of leaking cooking gas tanks in their air-conditioned apartments? I remembered, and in 1979 when I rented a townhouse on Soi 1 Sukhumvit in Bangkok, I had the landlady put an electric hot water heater in the bathroom for just this reason.

Jerry was living alone in an apartment on Soi Lang Suan, close to the U.S. Embassy. He'd been there for several years, and two months prior to his death he had moved to another apartment in the same building. I'd visited him once at the new apartment, and he commented that the louvered windows, just above the main windows in the bedroom, wouldn't stay open. They dropped shut every couple of days and had to be reopened—if you noticed they were shut. This relates in that the probable cause of death was incomplete combustion from the gas water heater in the adjoining bathroom, which allowed the CO gas to leak into the closed-off bedroom. After he died I heard from the U.S. Embassy folks that it looked like Jerry had taken a shower but then had not turned the gas hot water heater all the way off. He was found dead in his bed on Saturday morning, May 1, 1982.

I didn't view Jerry's body but I heard that it was "disfigured" since it had most likely been two or three days from the time he died until he was found. This was in the hot season and evidently the air conditioning in the apartment was not on when he died. I was told his body was "swollen and black" and not too pretty.

I had talked to Jerry by phone at his apartment on Wednesday morning. When he didn't come to work like he was supposed to on Thursday or Friday I was a little pissed off. I put off calling him until Saturday morning. When no one answered the phone I called Tom, a mutual friend from the embassy, and asked him to go over and roust Jerry's ass. It was Tom who found the body and notified the embassy security staff. We figured it was probably sometime Thursday morning when he died.

DEPARTMENT OF STATE cable from U.S. Ambassador John Gunther Dean, May 2, 1982

FM AMEMBASSY BANGKOK

TO SECSTATE WASHDC NIACT IMMEDIATE 7739

LIMITED OFFICIAL USE BANGKOK 24260

SUBJECT: BANGKOK PRESS REPORTS DEATH OF USG EMPLOYEE JERROLD B. DANIELS

REF: BANGKOK 24254

1. BANGKOK THAI AND ENGLISH LANGUAGE MORNING PAPERS DATED MAY 2 REPORT THAT REMAINS FOUND IN APARTMENT OF USG EMPLOYEE (SEE REFTEL) ARE REMAINS OF JERROLD B. DANIELS AND DEATH WAS ACCIDENTAL.

2. NEVERTHELESS, POLICE AUTHORITIES HAVE NOT YET REPEAT NOT YET CONFIRMED REMAINS TO BE THOSE OF DANIELS. SUCH CONFIRMATION EXPECTED TOMORROW MAY 3 AT THE LATEST BUT EMBASSY ATTEMPTING TO OBTAIN EARLIEST POSSIBLE CONFIRMATION.

3. [EMBASSY] POST HAS BEEN UNSUCCESSFUL IN LOCATING JERROLD B. DANIELS, AND EVIDENCE OBTAINED SO FAR INDICATES LIKELIHOOD THAT REMAINS ARE

THOSE OF DANIELS. IN VIEW OF PRESS COVERAGE, POST BELIEVES NOK SHOULD BE
NOTIFIED OF THE POSSIBILITY OF DANIELS DEATH ASAP.
   4. PLEASE ADVISE. DEAN

KENT "DAN THE ANIMAL MAN" DANIELS, brother of Jerry Daniels

When they called me and told me that Jerry was dead, I don't know where the call
came from but it was the middle of the night here in Montana, after bar-closin' time.
Some government officer said, "I've got some bad news." "Oh, yeah? How bad?" He
said, "The worst." I said, "Jerry's dead then." I don't think I had a reaction other than
it was just one of those deals. Why I was that blasé, I don't know. I guess I hadn't seen
him for a while. It wasn't like he died in my arms. You don't drift apart, but it's someone that's not there all the time. Jerry's a goner. Our brother Danny was a goner. And
my dad was a goner, too. That's all you can say about it.

I got up, got dressed. I called Jack, then I drove over to Louise's house to wake her
up to tell her the bad news.

Mrs. NANCY J. DANIELS, wife of Jack Tupper Daniels; sister-in-law of Jerry Daniels

It was really tough the night that Kent called Jack. We were living in New Hampshire,
and it was very early in the morning—still dark outside and we were asleep. When
Kent told Jack that Jerry had died, Jack screamed. I never heard him scream before.
He was lying on the floor on his back with his knees pulled up and he screamed. He
screamed really loud into the phone and kept saying *NO, NO, NO*. Then he rolled
over. That was hard.

CHA MOUA, Hmong friend; Hmong funeral organizer

May 1982. When Jerry died, Jack Stratton called me. Jack Stratton was a good friend
of Louise, Jerry's mother, and a good friend of mine. Jack Stratton called me at home
in the morning and said, "Cha, I heard very bad news." I said, "What, Jack?" He said,
"Jerry died. Louise called me, and I don't know what to do. She is very, very sad right
now. Will you go there and check up on her?" I asked, "What was the cause, Jack? He
got shot or what?" He said, "He died from gas leaking." That is all he told me. Then
he said, "We will find out more."

I went right away to see Louise. I didn't even call her because I wanted to see her
face to face. My wife and I found Louise at home, but we could not do *anything* to
help her because she was so, so shocked. She was so shocked. She heard the news
early that morning, then a little later she got a phone call from the State Department.
In the phone call they said, "A telegram will be delivered to you. The full description
is following and will be at your home soon." A couple hours later they sent her the
official telegram about Jerry's death.

GEU VANG, former colonel, SGU Army, MR2, Laos

Noi called from Thailand to Xang Vang, the director of Lao Family of Minnesota. Xang called about fifteen people to tell us the bad news about Jerry and asked us to meet that day. It was a group that knew Jerry well, people who worked directly for Jerry in Laos and also some former military officers. Xang told us that they will transfer Jerry's body from Bangkok to Montana. He said we need to organize a group to go to Montana to join the funeral.

BOB JOHNSON, former Highland Section chief, JVA, Thailand; regional director, International Rescue Committee (IRC), Seattle

I got the call from Nan Borton, probably six-thirty on a Sunday morning. Nan had been the head of the JVA, Joint Voluntary Agency, when it first started in Thailand and had worked with Jerry and Mac Thompson. She called me at home in Seattle, and I came out of a sleep and staggered downstairs to the telephone. I sort of sat in a stupor while we talked. She told me she had talked to Mac at some length, and he was pretty certain that it was legitimate and there was no foul play. She stressed that there was no foul play, "even though there are a lot of rumors circulating in the Hmong community that it is all a big plot." I wondered, *Rumors already? After only one or two days? What kind of a plot are the Hmong talking about?* I would guess it was that the communists got him or another Hmong faction was involved. Later the Hmong even hatched a plot that Jerry wasn't really in the coffin and that it was a ploy to convince people that he was dead while he was really back in Laos leading the resistance. I think the main reason for the conspiracy theories was because of Jerry's employment with the Agency, and it was the time of spy novels, don't forget.

JOHN W. TUCKER, former USAID Laos Refugee Relief Program; former Refugee Program, U.S. Embassy, Bangkok, Thailand; former Department of State, Bureau for Refugee Programs

I was notified of Jerry's death at home in Burke, Virginia, on a Sunday morning by a telephone call from Hank Cushing, who was my boss at the time in the Bureau for Refugee Programs at State. In the office the next day we worked on the eulogy on behalf of the State Department and discussed what to do. It was decided I would be the lead person to go to Missoula first, ahead of Jim Schill. Carol Leviton also decided to go as she had worked with Jerry and the Hmong in the refugee camps in Thailand.

Mrs. CAROL LEVITON WETTERHAHN, former Highland Section chief, JVA, Thailand

John Tucker called me at my apartment off Dupont Circle in Washington, DC. I knew John from the refugee program in Thailand. John was the ethnic affairs officer, the EAO, for the lowland Lao and Jerry was the EAO for the Hmong. They verified the stories of the military backgrounds for the refugees from Laos.

My initial reaction to John's call was anger. *Anger.* How could Jerry be so stupid? How could he let that happen? Shock and *anger* at Jerry for dying. I think you are always shocked when someone young dies before their natural time, and not ill. It's a shock. And I was angry because the death was stupid. Asphyxiation from a gas leak? That's dumb. Just dumb. It shouldn't have happened. It should have been prevented. But I didn't question it. I wasn't suspicious of it. Having lived in Thailand with those gas water heaters, to me it was all very believable. And that's what I initially heard, a faulty gas water heater.

JIM SCHILL, former USAID Laos Refugee Relief Program; former Department of State, Bureau for Refugee Programs

Sunday morning, May 2, 1982. I was in my apartment in Alexandria, Virginia, when I got a phone call that Jerry Daniels had been found dead in his Bangkok apartment. The shock was impossible. Maybe the commies had finally gotten to him. But the cause of his death really didn't matter. He was dead.

The next morning I arrived at Foggy Bottom, State Annex II, and found people deep in conversation, trying to make sense of Jerry's death, and reading a confidential cable from our ambassador in Thailand. Mostly the cable emphasized that no foul play was suspected.

Apparently, Jerry had been dead for two or three days before a friend got worried and went to check it out. He found the door to Jerry's apartment unlocked, even slightly ajar. There had not been a robbery or anything like that, but the door was not completely shut. When he knocked, the door went open and he smelled an awful stench. He walked into the apartment and saw a body on Jerry's bed. It was swollen and black, and the smell was horrific. Dead bodies do that, especially in the heat and all, because there are a lot of gasses that are trapped inside. Because of the disfigurement, he couldn't even guess who the person on the bed was. He notified the Embassy security office and told them, "That's not Jerry. There's some black person on his bed." The Embassy security staff and Thai police went to investigate and it *was* Jerry.

Many of us with the State Department in Washington, DC, had known Jerry in Laos, and others more recently in association with the U.S. refugee program in Thailand. Lionel Rosenblatt, Bill Krug, and John Tucker, all from State, began working on a draft eulogy. In spite of their sadness, they could still laugh about the code names Jerry used to identify refugee cases he was working on, such as the "Grimm Sisters" or others filed in the "Doom Drawer."

BOB JOHNSON, former Highland Section chief, JVA, Thailand; regional director, International Rescue Committee (IRC), Seattle

I talked to Mac Thompson and a couple of other people in Thailand. In my own mind the official explanation that I heard made sense. That he'd come home after a few too many beers and had taken a hot shower, then passed out and gone to sleep. From my perspective that story was as plausible as anything. Because the water heaters in Thailand are what they call geysers, which are direct heating from LP gas, liquid propane. When you turn on the hot water, they fire up and heat a wire coil directly, and he'd just left that on. Once the water heater got going the flame just kept rolling, and there is a pretty robust flame in those geysers. Over a period of time it burned up all the oxygen in the room. Basically he was asphyxiated because of lack of oxygen.

I did hear that when they found the tank it was all frosty. LP's a liquid form of gas in the tank and when it goes out it cools pretty rapidly. So they found the tank mechanism all frosted up. And it was absolutely empty. That made sense. Although I remember that the family questioned that. They were trying to figure out what that was all about.

JACK TUPPER DANIELS, brother of Jerry Daniels

I was still in New Hampshire when I got the first of several calls from the U.S. State Department about Jerry's death. I asked whoever called me how he died, and he said it was carbon monoxide from a faulty gas water heater in his bathroom. I'd been in his apartment so I knew exactly what they were talking about. There was this little heating coil with a pilot light. When you turned the hot water faucet on, that would ignite the little burner. When you turned the hot water faucet off, the little burner went out.

I don't know who I talked to, but I do remember getting back in touch with somebody and saying that it seemed strange that he could have died from carbon monoxide poisoning. The 4 May 1982 cable that we got said that his blood had 92 percent carbon monoxide. The cable referred to an autopsy report which we never received and really don't even know if it existed. But that is extremely high, 92 percent. It's hard for me to believe that someone could live and continue to breathe until they reached that high a level of carbon monoxide. You're not being *poisoned* by the carbon monoxide; you're being affected by a lack of oxygen to the brain. It's a deprivation of oxygen rather than too much of something else, so I think someone would pass out when they were down around 50 percent. There's no pain and eventually you don't have enough oxygen in your blood. When the brain doesn't get enough oxygen, then you lose consciousness. At some point ventilation would stop, which means he'd quit breathing, and the blood would stop absorbing the CO—which is why I don't know how in the world the blood saturation level of carbon monoxide got up to 92 percent. That means that the blood kept passing through the lungs for a long period of time, meaning he was still alive and breathing.

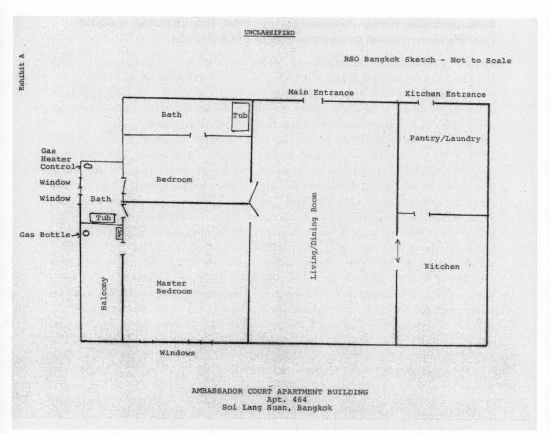

UNCLASSIFIED

RSO Bangkok Sketch - Not to Scale

Exhibit A

Main Entrance   Kitchen Entrance

Bath   Tub

Pantry/Laundry

Gas Heater Control

Window   Bedroom

Window   Bath   Living/Dining Room

Tub

Gas Bottle

Kitchen

Balcony   Master Bedroom

Windows

AMBASSADOR COURT APARTMENT BUILDING
Apt. 464
Soi Lang Suan, Bangkok

Diagram of the apartment of Jerry Daniels, Bangkok, Thailand. Exhibit A, Department of State, Office of Security, Special Investigation Report, May 14, 1982.

JIM SCHILL, former USAID Laos Refugee Relief Program; former Department of State, Bureau for Refugee Programs

We heard that Jerry had been drinking the night before he died. That didn't surprise any of us. When I first got to Laos in '73 and was up there in Long Cheng with Jerry and the guys, I lived in what was called the Thai engineer house, which was made of stone and cement surrounded by a sandbag bunker. When I moved in I found a closet full of beer, a pallet of forty or fifty cases of Olympia, a beer that's made in the state of Washington. That beer was eight months out of shelf life, and the cans were getting rusty. I made a few inquiries and it turned out that Jerry was an Oly drinker and he'd stashed them there. Oly was a 3.2 beer, but he still couldn't take more than two or three of them. He said that was because of his Indian heritage.

BOB JOHNSON, former Highland Section chief, JVA, Thailand; regional director, International Rescue Committee (IRC), Seattle

First thing I asked Mac Thompson was, "Is the beer still there?" And he said no. See, Jerry had a closet in his apartment in Bangkok. Every week when he was at the commissary he'd buy a case of beer. Oly Gold and Coors were the only two American beers you could get at the commissary. A case was the limit, and he kept stocking up. Jerry probably had twenty or thirty cases of Oly Gold in the closet.

See, Jerry was saving up for a rainy day because there was a point in time, I think 1979 or '80, when there were border threats from the Vietnamese.[2] There was this idea that maybe Thailand was going to get overrun. I mean, this was still close enough to the war period that maybe the Vietnamese being in Cambodia meant that they were going to move onto Thailand. The Royal Thai Army went out to repel the rumored invasion. According to some military types that hang out at the embassy, they clocked the Thai army doing the hundred-yard dash away from the Vietnamese in world-record time. Sailing out and sailing back pretty quick. So the Thai army wasn't going to be our biggest line of defense. Then we all figured the Vietnamese'd get stopped in the traffic jam on Sukhumvit Road and never get into Bangkok for a week anyway. You know, with 3 or 4 million Thais trying to leave Bangkok at the same time, the Vietnamese army definitely wasn't going to be able to drive their tanks in. That was our saving grace. We figured we would be saved by the traffic jam on Sukhumvit. We always joked that if the Vietnamese managed to surround the capital and the supply of beer got cut off, at least we could be up on the roof waiting for the rescue chopper with the proper refreshment.

XUWICHA "NOI" HIRANPRUECK, best Thai friend of Jerry Daniels

Jerry had a habit of "going wet," meaning get really drunk and drop out for a couple of days, so when he did not turn up for work nobody took any action. It was only on the third day that someone checked. After his dead body was found by the INS guy [Tom Prokopowicz, U.S. Immigration and Naturalization Service], police were called in with the Potr Teck Tung Foundation that takes care of dead bodies for the Thai police.

BOB JOHNSON, former Highland Section chief, JVA, Thailand; regional director, International Rescue Committee (IRC), Seattle

When Jerry was found dead we said what killed him was his government air conditioning allowance—because the official USG [U.S. government] employees got an apartment allowance with extra for the electric bill for air conditioning. Those of us who worked for nongovernmental agencies like JVA, we didn't get any extra for air conditioning. So our apartments had louvered windows that were kept open all the time, and those that were air conditioned were taped shut so they wouldn't leak and you could have the air conditioning on. That, in a sense, is what got him. It was the closed system.

JACK TUPPER DANIELS, brother of Jerry Daniels

You know, Jerry had *two* window air conditioners in his bedroom. He wanted to be cool, and it was a pretty big bedroom. And this was a tiny little bathroom water heater, not the exhaust from a Mack truck. I said, "You know, it's pretty hard for me to imagine that the carbon monoxide coming into that bedroom from an adjoining bathroom wouldn't just get sucked out by those two air conditioners." I knew Jerry hated hot, muggy weather. And April is a *miserable* month in Thailand. That's why he had two air conditioners! So I questioned that. I asked, "With the amount of square footage in that bedroom and two A/C units on, how would there be enough CO built up to kill someone?" Even one air conditioner probably would have done a decent job of clearing the fumes out of that room. When I mentioned that air conditioning to the State Department, they said, "Well, that's what was strange. The air conditioners were not running. They were both off." The air conditioners got eliminated as a saving device because they weren't functioning? Well, not in Bangkok in April. "What do you mean they weren't running? *Jerry* turned them off to go to sleep? *Both* of them? In April? I'm having a real problem with that. There's no way that he would go to bed in that room without air conditioners on. It was too hot." He wouldn't go to sleep with them not running unless somebody else turned them off. So we've got a problem here, you know?

And the next problem I had was that they said, "Well, we didn't find the body for two or three days. We figured this happened on Thursday and we didn't find the body until Saturday." I didn't know why they thought it happened on Thursday, but that the body was so badly decomposed from two or three days in the Bangkok heat, that it was too gruesome a sight to see, that it was "unrecognizable"—that bothered me, too. I've seen roadkill down in Texas that lasted more than two or three days in the heat of a Texas summer and it still was recognizable, so that story didn't hold up either. And the front door was found ajar and nobody in the apartment building reported that something was fouling the air? How could a body be so decomposed and nobody would notice and report it?

BOB JOHNSON, former Highland Section chief, JVA, Thailand; regional director, International Rescue Committee (IRC), Seattle

The front door being found ajar was another one of the conspiratorial aspects of it all. Like who had gotten in there? Or maybe there'd been a party there. Or maybe Jerry'd been out and just never closed the door completely. The open door wasn't explained, so it played into the whole conspiracy thing.

FARRETT DANIELS, nephew of Jerry Daniels; son of Kent Daniels

I might have been able to buy it if Jerry didn't just move from one apartment where he had lived for so long. That's what I heard, that he'd been in that one apartment and then he moved into another apartment in the same building and, "Oh yeah, that happens in third-world countries." You know, for me it's, "Love my country; don't trust my government."

JACK TUPPER DANIELS, brother of Jerry Daniels

Our talks left the investigation phase and went into the phase of what to do with Jerry's body. They said, "What do you want to do?" They said the Thai held Jerry in such high esteem that they wanted to have a cremation and put the cremated body in an urn and put the urn in a temple to honor him. They didn't say the Hmong or the Lao; they said the *Thai*. I thought that was strange that the *Thai* thought that highly of him. That the Thai wanted to keep him in an urn in some temple. I know he had some good Thai friends, but I don't know that the Thai people thought as highly of him as the Hmong did. So when they asked me, "Is it okay to have his body cremated? The advantage would be that we could satisfy the Thai by putting some of the remains in an urn like they want, and we could send the rest of the remains back for you to have in the States." Well, my first thought was, *How well will that sit with the Hmong?* And it didn't. The Hmong said, "No, we never cremate. And you can't divide the remains. We have to keep him all together." My understanding was that it mattered a great deal that the remains were kept together.

I deferred straightaway to the Hmong. I told the State Department to forget it: "We're not splitting up anything. Just send his body back without a cremation and we'll bury him here." Then it was another delay of a day or so before I got this message: "Okay, we'll send the body back but it's badly decomposed. It wouldn't be good to have an open casket, so we're going to send him back in a sealed coffin. Will you promise to leave it that way?"

When I got that message from the State Department my immediate thought was, *Maybe there's something going on and maybe Jerry's in on it. Maybe he wants to be "lost" and get on with something else. I don't want to mess that up for him. If I open the casket and he's not in there, that's going to cause a problem.* And I was thinking, *If that's the case I'm sure he'll let us know about it later.* So I said okay.

MACALAN THOMPSON, former USAID Laos Refugee Relief Program; former Refugee Program, U.S. Embassy, Bangkok, Thailand

Jerry's body was found in his apartment on 1 May, Saturday. On 3 May, Monday, I flew Bangkok to Udorn then took a taxi over to the Ban Vinai refugee camp to inform the Hmong leadership that Jerry had died. On 4 May, Tuesday, I flew back to Bangkok and at 1930 hours I went to Wat Mongkut to attend a memorial ceremony for Jerry. Noi, Jerry's good old Thai friend, did the organizing of the ceremony at Wat

Mongkut. It was a normal Thai funeral ceremony except for no cremation. Both Thai and Americans attended. The Ban Vinai folks sent a wreath to the ceremony. There was even a wreath from the Udorn-based taxi driver we usually used, Khun Duen. Jerry had ridden with Duen very often and Duen contributed five hundred *baht* [Thai money] for a wreath.

Shock and Dismay

HMONG leaders at Ban Vinai refugee camp are informed of the death of Jerry Daniels; a Buddhist memorial service in Bangkok; an article in the *Bangkok Post*; several conspiracy theories; more coworkers in Bangkok react; State Department cable and report; two condolence letters; the Daniels family continues to question circumstances of death, including the condition and whereabouts of a young Thai man.

NENG VANG, former lieutenant colonel, SGU Army, MR2, Laos; former Hmong chief of Ban Vinai refugee camp, Thailand

In May 1982 I was the chief of the refugee camp Ban Vinai. I was chief from 1979 until December 1982, at which time I resettled to the U.S.

One day in early May, about eight o'clock in the morning, there was a knock on my door. It was Mac Thompson. I knew Mac Thompson from when we lived in Laos. He walked into my house in Ban Vinai and broke out crying. He cried so hard that he was hardly able to speak. Then in Lao language he said that Jerry had died from a gas leak in the water heater. Mac was very upset and concerned about us, the Hmong in the refugee camp. He said, "Now that Jerry is dead, there is nobody else who can help you." He stayed about an hour, then left in a hurry.

When I heard this news I was sad, depressed, and most important of all I was worried. Jerry was the only person who really knew what went on with the Hmong in the clandestine war in Laos. Now he was gone. Who was going to watch over these thousands of Hmong refugees in Thailand?

After Mac left I sent out word for the Hmong camp council to meet in my house. The council members were the seven section leaders, former Hmong military officers and civilian leaders. It was the twenty or thirty leaders who were in charge of the social well-being of the people in Ban Vinai refugee camp. Of course they all knew Jerry. When they heard the news, everybody was upset and crying and worried because nobody would support us as much as Jerry had. At the council meeting we decided to send two representatives to Bangkok to attend his memorial service: Vang Bee [T-28 pilot Bee Vang] and Vue Mai. We choose those two because they were two of the most important people at Ban Vinai.

BEE VANG, former Hmong T-28 pilot, Laos

At the leadership council meeting everyone was so shocked and depressed. The leadership group decided that Vue Mai and myself would go to Bangkok to attend Jerry's memorial service. We would represent all the Hmong in the refugee camp. Vue Mai and I took one whole night to travel by bus from Chieng Kan to Bangkok.

XUWICHA "NOI" HIRANPRUECK, best Thai friend of Jerry Daniels

Jerry, Mr. Hog, was my best friend. He still is. He stayed at my house in Bangkok for almost a year before he moved to the dreaded Ambassador Court apartment. I shared years of friendship with Hog, and he is a man I am looking forward to seeing in the afterworld.

Before the departure of his body to Missoula, I organized a memorial service at Wat Mongkut. Wat Mongkut was, and still is, my temple. My mother was kept there for twenty-five years before she was cremated together with my father a few months before Jerry died. I have good pull there, so it was easier for me to arrange things there the way I wanted them, rather than at another temple.

Since Jerry was a Christian and Christians bury their dead, I arranged the parts of the Thai funeral process to fit his situation. The service allowed his friends in Thailand to ceremoniously send earth to accompany his body. That is a Buddhist and Thai tradition for burying the dead, although burial is not common as normally we cremate the bodies.

BEE VANG, former Hmong T-28 pilot, Laos

When Vue Mai and I arrived at the temple in Bangkok, there were about 200 people, American and Thai, gathering in a line outside of the hall. They were waiting to go look at Jerry inside the temple. Noi told us that inside the temple they will do Thai culture, but Vue Mai and I said, "Hey, we are Hmong and we don't know how to do Thai culture." Noi said, "Just follow General Saen. You do what he does."

Noi stayed with the people outside when the Thai army general pointed to two wreaths of flowers and asked us to carry them inside the hall. One of the wreaths had a written sign that said it was from General Vang Pao, who was living in the U.S. The other one said it was from the Ban Vinai refugee camp. Since Vue Mai was the vice-chief of the Ban Vinai refugee camp, Vue Mai took the big flowers that represented *all* the refugee camps in Thailand. I am from the Vang clan so I took the big flowers that represented General Vang Pao.

Vue Mai and I picked up the two wreaths and followed the Thai army general. Only three of us went inside first, before the other 200 people. We carried the flowers to the room for Jerry. Buddhist monks sat along the wall. The whole time we were in there the monks were chanting prayers. We followed the general and prayed to the monks like Thai custom. Then we gave each of the monks a new yellow robe. I think Noi bought all those things.

We showed respect to the monks, then we put the flowers in front of Jerry's name written on a closed cabinet wall. We saw only a picture of him, no casket. We placed the two wreaths in front of the cabinet wall, one from General Vang Pao and one from the refugee camps. The whole thing took about ten minutes. Not too long. Then we walked out, and they let all the other people go inside.

Xuwicha "Noi" Hiranprueck and Mike Eiland, U.S. Embassy refugee coordinator, make merit offerings to Buddhist monks after the chanting of Apidharma (cycle of life and death) at the memorial ceremony for Jerry Daniels at Wat Mongkutkrasatriaram, Bangkok, May 3, 1982. "Lucky" Lue Yang collection.

XUWICHA "NOI" HIRANPRUECK, best Thai friend of Jerry Daniels

The U.S. ambassador came to the evening service at Wat Mongkut, as did the chief of station and members of both Sky[1] and the State Department. Many Thai friends were there, including General Chuthai Saengtaweeb, "General Saen," an old associate of Jerry's from the war years in Laos. He was the highest-ranking Thai who attended, and he sat with the U.S. ambassador and performed the rite.

The ceremony in Wat Mongkut was a combination of a memorial service and a Thai funeral process concised to fit the odd circumstances, and it leaned towards content more than form. The ceremony was, in my view, what Jerry would have wanted. A funeral for a "real man." It went like a breeze, one event in memory of a fallen comrade.

BEE VANG, former Hmong T-28 pilot, Laos

I went to the service in Bangkok to show our respect to Jerry, but I did not believe it was gas that killed him. I don't believe that because for people like Jerry, I don't think it's easy to die like that. He's smart, very smart. I don't know what happened to Jerry but it must be something else, or possibly foul play if it was gas. Maybe somebody killed him? Nobody knows, because we never saw his body.

XUWICHA "NOI" HIRANPRUECK, best Thai friend of Jerry Daniels

It's true there was no body at the service. General Saen complained to me that night. He said that I should have put the body there, and in fact, Jerry's was the first and only memorial known to date in which circumstances did not permit the presence of the body because the body was in such bad shape. It was not easy to move him around, and I did not have the heart to do so. Only his photo stood as a symbol of his presence while his body rotted in the police morgue.

English-Language *Bangkok Post*, May 2, 1982

U.S. OFFICIAL FOUND DEAD IN APARTMENT

An American refugee official was found dead in his apartment yesterday. Lumpini police also found a Thai youth semi-conscious in the next room.

Police identified the American, believed to have died at least three days ago, as Jerrold B. Daniels, 41, a U.S. Embassy refugee official. . . .

In the next room police found 19 year old Vasant Daengnoi lying on a bed. He appeared very feeble and was unable to move or speak and was immediately rushed to hospital. . . .

Earlier in the afternoon, Vasant's mother reported to police that her son, a first year Liberal Arts student of Kasetsart University who worked part-time at Whole Earth Restaurant in Soi Lang Suan had been missing for several days.

Vasant was last seen on Wednesday night before leaving the Whole Earth with Daniels to the apartment across the street.

Police went to Daniels' apartment and found the two. Vasant was reported still in serious condition yesterday.

Ms. BERTA J. ROMERO, former JVA caseworker, Thailand

I met Jerry Daniels in Thailand in 1978 while I was working as a JVA caseworker in the U.S. Refugee Program, and later I attended his memorial service in Bangkok. The memorial service was a Thai Buddhist ceremony with incense and flowers. As is customary, a photo of the deceased was present.

Many Thai attended the service, as did almost all of us who had worked with Jerry in the refugee program. There were also other Americans, some whom I did not recognize, who we thought worked for the U.S. government in other capacities. The collective "we" asked a lot of questions of those in charge, and we were told only that Jerry was found dead in his apartment. There was a small article in the *Bangkok Post* that seemed to suggest mysterious circumstances around a possible "homosexual lovers" spat. Other rumors were around suicide, or that he was killed by the CIA. As some of the stories were out of character and just didn't make any sense, this added to the intrigue. The U.S. Embassy was not forthcoming in any exact details of his death. It was handled in such a way that those of us who worked with Jerry were kept in the dark.

Excerpt from a DEPARTMENT OF STATE cable, May 3, 1982

FM SECSTATE WASHDC

TO AMEMBASSY BANGKOK IMMEDIATE

INFO AMEMBASSY KUALA LUMPUR IMMEDIATE

AMEMBASSY SINGAPORE IMMEDIATE

AMEMBASSY JAKARTA IMMEDIATE

AMEMBASSY MANILA IMMEDIATE

AMCONSUL HONG KONG IMMEDIATE

USMISSION GENEVA IMMEDIATE

LIMITED OFFICIAL USE STATE 119289

. . . DEPARTMENT RECEIVED PRESS INQUIRY IN A FORM THAT REQUIRED THE FOLLOWING PRESS GUIDANCE TO BE USED ON AN IF ASKED BASIS. QUOTE. QUESTIONS. CAN YOU CONFIRM THE DEATH IN BANGKOK OF JERRY DANIELS, A USG REFUGEE OFFICER? DID IT OCCUR UNDER SUSPICIOUS CIRCUMSTANCES? ANSWERS. WE HAVE BEEN INFORMED BY THE EMBASSY IN BANGKOK THAT MR. DANIELS' BODY WAS FOUND IN HIS APARTMENT ON MAY 1. MR. DANIELS WAS A MEMBER OF THE STAFF OF THE REFUGEE SECTION OF THE EMBASSY. WHILE WE DO NOT HAVE A REPORT ON THE CAUSE OF DEATH AS YET, WE HAVE NO REASON TO BELIEVE IT OCCURRED FOR OTHER THAN NATURAL CAUSES. UNQUOTE.

JEFF JOHNSON, former Air America "runway guy," Laos

I believe I was with Jerry on the last night before he died. And I'll tell you this: absolutely it was *not* suicide. I knew Jerry up at 20-Alternate, Long Cheng. I knew he was the Customer there, the CIA case officer. After the U.S. pulled out of Laos in '75, Jerry worked in the refugee program in Thailand. I assumed, but didn't know for sure, that the refugee program was Jerry's new cover for the Agency.

This particular evening I was with Phil Doyle, another runway guy from Air America. We walked into the Napoleon that night. Napoleon was located on Patpong 1.

It was an upscale bar that served food. Women dressed well, and in the earlier days they had a jazz band on Sundays. It was a local hangout for wealthy Thai and the expat[2] community. Hard to say what time we got there. Maybe about ten-thirty. Phil and I walked in, and just by chance, Jerry was at the bar. I said, "Jerry, I'll buy you a drink." Normally he drank beer but it was some unusual drink he ordered, maybe a margarita, and he wasn't drinking as much as usual. I guessed he was on leave for a couple days because the only time I remember Jerry going into bars was when he was on leave or on vacation.

Jerry sat down with us. I'd never seen him talk so much before. He told me that he was tired of the refugee program. He said, "You know, it's been tough all these years. Working with the Hmong in Laos and now they're all refugees." He wasn't happy about that. Jerry was loved by the Hmong, right? When the U.S. left Laos the Hmong couldn't understand why. And Jerry was so respected and he had to sit in the refugee program and say to them, "I don't know why we left." That was seven years after we pulled out, and that's what was making it hard for him. Jerry said he was tired of it, and he asked me if I could get him a job in Saudi Arabia where I was working. I said, "Yeah, I think I can get you a job there as an administrator of some sort."

Then we started talking about his gold. He owned the mineral rights on some river up in Montana. He said, "You know, I've been thinking about going back and mining the gold." They'd been finding gold there. So I said, "You can get a little dredge and put it there." He was all excited about that idea. That conversation was about an hour or an hour and a half, and we talked mainly about him looking for new work and gold mining.

About midnight or eleven-thirty, Phil and I were leaving. Jerry said he was going back to his place. He'd had maybe three drinks. He was nowhere near drunk. He could *get* falling down drunk. Oh, I knew he could! I knew that in Vientiane. But the thing that I want to stress is that Jerry was in a very happy mood when he left the bar. He was upbeat, really upbeat. He was in a *great* state of mind. I want to eliminate this suicide thing.

We saw Jerry that night, and the next thing I knew, I was at the Super Star, a go-go bar on Patpong 1. A lot of expats went there. Good-looking women and loud music. You couldn't stay long because of ear damage. An INS officer [Tom Prokopowicz] from the American Embassy came up to me and said, "Did you hear about Jerry?" I said, "No. What?" He said, "Well, he's dead. I found him in his apartment." He was the first one into the apartment. He said, "The body was bloated beyond recognition." That it didn't *look* like Jerry, but it was. He said he found a young Thai guy in the apartment also.

Later I heard the rumor that there had been a party at Jerry's apartment. The INS guy didn't mention anything that would support a party theory, so I don't think that happened. Jerry never had parties anyways, as far as I knew—at least not any that he took home with him.

Excerpt from OFFICE OF SECURITY SPECIAL INVESTIGATION report, U.S. Embassy, Bangkok, Thailand

Title: DANIELS, Jerrold B.; AmEmbassy Bangkok
Date: May 14, 1982
Synopsis: Investigation conducted relative to death of subject. Source interviews provided circumstances of death.
[First several pages of interviews were sanitized by the U.S. Department of State and are blank.]

Page 11
... On Saturday, May 1, source was called by _____ asking that source check on subject to see if he was all right as he had not returned to work. Source then visited subject's apartment at about 1100 hours on May 1 and found the front door of the apartment open. Source stated that he entered the apartment and walked to the master bedroom where he discovered the body of what he described as a large black male in bed. He then looked into the other bedroom and saw a Thai male who appeared to be disoriented. He immediately reported this matter to the Regional Security Officer who, in turn, visited the apartment with two police officers. As background, source commented that subject had no financial or other concerns. He described subject as a dedicated officer with many years experience in Southeast Asia. He further characterized subject as a very stable individual and, moreover, he had never observed any signs of depression on subject's part. Source volunteered, to the best of his knowledge, subject had no family problems . . . that subject was well liked and that, as far as he knew, subject did not have any enemies. Concluding, source stated he had no reason to suspect that subject's death was other than accidental.

DOUG VINCENT, former JVA caseworker, Thailand

Jerry was supposed to be a "man's man." It wasn't until *after* he died that a few friends at JVA started suggesting that he was a closet gay. They had all worked with him, but those who said this weren't really close to the guy, at least I didn't think so. Maybe some people thought he was gay because of the Thai kid who survived the gas. I remember Jerry talking about having young Thai guys staying at his house, but I never thought anything of it. Personally, it wouldn't have shocked me if he was gay, but I didn't think he was. I knew the INS officer, Tom Prokopowicz, who found him dead, and Prok called the gay theory bullshit.

BOB JOHNSON, former Highland Section chief, JVA, Thailand; regional director, International Rescue Committee (IRC), Seattle

There were stories about the Thai guy who was found in the other room. That Thai kid worked across the street at the Whole Earth restaurant where Jerry ate all the time. Finding that guy in Jerry's apartment caused all sorts of weird stories that it was a homosexual tryst. Everybody who knew Jerry was pretty sarcastic about that: "Yeah, right. Jerry's a closet queen. I don't think so!" That was pretty strange stuff, but that was part of the conspiracy theory. Stories were kind of rampant for a while.

DOUG VINCENT, former JVA caseworker, Thailand

After he died there was the gay theory, and there was also the theory about his supposed sighting of U.S. MIAs in Laos. Also the idea that he died because the Agency wanted him to go to Afghanistan or Nicaragua and he was balking. Then I heard it was because he threatened to go to the press about the Hmong if they didn't let him stay in Thailand. Supposedly he was angry over the U.S. treatment of the Hmong after the war, that we promised we would take care of them, and now we were treating them like we usually do, breaking that promise. These were all theories that I got from others after his death, but Prok told me that he didn't think he died from any other cause.

XUWICHA "NOI" HIRANPRUECK, best Thai friend of Jerry Daniels

The memorial service was a grand send-off. We distributed black and white paper-wrapped soil packets to the attending guests—small, thin, white or black paper-wrapped packets, about the size of your thumb. White and black are universally associated with mourning, and the earth used was commercially available and provided by the temple. Each packet was a symbol of the burial so that the soil could go with the body to America and we could help bury Jerry there. We Thais do neat things like that because in Thai style, most actions in the funeral process allow friends to be with the family to help reduce their grief. At the end of the ceremony I collected a sack full of the black and white paper-wrapped earth packets and handed the sack to the U.S. Ambassador for shipment with the body.

Official Letter of Condolence to LOUISE DANIELS, mother of Jerry Daniels, from MICHAEL D. EILAND, U.S. Embassy refugee coordinator, Bangkok, Thailand, May 5, 1982

Dear Mrs. Daniels:

Accompanying this letter you will find a picture of Jerry that was displayed at the two-day memorial service for him, and a bag of small parcels of soil from both Thailand and Laos that his friends here hope you will see fit to bury with him. During this memorial ceremony each of several score friends of various nationalities placed these individual packages in a silver bowl before they were wrapped and tied as you see them by a monk.

The services were arranged and sponsored by Jerry's close friend Noi, and I might say that Noi went to extraordinary lengths in these arrangements; no one could have a closer or more devoted friend than Jerry has had in Noi. The services were, of course, basically Buddhist in nature, but were attended by members of all faiths and persuasions, including Ambassador Dean, General Saen, and—perhaps most important—Hmong tribesmen from Ban Vinai Camp. The services were simple but dignified, and afforded many old friends an opportunity to pay last respects.

On behalf of all of his friends and colleagues, allow me to use these inadequate words to express our heartfelt condolences and our profound sense of loss which we share with his family. A giant of a man is gone. He will be missed. His work lives.

XUWICHA "NOI" HIRANPRUECK, best Thai friend of Jerry Daniels

In truth, those small soil packets were only from Thailand. Saying some of the soil was from Laos was solely for the comfort of Jerry's mother. We all loved Louise, and there were many things we did to make it easier for her so that she, and all of us, would feel good about Jerry's tragic departure.

Excerpts from a Personal Letter of Condolence to LOUISE DANIELS from ELAINE and WALTER MCINTOSH, U.S. Embassy, Bangkok, Thailand, May 4, 1982

Dear Mrs. [Daniels] Reese,

Like Jerry's other colleagues and friends here at the American embassy in Bangkok, we were shocked and deeply shaken by his death. . . . You know government

Flower arrangements and a photograph of Jerry Daniels at his memorial ceremony in Bangkok, May 3, 1982. "Lucky" Lue Yang collection.

service is a peculiar sort of profession—a profession in which a man's accomplishments and truly great achievements often go unpublicized and unpraised in the world at large. Jerry never bragged or even talked much about his experiences and achievements in Southeast Asia. . . . However, the fact that he rose to so high a rank for someone of his age bears testimony to his achievements on behalf of his country.

. . . Yesterday my husband said a Thai army general with whom he deals asked about memorial services for Jerry saying, "He was my comrade-in-arms—we went back many years together to our days in Laos." He added that Jerry was loved and held in high esteem among many officers in the Royal Thai Army. . . .

I have no idea how the little gray bureaucrats from Washington, D.C. are going to extend the United States Government's official condolences to you and yours. My hope is that they shall do it properly. Knowing the bureaucracy as I do, however, I'm not sure that will be the case. . . . But be assured that unlike the little gray bureaucrats, the people that really count, both within and outside the ranks of American officers serving their country, viewed your son as a true hero.

Apart from everything else, Jerry was a beautiful human being. His warmth, compassion, intellect, courage, and good humor shone through to all whose lives he touched. We are going to miss him.

Ms. BERTA J. ROMERO, former JVA caseworker, Thailand

Jerry's memorial service was a simple and brief Buddhist ceremony. I remember feeling disappointed afterwards because it didn't recognize his work and contributions to the refugee program. He was a good man, and he was one of the few Americans who returned to help out the Hmong and Lao who had helped the Americans during the infamous secret war. Jerry's death haunted many of us, and I am still not comfortable with the circumstances around it.

That memorial was not a major event in Bangkok; it was well attended, but it was a small service. We later heard that the funeral service in Missoula was huge and emotionally powerful.

MACALAN THOMPSON, former USAID Laos Refugee Relief Program; former Refugee Program, U.S. Embassy, Bangkok, Thailand

After the ceremony at Wat Mongkut, Jerry's body was shipped home to Montana. I never saw his body, but, as with burn cases, a disfigured body is usually shipped in a sealed casket. Not sure if there was much recognizable in there. In any case, I don't believe that was a State decision, especially when the casket reached Missoula.

JACK TUPPER DANIELS, brother of Jerry Daniels

State had said, "We'll send his body back if you promise not to open the casket. He's too decomposed." I said okay, but it still didn't sound right to me. Why would he be so decomposed after only a couple of days? I don't care if it's 100 degrees, I don't think in two or three days a body's going to decompose that badly. So I didn't buy that. Other things the State Department said didn't add up either. Why were the two A/C units off? Jerry would not go to sleep in that intense heat with all the doors and windows shut and the A/C off. And then the gas hot water heater malfunctioned also? I mean, why then? Why were the *two* air conditioners off at the same time that the propane water heater went out? For all those things to happen at the same time, that was unbelievable. And then we heard a Thai guy in the second bedroom survives? Why did the guy in the other room survive? What was the level of CO in *his* room and in *his* blood? And who and where was he anyway?

Laos, Part I: Na Khang

FORMER colleague of Daniels remembers him during the years of the U.S. Central Intelligence Agency's secret war in Laos, 1961–75; letters home; stories about Lima Site 36, Na Khang, Laos, in the mid-1960s, including two major attacks.

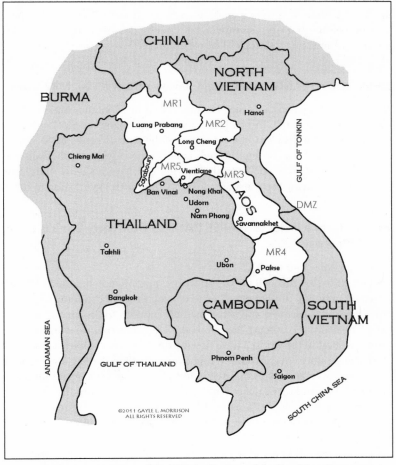

Map 1. Southeast Asia: Laos and the Military Regions of the Royal Lao Government

JIM SCHILL, former USAID Laos Refugee Relief Program; former Department of State, Bureau for Refugee Programs

Jerry Daniels was hired by the CIA and sent to Southeast Asia in the early 1960s. Montana may seem a strange place to hire covert agents for the CIA, but most of the group that was used in remote locations like Laos had been smokejumpers for the U.S. Forest Service. Jerry, too, had been a smokejumper. The smokejumpers who served in Laos were not the kind of covert officers that were brought to the Agency after they graduated from Harvard. Smokejumpers were people with special skills that were picked up during a time of crisis and told to keep their mouths shut. They did that superbly.

When Jerry started to work in Laos he was based at Lima Site 36,[1] Na Khang. A few years later he was reassigned to Long Cheng, LS 20-Alternate, as General Vang Pao's case officer, VP's direct link to the CIA in Laos. From 1972 until 1975 I was a USAID [U.S. Agency for International Development] officer and got to know VP and his CIA handlers well, including Jerry. Along with a host of Hmong, VP, former CIA personnel, and smokejumpers, I attended his funeral in Montana. I'll never forget the sadness, nor the stories I heard about Jerry.

NHIA "JUDY" VANG, former field liaison officer (FLO), MR2, Laos

In Laos, Jerry Daniels was Sky. He was raised in Montana, Big Sky Country, so he named the American CIA headquarters in Long Cheng the Sky compound. The U.S. government sent the Sky to Laos to work with General Vang Pao to stop the communist Viet Cong from coming through Laos on the Ho Chi Minh Trail. Sky supported General Vang Pao's SGU [Special Guerrilla Unit] troops with "hard rice,"[2] military hardware, all during the war years. Jerry worked with Sky starting in the early 1960s.

Excerpt from a letter to LOUISE DANIELS from Jerry Daniels at age nineteen, early 1961

Dear Louise and others,

I imagine that this will make you worry more than if you didn't know where I am or what I'm doing. But I'm now able to tell you this. I'm dropping cargo which mainly consists of rice, gasoline and some medical supplies to the Meo [Hmong] tribe refugees. The dropping is being done in Laos. The pilots that we work with are without a doubt the best in the world. I have flown with them over 1,000 hours already in C-46s. With these pilots I'm a lot safer flying over Laos than driving away from skid row.

When we've been working steady for a long time we are sent on R & R (rest and recuperation) and that is what I'm doing right now. I'll be in Bangkok for a couple of days then Hong Kong for a week (I haven't been there yet) then Taipei for a couple days then Okinawa then back to Vientiane Laos. I've been to Tokyo and Manila. So you might say I've been around.

Remember I'm safe and sound,

Jerry

TED O. "LITTLE O" LYMPUS, high school and college friend

As I understood it, there were two factions in Laos. There was the Royal Lao and the communist Pathet Lao. Vang Pao and the Meo, as they then called the Hmong, were with the Royal Lao. They were loyal to the anticommunist government. The Pathet Lao, the communist Lao, wanted to overthrow the royal government in Vientiane. So the United States was trying to support the Royal Lao without putting American troops on the ground. And they were doing it, among other things probably, by air dropping supplies to the Hmong troops. That's how Jerry first got involved—as a cargo kicker for the CIA.

BOB WHALEY, former smokejumper; lieutenant colonel, USMC (retired)

It seems like the jumpers, both the guys that joined the CIA and the guys in the military, we all tended to get together whenever we came back to Missoula. Mostly we would run into each other at the Flame Lounge. I ran into Jerry there. I had just finished my first tour in Vietnam; we were the first Marine helicopter squadron to go into Vietnam, down in the Mekong Delta. I was aware of activity in Laos because in Vietnam we had Air Force pilots who were flying VNAF T-28s. Later, some of those guys were getting sheepdipped[3] and flying close air support with the Ravens in Laos.

By 1962 Jerry already was engaged in things that were going on out there. Very much engaged. A lot of people didn't even know about Vietnam until the '63 to '64 timeframe when things started to happen. But in '62 things were really starting to happen across the border in Laos, and we talked about that.

Excerpt from a letter to LOUISE DANIELS from Jerry Daniels, November 2, 1965

Just a very short note to let you know every thing is fine. So far the job looks like a very great challenge. . . . I want you to send me for Xmas my 22 pistol with about 6 boxes of Ammo and a ammo belt. I know this is against the law but if you want send the pistol in two parts and no ammo. I'll pay the fine and would like to take the risk. Send air mail as soon as possible.

Excerpt from a letter to LOUISE DANIELS from Jerry Daniels, December 27, 1965

I'm a little busier than usual. I really enjoy the job. The weather is nice and cool up here in the mountains. Thought I might mention that I now also have a $150,000 policy that even covers guarilla (sp? can't even find it in my new dictionary) warfare.

Thank you again for the gun, etc.

MIKE LYNCH, former provincial advisor, Lima Site 36, Na Khang, Laos

I spent almost two years with Jerry at Na Khang sharing bunkers, a tin drum hut and the NVA [North Vietnamese Army] attacks of 1966 and '67. With the exception of the airfield itself, the facilities at Site 36 were concentrated within a trenched perimeter on a small hill at the northeast end of a 2,300-foot dirt runway.

Site 36 was sixty miles south of the border between Laos and North Vietnam. Once Jerry and I read an article about a couple of air force guys stationed in northeast Thailand at some listening post that described them as "the closest Americans to Hanoi," as if they were in daily peril for their lives. We laughed at that. We were much closer to North Vietnam at Na Khang. Jerry and I were together 24/7 except for brief times when one of us would make a trip out for a few days. Because of the nature of our work—someone had to mind the store—we were never away at the same time. Jerry and I probably spent 95 percent of our time there.

The third American member of the Na Khang team was Don Sjostrom, a young USAID employee who lived with Jerry and me. Don was the USAID refugee officer for the Sam Neua area. He worked for "Pop" Buell in Sam Thong and spent his time traveling to villages throughout the area, spending the majority of his nights at Site 36.

Jerry was away from Na Khang during the first major NVA attack on February 17, '66. He returned immediately as soon as he could find a ride. That afternoon we

Perimeter trench at Lima Site 36, Na Khang. This trench was built in 1966 after the site was recaptured by Vang Pao's soldiers. Photo credit: Mike Lynch.

Americans were ordered by the ambassador in Vientiane not to remain overnight, despite our strong arguments to the contrary. We believed that the friendly forces would withdraw from Site 36 in the event of another enemy assault if the Americans left. We lost the argument and departed on the last aircraft out, landing first at Moung Hiem to drop off wounded soldiers and some refugees. Moung Hiem, LS 48A, was about ten miles to the west of Site 36. "Pop" Buell and a USAF FAC, a forward air controller named Ray, had joined us at Site 36 earlier in the day and evacuated with us. They remained at Moung Hiem, and Jerry and I went on to Udorn, Thailand. As Don was the best Lao linguist and had an excellent knowledge of the terrain in Sam Neua Province, we brought him to Udorn with us.

On our arrival at Udorn, Jerry and I pled our case to the USAF for continued air support to the troops at Na Khang. We then went to brief the officers and air crews on the day's events, the current situation, and the anticipated enemy actions that night. We must have appeared as quite strange characters standing up in front of that group of immaculately groomed young men in pressed summer uniforms. We were rather grimy and unshaven with tattered clothes and dressed mainly in black. We had a few dirty bandages covering various cuts and scrapes and bloodstains from dragging wounded soldiers and examining enemy bodies. Jerry had a captured AK-47 rifle slung over his shoulder, which was a rather rare weapon for the friendly troops at this point in the war. I had my sawed-off 12-gauge Winchester double-barreled shotgun. Needless to say, we had their attention.

That night without the knowledge of anyone other than the USAF in Udorn, Jerry, Don, and I joined the air crews flying AC-47 "Puff the Magic Dragon" gunships for their first-ever close-support mission in Laos. Our purpose was to guide the aircraft to the precise target area by communicating by radio with the Site 36 defenders on the ground. Unfortunately, the first aircraft with Jerry and me on board had to abort short of the target with engine trouble and return to Udorn. The second aircraft, which took off a couple of hours later with Don on board, was successful in reaching Site 36 and provided protective fire for several hours. As this type of activity was well beyond the scope or authority of Don's USAID duties, we justified it by maintaining that he was on board to identify the friendly forces and assure that they did not become targets. He reportedly did an outstanding job. There is probably no official record of our presence on the flights that night. Earlier that day we had been told by "civilian officials" in Udorn, "We don't ever want to hear that you guys participated in a USAF combat mission." Well, they never did hear about it.

The Site 36 troops, probably less than 150 by that time, evacuated the position during the early morning hours on the day following the withdrawal of the Americans. I believe the attack had stopped by then, but the friendly forces were tired and frightened without the American presence that guaranteed air support and resupply. The soldiers and some of their families all moved overland to Moung Hiem. On the following day, Jerry and I rejoined our troops there, where we shared the territory for several weeks with a unit of neutralist[4] troops—a very uneasy "alliance." Adding to the ambience at Moung Hiem was the fact that the neutralist troops had some neat uniforms and equipment just provided to them by Sukarno's Indonesia. As a result

Standing: Captain Ray, USAF FAC. Seated: Jerry Daniels and Mike Lynch in front of bunker overlooking airstrip, Moung Hiem, LS 48A, February 1966. Mike Lynch collection.

Jerry Daniels and Mike Lynch at the abandoned French outpost of Moung Son, Lima 59. On backside of photo Daniels wrote, "Village of the Lost Ferrit Hoags." Daniels family collection. Used with permission.

they looked a lot smarter than our ragtag bunch from Na Khang, and they made sure that we were aware of this. Tension with the neutral troops steadily increased.

I was a poli sci major in college, but in Laos I just worried about the basics like who was liable to shoot at me, and who probably wouldn't. We didn't trust the neutralists, and the feeling was probably mutual. We had our doubts that the neutralist troops would be effective in defense of the area in the event of a major attack. Since there was never a plan to stay at Moung Hiem for an extended period as long as the neutralists were there, Jerry and I moved north with the remaining Site 36 troops. We were anxious to get to an area that we could control. We established a new base at Moung Son,[5] a former outpost during the French time. When we arrived, Moung Son was deserted, and the former French airfield and the remains of a few buildings were overgrown with vegetation.

Letter to LOUISE DANIELS from Jerry Daniels, March 9, 1966

Dear Louise,

Very sorry about writing no letters, but it may be this way for awhile. We have been extremely busy—moving. Needless to say my old home [Lima Site 36, Na Khang] became a thing of the past about one month ago. It turned to the color of the [black] ink I'm using here. Poor Phou Saly (our dog) bought the farm or is at least

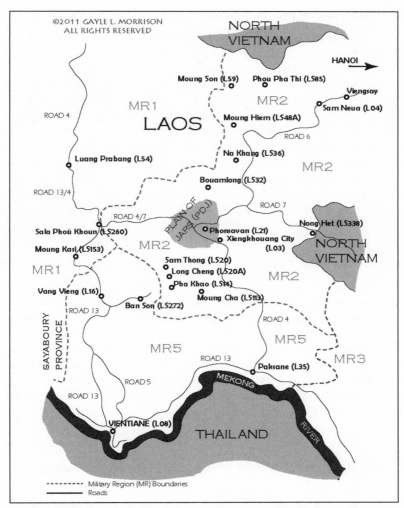

Map 2. Northern and central Laos, showing selected sites during the secret war in Laos, 1961–75

MIA (big dog talk for Missing in Action). We have since been moving to several different areas. It seems that it has turned out for the best because we are now at a place where no white person has been for at least 15 yrs. and there is old stone archways, deer, doves (just like ours!), a river that would put the great Rock Creek to shame, teeming with fish. I have seen some up to five lbs. I don't have any fishing material yet, but soon will. The ones I've seen were obtained by explosives. There is also many different exotic fruits. . . .

Jerry

I can't believe it, but I am actually learning the language some!

MIKE LYNCH, former provincial advisor, Lima Site 36, Na Khang, Laos

There were lots of fish in the stream, and our ragtag bunch of Hmong and Lao troops were using grenades to catch them for food. Our diet on the move was limited to sticky rice dropped by USAID and whatever greens the locals could scrounge with occasional pieces of pork. Once in a while the soldiers would trap or shoot a bird, so fish were a real luxury. Nevertheless, Jerry and I strongly discouraged using grenades for fishing. They were dangerous and killed more fish than could be recovered.

Jerry and I shared the available food with the troops. Sometimes we supplemented our diet with canned goods and leftovers brought in by the pilots. One of Jerry's favorites was the #10 can of corn meal from USAID. The locals usually wouldn't eat corn because it was considered pig food, but Jerry and I made corn meal mush and devoured it with Eagle Brand sweetened condensed milk on top. Jerry also drank coffee with Eagle Brand milk mixed about fifty-fifty. I guess we craved sweet stuff. It tasted good at the time.

Excerpt from a letter to LOUISE DANIELS from Jerry Daniels, April 9, 1966

Dear Louise,

I have been doing some wild chicken hunting, and have been quite successful. In each group of cocks there is only one that can whistle, if you down that one, the rest are very easy because they are lost without their whistler. Quite Funny EH?

My language learning is coming along amazingly well and I can now talk at random in my line of work. I have gone up to about 3 days of talking nothing but Lao—Mighty Pleasin. Mike Lynch is the guy who stays with me most of the time. He is a real good head to work with. Mike has been here in this part of the country for 3 years & he speaks French, which all the commanders here know. . . .

Jerry

MIKE LYNCH, former provincial advisor, Lima Site 36, Na Khang, Laos

After about four months in the field we made it back to Site 36 in June of 1966. All of our buildings had been destroyed, and unexploded ordnance ranging from small arms ammo to 500-pound bombs was littered all over the area. In addition to the damage done by the attacking enemy, the USAF had attempted to bomb into oblivion any usable equipment and ammunition left behind by the friendly troops when the site fell. We made an effort to clear the debris from the areas where we needed to operate, but much of the unexploded ordnance was just pushed aside or left in place.

One day a specialist in logistics and ordnance flew up to assist us in dealing with this hazard. Jerry nominally took the lead on matters relating to logistics, but he was not particularly concerned and went about his work as usual. The visitor arrived armed with rolls of yellow caution tape and little warning flags. He immediately set about marking the location of unexploded ordnance near the airstrip. There were hundreds of things to mark as the area was littered with shells. He finally recognized

Jerry Daniels shaving at Lima Site 36, 1965. Photo credit: Mike Lynch.

the magnitude of the problem and came up the hill to warn Jerry that the entire area was extremely hazardous to our health. When he saw Jerry just outside our front door sitting on an unexploded 500-pound bomb and shaving with his mirror propped up by the bomb's tail fins, he quickly retreated to his aircraft and departed.

About that same time, Jerry hung a rubberized body bag on the wall of our house—the standard Vietnam-era U.S. government model in olive drab—and each of us would sometimes find his name on the bag when returning to Na Khang after a few days away. It was our macabre joke. The three of us considered ourselves indestructible and often laughed about how we would get together in our old age and relive our adventures.

RANDOLPH "TOBY" SCOTT, former smokejumper; former Continental Air Services (CASI) loadmaster, Laos

In 1966 I worked there in Vientiane, Laos, as a loadmaster for Continental Air Services. Like Air America, Continental Air Services was on contract with the CIA. We'd haul 48,000 pounds of both "hard rice" and eating rice in a Lockheed 382, which is the same as the C-130. Hell, you ought to see hand loadin' and off-loadin' a C-130! Christ, we'd be on the ground for three or four hours. Then we'd drop it in four passes. Twelve thousand pounds in each pass. That's a lot of damn rice.

Sometimes I'd see Jerry in Long Cheng, and a couple of times I went up to Site 36 when he was up there. I guess Site 36 was lost to the bad guys for a few months in '66, but it went back and forth more than once. The NVA would try to take the place over when it got socked in. They always tried to get in there under real solid clouds because then our planes couldn't get in to provide air support.

Letter to ALAN DANIELS from Jerry Daniels, June 22, 1966

Dear Alan,

It's now the rainy season here, and things have slowed up a little, but not too much. The reason things slow down is because the clouds just hunker down low and cover most of the drop zones and landing strips.

I am now back to the very first place that I was when I first got here, but I travel around some about every day. The other day while hunkering on top of a mountain top, the big dog there gave me the best meal he could offer—bat meat—and to top it off the first piece I bit into was the head, they just fried them up whole—mighty pleasin'!

A few weeks ago I hunkered up on top of a high mountain peak for a week. I was the only white person within 100 air miles except for when a plane came droning over, which wasn't too often. (Planes couldn't land there.) I knew many of the people there with me though. Not one of them spoke a word of english, but I have not too much problem with their language, so I ended up giving many English lessons.

This countries' people (at least the people I work with) are much more different than the Viet. in that they are on your side or not. If there is a bad one in the group, he is recognized immediately, and things are handled accordingly. In other words you can depend on everyone behind you. I can leave things laying around at random, and have never lost an item yet.

Whenever I go to town I always try and take one of the guys down with me. Some are maybe 25 years old and have never been to town before, and they really let the good times roll.

Jerry

RANDOLPH "TOBY" SCOTT, former smokejumper; former Continental Air Services (CASI) loadmaster, Laos

Ol' Jerry, he'd get stuck up there at Site 36 for months. I'd see him every time he came into Vientiane, but it wasn't too often. When Jerry came down to town he usually had some little ol' Hmong with him, draggin' him around. Ha! That Hmong had never been to town before in his life. I mean it was like gettin' somebody from the 1700s back there with Lewis and Clark and turnin' them loose with things like airplanes, buildings, cars. He'd never seen anything like that. He'd be lookin' around, walkin' around sayin', "Oi-yoh!" That's their language, you know. That means something like, "My gosh!"

What usually happened, Jerry'd give the little guy a handful of *kip* [Lao money], show him where the whorehouse was, and turn him loose. Tell him to be back there at a certain time the next day. Ha! But Jerry said he had to be careful to not let them have a gun because in Vientiane they had Vietnamese around there. If a Hmong saw a Vietnamese they'd likely pull out a gun and shoot him. So he didn't let them take a gun when they'd come into Vientiane.

Sometimes he'd have trouble rounding them up the next day. He'd have to get them back up-country, you know? They'd be drunk and hungover. "Oi-yoh!" God, that little ol' Hmong would look like hell, but he was happy. He'd be back there yakkin', and Jerry said he couldn't shut him up for two days after they got back up-country.

Excerpt from a letter to LOUISE DANIELS from Jerry Daniels, July 17, 1966

Dear Louise,

. . . Now for Business—I want the check to the 1st Montana Finance to be used to pay off <u>in full</u> my debt there. I figure probably about 380.00. I hope no more, but give them no more than 500.00. The fifty dollars is for 3 pairs of those Levi "stay press" dark green pants (hope they're still making them, if not black can't bust-ems) with 33" waist and 33" length. 3 pair 34" underwear, 3 pair light wool type white socks (like gym socks) size 11–12. Send airmail. <u>Buy nothing more</u>. With remaining money—if any. You go fishing or eat some steaks or gut bombs what ever the amount warrants. . . . Say hello to all.

Jerry

MIKE LYNCH, former provincial advisor, Lima Site 36, Na Khang, Laos

Despite the rough conditions at Site 36, Jerry was rather careful about his clothes, especially those that he wore on his infrequent visits to Vientiane and Udorn. He constructed a crude wardrobe closet out of rice pallets and hung his shirts on a few wire hangers. One day when Jerry was away an American from another area of Laos caught a ride up to Site 36 on a supply flight and came up to our operations shack while his plane was being unloaded. As I was briefing the visitor, he absent-mindedly reached into our filing cabinet, picked up a .22 caliber survival pistol, waved it in my direction, and pulled the trigger. I froze in fright as the bullet apparently passed harmlessly through the wall and out into rice paddy beyond. I was amazed that someone would act so irresponsibly. I promptly sent the visitor back to his aircraft with appropriate comments.

The next day when Jerry returned, he went to retrieve a shirt from his closet and started yelling, "The dreaded rats have eaten a hole through the pocket of my shirt!" After discovering that all three shirts hanging in a line had holes through the pockets he exclaimed, "The dreaded rats can smell where I keep my snoose," his chewing tobacco. Once we discovered that the entry and exit holes in the closet ends matched up with the holes in the shirts, I told him about the pistol incident and how the visitor claimed that he did not expect that we would have a loaded gun in our filing cabinet. Jerry said, "Good thing I wasn't here. I would have shot him. What the fuck does he expect? There's a war going on up here!"

RANDOLPH "TOBY" SCOTT, former smokejumper; former Continental Air Services (CASI) loadmaster, Laos

One time I was doin' some cargo kickin' with Continental on the Porters. The pilots kind of liked to have a round eye in there for communication. They'd already had one mix-up in commo where they'd dropped a company commander out of a damn Porter. That company commander was helpin' them drop stuff and he was sittin' on the damn trap door when the pilot pulled the damn lever. Jerry said they got the message back, "We received our rice and our company commander." Ha! It killed him deader than hell.

Anyway, I saw Jerry when I was up there doin' some droppin' at Site 36. Site 36 was just some dirt hole. God, you wouldn't believe it. And Site 36 kept gettin' bigger and bigger because of the refugees pourin' in there and what not. When I got there, Jerry hadn't shaved, he was dirty and grubby looking. But he had all the radios runnin' real smooth and he's got his ammo stacked and everything's under control. Everybody knew what was goin' on.

MIKE LYNCH, former provincial advisor, Lima Site 36, Na Khang, Laos

Prior to the evacuation in February 1966, Jerry, Don, and I had lived in a house made of bamboo and wooden pallets used for rice drops. Although we slept under mosquito nets to prevent the rats from crawling over us, one managed to bite Jerry's nose while he slept. Jerry then declared total war on rats and would take his .22 cal revolver to bed with him and shoot at obvious rat movements as they scurried about on top of the parachute panels that we had hung to line the underside of our roof. This tactic was effective in reducing the rat population but scared hell out of me when a shot would ring out in the middle of the night. Even Jerry realized that it was time to quit when our parachute ceiling began to sag and discolor with the weight of dead and decomposing rats.

Failing to get support from the Vientiane embassy families for his project to recruit cats in Vientiane to join the war effort at Site 36, Jerry resorted to rat poison he ordered from Udorn. When ingested by rats, this poison caused them to drink large quantities of water, then crawl off and die in a dark place. The rats must have had the last laugh as several of them expired in the depths of Jerry's sleeping bag.

After we reoccupied Site 36 in June of '66 we shared a long tin house. The tin house was a new addition. More correctly, the house was built with fifty-gallon dirt-filled steel gas drums for outside walls and had a tin sheet roof. Our former bamboo house gave us no protection, but those dirt drums effectively blocked small arms fire and shell fragments from penetrating. They probably saved our lives more than once.

One foggy rainy day Jerry was bored because all the aircraft were grounded in Vientiane or Thailand due to weather. He decided to grab a pick and started digging a hole next to his bed. Although Don and I were skeptical at first, soon Jerry's version of "The Great Escape" became a group effort. We three Americans dug an underground tunnel from the floor between our beds out to a covered bunker so that we wouldn't get trapped in the house during an attack. When the time came, it worked as designed.

THOMAS J. "T. J." THOMPSON, former smokejumper; former air delivery specialist, MR2, Laos

Did you know that Jerry had geese there at Site 36? He had thirty geese he ordered from USAID, and then he turned 'em loose. At any given time, fifteen were on R and R and fifteen were on guard duty. Then he'd rotate 'em. This fifteen'd go back on duty so the others would go on R and R. The geese on R and R roamed around inside the position. The ones on duty were penned in clearings outside the perimeter that was trenched and had concertina wire around it. If the NVA'd come close those geese'd start squawkin'. If *anyone* came up they'd start squawkin'. They were quite effective, day and night. After some geese came up missing, Jerry put guards on the geese on R and R. He'd have a couple guys watchin' them, kind of herding them around. There was always a mess following those geese. You've heard that phrase loose as a goose? Well, it's the truth.

MIKE LYNCH, former provincial advisor, Lima Site 36, Na Khang, Laos

When several of the geese were reported as AWOL or mysteriously killed in action, Jerry investigated and could find no evidence of enemy activity. It became obvious that the deceased geese had ended up as the soldiers' dinner. Jerry recalled the remaining geese to headquarters and soon reported to Udorn that the geese were special guests at a dinner in their honor.

BILL LE COUNT, former pilot, Laos

It was probably around 1967 when I went into Site 36 and Jerry came out and said, "I need you to go to the jewelry store in Vientiane." He needed silver. About one hundred dollars worth of silver. He said the Meo had their big festival and they had all these chicken fights, and he bought the winning rooster, the grand champion of the whole festival. But the owner of the chicken wouldn't take any *kip*, any Lao paper money, so that's why I had to bring the silver up there. So I brought the silver up and we owned the chicken. A pretty valuable bird. We wanted to take him down to Bangkok and enter him in the big rooster fights down there, the big money.

Well, I never personally saw that chicken, but I'd say to the other pilots, "How's our rooster doin'?" They told me that Jerry had him on a health diet and was exercising him and had him in a special little cage with a guard on him. Inside the cage they even built a little treadmill for the chicken to walk on. They'd say, "Well, he's walkin' the treadmill. He's building up his leg muscles."

The next time I came into Site 36 Jerry had a big sad face. I said, "Uh-oh. What's gone on?" He said, "The chicken's dead." He said, "A Meo came in here with his wife and kids. Came in from nowhere. He's walking a little pony and has a chicken that's riding in a cage on the horse. That should've given me my first clue about who was important in that group. He said he'd heard about our bird and he wanted his bird to fight it. I couldn't refuse. I would lose face." Then Jerry said, "His bird made really short work of our chicken." I said, "Well, hell! Why can't we buy that one?" He said, "He wouldn't sell." He'd already put the bird back on the pony and away he went. That was it. One hundred dollars in silver, and I don't think we had that chicken a whole week. The Grand Champion. Ha!

BARRY REED, former smokejumper; former Air America loadmaster, Laos

I worked for Air America in Laos from '66 to '74 as a loadmaster. Loadmaster, kicker, air freight specialist. Whatever you want to call it, they all mean the same thing. In November 1966, roughly, I was on a Caribou and we landed with a full load in Na Khang, Site 36. In a roaring cloud of dust we came to the end of the runway and then turned around. The pilot let the engines idle. We never did shut down the engines up there at Na Khang because Site 36 was narrow, sometimes it was under fire and we never knew when that would happen, and it was cluttered with cargo because it was a very busy small strip. We kept the engines running at that site because you want to get in and get out of there.

That day we landed the Caribou, and I was on the cargo ramp in the back, just opening things up and waiting for whoever was coming up to off-load the cargo. I saw a guy walking through this thick cloud of dust in a cowboy hat. As the dust finally settled he took off the cowboy hat and slapped it against his leg. He was just *covered* with dust. He looked up and pointed at me and said, "I know you!" I said, "I know you, too!" It was Jerry. We didn't have much time to talk that day. Just quick. I'd known him since we were both smokejumpers, and I'd seen him earlier that same year in Missoula, shopping or something. He was one of the last people I'd expect to see out there. In fact, I never dreamed that there were other people from Missoula *anywhere* in Laos!

LEE GOSSETT, former smokejumper; former pilot, Laos

I first met Jerry when I was a smokejumper for the Bureau of Land Management, the BLM, jumping out of Fairbanks, Alaska, in the summer of 1963. Jerry was one of the crewmembers on the Intermountain Aviation B-17 that arrived from their home base in Marana, Arizona. That B-17 was equipped with the Fulton Skyhook system.

Caribou and Pilatus Porter on airstrip at Na Khang (LS 36). 1965. Photo credit: Mike Lynch.

By 1964 I was working as a kicker for Air America in Vientiane, Laos, but by 1966 I worked for Air America as a Caribou copilot and would see Jerry up-country at LS 36. Jerry would live in the trenches with the Hmong soldiers, sometimes for sixty days at a time. Once while we had some time Jerry showed me around his humble trench. I couldn't believe how he lived, but for Jerry, if it's good enough for the Hmong troops then it's good enough for him.

Whenever I was on fuel shuttle flights from Vientiane to LS 36 I would take Jerry two cheeseburgers from the Air America restaurant at the Vientiane airport. The flight was one hour each way and we could only do three round trips per day, so I would bring the cheeseburgers on the second flight after I knew he was in camp. You should have seen his face light up when I arrived with those cheeseburgers.

MIKE LYNCH, former provincial advisor, Lima Site 36, Na Khang, Laos

In 1966 Don, Jerry, Ernie, and I were at the small Lao village of Moung Het on the Song Ma river in the far north of Sam Neua Province only six miles south of the North Vietnamese border. The friendly forces briefly moved into this village with little or no resistance. As it turned out we were the first Caucasians that the locals had seen since the 1950s; we were really objects of curiosity. As the village had never been fought over or bombed, it was a breath of fresh air to see people who were growing food and raising a few animals. We were there for two days, during which time Jerry managed to purchase three fat ducks that we roasted and shared with some of our troops. That was a real treat for all. Only Jerry would know how to prep and cook a duck using only bamboo skewers and a fire augmented with powder charges from a 60 mm mortar. That day he was the Julia Child of Sam Neua.

BILL LE COUNT, former pilot, Laos

I was a pilot in Laos from 1964 to '69. When we flew up-country we always asked all the guys, "What do you need us to bring you from the commissary in Vientiane when we come up?" We'd take them whatever special deals they wanted. We were kiddin' around one time, and Jerry said, "Bring me a girlfriend, an American girlfriend. I haven't been home in a long time." I said, "Okay, we'll see what we can do." So we mail ordered for an inflatable woman and eventually she showed up. When we were going up to Site 36 in the Caribou, the guys inflated her and they'd bought all the extras. They had lipstick, panties, shoes, everything. They stuck a wig on her. We brought him a big blonde. We presented her to Jerry, and I stood up in the hatch of the Caribou and took a picture of him with his inflatable woman. Jerry's standin' there grinning ear to ear. We were in range of enemy fire so we didn't spend a lot of time on the ground. I took a picture and we got right back out. I heard later on that it caused quite a commotion with the Hmong. Americans are crazy anyway, but now they've got fake women, artificial women! Jerry said they just went nuts. That's what he said.

Yeah, we'd see Jerry on site and then we'd party when he came down to Vientiane. And that's not publishable.

MIKE LYNCH, former provincial advisor, Lima Site 36, Na Khang, Laos

By coincidence, Jerry had taken a rare night off to visit Vientiane and thereby also missed the second attack on Na Khang on January 6, 1967. That one came about four or five o'clock in the morning when Don and I were sleeping. We were awakened by the sound of AK fire up close. Don provided cover for me with my shotgun while I attempted to raise someone on the radio. I eventually made contact with the American military attaché in Vientiane, who made contact with Udorn, who then assisted in diverting a pair of USAF fighter-bombers that were returning to Thailand from a mission in Vietnam. Probably the whole process took less than half an hour although it seemed longer as we were under heavy fire at the time.

As soon as Jerry heard of the attack he insisted on departing from Vientiane on a small plane, a CASI Pilatus Porter. In several radio conversations between me at Site 36 and Jerry in the Porter, he kept saying he was pissed off at the "dreaded enemy" for not waiting for him. Jerry's eventual arrival at Na Khang that morning was quite spectacular. Even though the strip was closed and bullets were still flying about, Jerry convinced the pilot to do a touch-and-go on the runway so he could jump out. It appeared to me that when the plane touched down briefly, Jerry exited through the drop door in the floor and the aircraft immediately accelerated and took off as he

Jerry Daniels and the inflatable woman, Lima Site 36. Photo credit: Bill Le Count.

rolled out from under it. As the dust started to clear I could see Jerry roll to the ditch at the side of the runway and scamper up the hill to our house, only to find Don's body covered with a blanket lying just outside our doorway.

Jerry asked me what happened. I told him Don was providing cover for me while I made radio contact with the inbound aircraft. I was crawling forward to inform Don when he was shot in the head. Jerry said, "Jeez, I'll bet the last seconds of his life were interesting as hell."[6] That was Jerry's own way of showing respect for Don while trying to boost the morale of the beleaguered defenders. His next comment was something like, "Well, let's get back to work." Because about the time he arrived I was a crazy madman juggling several radios and calling in air strikes on enemy attackers who still surrounded our position. Later one of the pilots reported that I said something like: "See the hill next to the runway with someone waving? That's me, so shoot everyone else within fifty yards—no, make it twenty-five yards!" I was trying to keep Vientiane, Udorn, and Long Cheng informed, and attempting to communicate with a bunch of frightened Lao and Hmong who had suddenly forgotten all of the French and English they could speak so well the previous day. By the time Jerry arrived we had two A1-E Skyraiders overhead making firing passes so low that we could see the faces of the pilots and the glow of their exhaust stacks. They made a heck of a roar when they were flying by at low altitude and full power.

Jerry relieved me of most of the air support duties so that I could talk to the local commanders and try to pinpoint additional targets. By late morning the enemy fell back under the close air support by the USAF and the actions of the defenders. We were then able to open the airstrip and start coordinating the resupply of our troops and the evacuation of the dead and wounded to Long Cheng. We also received reinforcements of fresh Hmong soldiers and weapons from Long Cheng.

Meanwhile, Vientiane was insisting that we Americans be evacuated prior to nightfall while Jerry and I pleaded that we needed to remain with the troops to prevent them abandoning the site, as they had done the previous year when we evacuated. It took us a couple of hours to get approval, which ultimately came from Ambassador Sullivan.

That night Udorn and Vientiane pulled out all the stops in getting air support for us. Throughout the night Jerry and I took turns talking to the pilots to provide targets and encouragement to the jet fighters and World War II–era B-26 bombers. The last C-130 Lamplighter flareship was still dropping flares as the sun came up the next morning. At this point Jerry and I were, in his own words, "farting through silk." We had avoided a mandatory evacuation and proved that if the Americans remained on site and provided the tactical air and logistic support and didn't bug out in the face of an attack, the local troops would stay and prevail, and they did.

English-language *BANGKOK POST*, January 10, 1967

50 REDS KILLED IN LAOS

Vientiane, Laos, Jan. 10—(UPI)—The bodies of 50 North Vietnamese and Pathet Lao troops were found over the weekend on a battlefield near Nakhang where government and Communist troops clashed in a ten-hour fight Friday night.

A Laotian Defense Ministry communique issued Monday said three battalions of Communists attacked a government strongpoint near Nakhang village.

The communique said the North Vietnamese and Pathet Lao were met by strong government resistance and were driven back with the help of air raids.

Government troops lost seven killed and 30 wounded.

It was the second time in less than a year that Communist forces have tried to take control of the strategic strongpoint at Nakhang.

MIKE LYNCH, former provincial advisor, Lima Site 36, Na Khang, Laos

Don's death was particularly hard on Jerry, who was a close friend. Despite his sometimes outward cockiness and apparent indifference, I found Jerry to be a compassionate and sensitive guy. We lived and worked in very close proximity in a small world that could often be chaotic, stressful, intimidating, and at times scary. It always bothered him that he had missed the brunt of the NVA attacks as he seldom left Na Khang during periods of heightened enemy activity in the area—usually the entire dry season.

THOMAS J. "T. J." THOMPSON, former smokejumper; former air delivery specialist, MR2, Laos

Site 36 was called "the Alamo" because it was surrounded by enemy. You flew in and you flew out and you could get fire anywhere you went. By the fall of '67 there was no village at Site 36; it was strictly a military post with maybe 150 Hmong and Lao soldiers. It was very heavily fortified with trenches and barbed wire surrounding the site, and the troops were on alert twenty-four hours a day.

I stayed up at Lima Site 36 with Jerry in the fall of '67. Jerry was tellin' me about coming off an operation on Route 6, the main road to Sam Neua and Hanoi. I guess he was the only American on the operation with quite a few Hmong and Lao troopers. I imagine there must have been forty or fifty of 'em, all on foot, of course. The troops were moving out after the operation and trying to get back towards Na Khang. As they moved out they came under mortar fire from the NVA. Jerry was on the radio to a FAC overhead to call in an air strike, saying the mortars were coming in. His radio boy was with him when one round came down and hit on Jerry's right side. The

Hog Daniels and Hmong forces during an attack by enemy troops on Phou Mok Lok Mountain near Road 6, Sam Neua Province, December 1966. Mike Lynch collection.

radio boy was standing between him and the mortar round and the boy took all the shrapnel that was meant for Jerry, I guess. The ground commander hollered, "Move out! Move out!" Jerry said, "Well, I couldn't do it. I picked up the boy. I knew he was dying." He probably slung him on his back somehow. Jerry was real strong, you know, used to backpacking and carrying heavy loads, and that young soldier couldn't have weighed all that much. He carried him about a mile through the jungle, which isn't easy to do. When he stopped and set the soldier down he was dead. The fragments had peppered him with holes, just like a sieve. But Jerry said, "Well, I just couldn't leave him." See? That sort of tells you about his moral character and his steel under combat, under fire. But to me the big thing about Jerry was his invincibility. He couldn't be destroyed. That was one story that he told me as we were sittin' in his bunker up at Site 36 at night. Jerry told that story without showing emotion; that's just the way he was.

Up there at Site 36 I lived, ate, and slept in Hog's bunker. You go down in there and you'd keep yourself as clean as you could but it was a dirt hole, maybe ten feet wide and twelve feet long. It was dug into the ground with two feet of sandbags over the top, timbers over that, then tin, then more timbers and another layer of sandbags. There were three or four bunks. I stayed down there in Hog's bunker with the radios and the rats. The rats were all sizes and very active, very aggressive. They roamed all night and kept you awake clattering about. The Hmong would shoot them with crossbows—cook and eat them. I didn't try any rat meat, but there were a hell of a lot of 'em.

At night there was hardly any movement inside the position. Movement was taboo because you could get shot real easy. You'd try to sleep and the radio was always breaking in. There was constant radio talk, murmurs from around the perimeter. There was always spontaneous gunfire and there were flares going off. The night would slowly quiet down. When you did get to sleep you slept good but it was interrupted. You slept fitfully 'til early in the morning when things started again. Air choppers and planes started coming in. It was very long days. And there was no drinking. There was no way you could drink and be mentally alert. No way. Those days just started early and lasted long, and you were on the edge all the time.

I flew with Hog to several sites each day. We covered all of Sam Neua Province and part of Xiengkhouang Province. In each village Hog introduced me to the Hmong officers, village leaders, and gave me a tour of the village and their defensive positions.

RANDOLPH "TOBY" SCOTT, former smokejumper; former Continental Air Services (CASI) loadmaster, Laos

Boy, the Hmong thought the world of Jerry. I mean he was like a god. The reason Jerry got along so damn good with the Hmong—he was probably the only ranking CIA guy that worked over there that had ever grown up in the woods, packed in, hunted, fished, stayed in a tent, all that kind of stuff, which is the way the Hmong lived.

Jerry stayed there and lived with them. Whatever food they were eatin', he never turned it down. If he had to eat monkey or bat, he'd sit right beside them and join in.

Hog Daniels sharing a meal with Hmong soldiers. Toby Scott collection.

If they went two weeks without a bath, he did, too. Sometimes we'd tell him, "Oh, my God, Jerry! You stink!" He was the only guy the CIA had that would go out and live with the Hmong and respect them and talk to them and not lie to them or feed them a bunch of crap. They trusted anything Jerry told to them. He never lied to them. He'd rather lie to the CIA than lie to the Hmong!

BILL LAIR, former CIA paramilitary officer, Thailand and Laos

I think of all the Americans there, Jerry probably had better communication with the Hmong than anyone else. The big thing about him, he was willing to stay up there with them for months at a time. Most other people would be climbing the wall, but Jerry liked that. He got along so well with the people. He liked them, and they all liked him.

GLENN F. HALE, former smokejumper; former Continental Air Services (CASI) Air Operations, MR3, Laos

Jerry always worked and did a good job, above and beyond. You respected him for what he was, but basically he was really an animal. He lived up at 36 in a dang cave and shot rats. I never saw Site 36 myself but to live like that, live with the Meo, live in a bunker cave and shoot rats, it takes a special kind of person.

I've thought a lot about that. In the Agency they have a saying, "going native." I believe Jerry did that, went native. Going native was a phrase we used when someone got so involved with the project and even more so with the people, that he would just stay on and be dedicated to the cause of these "natives." You get up there and you recognize the important part that you play in the puzzle. And so you have a dedication to make it as good as you can. This is not a bad thing in my estimation. I think the biggest problem of our government today is no continuity of support for the causes. It's just get in, kick ass, and try to get out. But Jerry stayed and he went native for the Meo. He loved the Meo and vice versa. So he took care of them and stayed there, really at the expense of most of his career with the Agency.

BARRY REED, former smokejumper; former Air America loadmaster, Laos

Na Khang, Site 36, was overrun for the last time around March '69, about a year after Phou Pha Thi was lost. Phou Pha Thi was nicknamed "North Station." It was a mountaintop that we had used as a beacon, a TACAN and TSQ-81 radar station for the air force tankers and also the fighters. The tankers and the fighters used it as a reference point for bombing runs on Haiphong and Hanoi. Phou Pha Thi was lost about the same time as the Tet offensive in Vietnam. After we lost Phou Pha Thi, the NVA kept pushing across northern Laos. The communists usually made their big advances during the dry season. By then Na Khang was the only major outpost left in northern Laos.[7]

In March '69 I was based in Udorn, Thailand. We had a core of people that were volunteers to do night drops. A night drop was so we wouldn't get shot down during the daytime. It was a hazardous mission and we got extra pay, fifty bucks for each night drop. The crew I was with was in a C-47, dropping supplies pretty close to Phou Pha Thi, Site 85. Before we left Udorn, the pilots were told in the FIC [Flight Information Center] briefing that Na Khang, Site 36, had been overrun the evening before. The Agency people had gotten a radio transmission that Site 36 was under heavy attack from the NVA and that our people were leaving. Since Site 36 was almost on our direct flight back to Udorn, the pilots were told to overfly it and see if there was any friendly activity because the Agency people had lost all radio contact with their people on the ground. We should watch for survival flares, fires, strobe lights.

We made the air drop at a drop site south of Phou Pha Thi. Site 36 was maybe thirty to forty air miles south of the drop site. We were about ten miles southwest of Na Khang, looking around, when we saw these little hand-held flares going up from a ridge top. So we figured, "That's gotta be them." That was Jerry and his Hmong group that got away. We didn't make any radio contact. Just saw the flares and reported back to the Agency so that our helicopter pilots, along with Jerry's bosses, could make contact with them.

Many years later I found out that it wasn't Jerry on the ground that night after all. Turned out Jerry was in Missoula, enrolled at the University of Montana! He'd been at Site 36 for so long I just assumed he was down there in the jungle with his Hmong people. He was in Missoula for about eighteen months, then he came back to Laos again.

Two

MISSOULA

May 2–8, 1982

Hometown Friends

FRIENDS of Jerry Daniels in Missoula share the news of his death; Louise Daniels; a State Department cable; suspicions voiced by Missoula Hmong and the family of Jerry Daniels; decisions about estate administration; a reporter files a Freedom of Information Act (FOIA) request.

LEE "TERRIBLE TORGY" TORGRIMSON, grade school friend; Missoula crony

I would suspect it was the Animal Man who told me Jerry was found dead. My initial reaction was sadness, but not surprise. Because of his last homecoming.

Knowing what I knew of Jerry, when I heard the circumstances I knew immediately that that's not how he died. You know, it's not beyond possibility that the gas could have gone off and he would have suffocated. Because he could get pretty well hammered. But my mind-set was our last conversation prior to him dying. That he was gonna quit the Agency. When you're in the kind of operation that he was in, and what he told me was happening and what he insinuated, it was just a matter of fact in my mind that he's dead. And our government killed him. Because I don't trust *anybody* in our government. George Bush, Secord, Ollie North, Colby. That bunch are no good. They're rotten people, and they'd do anything to present their own programs, further their ends.

Conversation between TED O. "LITTLE O" LYMPUS, high school and college friend, and LEE "TERRIBLE TORGY" TORGRIMSON, Missoula crony

TED: Torgy called me and said, "I have bad news. Barker's dead." To us, Jerry was J.B. or Barker, because Barker was his middle name.

TORGY: Yeah, we called him J.B. or Daniels or Barker or Shithead or whatever was needed to catch his attention. Black Man, Black Meat. Anything that would come along. That name Hog probably came from overseas. Here in Missoula mostly we called him J.B. or Barker.

TED: Anyway, Torgy said he was dead.

CHA MOUA, Hmong friend; Hmong funeral organizer

When Jerry passed away Louise cried and cried, and I stayed with her all day long. When I talked to Louise I seriously questioned her because I wanted to make sure if it was Jerry or somebody else and they made a mistake. I said to Louise, "Mother, are you sure this is the right one? There are so many Jerrys. What identification leads you to believe that it is really *our* Jerry? Why are you so sure?" Then she pulled out the telegram that they sent her. And Louise said, "Honey, I think so. They said the dental information matches Jerry's dental records. Honey, everything matches."

Louise was very sad. She was crying, and I tried to calm her down. I said, "Please reduce your crying, Mother. In Jerry's position it could be many other things. Even though the telegram words sound true, I still don't believe 100 percent that he really died." That time Louise said, "Do you think so?" I said, "Maybe. For the time being, I assume that it is a fifty-fifty chance, dead or alive." Louise said, "Okay, I will hope for that." We believed he may have died or he may not have died, but we had hope. That was the only chance we hoped for.

DEPARTMENT OF STATE cable from U.S. Ambassador John Gunther Dean, May 4, 1982

FM AMEMBASSY BANGKOK

TO SECSTATE WASHDC IMMEDIATE 7964

LIMITED OFFICIAL USE BANGKOK 24596

SUBJ: DEATH OF REFUGEE OFFICER, JERROLD B. DANIELS

1. RMO WILDE HAD CONFERENCE WITH POLICE GEN. PHAITOON LIMRAT, CHIEF OF PATHOLOGY AT POLICE GENERAL HOSPITAL AND STAFF CONCERNING CAUSE OF DEATH OF SUBJECT.

2. IDENTIFICATION OF BODY OF J. DANIELS IS 100 PERCENT POSITIVE ON THE BASIS OF:

(A) APPENDECTOMY SCAR

(B) FRACTURED RIB

(C) DENTAL RECORDS OBTAINED FROM LOCAL DENTIST ON 3 MAY. DUE TO ADVANCED PUTREFACTION IT WAS IMPOSSIBLE TO OBTAIN READABLE FINGERPRINTS.

3. CAUSE OF DEATH IS CARBON MONOXIDE INTOXICATION. THIS DIAGNOSIS IS BASED ON:

(A) CARBOXYHEMOGLOBIN OF 92 PERCENT

(B) SETTING AT SCENE

(C) POLICE REPORTS - INTERVIEW OF SURVIVOR. A 19 YEAR OLD THAI BOY WHO IS NOW HOSPITALIZED WITH CLINICAL SYMPTOMS CONSISTENT WITH CO POISONING.

4. WHILE THERE IS PRESENTLY NO INDICATION OF FOUL PLAY OR DRUG ABUSE, WE WILL NEVERTHELESS WAIT FOR THE COMPLETE POLICE REPORT PRIOR TO COMMENTING ON THE CIRCUMSTANCES OF DEATH. AN SY [SECURITY] CHANNEL CABLE WITH PRELIMINARY INVESTIGATION RESULTS IS BEING FORWARDED SEPARATELY.

5. GENERAL PHAITOON WILL PROVIDE COMPLETE AUTOPSY REPORT TO THE EMBASSY LATER. DEAN

"LUCKY" LUE YANG, former field liaison officer (FLO), MR2, Laos; Hmong funeral organizer

Many of our Hmong people could not quite believe the story about how Jerry died from a gas leak. Some of us thought that maybe there was some kind of a political question; others thought maybe Jerry did not want to live in the U.S. anymore, or that the U.S. government sent him somewhere and now he lived in some other part of the world in secret. Everybody was kind of frustrated. We didn't know exactly what was going on. Many people tried to put together ideas from many different angles.

PAO K. MOUA, younger brother of Chou Moua and Cha Moua

When I heard Jerry passed away, first question in my mind: *How many died with him?* Answer: *Oh, there was poisonous gas in his bedroom but one Thai houseboy escaped.* Blah, blah, blah. The mystery question was if there were two of them there in the apartment, why didn't the Thai die? Why only Jerry died? That means something. That's an unexplained something. We talked about these things. We put the puzzle on the table to see whether it made sense or not. One survived, one died. We thought: *Oh, that's a setup.*

Mrs. MARY MAO HEU VANG, wife of Chu Vang; daughter-in-law of General Vang Pao

Chu came home and told me about Jerry. I felt pretty bad because he was Louise's son and he was *Jerry* and everybody knew him. He was *so* popular. He was someone! So when you heard that he passed away everybody was shocked. "My God! How did he pass away? Why? He's a *good* man. We still want to see him, to meet him!"

When Chu and I stayed in the Nam Phong refugee camp in Thailand, Jerry was the one who watched over us every day. He gave some spending money to each member of VP's family. He gave so much per day per person. He didn't talk too much but he talked very seriously. He was a good man, *very* nice, and you don't want anything to happen to him. I was not close to him but I was with VP's family so there was an impact. He was someone that you wanted to have there. He watched over us like he was a sponsor to us in Thailand.

It was so sad when he passed away, especially because of Louise. When we first came to Missoula, Louise said to me, "Oh, you are Chu's wife? You know my son?" She was *so* sweet. Louise was so happy to see me, she hugged me and she took us to a restaurant. Not many people take you to the restaurant to eat steak or do good things for you like Jerry's mom did. Louise was *so* nice to us. You don't want a mother to lose her son like that. You feel so bad for the mom and you feel so bad for Jerry, too. That is how I felt. That was the personal impact on me. I felt *bad* when Jerry passed away, even though I was not so close to him.

Telegram to Louise Daniels from NAN BORTON and HANK CUSHING.[1] Washington, DC, May 2, 1982

WE SHARE WITH YOU AND YOUR SONS THE PAIN AT THE LOSS OF JERRY. HE WAS, YOU KNOW, OUR LOVED AND ADMIRED FRIEND. YOU HAVE OUR SYMPATHIES AND AFFECTIONS.

JACK TUPPER DANIELS, brother of Jerry Daniels

Right away the 92 percent level of carbon monoxide in his body struck me as odd, and it continued to bother me. My PhD is in physiology so I know the human body. And exercise physiology, which is my field, deals with ventilation and oxygen consumption, gasses in the blood, things like that. So that cable concerned me, and I said to the State Department people, "You know, there are several things that don't add up. There is a Thai guy in another room, which is connected to the same bathroom, and he lives through this when Jerry in the opposite bedroom doesn't live through it?" I said, "Gee, that's strange. Somebody gets enough CO to die and somebody else gets enough to pass out and stay unconscious for *two or three days*, without either dying or coming to?" I said, "We've got a dead person in one adjacent room and a living person unconscious in another adjacent room—albeit two different rooms. The only possible way that could happen was if the door to Jerry's room was more open than the door to the other room so that his bedroom got a higher dose of CO. Enough carbon monoxide in his system to kill him. Then if the supply of gas ran out after Jerry's bedroom had filled with monoxide but before the other bedroom had filled with monoxide, the concentration would not be as high and that person would be put unconscious, into a state of mid-death, and live through it somehow." And the answer I got back after some hours or a day or whatever was, "That's exactly what we figured happened." So every time I would suggest something, I had given them the answer as to how it could have been that way. I was giving them the answers. And everything I said, they agreed with. So that was always troubling. Not to mention the fact that the unconscious Thai guy found in the next room had disappeared. The first time they called me, he was *in* the hospital. And *alive.* Then he vanished from the hospital and was never again to be found to my knowledge.

Ms. DEIRDRE MCNAMER, former newspaper reporter

In early May 1982 I was working as the police and courts reporter at the *Missoulian* newspaper. That day an obituary came in from the mortuary where Jerry Daniels' service would be held. It was routine, just a brief obituary. I had never heard of Jerry

Daniels, but what I noticed about it was that there were questions that seemed immediately apparent to me. There were discrepancies.

For one thing, it seemed to me that there was a long amount of time, several days, between the time that he was thought to have died and the time that anybody found him, and I thought, *Why those gapped days? He has a pretty easy job or a pretty strange job that nobody discovers that you're gone from it for several days.* That question came up. It also said he was in Bangkok and worked as a liaison with the State Department. I saw "State Department" and I thought, *Well, he was a spook!* Also the cause of death was vague, "unknown cause." And there was no mention of an autopsy. A few little things like that.

Well, if a prominent local person had died here in Missoula and there had been that kind of obituary, I would have called up somebody to iron out these discrepancies, especially after the description of the funeral that I got from my sister a week or so later. My sister, Meagan, was studying ethnomusicology at the University of Montana and already knew a fair amount about Hmong music. She went to that funeral to observe the Hmong rituals. She said it was "a very big deal," that this Jerry fellow seemed to be someone of *real* stature. That there were these people who showed up who looked like old Asia hands with white linen suits on and yellow skin—a look that you don't often see walking down the street in Missoula, Montana. And the obituary itself was very little and matter of fact. So I wanted to find out more about this guy. I was just trying to be a good newspaper gal, trying to clarify an obituary with holes in it and one that seemed rather slight for the subject.

Not long after that I filed a Freedom of Information Act request. I'm not even sure I expected to get anything. I just wanted to try it. So I sent off a request as a member of the press. I sent it to both the CIA and the State Department, and I got back very quickly this, "We don't confirm or deny if anybody, alive or dead, ever worked for us," from the CIA. And my request was still sitting at the State Department.

Ms. CECELIA CHRISTENSEN (formerly Mrs. Jack Stratton), friend of Louise Daniels

Louise was just so sad. Several years before, she'd lost her oldest son, Danny. A drunk driver hit him, and that was devastating to her. It truly was. Jerry's death was bad, but I think it was the combination of both of them dying. So it was *hard*. And there was a lot of disbelief on what really happened to him. Was it the accident that they said it was? Or was it something else that they were trying to hide? I don't think that was ever resolved in her mind.

JACK TUPPER DANIELS, brother of Jerry Daniels

In his will, Jerry made me the executor of his estate. For all those years, Jerry never had a will. He only wrote one a year before he died. He wrote it out by hand on blue paper, and he sent it to me from Thailand. He explained that he had checked with an

Danny, Alan, Jerry, Jack, and Kent with their mother Louise Daniels at the funeral of their father Ronald L. "Bob" Daniels. Deer Lodge, Montana, December 1969. Daniels family collection. Used with permission.

attorney friend in Montana and it was acceptable. That there was such a thing as a handwritten legal document that didn't have to be witnessed by a lawyer as you filled it out, that he could do it himself. I always thought it was kind of strange. He'd been there for twenty years and the year before he dies he finally writes a will. That's a coincidence, isn't it?

Ms. DEIRDRE MCNAMER, former newspaper reporter

Sometime after I filed the FOIA request I was in the *Missoulian* newsroom and there was a call for me. Some guy on the phone said, "I just want you to know that a lot of people are pretty concerned that you are looking into the death of Jerry Daniels." And I said, "Why are they concerned? I'm just functioning as an ordinary police reporter trying to amplify a story that has holes in it. Why the concern?" And he said, "Let's just say a lot of people are very concerned." I said, "Well, where are you calling from?" And he said, "Virginia." I said, "And what's your name?" He said, "Dan O'Dell." I said, "Well, Mr. O'Dell, why don't you come to Missoula and you tell me about Jerry Daniels? Or tell me why people are concerned? Why don't we talk?" He said something like, "Maybe I'll just do that," in a really threatening kind of voice. I said, "Well, why don't you!" By that point, I was in my obstreperous reporter voice. Then SLAM SLAM. He slammed, then I slammed.

At first I was just laughing. I thought, *If that really is someone connected with the CIA in Langley, that is the most heavy-footed, heavy-handed, stupid, clownish way to deal with it.* I just couldn't believe it! But what was interesting about it was that not many people knew I had filed this request. Then I thought, *Well, if it isn't the CIA, if it's some adventurer who knew somehow that this request was filed and he has taken it upon himself to issue some sort of warning*—and it was very distinctly a warning—*then* that *person is pretty inept.* I just thought the whole thing was so inept. I might have just let it all go but then that call came and I thought, *Hmmmmmm, let me look again at this.*

Missoula Hmong

SOME background regarding the Hmong community in Missoula, Montana; Hmong friends meet and prepare to conduct a traditional Hmong funeral ceremony for Daniels; comments by Hmong Christians. Brief description of the required positions in a traditional Hmong funeral ceremony; Cha Moua and "Lucky" Lue Yang take on duties as funeral organizers; Hmong women cook.

BARRY REED, former smokejumper; former Air America loadmaster, Laos

By 1982 there were a lot of Hmong in Missoula, mainly because of Jerry's refugee effort. I knew that the Hmong were very superstitious, and that there was a superstition among them that they could not live below 3,000 feet. They would just wither and die. I heard that when I was working in Laos, from people who worked for the Agency and worked with the Hmong.

Missoula is 3,200 feet in elevation. And because this was Jerry's hometown and some of Vang Pao's sons went to school here at Jerry's urging, that's how the first Hmong came to Missoula from Laos in the early '70s. Later a lot came to Missoula from the refugee camps in Thailand. Eventually most migrated to other places where they could find work, and they found they could live below 3,000 feet.

CHA MOUA, Hmong friend; Hmong funeral organizer

Originally my family was from Houa Phan, from way north Laos. They moved down to Long Cheng in Xiengkhouang Province in 1968 because of the heavy fighting in the north.

In 1963 I started as a soldier in the Hmong Special Guerilla Unit, General Vang Pao's SGU Army. First time I met Jerry was late in 1965 at Site 36, a U.S. military operation post in northern Laos. A year later I got to know Jerry better because Jerry and I went together to rescue many soldiers who got shot at the battle zones on the Plain of Jars, the PDJ, and other areas.

By 1971 I was a planning officer with the Royal Lao Army. I took English class for a whole year at the military headquarters in the capital city of Vientiane. Then from January 1 to June 30, 1972, I came to the United States and received training in military tactics at Fort Knox, Kentucky. When we finished the training I went back to Laos and went to work with the SGU Army both at Long Cheng and Bouamlong.

This time I worked with Jerry as a field liaison officer, a FLO, from August '72 to August '73.

In February 1973, a few months after the ceasefire started, Jerry came to Bouamlong, Site 32, to check it out. We sat together on top of the bunker to discuss future plans. At that time I was twenty-four or twenty-five years old. I told Jerry that I wanted to quit my job as a field liaison officer because I would like to go back to school in the United States. Jerry said, "Why do you want to do that?" I said, "I want to get a better education to help my Hmong people because the war will be over soon and the Hmong will really need help." Jerry told me to go down to Vientiane to check with the American Embassy to find out all the requirements for me to apply for a student visa. I did so and I got it.

I left Vientiane, Laos, on August 28, 1973, and I got to Missoula, Montana, on September 2, 1973. The next day Jerry's mom Louise said, "Honey, today you will go to school." I said, "*Louise*, can I wait another day?" Ha! Montana was just like a dream. Because of the change of time, day and night, I had no idea what was going on. I didn't go to school until September 5. Then I went to Hellgate High School as a junior.

In 1973 I was not the only Hmong in Missoula. Mouasu and Bao and three of VP's children were there also. And also Colonel Ly Teng's son, Khamsene, and Colonel Cher Pao Moua's son, Saykham, and Colonel Tou Lu Moua's son, Chong. I went to a *little* town in Montana, but in 1973, the *majority* of the Hmong in the U.S. lived there!

Before Jerry's body arrived I talked to Louise about his funeral. Jerry's brothers were not there much that week so I said to Louise, "Mother, how we gonna do his funeral? What do you want to do?" I asked that question on behalf of myself and my family because Jerry helped me a *lot*, and we were so close. Louise said, "Honey, I think Jerry loved the Hmong so much. He is part of your family. I want you to perform the funeral the way you want to do it. Can you do this for him?" That is what we were waiting to hear. I told Louise, "I would be happy to do that. In that case, we are going to do the Hmong spiritual system and perform all the Hmong ceremonies." She said, "My Jerry will be very pleased. He will be much more happy with your Hmong traditional ways." Louise told me that she did not need any Christian pastor to speak or do anything at all.

After she made that decision, when Louise gave us the body, at that moment I took all the planning and responsibility into my own hands. I called the clan elders together to talk about how we were going to do it. Mostly it was Lucky, me, and my brother Chou who made that commitment.

PAO K. MOUA, younger brother of Chou Moua and Cha Moua

I was in our family meeting at Nhia Chu Moua's house. Nhia Chu was the elder of our clan at that time. It was just four or five people, not a big meeting. Just a brief presentation by my brother Cha. Cha said, "This is what we're going to do for Jerry. This is what will happen."

Cha Moua hiking at Jocko Lake near Arlee, Montana, 1974. Daniels family collection. Used with permission.

Actually, the clan elders were somewhat concerned about his plan. Nhia Chu mentioned, "It's not common in our culture to perform the funeral rituals if the person is not really a member of the family and does not belong to our belief system." For Hmong, there are spirit beliefs [*peb cov dab quas*] that belong to each specific family and clan group. The funeral rites differ based on those particular beliefs. The elders said, "If you bring in someone from outside our belief system, it is not right." It had nothing to do with Jerry personally. The elders just didn't want this action to stir up any bad spirits. When spirits are stirred up, they can hang around and cause problems. But the decision was already made. In our culture, when something is presented like that, even if you reject the idea pretty strongly, there's no argument. In our culture, if we reject your idea and you stop there, that's good. But if you keep going, we don't say any bad words. Any argument is bad luck. So when the decision was presented to perform Jerry's funeral, the elders just tailed along quietly. They didn't say anything more about it.

For the younger, more modernized generation, we say, "Well, Jerry did lots of good for us. We do this just for him."

CHA MOUA, Hmong friend; Hmong funeral organizer

When I met with the clan elders there was some concern. The ritual performer would be Kia Moua Thao. His concern was how much authority Jerry's mother would give us to do what we needed to do. Can Jerry's family *really* give him to us? Is it that simple? Will the funeral facility allow us to do everything we need to do? Those were the main concerns because this would be the *first* time that the Hmong community ever performed our funeral rituals for another person. Jerry was a *big* name to us. And Jerry was American.

For the Hmong traditional ceremony, each Hmong clan—the Vang, the Moua, the Ly, the Lor, the Thao, the Vue, and others—each one has separate rules and requirements for a funeral. Jerry didn't belong to one of the clans, so how do we do it? I said, "Okay, how about we adopt him after death and just make it simple?" We can do that. The ceremony can be general to Hmong rules and regulations. Just make it simple and send Jerry to *his* ancestors and don't use the complicated rules and regulations specific to a particular clan.

I talked to Louise first, then the clan elders, then I went to talk to General Vang Pao. I said, "General, Louise wants Jerry's funeral to be performed according to our Hmong ritual way." General Vang Pao nodded his head okay. I said, "You do not have to do anything except prepare your speech."

I made the reservation at the Mountain View Mortuary in Missoula, and I started to contact all the necessary people we need for a traditional Hmong funeral. We tried to do everything without putting any burden on Louise. We chose a simple way to perform the rituals, and we focused on what was required for Jerry's spirit to progress. We focused on the requirements for the dead, not the parts of the ceremony that are for the living relatives left behind. The purpose of this ceremony was not for the living; it was for the spirit of the dead.

GEU VANG, former colonel, SGU Army, MR2, Laos

I'm not sure why Jerry's funeral turned to be Hmong traditional. I became Christian since 1947 in Xiengkhouang, Laos. My family was the *first* Hmong family to become Christian. So it felt strange to me that Jerry's mother was a Christian woman and Jerry died and she said, "Do whatever you want to do, General Vang Pao." I don't know why she did that since she was Christian. That was a question in my mind.

NHIA "JUDY" VANG, former field liaison officer (FLO), MR2, Laos

Jerry had a traditional Hmong funeral. I am Christian since I got married in Laos in 1972. Would I be happier with a Christian funeral for him? No, because he and I argued a lot about religion when we worked together. Most of the time he said, "You know, Jesus is out of date. He's 1,000 years ago, and he no longer exists." Jerry is the one that pissed me off when he said Jesus was too long ago. He no longer exists. So it was okay to have a Hmong funeral for him. He rejected Christian so he fit into the traditional Hmong funeral fine. Blow the bamboo pipes for him to go! He loves that!

THE TRADITIONAL HMONG FUNERAL CEREMONY

When a Hmong person passes away, there is an immediate need for the family to find and designate the critical people to perform the many duties of a traditional Hmong funeral. The funeral ceremony as performed in Laos is somewhat more complicated and requires more positions than when it is performed in the United States. In the United States, the positions that are most necessary are:

1. Family ritualist [*txiv cuab tsav*]
2. Funeral coordinator(s) [*kav xwm*]
3. Soul guider [*txiv qhuab ke*]
4. Kheng player [*txiv qeej*]
5. Butcher [*tshwj kab*]
6. Rice cook [*niam ua mov*]

The family ritualist [*txiv cuab tsav*] is the man who represents and acts on behalf of the family. He knows the specific funeral rituals that the family follows [*peb cov dab quas*]. His main job is to take care of feeding the spirit of the deceased.

The funeral coordinator [*kav xwm*] is the second-ranking person. He is like a general manager and is responsible for organizing everything at the funeral home. He organizes the cooks and makes sure the guests are fed on time and that everyone has enough to eat. He is also responsible for shopping, safety, and cleanup, and for receiving and counting all gifts of money, chickens, drink, and anything else. Usually there are four funeral coordinators.

The soul guider [*txiv qhuab ke*] is the man in charge of talking to the spirit of the deceased and guiding the spirit all the way to the ancestors during the first part of the funeral ceremony, called "showing the way" [*qhuab ke* or *taw ke*].

The kheng player [*txiv qeej*] is the man who blows the kheng [*qeej*] instrument, the bamboo musical pipes that can mimic and "speak" the tonal Hmong language. For a funeral there are usually three or four kheng players.

The butcher [*tshwj kab*] is the man who butchers and cooks the meat and vegetables to feed the guests. Usually there are four butchers and four rice cooks as well.

The rice cook [*niam ua mov*] is the person in charge of cooking the rice. All of the other positions are for men, but the rice cook is usually a woman.

In Hmong tradition, it is preferable to use a different person for each of these positions, but sometimes it is necessary for one person to perform multiple positions. If it is a short ceremony or if it is not possible to find people nearby who know what to do, even one person can do almost everything. In the Missoula area in 1982, Kia Moua Thao is the only experienced funeral specialist. Kia Moua is asked to be the family ritualist and he also performs several other jobs at the funeral for Jerry Daniels. Khoua Ker Xiong is asked to be the funeral coordinator.

In a traditional Hmong funeral, a butcher is required because at least one cow is killed for an important funeral.[1] For Jerry's funeral, the decision is made that it will be a little more formal than usual because the American funeral home and the American guests are not used to having people cook freshly butchered meat on site. The Hmong organizers don't want to shock anybody. They decide to buy meat from the supermarket and cook off-site, so there is no need for a butcher.

For Jerry's funeral, Cha Moua will act as the "host family" [xyom cuab], and both Cha Moua and "Lucky" Lue Yang will act as "facilitators" at the funeral ceremony because they speak both Hmong and English. "Facilitator" is not a traditional position, but in 1982 only a few Hmong in Missoula speak much English. Those two men will have the job of translating back and forth between Jerry's American friends and the Hmong people. Both of them were very close to Jerry, and they know most of the Americans and all of the Hmong who attend the funeral.

Mrs. MARY V. YANG, wife of "Lucky" Lue Yang

For Jerry's funeral there were a lot of people who came from out of town. Lucky invited them to dinner every day, so seven or eight women came to my house every afternoon to cook—my sister and Moua Cha's wife, Moua Cha's mother and my mother, and a couple other ladies. Mostly we baked pork and chicken and beef, but also we made spring rolls, soup, rice, and stir-fry. Usually for Hmong funerals there is a lot of meat because we kill so many cows and pigs for the dead person. We have to cook all the fresh meat first because it will spoil and we don't want to waste it.

The cooking was not hard, but we had to hurry because thirty to forty people came to my house every day. There were a lot of Hmong from out of town and also Bob Johnson, T.J., Shep's brother Miles, and a few more Americans. For three or four days they came every day until the funeral was over.

Laos, Part II: Long Cheng (1968–73)

THE importance of Long Cheng during the secret war in Laos; Daniels as operations officer; smokejumpers working in Laos; Richard Helms visits Long Cheng; Daniels at work; the intensity of war in Laos, especially Military Region 2 (MR2); some letters; bar stories. [See Maps 1 and 2 on pages 33 and 39.]

Excerpt from the English-language BANGKOK POST SUNDAY MAGAZINE, December 9, 1973

THE "FORBIDDEN VALLEY" BY BANGKOK POST
CORRESPONDENT AND PHOTOGRAPHER DON RONK

In early 1967 it was from volunteers in Laos I first heard of Long Cheng. Not that they gave it a name, nor that they were certain it even existed. A "secret city" was rumoured to exist in the mountains of Laos from which the then-mounting Laos war was being directed and conducted by the American Central Intelligence Agency.

The whole idea of a secret city was preposterous to this cynic in those days. Reason asked, how could a city be secret? Someone would have stumbled across it. Nothing could be so distant from where people could see and talk.

I did not know the vast wilderness that northern Laos is.

I was wrong, of course. There was a city. It was called Long Cheng, and although it took years for its precise location to become generally known even in Vientiane (only about 70 miles away by airplane), it did slowly emerge from the mists that shroud the vastness of up-country Laos, mists created both by act of God and the CIA.

Even after I moved to Vientiane in 1969 as a journalist and began reporting developments in Laos, Long Cheng remained a vague entity, still not precisely locatable on available maps.

BILL LAIR, former CIA paramilitary officer, Thailand and Laos

When I first went to Thailand in 1951 I began to think about what were the total problems over there. Communism was coming, and as we put people in the field, we began to realize that the local people living in the remote areas in Thailand—and Laos, too—along the border and everywhere else, had very little contact with *any* government. They were isolated and at the mercy of anybody who comes along with a gun. And that's what the communists were going to do: Come along. Those people were going to have to go along with whoever had the gun. They needed physical security for themselves and their family and their village.

The people who were going to be coming in there were trying to spread communism—that was *our* enemy, too. So if someone goes in and trains the villagers and arms them, they're just going to take care of themselves because there's nobody else who's going to protect them. They're going to do it themselves. So our requirements meet right there, see? That's what I saw coming. That's why I started the idea of creating in Thailand a unit of PARU, the Police Aerial Resupply Unit.[1] See, at that time, it wasn't like Laos was a different country from Thailand. If you were on the Mekong River, the people on the Thai side of the river all knew everybody on the Lao side. Ethnically it's the same people, so you could find out a *lot* about what was going on in Laos. More than if you went to the capital city of Vientiane. That was how we studied the situation before the PARU ever went to Laos.

In 1960 I already knew who VP was. I knew that he was an officer in the Lao Army and was the highest ranking of any Hmong. I knew VP was a pretty obvious leader that we needed to get in touch with if the PARU had to go into Laos. And after

Already paratroopers, a special unit of thirty Thai PARU were trained to jump into jungle/timber for special operations, and to use power saws and explosives to construct STOL airstrips in remote areas. The trainers were former U.S. Forest Service smokejumpers, left to right: Ken Hessel, George "Pappy" Smith, and Miles Johnson. The Helio Courier was one of several aircraft used for jump training at Pitscamp, Thailand, 1964. Ken Hessel collection.

we studied the situation we *were* looking for a way to get there. So when Laos started percolating, I already had Thai PARU teams along the border.

The first time I met Vang Pao was in 1961. I asked him, "What are you going to do about the communists?" He said, "We cannot get along with the communists. We have to either fight them or we have to leave Laos. And if you give us the weapons we will fight." Most people thought you couldn't make an effective soldier with a lot of the ethnic people. But I believed they would be *better* than the average American soldier sent overseas simply because they lived in that area and were used to it. In the mountains, the Hmong could walk faster than anybody because they'd never taken a step that wasn't up or down. They were uneducated so they couldn't read and write, but they were very bright and easy to train. That's what impressed me. And they were fighting for *Laos*, not for the U.S. There was no mention of the U.S.

I knew Jerry in 1961 when he started as a kicker with Air America, a guy who pushed cargo out of an airplane. When he first came out to Thailand, his association with the Agency was very nebulous. It had nothing to do with operations in Laos. At that point he hadn't done anything that would make anybody think he was going to be good at operations. But after he'd been there a little while, Jerry wanted to go to Laos and he didn't want to go as a cargo kicker. He wanted to go as a case officer. He went home to go to college, and when he came back in 1965 he worked at Lima Site 36, Na Khang. In 1970 he became an operations officer assigned to 20-Alternate,

Long Cheng valley and the air base at Lima Site 20-Alternate, looking east from about 5,000 feet above, 1969. Photo credit: Dan Gamelin.

Long Cheng, LS 20A, headquarters of both General Vang Pao's SGU Army and CIA operations in Military Region 2, Laos. G. R. Jenkin collection, Air America Archives, University of Texas at Dallas.

Long Cheng. The Hmong project ran from there. All the Agency operations officers were assigned to Alternate, and from there they could go anywhere.

Over the years, Jerry became a very good friend of mine. We understood each other and we operated in much the same way. See, I didn't give a damn if the case officers knew about tactics. The most important point was to know how to work with the people—the Hmong and the Thai PARU. Because the Americans up-country didn't add to the tactical. What they did was make sure that the troops had food, ammunition, all that support stuff, and that the stuff kept coming.

JIM SCHILL, former USAID Laos Refugee Relief Program; former Department of State, Bureau for Refugee Programs

Long Cheng was the secret CIA base in northern Laos where most of the covert operatives were based. It had been built and upgraded over a period of years until eventually there was about a 4,000-foot all-weather runway that could take C-130s, and serve as an emergency landing strip for U.S. military aircraft that were flying sorties over North Vietnam and Laos. Long Cheng was also Vang Pao's headquarters in Military Region 2, MR2. It was a major staging area for General Vang Pao and his Hmong troops, as well as home to many of their family members. There were also Thai mercenaries, Thai PARU, stationed there to help the Hmong fight a war against the communist Pathet Lao and their North Vietnamese colleagues. Long Cheng was the heart of the secret war in Laos.

CHOU MOUA, former chief of Forward Air Guides (FAGs), MR2, Laos

Until 1968 Jerry was at Lima Site 36, Na Khang, and he worked mainly with the northern province in Laos, the Sam Neua area. Site 85, Phou Pha Thi, was the secret U.S. radar station in the north, very important.[2] Four SGU battalions were stationed there to protect it. And that was my area. When Phou Pha Thi and the north was lost to the communists in '68, both the SGU soldiers and the civilian families moved south to Long Cheng.

When we moved south Jerry left, too. He was gone about a year and a half, probably until early '70. When he came back they wanted Jerry to be the Number Two Sky person in Long Cheng, but Jerry said he didn't want to be the Number Two man. He wanted to be the Number Three man, in charge of operations. Jerry *loved* operations. Number Two was mainly to help the Number One. So Zack was Number Two. Jon was Number One.

When I was stationed in Long Cheng, mostly I go north as a forward air guide, a FAG, because I know that area. FAGs are on the ground, and they make radio contact with the Raven pilots about air strikes. Give a Raven pilot the target coordinates, then the Raven shoots the smoke to show the F-4 jet or the A1-E Skyraider where to strike with rockets or bombs. After Jerry came back to Long Cheng in 1970, they asked me to be the chief of forward air guides, the FAG leader. Then Jerry and I worked together for the whole MR2 region, not just the northern area. At that time, we Hmong followed what Jerry said. We did discuss what to do, but there were so many things going on and we trusted him, we believed him, and we did things the way he wanted us to do. He handled many things about commando activity and the whole military situation. There were a lot of things for him to handle.

BILL LAIR, former CIA paramilitary officer, Thailand and Laos

We were trying to fight against communism in Southeast Asia. That's what the whole thing was about. So you have to get those people who have a reason for fighting communism, too. Our whole purpose for being there was to get those people to do what we wanted them to do when we had no *real* authority over them. I worked my whole career trying to get people to do things when I had no real authority over them. You're trying to talk people into doing things that are either illegal or unpleasant or that may get them killed. You get them to do what they want to do, but it also has to be what you want to do.

Excerpt from "The Legend of Long Cheng: War's End Unveils a Forbidden Valley," by DON RONK, *Asia Magazine*, Hong Kong, April 21, 1974

The fall of [Phou] Pha Thi [in March 1968] was more than a simple military loss. It marked the beginning of retreat, what "Pop" Buell was to call the "running and dying, running and dying" of the Meo. The battle to reclaim Pha Thi marks the first major defeat of Vang Pao's army and the beginning of the long retreat back toward Long Cheng. From that defeat, an increasingly ferocious war closed ever more tightly on Long Cheng.

KEN HESSEL, former smokejumper; former Continental Air Services (CASI) Air Operations, MR3, Laos

I got to southern Laos in October '68 as the air ops officer in Savannakhet, LS 39 in MR3. When I got there I found out that the NVA were pushing hard all over. There was the Tet Offensive in South Vietnam early in '68, and not long after that they overran our radar station at Phou Pha Thi in northeast Laos. The NVA kept pushing southwest across northern Laos. Of course the PDJ was directly in their sites, and a lot of heated battles were pitched there. Control of the Plain seesawed back and forth between wet and dry seasons, but it all got a lot harder as the bad guys got stronger. VP's troops were taking a hell of a beating even with air support. Total friendly forces may have slightly outnumbered the enemy forces,[3] but the difference was made up by the caliber of NVA troops that showed up on the front lines. When it came down to actual combat, the NVA troops were simply better soldiers than most of the troops they went up against. So the odds weren't looking too good.

THOMAS C. "SHEP" JOHNSON, former smokejumper; former air delivery specialist, MR2, Laos

I went to Long Cheng in July 1969. It was the same month they fired that Apollo 11 to the moon. When I first got to Long Cheng, Jerry wasn't there. He was in school in Montana. Course, I knew him before Laos. In 1960 both of us jumped the Waterfall Creek fire on the Middle Fork of the Salmon River in Idaho. We was on that fire, and then I worked with Jerry on that Tibetan night drop deal out of Thakli in '62, so I knew him. After Jerry finished school, he come back maybe eight months after I got there. Basically as the operations officer for General Vang Pao. My two years over in Long Cheng, Jerry was the ops officer most of that time. He handled everything that went on.

When Daniels come back to Long Cheng, the riggin' operation was so damn disorganized. We had the gear and the equipment but no people. I couldn't get but maybe two or three riggers to rig the bundles for the parachutes. Air America would come in in a Caribou or something, and we had to hand up the ammo boxes or rice or whatever it was, then we'd rig it right on the airplane. Well, the kickers'd get pissed off, and the pilots and everybody. We wasn't gettin' up to the sites to resupply like we should. We was way behind. And especially General Vang Pao was pissed off. It's the only time that General Vang Pao chewed my butt out. He come up and he says—General Vang Pao can speak English if he wants to—he says, "Shep, you're not gettin' our troops supplied out there like you should." He didn't say it quite like that but he jumped on me and it was short and sweet. Well, anyway, it hurt my feelings.

I told Jerry. I says, "Jerry, damn it, VP just come and chewed my butt out. He said he wondered why I wasn't gettin' the troops resupplied." I says, "I can't get this stuff out if I don't have anybody to do the work. I'm riggin', and the kickers are riggin' the bundles right on the airplanes." Jerry says, "Then go down there to VP's house and tell him." "No," I says, "*you* go tell the general. You speak his language and you're closer to him than I am." Besides that, VP just chewed my rear out so I didn't *want* to talk to him. Jerry said no. So, anyway, I says, "Awright."

I went on down to VP's house. I says, "General Vang Pao," I says, "I don't have anybody to help me. You've got to get me the troops to rig. If I don't have the help, I can't get your bundles rigged. I already went up to see that lieutenant but I got no help." There was a Lao lieutenant that was supposed to be in charge of the riggers, but he was always in his little room, all doped up. The door was covered with a blanket and he used a can to make a water pipe and he'd smoke opium in there. He was out of it. You'd pull the blankets apart at the door and stick your head in his little office and you'd almost get drunk yourself just lookin' in. Anyway, I couldn't get the people that lieutenant was in charge of.

Well, General Vang Pao left the house with his two jeeps full of troops, his entourage of bodyguards that he always had with him. Two jeeps rolled out and went up and made a tour around the riggin' site—no troops, no riggers. Later that day VP come up and went around the place again—no troops, no riggers. And I think he probably looked in at that lieutenant and he was probably bombed.

The next morning there must have been a hundred Hmong there at the riggin' shed. God! I had so many people I didn't know what to do with them. Boy, I really had to do some reorganizing but anyway, I says, "Jerry," I says, "Jerry, *damn*, what did VP do to get all these people up here?" He says, "He shot the lieutenant." I says, "Oh, no, he didn't do that." Jerry says, "Like hell he didn't. He shot the lieutenant." And I believe it after Jerry emphasized everything. I doubt that General Vang Pao shot him himself. Probably it was one of his people, but I felt like he probably did. I never saw that lieutenant again. He was gone.

JIM SCHILL, former USAID Laos Refugee Relief Program; former Department of State, Bureau for Refugee Programs

The Hmong had no indigenous military leader until Vang Pao showed up. He was tough, charismatic, and exhibited leadership. This got him noticed and supported by the CIA. And the U.S. backed the right guy.

Jerry was General Vang Pao's case officer, VP's direct link to the CIA in Laos. Jerry was a covert agent covered by USAID, United States Agency for International Development. He was totally dedicated and was liked and respected by the general. Like quite a few other Americans who worked in Laos, he had been a smokejumper and was well prepared to work under rough, primitive conditions.

Thai PARU Nob Intrachat supervised all cargo riggers at Long Cheng. Nob is on top of the cargo (wearing hat) with Thai, Lao, and Hmong riggers, c. 1970. Thomas "Shep" Johnson collection.

BILL LAIR, former CIA paramilitary officer, Thailand and Laos

At that time, everybody thought people from the Ivy League schools were the smartest people in the world. They were liberal arts majors or something theoretical. I went to Texas A&M and I was trained as an engineer. Practical. You have it in your head that 2 + 2 makes 4. The way I saw it, the Ivy League tended to think that something was true because it morally *ought* to be true. Not because it really *was* like that. Those guys would more or less say, "Well, 2 + 2 really ought to be 5. It would be more humane if it was 5."

Now I'm not putting the Ivy League down. They were good people, and in the end we all worked together extremely well. But for me, 2 + 2 makes 4 no matter how immoral it might be. There is nothing else you can make out of it. No matter how wrong or right or theoretically how it should be, it's still 4.

Dealing with intelligence is the same. You've got to treat it in the same practical manner. If we recruited case officers from places like Texas A&M, and particularly engineering graduates, they were more practical. And the smokejumpers we recruited from up in Montana and Idaho were also very practical types. I think they fit well into this organization, especially overseas, because they were dealing with people who were more like them than they were like the guys from the Ivy League.

THOMAS C. "SHEP" JOHNSON, former smokejumper; former air delivery specialist, MR2, Laos

As the operations officer, what was good about Jerry was that he didn't care about anything as long as you got the job done. Any way you could do it, do it. And sometimes we had to use unsophisticated-type ideas, and that's where the smokejumpers could really think things out and come up with practical-type solutions.

There was one position near Site 15, Ban Na. We had a position four or five kilometers off to the southwest of Ban Na landing strip. It was a hilltop site and there wasn't any natural source of water. They were under fire from the North Vietnamese, the NVA, so we couldn't land to resupply them. What can we do? Well, Jerry and I decided to try to drop water containers using the impact system. That's a ground-opening parachute device. It was something we developed at Marana to cut out the wind drift factor when dropping from a high altitude. What it was is, when the parachute come out of the bag, a reef line sewn around the skirt of the parachute keeps the canopy tied almost closed, and at the same time a lead foot drops down. This lead foot had 150 foot of nylon line attached to it, little skinny line. The line connected the lead foot to an electrical device attached to the skirt of the parachute. When the foot hit the ground, well, that device would close the circuit that fired a detonating device that cut open the reef line around the skirt of the parachute so the chute popped open 150 feet off the ground. That was the purpose of it: freefall down to 150 feet so the pilot could stay up and out of range of ground fire.

The hilltop position that we were droppin' on was so small, even droppin' those cube water containers in there with the impact system, we couldn't get them in on top of that little knoll. The impact would go to one side or another. And the soldiers couldn't get out of their bunkers to retrieve the drops, because the NVA was all around them. The impacts were far enough off that everything just went to the NVA. We couldn't do it. And it was pretty hot conditions up there. While we were makin' the drops we started receiving some small arms fire that was hittin' the Otter that we was in. Jerry says, "Well, we got some little bees flyin' around." Hell, I looked around and I could see the holes.

Well, like I said, they was out of water down there. Jerry says, "We can't drop any water into 'em. They all miss." "Jerry," I says, "we've got a ice maker up at the mess hall in Long Cheng. Let's just drop bags of ice into 'em." And that's what we did do. We had to try to pinpoint and freefall the bags of ice right into their position, and it worked.

GLENN F. HALE, former smokejumper; former Continental Air Services (CASI) Air Operations, MR3, Laos

Anywhere I ever have been around Agency people or jumpers, the one personality trait that I think *all* of us guys had in common was that you could give us a job and leave us alone. It was always can-do: "Whatever you need, just tell us and you don't have to bother us or check on us. We'll get 'er done." To me that's a *special* trait, and a pride as well.

The can-do attitude proved itself many times when we were in Laos. The station chiefs would want some capability for different projects such as special night drops or picking up teams of operatives. They would ask us to set it up, get the aircraft necessary, design systems for the aircraft that would be necessary for the job, do the parachute rigging, do the dropping, and get it done.

LEE GOSSETT, former smokejumper; former pilot, Laos

The first time I met Jerry was when I was smokejumping out of Fairbanks, Alaska, during the summer of 1963. He arrived from Marana, Arizona, in the Intermountain B-17 with several other smokejumpers. That B-17 was equipped with the "Fulton Skyhook" system. A few years later I worked with Jerry in Laos.

In September 1970 I was picking up a load at Long Cheng when a CASI Twin Otter arrived. I knew something was up with all the security around but didn't pay much attention to it. As the door to the Twin Otter opened, a tall, distinguished-looking man got off. I was standing next to Jerry and I asked him, "Who is that guy?" Jerry looked at me with a smile and said, "Don't you know who that is?" "No." Then Jerry went on to tell me his name was Richard Helms,[4] then the director of CIA.

I went back to work, and several hours later I was back at Long Cheng for another load. Again I was standing next to Jerry when VP's convertible jeep station wagon arrived. Richard Helms was in the backseat with VP. Rather than open the door, Mr. Helms leaped over the side of the jeep, and when he hit the ground, a snub-nosed .38 fell out of his belt and went *clunk* on the ground. Mr. Helms immediately looked at Jerry and me and said in a sheepish way, "Sometimes I am my own bodyguard." We all had a chuckle over that event.

Letter to LOUISE DANIELS from Jerry Daniels, September 26 (year unknown)

Dear Louise,

I have something for you to do. I need 5 (five) .38 Special Smith & Wesson's with a four inch barrel. . . . I would like these pistols as soon as possible. Find out if there is any possible way for you to buy them and get them to me legally. . . . These pistols are gifts from me to some of my friends, who by the way will never leave the mountains. . . . I am enclosing a blank check. . . . If you cannot buy them please take the blank check to the Registares office at the University and pay my bill there, I believe about 40 dollars.

The dry season is now upon us, and things will be busy again soon.

Jerry

MACALAN THOMPSON, former USAID Laos Refugee Relief Program; former Refugee Program, U.S. Embassy, Bangkok, Thailand

During the dry season, the bad guys can move their support gear, ammo, food, etc. Wet season they can't. Wet season the baddies are restricted in their movements so they hunker down waiting until they can become mobile again. Meanwhile the SGU can move troops around during the wet season via air and be supplied by air.

KEN HESSEL, former smokejumper; former Continental Air Services (CASI) Air Operations, MR3, Laos

During the dry season of 1969 the NVA had their way with things in MR2 by committing large troop numbers, 130mm guns, and even tanks. Even with our reinforcements from the Thai troops and SGU and FAR [Royal Lao Army] troops from other military regions in Laos, the NVA for the most part went where they wanted to go, when they wanted to go there.

In 1970, things heated up in southern Laos, too. Now both the north and the south were under heavy attack by communist troops. The Thai troops were a great help, but we continued to take a beating. Up north, MR2 had more and more Hmong kids recruited to the front line because of the number of casualties. Many of them didn't last long.

Hog Daniels (dark glasses and radio) and General Vang Pao (second from right) overlooking a battlefield in northern Laos. Daniels family collection. Used with permission.

THOMAS J. "T. J." THOMPSON, former smokejumper; former air delivery specialist, MR2, Laos

In 1971 Jerry and I were flying over a position southeast of Long Cheng. We were in an Air America Porter, on recon. Jerry was up front with the pilot, and I was in the back. It was the dry season, and as we circled over, we saw where the NVA troops just crashed through the jungle and beat it down comin' in to one of our positions. It was real easy to trail them, even from the air. Probably we were between 1,500 and 2,000 feet, not any higher than that, making left to right circles over the position. We could see there was TIC going on—Troops In Contact.

I looked down and I could see the NVA very clearly. Many of them had nice, new green uniforms, so they were fresh troops. And they were shootin' at us. Every time those NVA rifles went off, the flash from the ground looked like it was hitting you right in the face. I told Jerry, I said, "God, we'd better get out of here. They're shootin' at us!" He looked back and said, "Oh, not to worry." I thought the pilot wasn't going to make another round but, well, he *did*! The next thing I know, there's the NVA and they're shootin' at us again. So I ran to the front and said, "Let's get the hell out of here, Jerry! These bastards are gonna hit us!" He turned around and said, "Oh hell, we're just like whackin' a wild goose, a big old honker. We're hard to hit." Jerry always related to animals, like the big gander goose, the Canadian honkers he liked to hunt in Montana. So we made one more pass over, and true to form, we weren't hit. And I don't know why. But it was so typical the way he said, "Aw, not to worry. We're just like a big ol' goose. We're hard to hit." My God! I just wanted to get out of there! That was so true of the way Jerry thought. I do not think he was ever scared.

Excerpt from "The Legend of Long Cheng: War's End Unveils a Forbidden Valley," by DON RONK, *Asia Magazine*, Hong Kong, April 21, 1974

A quick look at those making up Vang Pao's army says something important about the situation in 1971. In 1969 it had been basically a Meo army; in 1971 it was basically a Lao Theung[5] army heavily peopled with Thai irregulars brought in for static defense work. In a sense the Meo were finished; there were no more available.[6] Small boys were used to bulk out units.

The attrition of troops also represented an attrition on the ground. Every year the North Vietnamese eased closer to Skyline Ridge, overlooking Long Cheng valley.

THOMAS J. "T. J." THOMPSON, former smokejumper; former air delivery specialist, MR2, Laos

Long Cheng, 20A, was hit badly on February 14, 1971. That was the St. Valentine's massacre. Shep was wounded, and I took over his position up at Long Cheng. After the St. Valentine's attack, the big dogs in Vientiane got nervous about us spendin' the night up at Long Cheng. They didn't want any of our tender white asses to end up being captured by the NVA, so all of us except Jerry started flyin' down to Vientiane before dusk each night, and we'd fly back up the next morning, which was a hell of a lot more dangerous than stayin' up at Long Cheng.

After we'd get down to Vientiane at the end of each day there'd be a sit rep briefing at the CASI compound at the airport, a situation report about the day's activities. It was usually fifteen to twenty-five people: a bunch from the Embassy, Ambassador Godley,[7] sometimes the chief of station, sometimes some Hmong representatives. Well, that was okay. Then there'd be these other captains and lieutenant colonels, from where I don't know. Wannabes and hangers-on. I guess they were there to hear war stories so they could impress everyone in the bar that night.

Anyway, Jerry was doin' a briefing. See, the PDJ had been lost to the NVA, and the NVA had been pushin' south from there, building a road that would bring them right to Long Cheng. Jerry'd been watching their efforts for a while. Mostly it was one NVA guy on a bulldozer, pushin' that dirt, buildin' that road. Well, Jerry decided it was time to call in an air strike and put an end to it. He called in two F-4s and they made a run on the guy. They both made bombing runs, and that soldier just kept runnin' that dozer and glarin' up at 'em. When the F-4s expended all their ordnance and had to return to base, the NVA guy was still workin' his dozer.

After Jerry made his report he started to return to his seat. Someone in the meeting asked, "He wasn't hit? There was *no* damage? None at all?" Jerry said, "No, they only nicked his wheelbarrow." "Nicked his wheelbarrow? What wheelbarrow?" Absolutely deadpan Jerry said, "The one he hauls his balls in." That even got a chuckle from Ambassador Godley. That was Jerry's sense of humor.

JIM SCHILL, former USAID Laos Refugee Relief Program; former Department of State, Bureau for Refugee Programs

Ambassador Sullivan[8] and all subsequent ambassadors to Laos were directly involved in the prosecution of the war from the U.S. side. The embassy and its central ability to disseminate and control information, and work to ensure that the big secret remained so, was very important to each administration. Its focus was primarily confined to keeping the lid on, and the U.S. operations in check. And this was a huge responsibility with the U.S. military, CIA, and others deeply involved in carrying out interdictions against the Pathet Lao with the Royal Lao Government, Hmong, and Thai surrogates. It got hot on the ground, and many times keeping the lid on was iffy at best.

BEE VANG, former Hmong T-28 pilot, Laos

You know, one time I flew Jerry from Long Cheng to Vientiane. That day Jerry goes to meet with the U.S. ambassador at the ambassador's office at That Dam. But Jerry stays too long in the ambassador's office. In only two hours the sun will go down and it will be dark. The Long Cheng airport has the mountain and no lights, so the aircraft cannot land there after dark. We have to land in the daytime. So I have to go to the ambassador's office to find him.

Hog Daniels with General Vang Pao and soldiers, 1970s. Daniels family collection. Used with permission.

The guard is an American black man, a *big* guy! I say, "Hey, mister. Do you know Mr. Jerry?" The guard has a big book on the table. He looks in there, then the guard talks the big words opposite: "No Jerry here." I say, "What about Hog? Hog Daniels?" He says, "I don't know that name either." The CIA people have too many names. They have a *lot* of names. "No Jerry here. No Hog here." I say, "Hey, mister! I flew him here. Right now I need to take him to the airport to go back to Long Cheng because we have no more time." *Now* the guard knows Jerry. He knows Jerry, but the name is not in the book. He calls on the phone and in about five minutes Jerry comes out. Jerry Daniels, Hog Daniels. Oh! A *lot* of names!

Jerry and I worked together for fifteen years in Long Cheng. The CIA has *very* secret information about the situation there. And Jerry knows *all* the situations.

Excerpt from "The Legend of Long Cheng: War's End Unveils a Forbidden Valley," by DON RONK, *Asia Magazine*, Hong Kong, April 21, 1974

This secret place could only have been peopled by characters from [an] adventure story—shadowy civilian-soldiers called Bamboo, Hog, Kayak, Clean—men who peopled a legend simply because they would not talk, nor would those who knew about them. . . . The men here are referred to in Vientiane as "the spooks," and are shy of the camera. . . .

Clean is huge, trim, hard, not much of a talker. His head is shaved. Legends are made of people like Clean.

Hog is young, perhaps 30. He talks like an alumnus of the Peace Corps, a gentle man obviously much taken by the Meo he works with, but hard-nosed enough so that there is no chance he will ever be called a bleeding heart. He is a favorite of General Vang Pao.

RANDOLPH "TOBY" SCOTT, former smokejumper; former Continental Air Services (CASI) loadmaster, Laos

Oh, that time in Laos had a lot of excitement. When you live like that you don't ever think you're goin' to die. Like Jerry said, when we hit forty years old we was gonna jump off the Higgins Avenue Bridge in Missoula! He said he'd be over the hill if he lived to be forty.

THOMAS C. "SHEP" JOHNSON, former smokejumper; former air delivery specialist, MR2, Laos

We Americans got moved down to Vientiane in February 1971. After that, sometimes we went up and stayed with Jerry in Long Cheng just to help out, but we didn't stay long. A couple of days, then we'd get out of there. That was when Jerry lived in his bunker up in that banana grove to the south of the king's house. He lived in the ground in a hole about sixteen feet deep. I stayed in that bunker with Jerry for a couple of nights, but it was too hot up there for me! I mean, there was a lot of *action* goin' on.

THOMAS J. "T. J." THOMPSON, former smokejumper; former air delivery specialist, MR2, Laos

Up at Long Cheng we were always gettin' rocket attacks. One day Jerry and I and Dutch, another American case officer, were standing there on the ramp talking. This was two months after that pretty hairy NVA attack on February 14, 1971, when we lost the rice warehouse, the Air America hostel that was down on the ramp, the parachute loft and rigging site, and the barracks. In April some soldiers were rebuilding the warehouse and they were diggin' holes for abutments. I always kept my mind open as to where was a good place to dive if the rockets started. I knew where those holes were, and I always picked one close that I could get into.

We were talking—Jerry, Dutch, and I. Then Nob, a Thai PARU who supervised the riggers, called me over. I walked over by this hole and looked down in there. I was thinking as I passed it, "Well, if anything happens I'll just dive into that hole there." I talked with Nob. Jerry was over to my right. Nob and I finished talking, and I started walkin' up the hill. I was probably forty feet beyond that hole when there was a big explosion on my right, and I knew we had come under another rocket attack. It flashed through my mind that I had a choice of goin' back to that hole forty feet behind me or to the bunker which I was looking at. My attitude is always pretty much, *Don't turn around.*

At the same time, I heard another rocket pull right over my head. It had burned out, and it was just coasting. Just *whoo-whoo-whoo*, coasting right over my head. When I heard it comin' in, I hit the ground, straight down, and that thing went off *so* damn loud and *so* close that my ears rang, rang, rang, rang. I laid there, stunned. I actually thought maybe I was hit, but I couldn't see anything wrong. So I got up and there was a bunker right ahead of me. I made it to that bunker as all hell was breakin' loose with another four or five rockets coming in. I think the NVA dumped in about six of them; they make a *tremendous* noise.

When the attack was over I got out of the bunker and started walking down the hill, wondering where was Jerry? My ears were ringin', ringin', and I was walking sort of numb, I guess. I looked over to where I'd been talkin' to him, and there I see some guy with his head cut off and the blood was just draining all over him. His whole body was just all red, covered with blood, and my first thought was that that was Jerry. There was no way I could tell it was *not* Jerry. That's where I'd seen Jerry standing, still talking to Dutch, when Nob called me back.

I kept walking. When I got closer and looked in the hole I was going to jump in, I saw the rocket that went over my head had landed in that hole. And one guy did get into that hole and he was thrown out. Dead, dismembered. Just a torso. There was nothing left in the hole but the rocket. It went straight into the hole and everything went *up*. That's why I wasn't hit.

I looked over and Clean[9] was already up and moving. Clean and John Kerns were up, and they were already sackin' bodies. I said, "What's the hurry?" Clean was pickin' up the guy who'd been thrown, I'd guess, forty feet from the hole. He had his hands around his neck and the guy's hair was standin' up. It was fairly long and it was straight up, I guess from static or shock from the shell. He had no arms, no legs, just a torso. Just a chest that was all hollow. Clean was pickin' him up. He had the guy by his head and neck. He laid that torso in a body bag and the rest of him was just all over the place. I looked back over at Jerry, where I had seen Jery last, and I thought: *They killed a deer. What'd they kill the deer for?*

And then George was screamin'. George was a Thai worker in the warehouse. A rock from a rocket was in his head and he was just screamin'. He was screamin' all the time, and it took him fifteen or twenty minutes to die. And then I turned around and there was a dog that had a fresh kidney with ten or fifteen foot of gut on it. A damn dog draggin' a kidney with a gut on it.

Well, everything was goin' to hell, but they'd quit firin' so I just stood there looking around. I was in a daze, there's no doubt. I just looked at the carnage going on. I was sort of ineffective because I couldn't pull myself together to help the wounded. When they counted there were fourteen wounded, six dead, and seven soon to come. We'd been under fire before, but to see that, and think that was Jerry—I was embarrassed of how rattled I was. I just backed off until I could think a little better.

I watched Clean pickin' up bodies. I walked over there, and they'd already sacked up and hauled off the guy whose head was cut off. Clean was over another twenty or thirty feet. They were haulin' wounded, and the next thing I know here comes Jerry runnin' out of Air Ops. Jerry runs up to me and he says, "I thought that was you over there all dressed in red! I was just comin' to get your watch." I looked at him, and I was relieved that there he was. Then he was pullin' his bullshit on me so that started relieving things.

Oh, it was a mess that day, yeah. We recovered, picked up the dead and the body parts, and went on with the job. The planes had all scrambled to get off the ground and then they started comin' back in. We started loadin' cargo and goin' on with what we had been doing. There was no break and no counseling like they do now. Now someone gets shot and the counselors come in.

Months later when I was leaving Long Cheng, I hadn't told anybody about what happened to me that day, especially not Jerry. Dick Eppard, the logistics officer, and I were sittin' at a little ol' place havin' a beer at Long Cheng. So I sort of told him that story about this thing that I thought was a deer. And when I told him, he sat there for a while and said, "You know, I saw that guy too, and I thought it was a pig." So there were other people that were affected by that, too. And I began to recover, not thinkin' I was the only one.

CHU VANG, son of General Vang Pao

Long Cheng was again under a war situation in January 1972. That was a sneak attack when Vietnamese commandos came all the way through town, sneaking past all the security checkpoints. They were cutting the fence outside VP's house when one

Vang Pao inspecting an 81mm mortar. Photo credit: John Willheim. Used with permission.

of the soldiers guarding the house saw them and fired. The Vietnamese got all the way into VP's house, but they could not control it. They fought until the NVA withdrew to Skyline Ridge. For more than one month VP's soldiers tried to push the enemy soldiers back from Long Cheng.[10]

KEN HESSEL, former smokejumper; former Continental Air Services (CASI) Air Operations, MR3, Laos

Down in the Lao panhandle it was a different situation from MR2, but it wasn't much better. The NVA were making big improvements on the Ho Chi Minh trail. We just couldn't stop them even though we tried our best to interdict the flow of men and materials to South Vietnam. We used road watch teams and made numerous air strikes. We continued to probe the trail system with SGU operations and raise as much hell as we could, but when we did that the NVA would respond by committing more troops until we had to leave the area.

Things were deteriorating. In the north the PDJ was lost, and the bad guys pushed hard all the way to Long Cheng. In February of '71, 20A was raided by NVA commandos. Then the NVA made a second heavy attack on 20A in January 1972. They camped out on Skyline Ridge above the valley and kept up the attack for a month or more. In southern Laos we had our own fierce fighting going on by now, so we couldn't support VP with the number of troops that he was used to getting from MR3. Fact is everyone was getting worn down.

BILL LAIR, former CIA paramilitary officer, Thailand and Laos

In '68 I left the operation in Laos because I could see what was coming. They[11] were getting away from guerrilla warfare. They wanted to force the Hmong into fighting regular, not as guerrillas.

VP was a mountain guy. Guerrilla fighting is what he really did well. The Hmong would fight, then run into the hills. Keep the Hmong units small—a little ambush here, a quick attack there—then melt away to reduce Hmong casualties. But when they offered VP a more regular force, he went along with it. So once those soldiers get into pitched battles with the North Vietnamese infantry, they're gonna lose, and they're gonna lose a lot of people.

My expertise was guerrilla warfare. If you get away from that, then there's no use for me to be there. I believed 100 percent that we were heading downhill, and I thought it was probably better to avoid being at the funeral.

THOMAS J. "T. J." THOMPSON, former smokejumper; former air delivery specialist, MR2, Laos

In Long Cheng we were very, very busy. At the air delivery end, on a slow day I was putting out 100,000 pounds of cargo. But the biggest day I ever had was in 1972—

309,000 pounds of cargo, rigged from scratch. That's what we started rigging that morning for that day's requirements. Not what was rigged yesterday for today. Since all the American aircraft had to be out of Laos and across the Mekong to Thailand when it was still daylight, those were very, very active days, no doubt about it.

Every day the GM commanders, Guerrilla Mobile, would assign three or four soldiers from each GM to do the rigging. They would receive the requirements from their GM on paper, then we'd pull all that stuff and rig it. All the GMs worked together in the rigging shed, stackin' ammo pallets, putting slings on them, D-rings and parachutes. Then the Air America and Continental planes would come, and we'd load the cargo.

Most of the drop birds for the small positions were Caribous and Twin Otters. We dropped with the small birds because you can stay in closer. Those positions were usually surrounded with enemy so you didn't want to get out too far. And most of the small positions had a lot of TIC, Troops In Contact. You made tight circles, tight turns so you could drop right into the position. Of course I flew on quite a few; as air delivery specialist I had to know the drop zones.

People don't realize that we were using an average of 4,000 cargo parachutes a month, just out of Long Cheng. And the biggest *month* I had in Long Cheng was

Cargo drop from a Prestwick Twin Pioneer over northern Laos, 1968. Daniels family collection. Used with permission.

when we dropped 4 million pounds and we slung-load by helicopter another 2 million pounds. The month that we dropped 4 million pounds of cargo, I used over 16,000 cargo parachutes. We were making anywhere from 700 to 800 landings and takeoffs a day. And people don't realize it. If you start tellin' people that, they think it's a bunch of bull. But it is not. It's the absolute truth. That was at Long Cheng in '72.

JOHN R. GREENWAY, former Air America pilot, Laos

I was a pilot in Laos, '70 to '74, a captain with Air America. When we went up to work out of 20A we stayed there for six days and we flew twelve hours a day. We *really* got our twelve hours a day flying in. Even on a bad day we got ten hours. You should have seen the *black* circles under my eyes from all those twelve-hour days.

Probably the best part of the whole war was during the early '70s. Now that was a proper war. What we were doing was right, so it was great for the warrior groups. I can't say it was enjoyment, but it was an intense feeling of being alive. It was a *huge* challenge and everything was so *intense*. When you're looking at a piece of Plexiglas and there are holes being ripped in it as you watch, it's *really intense*! Or you look down and you see your copilot's rudder pedals are gone and all of the instrument panel on his side is gone. "Well, that's okay. My side's still all right." That's *intense*.

I know it wasn't great for the Hmong. It wasn't great for the poor little kids that

Lieutenant Colonel Vang Geu prepares Regiment 21 before an attack on a North Vietnamese Army camp near the Plain of Jars at Lat Boat, west of Khang Khai. June 1971. Geu Vang collection.

got all blown to pieces. Like the fourteen-year-olds I'd take out in the morning and carry them back dead in the evening. For them it certainly wasn't great. That wasn't good.

KOUA YANG, former Hmong SGU soldier, MR2, Laos

In August 1972, early in the morning nine helicopters drop 100 Vang Pao soldiers on the Plain of Jars.[12] We know the Pathet Lao and North Vietnamese troops are already there. The American pilots say it is too foggy. No one can see anything, but we all have to drop twenty-five feet down into the fog. When we jump from the helicopters the enemy shoots at us. Some of our soldiers are killed before they reach the ground. When we hit the ground we break into small groups and scatter. We have food and water and supplies for one or two days. The helicopters leave and go back to Long Cheng to get more soldiers. Over the next couple of days about 1,000 soldiers are dropped there.

The first 100 soldiers go to fight right away. It is cold, raining, and foggy the whole time. Very, very cold. We fight daytime and nighttime, but the communist soldiers fight too hard. After four or five days there is no food to eat. The helicopters and planes are not bringing in supplies because they are afraid they might be shot down. A *lot* of our people are hurt from the land mines. The helicopters didn't come back to pick up the wounded soldiers. A lot already died.

We have to keep moving. Keep moving. Keep fighting. The communists have a lot of powerful weapons, big guns, to use against the government troops. We call by radio to Long Cheng and ask for help. We ask for backup troops, but no one comes and no helicopters come to pick us up.

It just keeps *raining*! Heavy rain and cold and our feet hurt so much. For one week our boots are wet all the time. The skin is peeling off our feet. We cannot walk. Some people don't have enough to eat and they cannot survive. They just die. The conditions are very bad.

After five or six days of fighting, moving, some of us try to walk back to Long Cheng. We want to escape the place we are in because there are enemy soldiers everywhere. We want to get to a place where the plane can come and pick us up.

When we fall back we try to cross the Nam Ngum River. It is still raining and the river is too *big* and too fast. Some of our soldiers cannot swim. They drop into the river and drown. They are carried away. Maybe ten or twenty die that way. The communist soldiers are still fighting us while we cross the river. They never stop fighting us. More communists are hiding and waiting for us on the other side. They know we will try to walk back to Long Cheng. We use the CB radio to call for the helicopter to come pick us up but it doesn't come, and we cannot get through the communist lines. The communists keep fighting a lot.

We had no food for five or six days already, but we still have our guns and ammunition so we fight. Now there are only two people in my group, me and one other soldier. I am fourteen or fifteen years old. The other soldier is about the same age as me.

After nine days we have nothing left. My group is only two people when the communists capture us. They capture us because we are young and we don't know which way to go. Forty-nine of us soldiers are captured and put in jail. I don't know how many of our soldiers had died by then.

Another soldier is caught at the same time we are caught. He is a little older, and the communist soldiers ask him questions because he looks like he knows more. The boss of the Hmong people, General Vang Pao, already told us, "If the communists catch you, you don't say anything. You keep your secrets. You don't say *anything.*" That is part of our training. When the communist soldiers question the other soldier I think, *If he tells the truth, he is going to die. If he doesn't tell the truth, he is going to die.* He says nothing. He closes his mouth and they kill him.

KENT "DAN THE ANIMAL MAN" DANIELS, brother of Jerry Daniels

In June 1972 Jerry and VP came to Missoula along with VP's brother-in-law, Colonel Ly Tou Pao, and his father-in-law, Colonel Moua Cher Pao.[13] Here were these nattily dressed gentlemen that looked like Asian businessmen stepping off the plane carrying all these tubes. Jerry explained how tough VP's father-in-law was. That he was a warrior who had never lost a battle. Jerry said later that those tubes held their maps. So here were these nattily dressed gentlemen with tubes of maps and battle plans from a serious war zone.[14]

Letter to RANDOLPH "TOBY" SCOTT, former smokejumper; former Continental Air Services (CASI) loadmaster, Laos, from Jerry Daniels, July 31, 1972

Tobius,

. . . I pushed off on a round-the-world trip with VP (real good fuckin deal since that took up 36 days of my 60 days off and it was more work than at Long Tieng). I left the 1st of June and got back to Bangkok on the 6th of July. Left VP. Then immediately pushed to Sydney [then] to Queenstown NZ.

. . . Right now I'm flying back to Bangkok from Sydney. I have to start back to work again tomorrow. Actually I'm glad to get back, I just can't take the whooping & hollering like some of these shit-birds. In fact I haven't had a drop since the 25th. I just walk around like granny Peters looking at shit. The reason being is I didn't want to return to work all shaky and red-faced so I decided to knock off a week early and so far I'm glad I did.

. . . I'll get 2–3 weeks off probably next July, at which time I plan on going to Flathead lake and do nothing but fish and drink Bud.—You ought to think about coming up there. . . .

Well try and drop me a line.

Fuck you very much,

J.B.

KEN HESSEL, former smokejumper; former Continental Air Services (CASI) Air Operations, MR3, Laos

I could tell you a story about Jerry at Phitsanulok, Thailand. Jerry and two other jumpers working with us in Laos came down to visit Miles and me. Pitscamp was out in the jungle. It was about fifteen miles from the jungle camp into the town of Phitsanulok. Miles and I, we kept a little house down there in Pits Town that we paid for in case any of us were out on the town and couldn't get back to the jungle camp. It was a typical Thai house set back off the road with a rice paddy out in front of it and a plank walkway on top of a dike. You could walk across the planks to get out to the road.

Anyway, Jerry came down and we went into Pits Town, and of course we got just completely smashed. Jerry got sick. He had diarrhea. Well, that wasn't unusual, livin' over there. What you ate had a lot to do with it. Anyway, Jerry crawled into the bathroom because he'd "messed himself" that night while the rest of us were sleeping. The next morning the sun came up and the day got hot, and the flies started buzzin' around. I woke up and found Jerry in there tryin' to clean himself up but he didn't do a good job of it. I mean he had it all *over* him. It was terrible. It was hot and just a *bad* smell.

Finally he came out of there and he was blinkin' his eyes and adjustin' himself. He didn't say anything to anybody, just went out the front door and walked out to the street. I was watchin' him. "Where you goin'?" "Goin' down to the bar," he said. The bar was less than a mile away, but we always took a taxi. A few minutes later this taxi came by, and Jerry waved this guy down to get a ride into town. He got in that car and that guy went about fifty yards and he just *slammed* on the brakes and there was a big yellin' match. He was tryin' to get Jerry out of his taxi because he smelled so bad. And Jerry was just hanging onto the door, and he made the guy take him down to the bar.

When *we* got down there thirty minutes later, everybody in the bar, all Thai, had gotten up and moved to the other side or left. Jerry was just sittin' there in the middle of the bar, drinking by himself. At that point he was one "ugly American." He had crap all over him, and we grabbed him and got him out of there.

After he got cleaned up at the house, we took him to Pitscamp and got him on the plane back to Long Cheng. I didn't see him after that for a *long* time. But you know, like I said, Jerry'd go stay up there and he wouldn't touch a drop for months. But when he came down, boy, I tell you, he'd just clear the decks. And it was the same deal in Vientiane. Jerry almost never came out of the jungle, but you could always tell when he was in Vientiane because every vendor in the whole town had a stand out in front of Lulu's and Jerry'd just buy everybody whatever they wanted. He'd throw money around like a drunken sailor. All the peanut and pineapple vendors in town would be outside the door if they knew Jerry was in there! Hell, he'd stay in there for a week!

ROBERT H. NICOL, former smokejumper and pilot

When Jerry wasn't working he rarely drew a sober breath. But when he was on duty, he was definitely on duty. No one ever saw him do any drinking up-country.

Letter to LOUISE DANIELS from "LUCKY" LUE YANG, October 15, 1972

Dear Mother
You should know that we and our brother Jerry as usual had a lot of work to do. I know that you may worry about our brother Jerry too much, but you might not [be] thinking we both stay together and work help each other. Brother Jerry he loves us and helps us so we feel very happy to have him with us all of our lives.

from very sincerely yours
Yang Lue (Lucky)

JOHN R. GREENWAY, former Air America pilot, Laos

In December '72 there was another great big NVA assault coming over a ridge to the east of the PDJ. The North Vietnamese had been building *big* roads with Russian bulldozers for the past couple of months, preparing for this assault. I took an ABC newsman, Steve Bell, out to that area. We were landing Caribous at that dirt strip, LS 353, dropping off troops and supplies. There were six or eight Hmong soldiers there at a gun emplacement that wasn't being mortared right then.

Steve was using a lot of my work time so I dropped off him and his camera crew—all of his equipment, his cameras, everything—so we were there a little longer than usual, offloading. As I left, the NVA started mortaring the site again because the helicopter had been there. They mortared the bedevil out of it for about four hours. I worked until they let up on the mortaring and then I went in and picked up the news crew. Steve's eyes were very wide. He had thought this war was not really happening because of the imminent ceasefire. But when a mortar's landing in the same ditch that you're laying in, you know it's happening.

Starting in February '73 there was supposed to be a ceasefire in Laos, but I never saw a ceasefire. If they had one it was only on our side.

KEN HESSEL, former smokejumper; former Continental Air Services (CASI) Air Operations, MR3, Laos

Nineteen seventy-two's about the time that Washington, DC, started thinking about how to get our butts out of Southeast Asia. Political talks started, but the fighting never let up until a ceasefire began on February 22, 1973. By then the writing was on the wall for us and our allies. In March '73 the U.S. POWs who were captured in Vietnam started to be released by the North Vietnamese in Operation Homecoming. The downside of the secret war in Laos is that it "never happened," so none of the American MIA/POWs captured in Laos were returned or even acknowledged.

We still have no idea what ever happened to many of those guys, except that now the Lao government is beginning to allow investigators into known crash sites, and a few remains have been identified over the past few years. It's a fact, however, that we'll never know what happened to most of the Americans known missing in Laos.

During the five years I spent in Laos, I felt like we did everything we could do, and more, to tie up NVA forces and equipment in that country, thereby denying participation in South Vietnam. In the end, of course, it was all for naught, but I have always taken pride in the fact that, along with the other Americans involved in the theater, we did what we could to stop communism in Southeast Asia, even if just for a few years. I left Laos on October 1, 1973, seven months after the ceasefire started.

Excerpt from the English-language *BANGKOK POST SUNDAY MAGAZINE*, December 9, 1973

THE "FORBIDDEN VALLEY" BY *BANGKOK POST* CORRESPONDENT AND PHOTOGRAPHER DON RONK

Long Cheng remains a highly restricted area in terms of visiting. . . . The road into Long Cheng from Ban Xon is lined with Meo and Lao Theung (mountain Lao) villages inhabited by extraordinarily likeable people. Along this road, probably more so than anywhere else in Laos, the visitor is plunged into the reality of how greatly the war just past has taken from the mountain people.

Tens of thousands are crammed village upon village along its length and even the most unlearned about mountain life knows the land along the road cannot sustain this many even marginally.

A trip into Long Cheng the long hard way is an educational experience of the first order, every mile of it. . . .

The certainty of an idyll of peace has not yet come to the mountains of Laos. Two ridges north of Skyline is an opposing army. Its positions can almost be seen from that vantage. Though there is no fighting, there is wary watching of one another and the potential for a renewed war.

General Vang Pao's [American CIA] advisory staff remains; they want to maintain their anonymity.

BILL LAIR, former CIA paramilitary officer, Thailand and Laos

I think the Americans really believed they would have a coalition government that might work. I think they really did. And *I* knew it wouldn't work because no coalition with the communists had *ever* worked.

Excerpts from an audiotaped letter to LOUISE DANIELS from Jerry Daniels, May 5–10, 1973

Everyone's status here depends a great deal on the new government [in Laos]. Even after the new government's formed, things still aren't firm yet. It depends on how the new government *is* formed, who's involved in it, how much the *Neo Lao Hak Sat*, the communist side, gets their fingers in the ministries. They, of course, like us, are making some pretty strong demands and these things will have to be negotiated, but it's definite that there will be quite a change afterwards. . . . Everyone's status is kind of in limbo now, waiting to see—Air America and all agencies over here. So, just not too sure about that.

. . . . I'd appreciate it very much if you could unlimber some or all of the opening seasons. All the literature on the honkers and the elk and the an-TEL-opee and all that good stuff. . . . but like I said earlier, I don't know when I'll be able to get off. . . .

Mrs. MOE GEARY, wife of Helmville rancher Bill Geary

My contact with Jerry was through T.J. and his friends, usually smokejumpers. In the '70s T.J.'d come up to Helmville and he'd bring people through. They'd be on what they called a "D and D," drinkin' and drivin'. Bill, my husband, always asked, "Where's Jerry?" Bill knew Jerry well when Jerry was a kid growing up in Helmville. There was never anything but respect for that Daniels family because they worked hard. Kent and Jerry had good reputations as workers, just like their folks.

Bill would always ask about Jerry, and Jerry'd always still be over in Laos. He was pretty involved over there so we didn't see him much. Then they'd laugh and "have a fifth for Jerry." That was always the expression. To this day T.J. says nothing went on in Laos that Jerry didn't know about.

THOMAS J. "T. J." THOMPSON, former smokejumper; former air delivery specialist, MR2, Laos

Those stories I've told about Jerry sort of fill out his character. Control under fire and humor at the same time. I thought about those things a lot, and I believed in his invincibility. Then when he died I figured, well, he's not invincible at all. You know what I mean? When it comes right down to it, I was totally surprised to hear Jerry was dead. I was shook. I mean it really rolled me up. Of *all* the people, that was hardest to believe.

Three

MISSOULA

Hard Landing

F RIENDS gather in Missoula for the funeral for Jerry Daniels; the Missoula airport scene when the casket arrives; the process of sealing a casket; tension at the funeral home.

CHA MOUA, Hmong friend; Hmong funeral organizer

About a week after we heard Jerry was dead, the body was flown from Bangkok. The day before the casket arrived, somebody called from Washington, DC, to let us know the schedule. John Tucker also arrived the day before. John reported to me that the casket will be there at the Missoula airport at such and such a time the following day, accompanied by Jim Schill. We went to tell the funeral home what time to pick up the casket the next day.

JOHN W. TUCKER, former USAID Laos Refugee Relief Program; former Refugee Program, U.S. Embassy, Bangkok, Thailand; former Department of State, Bureau for Refugee Programs

On Friday, May 7, I went from Dulles Airport to Salt Lake City, then flew on to Missoula where I was met at the airport. The Hmong had organized a meet-and-greet detail as so many of Jerry's OGA colleagues were going to arrive. OGA is Other Government Agency, meaning Central Intelligence Agency.

From the airport I was taken to my hotel. Many of Jerry's friends had already checked in by the time I got there. There was a lot of beer drinking that night, and I heard a lot of stories about Jerry.

Mrs. CAROL LEVITON WETTERHAHN, former Highland Section chief, JVA, Thailand

I flew from Washington, DC, to Missoula with John Tucker. John went on behalf of the refugee section of the U.S. State Department. We were so sad and still in shock that Jerry was gone. He was such a huge personality. It made an impact on everyone who knew him. He was a real straight shooter. He didn't mince words. He was fun, he was nice to be around. And he knew the Hmong better than anybody *ever*, I think. Anybody who is not Hmong. He was a part of that refugee family history. It was a terrible loss for everybody. He was someone who just wasn't ready to die. It seemed that there would be more of Jerry in everyone's future. It just was a total shock.

It was so emotional, the trip going out. It was part of the whole mourning period, the traveling out. I think that's probably why I wanted to go. I wanted to be part of it. I wanted to say good-bye. I wanted to have a long good-bye.

At the airport in Missoula, there were a lot of people there when our plane arrived. I'm not a high-profile person. When we landed, I just melted into the group. But I remember being greeted by one young Hmong man. He said, "Oh, it's the urine lady!" Ha! That young man remembered me from the refugee camp when I used to go in with the opium detox program for urine testing. I guess the Hmong referred to me as "the urine lady." That young man was resettled in Missoula. By then he was an American teenager, college age, and he remembered me. I was kind of blown away when I heard, "It's the urine lady!"

GEU VANG, former colonel, SGU Army, MR2, Laos

Eight of us went in a van to Jerry's funeral to represent all the Hmong people living in the Midwest. Our group was Colonel Tou-Fu Vang, Major John Xiong Yang, Major Shoua Vang ("Snoopy"), Lieutenant Tou Ly, Leng Wong ("Sancho"), Vang Kao, myself, and Cheng Vang. All of us were from Minnesota, except Tou-Fu was from Chicago.

We left late from St. Paul on Thursday night, and it took us sixteen or seventeen hours to drive to Missoula. When we got there it was late in the day on Friday. Jerry's body did not come yet. The next day all eight of us went to wait at the airport.

JOHN W. TUCKER, former USAID Laos Refugee Relief Program; former Refugee Program, U.S. Embassy, Bangkok, Thailand; former Department of State, Bureau for Refugee Programs

The next day, Saturday, more than 100 Hmong went to the airport to meet the casket. According to the cable traffic I had read back at State, Jerry had to come from Bangkok on Pan Am via JFK New York instead of other airlines via the shorter Pacific route. This was because the casket could not be opened for inspection as required when transferring airlines via the Pacific route. Pan Am could bring him directly from Bangkok to New York without opening the casket.

That day we drank beer in the airport bar, periodically checking on the status of the flight Jerry was due in on. At one point there was an announcement posted that the flight was delayed. We were disappointed and it looked like we might have to return later to meet the casket, so we continued to drown our sorrow in beer.

BOB JOHNSON, former Highland Section chief, JVA, Thailand; regional director, International Rescue Committee (IRC), Seattle

I'd been in touch with Jim Schill and Bill Sage at the State Department. They said, "You should represent the IRC at Jerry's funeral. We'll pay your trip out there." So the plan was for me to fly from Seattle and meet up with Jim Schill at the airport in Salt Lake City. We'd arranged to be on the same flight to Missoula as Jerry's casket.

Jerry left Bangkok and came into JFK first, where somebody from the State Department met the plane and did the paperwork. Then they got him on the flight to Salt Lake City. We'd set this route up to have people meet the casket all along the way to make sure Jerry didn't go astray.

Jim and I were sitting there in the lounge in Salt Lake City, waiting for the flight. I looked out the window and I saw this big shipping container on one of those little airport trucks, going in the opposite direction from us. I said, "You know, I wonder if that's Jerry?" Jim jumped up and got ahold of the airline supervisor who radioed out to the cargo handlers. Sure enough, that was him. They were putting him on the wrong flight.

JIM SCHILL, former USAID Laos Refugee Relief Program; former Department of State, Bureau for Refugee Programs

That big aluminum transfer container was standard for caskets being transported by the airlines. It is required to be that way. The container is about seven feet by three feet by two and a half to three feet high. They're pretty large, and they have to be moved on big transfer rollers. When I saw that transfer container moving off I said, "Bullshit! Jerry is going on *our* flight!" I prepared to pull a flimflam on the airline officials. I showed them my ID and said with authority, "Sirs, I represent the United States government, including the State Department and the Congress. I have been instructed to ensure that the body of one of the most important heroes of the Indochina conflict be directly and expeditiously transported to Missoula, Montana, on the next flight. Your assistance will be gratefully appreciated." They paid attention with unusual zeal and assured me that Jerry's body would receive priority off-loading and transfer to my aircraft. They even drove me to the transfer point.

From the transfer point I pointed my finger down there and said, "That's it! You don't lose him!" Oh, I was *really* upset. But as I watched that aluminum transfer container being moved to our outbound aircraft, I choked up and could not speak. Hog's remains were with us, but that didn't lessen the fact that this friend would only be with us in spirit from now on.

BOB JOHNSON, former Highland Section chief, JVA, Thailand; regional director, International Rescue Committee (IRC), Seattle

Suddenly the forklift reversed and headed back toward our plane. Jim and I kind of laughed about that, saying Jerry was already trying to get away from this program. That he was trying to avoid his own funeral! We got the casket on our plane and we headed off to Missoula.

THOMAS J. "T. J." THOMPSON, former smokejumper; former air delivery specialist, MR2, Laos

Toby and I flew up from Texas. We were in Missoula for two days before Jerry ever showed up. He kept us waiting; you know how he is. Then on the second day we went to the airport when Jerry was arriving. The airport scene when they brought Jerry home, it was pretty heavy.

There were more than 150 people there. The Hmong and us, we filled the old airport. People were in the bar, in the restaurant, and out in the lobby. While we were waiting, we all were drinking and talking. It was very noisy with everyone in the bar. I watched it all.

CHU VANG, son of General Vang Pao

At the airport my dad and the American friends, three or four people that used to work with Jerry in Laos, they ate lunch and were talking and laughing and enjoying conversation because they didn't see each other for so many years. I asked one of them, "Where are you now?" And he said, "I'm in Africa." We were talking, laughing. CIA style is that way! They aren't sad for anybody who dies. They don't feel that that is the end of life. They don't feel that way! Life goes on, and to live and die is normal, everyday life. They could go anytime. It could be them, it could be anybody. They *know* that. So nobody looked real sad. That is the CIA style. For the American friends, everybody seems to be more happy to meet each other than sad to have Jerry lay down in that casket. More happy than sad. Because they knew it could be any of them next.

JIM SCHILL, former USAID Laos Refugee Relief Program; former Department of State, Bureau for Refugee Programs

We landed in Missoula, and the small airport seemed mostly deserted until we entered through the terminal doors. Inside was Zack and Mr. Clean—retired spooks, John Tucker from State Department, and a group of Hmong, including General Vang Pao, Judy, Lucky, and Glassman—all of whom had worked closely with Jerry. I hadn't seen this particular group of Hmong since they were all evacuated from Laos in '75. But I don't think *any* of us were surprised to see each other. It was like coming back home, only everything was overshadowed by the pain of the event.

At a restaurant during the funeral for Jerry Daniels in Missoula, May 1982. Seated left to right: Joe Glasgow, "Judy" Nhia Vang, Chu Vang, Tou-Fu Vang, Chong Vang, Xiong Moua, "Sancho" Leng Wong. Standing left to right: Jon Randall, Ken Hessel, General Vang Pao, Miles Johnson. Thomas "Shep" Johnson collection.

Someone told me that Jerry's remains would not be in until later, and motioned me to sit down and have a beer. I spoke with difficulty. "The Hog came in with me. I think we should go outside and be with him when he is off-loaded." Lucky, Judy, Glassman, and others immediately stood up and began to move toward the outside of the terminal.

"LUCKY" LUE YANG, former field liaison officer (FLO), MR2, Laos; Hmong funeral organizer

Jim and I started to go over to the plane, but they didn't allow me to go. Usually they don't allow people to walk to the airplane to pull the casket out, right? Jim pulled out his State Department ID, and they opened the door and we went over there together. I was the one who pulled the big metal box out while everybody waited. Jim said the casket was inside the metal box.

CHA MOUA, Hmong friend; Hmong funeral organizer

When I saw them pull out that big metal box, my first reaction was shock. We all felt shock. We put it on the rollers and rolled it from the airplane to the pickup area outside.

JIM SCHILL, former USAID Laos Refugee Relief Program; former Department of State, Bureau for Refugee Programs

As Jerry's big transfer container was moved, Lucky, Judy, and others began to show their emotions by stroking the casing. They're putting their hands up and they're rubbing it and stroking it and caressing it. Then one or two of the Hmong put their arms around the edges of it and just kind of hung onto it. Maybe for five minutes they hung on as if they did not want to let it go. It was very moving. And you could hear these guttural moans coming from them while the tears welled up. There was such overwhelming pain that they were feeling, both emotional and physical. We all looked at it and felt it in some way, but especially the Hmong were just bereft.

VP stood in the background silently. Everybody knew he was hurting, too, but the general didn't flinch. VP had been brought up to be strong, and he stood there with the pain. He was a very proud general and these were his people. He took it as a leader would; he was very stoic. I know he felt the pain and the anguish of his own people and thought about his friend Jerry. The relationship between Jerry and VP had been very close, but it wasn't father-son because Jerry was a CIA case officer. VP knew that Jerry was his principal contact with the outer world of support, that Jerry was in Laos as a principal go-between on behalf of the U.S. government.

Finally some of us put our arms around the Hmong and said, "Come on. Let's help load Jerry into the truck. It's time to load him." Absolutely lovingly gentle, we helped them back away.

BOB JOHNSON, former Highland Section chief, JVA, Thailand; regional director, International Rescue Committee (IRC), Seattle

We looked for the funeral van that was going to take the big shipping container over to the funeral home. The van wasn't there. We called and they said, "Oh, we heard the flight was canceled so we reassigned the van." We said, "Is there something else you can send out?" They said, "All we've got is the landscaping truck." We said, "That'll be fine. We don't think Jerry will care!" So what they sent out was just a big open truck with a bunch of loose dirt and tools in the back. We laughed. That would work out just fine.

THOMAS J. "T. J." THOMPSON, former smokejumper; former air delivery specialist, MR2, Laos

When the crew off-loaded Jerry from the airplane there was absolute silence. It wasn't anything like years earlier when we would arrive at this same airport and meet our buddies and drink beer at this same bar. This time, Jerry was home and there was no talking.

VP was standing about three feet from me. I hadn't seen Vang Pao since he came to the States. To see him out of uniform, that was a surprise. The last time I'd seen him was in Laos at the Long Cheng airport when I left in February '73. They had a *baci*, a well-wishing party for me and it was a big deal. That was the last time I saw him until almost ten years later in Missoula. Our eyes met and he looked at me funny, sort of inquisitive, like he couldn't quite place me, and then he lit up just a little bit. Our eyes locked for a second or two. Actually it was quite emotional, no doubt about it; even for VP, I could see that. Then we both looked away, understanding each other's thoughts and feelings without saying a word. I watched as the Hmong and the Americans put down their half-empty bottles and quietly left. Reality had set in.

I was one of the last to leave the bar. Why? Because I really didn't *want* to leave. There were just so many things I was thinkin'. I was rememberin' when I used to tend bar at the Missoula airport when all the jumpers hung out there. The core group of us used to gather at the bar when everybody came home from winter work with the Outfit. We just had really good, hell-raisin' times. If one of the guys was coming home, you could bet your sweet ass they'd be waitin' for you and you were gonna get shitfaced! And when we'd leave and go away on missions we'd do it again. We were all young and full of life, and our sayin' was, "Let the Good Times Roll!" Back then, we couldn't have foreseen a gathering like this. So that was part of it. This homecoming was so different. It was a kind of closure for me, you know? And it hurt.

Everyone left and when I looked at the empty room there must have been over a hundred unfinished beers sitting on the tables and the bar. I guess that no one felt like drinkin' anymore. I thought, *Well, this would not meet with Jerry's approval.* I finished my beer and reluctantly departed with a big pit in my stomach and a very lost and lonesome feeling.

BOB JOHNSON, former Highland Section chief, JVA, Thailand; regional director, International Rescue Committee (IRC), Seattle

At least for the Americans, there was a certain amount of mirth in the fact that the funeral van wasn't at the airport and we had to ride in the back of a landscaping truck. I remember thinking that Jerry might have preferred the work truck to the Cadillac hearse anyway. We figured that was probably Jerry's doing. We were on a roll after he tried to get away from us in Salt Lake City. There was a little bit of gallows humor in that. So it was the continuing saga, getting Jerry home and to the right place.

Two or three of us rode in the back of the truck with Jerry to keep him company on the way through town. The Hmong were all pretty upset, but the Americans were a couple of beers into it so it wasn't quite such a big deal. The funeral home was probably a bit surprised to find a few empties in the back after we unloaded the container.

JIM SCHILL, former USAID Laos Refugee Relief Program; former Department of State, Bureau for Refugee Programs

The State Department has hard and fast rules, as do the transport companies, on how bodies should be handled. When State sends bodies home, they have to be sent home in a certain way. That's required by law. I think in the case of Hog it was no different. The information we had from the Embassy in Bangkok was that after the autopsy, Jerry's remains were so decomposed and smelly he was wrapped in a heavy plastic bag by the Thais. Some embalming fluid was put into the plastic bag to preserve the body long enough to have it laid to rest. Then the bag was sealed and put inside the wood casket. With the remains inside, the wood casket was sealed with some kind of a sealant along the rim and then the lid was secured by screws. The wood casket was then placed in the standard aluminum transfer casing for international shipping to the United States.

After all of us arrived at the funeral home, the metal transfer container was off-loaded onto a gurney and moved into a room where normally they would embalm people. There were probably eight or nine of us in the room when the container was opened.

BOB CLIFFORD, funeral director

Rick Evans and I were the two funeral directors for Jerry Daniels' funeral. When we removed Mr. Daniels' casket from the shipping container I recall he was in what we call a "toe pincher," a casket that is broader at the shoulders, then tapers in somewhat as it goes to the feet. That style of casket was something foreign to us—a different style casket that was not like anything we have here in the U.S. It definitely came from overseas.

JIM SCHILL, former USAID Laos Refugee Relief Program; former Department of State, Bureau for Refugee Programs

When the Hmong saw the wood casket come out of the transfer container they said, "Can we open Jerry? We have to make sure it's Jerry in there." The funeral director said to me, "They did a very good job of putting his remains into the casket and sealing it," then looked at me and said, "but there's still a whiff. Can you get a whiff?" And I said, "Yes, I can." You could still get a slight whiff of the body when the casket passed by. That smell can only be described as putrefaction with little evidence of formaldehyde.

CHA MOUA, Hmong friend; Hmong funeral organizer

At the funeral home, that is when we lift the wood casket. Lucky and I and Chou and Glassman and a couple of others. When we put our hands on the casket and lift it up, we feel we can still run! We all question each other: "Why is it so light? And why is it so short when Jerry was so tall? Jerry should not be this light, this short." We talk among ourselves like that, immediately. We all complain: "Maybe Jerry is not in here!"

RICK EVANS, funeral director

The remains were hermetically sealed. Hermetically sealed caskets we get very rarely. The casket had a sealant that went around the lid to keep odors, leakages, anything like that, inside of it.

In reviewing the notes in the mortuary file, a May 6 telegram we received from the American Embassy in Bangkok said, "Thai mortuary officials have informed us that the embalmment of the remains are not expected to be completely satisfactory. Remains are in an advanced state of decomposition. Container seals should be carefully examined." And there were phone calls, too, that said the body was in an advanced state of decomposition and there wasn't really anything they could do with it. "Advanced decomposition" usually means general arterial embalming is impossible. So I would think that they probably used an external pack or embalming formaldehyde. They would probably put a liquid over the skin and then wrap it maybe with cotton or a blanket of some sort to hold it in. At least that's what *we* would do for an external embalming. Pour fluid over the body just to try to squelch the odor and to keep it from going too much further.

JIM SCHILL, former USAID Laos Refugee Relief Program; former Department of State, Bureau for Refugee Programs

The funeral director said, "We're not going to open this." He explained that the casket could not be opened because it had been permanently sealed by the health authorities in Thailand. "Here are the transfer documents from the U.S. Embassy that say these are Jerry Daniels' remains." He showed the documents from Bangkok attesting that the remains inside were those of Jerry Daniels. This did not convince the Hmong. Glassman put his hands on the casket and started to weep. He hugged the casket and said, "I don't believe Jerry's in here."

CHOU MOUA, former chief of Forward Air Guides (FAGs), MR2, Laos

There was a person from the State Department at the funeral home. We were standing around the casket and we said to him, "We want to see if that is really Jerry or not." And he said, "I promise that is Jerry Daniels. If not Jerry Daniels, I would not be here." That was *exactly* what he said at the funeral home. He would not allow us to open the casket.

NHIA "JUDY" VANG, former field liaison officer (FLO), MR2, Laos

We ask to see the body but they say no. That's why we think it may not be true. What came to our minds is, probably something in there is not right. Maybe it is a piece of wood or rocks or maybe dead pigs or maybe some other body in there, but not Jerry.

BOB JOHNSON, former Highland Section chief, JVA, Thailand; regional director, International Rescue Committee (IRC), Seattle

The Hmong *really* wanted to look inside. That was one of their big goals. That would have been their way of verifying it was Jerry. But we couldn't do it. Because of the decomposition.

JIM SCHILL, former USAID Laos Refugee Relief Program; former Department of State, Bureau for Refugee Programs

It was about a twenty-minute standoff at the mortuary until we decided everyone should leave and think about it for a while. That would give the Hmong time to calm down.

We all left the mortuary. I went with Tucker back to the hotel where Tucker and I, Zack, Mr. Clean, and another few spooks, five or six of us, sat around and talked about Jerry and our years in Laos. It was so sad. We talked and drank until we were blitzed out and just cried. Later, with some composure regained, Tucker and Zack and I were given a ride to the Daniels residence. We gave Mrs. Daniels and her sons the letters of condolence from the Hill, State Department, and cables from abroad. We sat with her and held hands. She was composed as she showed us photographs of her recent trip to visit Jerry in Thailand, and she thanked us.

Letter of condolence to LOUISE [DANIELS] REESE from MORTON I. ABRAMOWITZ, former U.S. ambassador to Thailand

DEPARTMENT OF STATE

Washington, D.C. 20520

May 5, 1982

Mrs. Louise Reese and Family
1701 Cooley, No. 1
Missoula, Montana 59801

Dear Mrs. Reese:

    I was the American Ambassador to Thailand from 1978
to 1981 and worked with Jerry on refugee programs.
I was shocked and deeply distressed to learn of his
death. Please accept my heartfelt sympathy.

    Jerry was an outstanding official. He was deeply
devoted to his work and to helping the Hmong people.
They will miss him greatly and so will we. It was a
privilege to be associated with him. All of us in the
United States Government who worked with Jerry mourn
his untimely passing. Our thoughts are with you.

                    Sincerely,

                    Morton I. Abramowitz
                    Ambassador

JIM SCHILL, former USAID Laos Refugee Relief Program; former Department of State, Bureau for Refugee Programs

From Mrs. Daniels' house we went back to the hotel for a while, drank more beer and sat around and cried some more, but we were still functioning. Later that evening we would go over to Moua Chou's house to talk with the Hmong again.

Personally, I had no doubts about who was in the casket. Having worked in the U.S. Embassy for eighteen years, I had taken care of some of these unfortunate things before. And, frankly, the U.S. Embassy would not try to create a conspiracy that would require them to do something different. There is a very well-numbered process that has to be gone through in the consular services for notification of kin and disposition of remains. It is a step-by-step process, and certain requirements mandate that body identification be accomplished at post. And there are additional requirements if the casket is to be sealed. It has to be certified and authorized by many authorities along the way. I'm sure that's what happened to Jerry. The health officials permanently sealed the casket because the body was too far gone. So there was no question in my mind. I mean, nobody *wanted* to believe it. But it's there. That's Jerry. And you have to accept it on faith.

"GLASSMAN" YANG SEE, former liaison between Jerry Daniels/Sky and General Vang Pao/MR2 staff, Laos

Technically, according to Hmong culture, the casket *has* to be opened before the funeral ceremony starts. But not according to public health. Public health was very terrible and very insistent that the casket could not be opened. We had no choice but to accept it for the moment. We needed to start the ceremony that day.

BOB JOHNSON, former Highland Section chief, JVA, Thailand; regional director, International Rescue Committee (IRC), Seattle

The Hmong ritual would start late that Saturday afternoon. It was already set up and ready to go. The American part of the funeral was set for the next morning, a Sunday service with the eulogy and so forth.

Mrs. MARY ELLEN STUBB, Sexton, Missoula Cemetery

When I look at the notes in the funeral records from Mountain View Mortuary, they openly state that this is a sealed casket and that it is "SEALED FOREVER. NOT TO BE OPENED." In capital letters and underlined four times. I find that interesting.

BOB CLIFFORD, funeral director

The truth is, I was *told* the body was not in good shape. I can't confirm that because I never saw it. I had talked to some State Department people in Washington, DC, by phone. More than likely I had several conversations at different times with different people. I may have used the public health issue simply with the knowledge that *if* the body was in bad shape, as we were told, and *if* we opened it, yes, it could have been a public health nuisance. The body had the *possibility* of being a public health issue, but I couldn't say 100 percent that it would be.

Badly decomposed bodies are not pleasant sights. The Hmong probably would not have been as appalled at it as we would be because more likely in their environment and their culture they would have seen that a lot. They go out in the jungle where it's hot and humid and they may not find a body for four or five or ten days; they're going to be in pretty bad shape. "Let's retrieve it, let's do our ceremony and do what we have to do." But for us, a body that's in bad shape is somewhat appalling.

There was no *legal* constraint, but the State Department was *very* adamant that the casket not be opened. Frankly, I was somewhat intimidated. I can't use the word "threatened." I never thought anything would happen to me or my children. We were not threatened, but we were intimidated to some degree. It was very, very clear that under no circumstances whatsoever would that casket be opened. It was said so many times by the State Department that it became ingrained in me. There wasn't any *legal* reason for it not to be opened, but there was *no way* I would have gone against that order.

Laos, Part III: The Fall (1973–75)

A CEASEFIRE begins in both Vietnam and Laos; several letters home; a parade for the Pathet Lao in Vientiane; the air evacuation of Long Cheng, Lima Site 20A.

Excerpt from a letter to LOUISE DANIELS from Jerry Daniels, January 23, 1973

I can't really say too many words of wisdom on the peace deal,1 just hope it does come through one of these days so things might be a little different for awhile. The enemy has not yet probed Long Cheng this year with the exception of a few shellings which were kids play. Don't know what their intentions will be the remainder of the dry season. Can only say that if negotiations are settled then NVA must be really getting a good deal, because they sure aren't hurting as far as I'm concerned.

Excerpt from a letter to LOUISE DANIELS from Jerry Daniels, March 24, 1973

To boil it all down I still do not like the bad guys and realize they have gained more, as usual, and [are] now ready to sit back awhile. But for immediate future believe all concerned want to stop the fighting and try the politic and economic battle.

Excerpts from an audiotaped letter to LOUISE DANIELS from Jerry Daniels, May 5–10, 1973. Sound of steady rainfall can be heard in the background.

The rainy season's begun. . . . It's really mighty pleasin'. This is the best time of year, as far as I am concerned, because you're used to everything being kind of brown and now it gets real green and the air gets clear and the smoke is cleared out. In fact we just had pretty much of an elephant rain. . . .

I am hunkered in my room down at VP's house. Got down here and the rain came in and trapped me so I decided, well, I'll just start on this huckleberry [cassette tape recording] right now, before I go back up to the office. . . .

Excerpts from an audiotaped letter to LOUISE DANIELS from Jerry Daniels, August 9, 1973

Before, when I worked up north, the weather would get bad and we'd get socked in and we'd have a chance to read and lay around, but once I started working here in dreaded Long Cheng it's been nothing but a big whirlwind for about three years. Last year when I came back on the fourth of August [1972] up until now, I've only had three six-day time-offs, that's only eighteen days. Now it's finally gearing down some. I probably shouldn't tell you that because then you'll expect more letters. It's getting free time to watch a movie and everything else. God, it's mighty pleasin' just shirking at random. Like today, I've just shirked the whole day not even working. . . .

A couple weeks ago I took a road trip south of here [to Pha Khae]. First time I ever had the time to do something like that. Just a beautiful day. Burr [Burr Smith, "Mr. Clean"] went along with me. We took a shotgun and raked a few sparrows. It's about a two and a half hour drive down there. . . . When we got to Pha Khae it was getting fairly late. We'd like to have somebody come back with us. We figured that quite a few of the Hmong folk would want to come back since it was a free ride. But I guess they thought we were crazy old Americans, leaving too late, except for one guy who said he'd go with us.

On our way down there we'd gotten high-centered in a couple of places and broke a spring off the accelerator so after I pressed down on it, it wouldn't come back up automatically. I had to stick my toe under it, and then the radiator was steaming. So when we got down there we bought some rubber bands. We figured we could get the accelerator fixed again.

So anyway, we picked up this guy and we were D and D-in', had nectars in our hands. We pulled up to this stream about half a kilometer out of the town so we could put in some water and lift the hood up and fix the accelerator. It was late and, God, this poor guy took one look at us after we put the hood up and poured the water in, nectarin'. And then when Clean hauled out the rubber bands and started hunkering over the controls of that accelerator the guy said he had a headache and he didn't think he could go any further. We thought that was really funny. But he got out and he said, O, *chop houa*, the old "sick head." So, needless to say, he didn't go with us. What was good though, the darn rubber bands worked perfect and we didn't get stuck at all going back. We made it back before it got dark and we really had a good time.

[By the way] I wanted to mention to the Animal Man, in that one picture where I am striding along with Mr. Clean, that I have halfway the watermelon arms again. I've been doing some exercises, weights, push ups, stuff like that. I figure that before I get back I'll be able to down him in an arm twist.

Two CIA case officers: Hog Daniels with his "watermelon arms" and "Mr. Clean" (Burr Smith), 1973. Susan Smith Finn collection.

Excerpt from a letter to LOUISE DANIELS from Jerry Daniels, December 5, 1973

The Muong [Hmong] new year this year began on 25 Nov and lasted until around 04 Dec. It was not as memorable a one as last year since the King's son (the Crown Prince) was here during most of the time and I had to spend a lot of time in Vientiane. I never even got to ride a bull let alone go to many of my friend's parties. However, there will still be some more activities for the Sam Neua Meo will not be having their New Year until 25/26 Dec, something to do needless to say with the lunar new year. So I may still get to ride a bull yet, plus the Sam Neua Muong are my old friends.

Letter to TED O. "LITTLE O" LYMPUS, high school and college friend, from Jerry Daniels, January 20, 1974

Dear "O",

No big haps in this area. My tour this time is up 04 Aug 74 and I figure on stacking my arms and pushing on, don't know where to yet. Perhaps I'll just unlimber a skidrow somewhere for a few months.

. . . I have been meaning for some time to unlimber a will or at least some ideas on such a document and forward to you, however, to date nothing has been pro-

Watching a bullfight at Hmong new year, Long Cheng, 1971–72. In the crowd (left to right): Colonel Shoua Yang in fatigues, J. R. Johnson with pipe, Pat Landry with stick, Chao Saykham with dark glasses, General Vang Pao in suit and tie with several of his sons, Touby Lyfoung with cane, and Hog Daniels. J. R. Johnson collection.

duced. I expect to have this completed within the next few weeks and <u>will</u> send to you for your scanning and input. . . . I guess that's enough man talk.

I've been on a health kick since 01 Jan but the indian blood is flowing and am about ready to break down and have just one, few beers never hurt anyone.

Jerry Barker

KENT "DAN THE ANIMAL MAN" DANIELS, brother of Jerry Daniels

When we were still youngsters in California, Louise used to say we were supposed to have some Indian blood, and I'm using the words "supposed to have" because we never probed at her. Our great-something grandfather on Louise's side was "supposed to have" been Chief Powatan,[2] Pocahontas's dad. It was one-sixty-fourth or something Indian blood; it was just that small amount. Jerry and I played it into it bein' the Indian blood that got us when we were drinkin'.

GARRY R. JENKIN, former communications officer, MR2, Laos

When I arrived in Long Cheng in January 1973 I was one of four American CIA communicators working under Air America cover. I lived in the Sky compound and

Two Hmong girls at new year in Long Cheng, December 1973. G. R. Jenkin collection, Air America Archives, University of Texas at Dallas.

worked at Sky headquarters. I was a communicator, connecting Long Cheng with the world via secure high-frequency radio communications.

In 1973 the Vietnam War was slowly grinding to a halt. The ceasefire agreement was signed in Vientiane in February 1973, leading to the formation of a coalition government for Laos. During the months that followed, U.S. personnel reductions were taking place, including the number of communicators. By early 1974 I was the sole communicator left at Sky compound and knew I wouldn't be there much longer. Before I left Long Cheng at the end of May 1974 I trained Jerry as the stay-behind communicator. Communications security is always a top priority, and I was determined to make sure he would have no problem. Not surprisingly, he was a quick learner, and by the time I left we were both confident in his abilities.

NHIA "JUDY" VANG, former field liaison officer (FLO), MR2, Laos

Sky supported General Vang Pao and MR2 soldiers all during the war years. Then the ceasefire in 1973 changed everything. In 1974 the coalition government in Laos starts to release some of our SGU soldiers to return to civilian life. Every year they will reduce the SGU military because they say there is peace.

Almost 200,000 Hmong live in the Long Cheng area, including the outposts. These people left their villages and farms a long time ago when the communist soldiers came to fight. Without any land to farm, almost every family relies on financial support from their soldiers. Without a military salary, how can this population survive? We need to create some income for the Long Cheng population, so Sky reorganizes and develops projects that will create jobs. The development projects are paid for by Sky and USAID and General Vang Pao. They will help to establish some other source of income for the military families now that the government says there is peace.

JIM SCHILL, former USAID Laos Refugee Relief Program; former Department of State, Bureau for Refugee Programs

Maybe I'm wrong, but what the spooks did in terms of development, they did unilaterally. They never checked with anybody in USAID to ask, "What do you think? Does this make sense?" The Agency had a lot more money to spend than USAID, and they weren't confined to *anything*. They set up pig and chicken farms, created Xiengkhouang Development Corporation, and such. It is my impression that there were some great ideas, but for them to hatch and have some lasting effect, it would take years to integrate those projects into the culture and the governance of the Hmong and maintain the blessing of the new government. So there was tension between Agency people and USAID, but it wasn't competition, more like different kinds of support to VP. So you had VP saying, "I want to do this and that." And the spooks saying, "We want to do that and this." They all went through Jerry, and Jerry helped out as best he could, but creating this push came too late in an already tough game. In my opinion, the Agency just wanted to spend the damn money, keep VP and the Hmong happy, and get out. That's all. The spooks were leaving Long Cheng, and they wanted to get out without causing a great deal of concern.

BARRY REED, former smokejumper; former Air America loadmaster, Laos

My last Air America flight into Vientiane was in a C-130. This was very early April '74, not long before Air America pulled out of Laos for good in June '74. We landed at Wattay Airport in Vientiane. Dropped off whatever cargo there was, nothing really to speak of. We had been doing that for the past two months. Evidently the Customers had been told to shut down their sites so they had been evacuating their assets, mostly to Udorn.

Anyway, we landed in Vientiane. There was almost nobody around the traffic department where cargo was stored, and the warehouse was almost empty. We stopped in Operations and Oscar Mike, the Air America operations manager, said a parade was starting to come through town just past the compound. I think it was the welcoming parade of the coalition government for the Pathet Lao.[3] There was nothing that needed to go to Udorn, so we left. As we were going out to the airplane, the parade vehicles started to come by. We could hear the trucks but we couldn't see them.

We took off and went around the landing and takeoff pattern. The pilots saw the parade approaching the airport west of us. They were curious to see what was going on so they did a 180 turn and flew overhead the parade route. This was a fly-by about 500 feet off the ground down Wattay, which was the main road coming into Vientiane from that direction. Somebody said, "If you want to see the Pathet Lao, look out the window." We all were curious so we looked. From the airplane we could see the lead vehicles. It looked just like a homecoming parade you might see anywhere. The grand marshal, whoever that was, was sitting out in the open, waving to the crowd. Both sides of the street all the way downtown were lined with people waving flags and cheering. There were several vehicles full of soldiers.

I was in the back end of the plane looking out the window. Everybody else was looking, too. It was a quick look. When you're buzzing by at better than 100 miles an hour you don't have much time to see, but I was thinking, *Wow. History.* I'd been there for almost eight years. Seven years, nine months, and nine days was my period of employment with Air America. So this was poignant, in a way. This was the end of an era. And the start of a new one for somebody else. We did a little cruise and then broke right for the Mekong River and kept on going.

JIM SCHILL, former USAID Laos Refugee Relief Program; former Department of State, Bureau for Refugee Programs

In 1973 the CIA was spending about $50 million per year in Long Cheng alone to support the military efforts of the Hmong to keep the Pathet Lao and NVA from overrunning northern Laos. That money came in each month in cash to pay the salaries of the Thai mercenaries and others on the CIA payroll—the Hmong who worked directly for the spooks, the CIA case officers, and various ancillary military efforts such as the Commando Raiders. In addition, the Hmong received about $5 million from USAID for education, health, economic development, and humanitarian aid. This support had been building over the last ten years, and now that things were slowing down due to the peace agreement as well as public perceptions of the cost of the effort, the money approved by Congress was also drastically reduced and limited to technical assistance.

In 1974 the umbilical cord is beginning to be severed between Sky and the Hmong, not only because of the ceasefire but because the CIA is beginning to move out of Long Cheng anyway. By the end of '74 CIA funding had dropped off exponentially to maybe $3 or $4 million. The CIA had all but left the Long Cheng valley, all except for Hog.

By early 1975 the military situation in neighboring Vietnam was going from bad to worse. The North Vietnamese were on the move, and the South Vietnamese army was falling back in disarray. In Laos we ended up with fewer resources—both human and financial—to help secure a development effort in the country. USAID officers and others were asked to leave their posts in northern Laos to return to the capital city of Vientiane and work in the USAID headquarters only. I have always held the notion that to make development happen you have to be on the ground, on site where it is to occur.

VP is a very savvy guy. He sees the writing on the wall. He knows Sky is closing down in Laos. Jerry may be there with him forever, but Jerry is going to have less and less money. I think it boiled down to a lack of political commitment from Washington, DC; a lack of support from Congress; and the lack of will on the part of the American people to stick it out.

By March 1975 there was a general unease in Vientiane as the newly formed coalition government, which included the Pathet Lao, made it clear that there would be a changing of the guard. There was a lot of confusion, and the Pathet Lao were beginning to make sounds like they were going to become the military enforcement authorities of Laos.

Excerpt from English-language *BANGKOK POST*, April 24, 1975

PATHET LAO GAIN VITAL POSITION
BY IBRAHIM NOORI

Vientiane (Reuters)—The pro-communist Pathet Lao have made a major territorial gain,[4] making it easier for them to take over the country militarily if they wished. . . .

The Right-wing Defence Minister Sisouk na Champassak told a Press conference, that two Pathet Lao battalions supported by one North Vietnamese battalion had launched the attack on positions held by the Vientiane side using tanks, long range artillery and 122 millimetre rockets. . . .

The fighting was the most serious since the two factions signed a peace agreement on February 21, 1973, ending a decade of civil war in Laos.

Excerpt from a letter to LOUISE DANIELS from Jerry Daniels, March 23, 1975

Dear Louise,

. . . I guess it is pretty easy to see that the months ahead won't be too pleasin for us American huckleberries left here. I will probably remain here now until July of 76. . . . It will probably be unpleasant but an interesting time which sees our previous world influences and prestige vastly diminish, particularly in Indochina. But I guess times change and to get too carried away about it doesn't help any. So don't worry, we'll probably just end up shipping all the Muong [Hmong] folk to Montana. . . .

Jerry

NHIA "JUDY" VANG, former field liaison officer (FLO), MR2, Laos

Starting in February 1975, Jerry and the high-ranking officers in Military Region 2 knew that something would happen soon. When the U.S. withdraws from Vietnam, MR2 will have no American support because the U.S. mission to Laos is *part* of the mission to Vietnam.

When Saigon fell on April 30, 1975, VP, Jerry, and the U.S. Embassy talked about getting the Hmong out to Thailand because now the situation was critical. VP gave Jerry the rough number of 2,300 to 2,500 people that needed to be moved out, mostly officers and their families. Jerry called for American pilots and planes to lift us out of Long Cheng to Thailand. When the American planes start to fly on May 12, Jerry and I are very busy, working about sixteen hours per day. We are on the airstrip talking by radio to the American pilots about where to land.

When the Hmong people hear about the air evacuation at Long Cheng, they are scared and they are mad. They rush in from the countryside and camp at the airstrip. Thousands of people are all jammed up there, waiting for the planes to take them to Thailand. Jerry and I work hard the whole time. Everything is so tense, and at night it is not safe. Every enemy gun points at the Sky compound and at VP's house. If the enemy attacks, those are the two places they are going to hit. Some nights Jerry sleeps at my house for security.

The Sky Compound at Long Cheng nestled behind rocky karsts with curving market road below, 1973. G. R. Jenkin collection, Air America Archives, University of Texas at Dallas.

DANIEL C. ARNOLD, former chief of station, CIA

By 1975 I had worked with Jerry Daniels for many years. I knew him well; he was an absolutely outstanding young man—totally dedicated, very honest, and very courageous. He epitomized, in my opinion, the very best that this country can produce. That's why, when it came down to one person, Jerry was the one man retained at Long Cheng. He had been there for years and had a close personal relationship with VP and the others. They saw him for exactly what he was—as long as *he* was there, *we* were there.

By the time the request for a U.S. airlift came, it was not a surprise. The American drawdown was in progress, but there was never any question about honoring the commitments that had been made in the preceding fourteen years by every U.S. ambassador and every senior Washington official who ever visited the area and met with the insurgency and/or Lao government leaders. There was never any question that a commitment had been made. There was every intention to honor that commitment.

When the time came, it was imperative that the evacuation proceed without delay. We moved very quickly because the objective was very clear: to get as many people out as possible and as quickly as possible. The intent was always defined in terms of the key leadership and their families, to the extent we had the capability to get them out. Jerry and I had discussed ahead of time the need for him to get himself and VP out safely. When it came time, I looked to him to devise a plan, which he did, and that's what we implemented. The trickiest thing was to pull it off without getting somebody killed or causing a panic.

Mrs. MAOSAY LY SAYKAO, mother of eleven children

My son Sam [Sao] told me to stay with the American Jerry. Jerry will help the people, and he knows me. Jerry said to me, "One airplane will come to pick up all the ladies whose husbands and sons work with us. I am going to send those ladies to Thailand. You have to stay with them, stay with the group, so you can go. You will have to rush to that plane." The American Jerry wants me to go because my son Jerry [Ger] is living with the American Jerry's mother in Montana, and my older son Bruce [Pao] had been in the United States as a student.

I wait to get on that airplane. The little airplane comes but too many ladies get in there before me. I cannot fit. Jerry got mad at me and he said, "What did I tell you? I told you that when the airplane gets here you have to *rush* in!" I said, "No, I cannot do that! I have a child. By the time I grab my child the airplane is full! I cannot go!" Jerry said to wait for the next airplane.

The next day my family and I wait at the airport all day long until all the planes left. That night all my kids and my husband and I stay outside close to the airfield. If you want to sleep you sleep on the bag you packed. We don't really sleep; we just sit there with our eyes open waiting for the airplanes.

The next morning, May 12, the airplanes start to come at seven o'clock. We wait for the American Jerry to tell everybody when to go. Jerry is the one who reports to the people, "The airplane is almost here! It's just on the other side of the mountain! It's coming right now! Get ready!" He is the one who controls the CB radio, and he always reports to the people. That morning the airplane comes and Jerry tells us to *GO!* But when we get to the airplane everyone just *fights* to get in there! Three times we tried to get on an airplane but there are too many people. Full, like fingers on your hand! Again we sit and wait all night. We are so scared that we may not get onto the airplane the next day. There are a lot of people waiting there at the airport. If anyone asks the soldiers, "Is General Vang Pao still here?" The soldiers say, "Still here." But we don't really know if he is still there or if he has gone away already.

On May 13 when the first plane lands, the soldiers announce that nobody can go into the airplanes until the high officers and their families are already gone. The soldiers keep the civilian people back with their guns. Second plane, third plane. They only let the soldiers and the high-ranking officers and their families go. A fourth airplane came very late in the afternoon. Soldiers and their wives and children again. Later that day one *big* airplane lands.[5] Everyone runs. There are so many people! People hit each other's heads and just rush, rush, rush! There was one old man who almost got into the airplane. He was on the ladder but other people knock him down, then they run over his body.

After that last plane leaves we are really mad and sweating. Sweating mad and hungry! We did not eat all day. We don't have another plan. If the airplane doesn't come back to get us, probably we will die. We tell the children how important it is for us to get onto the next airplane.

CHOU MOUA, former chief of forward air guides (FAGs), MR2, Laos

By May 13 the situation in Long Cheng is very difficult. We stay in the Sky compound and ask Jerry to help us. Jerry tells us there will be one C-47 plane for our group, for the families of the people that work with the Americans. But when we get to the airport there is a lot of argument and some Hmong officers point pistols at each other and kick each other saying, "If you kill me, I will kill you, too!" It is a bad time! Not easy at all.

CHU VANG, son of General Vang Pao

That day, May 13, we lose control. So many people are at the airport. As soon as a plane arrives people just run and climb into it. Things are out of hand. I see a family push a little kid onto a plane and they close the door. The mother is still on the ground. That little kid is sent to Thailand with no relatives. What a situation!

Excerpt from an audiotaped conversation between DAVE KOUBA and GENE ISAAC, former Continental Air Services (CASI) pilots, May 13, 1975, Vientiane, Laos

KOUBA: I tell ya, I never saw so many people at Gate 1 up there at Long Cheng as I did this morning. It was a *madhouse.*

ISAAC: We just got a radio call. Jerry's going to spend the night there.

KOUBA: Well, that fuckin' Hog better come out tonight, the dumb shit. What the hell good is Jerry going to do stayin' there tonight?

ISAAC: Seems like it would be a good idea to me, too, but that ain't the way they got things planned. By morning you go overhead and talk to people. Ski [Stan Pelzinski, CASI pilot] reported off and on overhead Ban Son [LS 272] and two minutes later they got the word that Ban Son was being hit.

KOUBA: You know how long it takes to drive from 272 to Long Cheng? What makes you think the PL won't be in Long Cheng by tomorrow morning when I get up there?

ISAAC: We don't.

KOUBA: I'll be damned. Ain't it the shits. And they think everything is so fuckin' peachy cream down here in Vientiane.

ISAAC: Goin' down the drain in a hurry, isn't it?

NHIA "JUDY" VANG, former field liaison officer (FLO), MR2, Laos

No matter what, we know the Embassy assigned Jerry to stay with VP to the end, dead or alive. Jerry was a good personal friend with VP, and at the same time he was the person assigned to make sure VP was safe. Jerry was the only American person that VP trusted and saw all the time.

It is tense in the daytime, but when it gets dark the communists move closer, so more and more pressure and danger. We hear that tanks are coming up the road to Long Cheng, but we can't confirm that. There are so many rumors saying different things. On the night of May 13, Jerry and Sky make a secret plan to get VP out the next day. We keep our plan secret because security is very shaky. There are hundreds of soldiers and civilians at VP's gate. They want to know his plan. What will he do? They say, "Hey, not only you fight for the country! We do, too!"

NHIA YANG VANG, former first lieutenant, SGU Army, MR2, Laos

General Vang Pao had promised to take *everybody* to Thailand with him if they served under his military command. Because of that promise, all the military commanders and all the Hmong community in Long Cheng have a strike around the general's house. I cannot count how many thousands of people are there, but many, many people—*everyone* comes to surround his house!

LY TOU PAO, former colonel and chief of staff, MR2

Why doesn't VP face all the people? Why does he stay in his house? Because there is talk about possible assassins. People are coming in from everywhere, and there are too many strangers in town! We cannot control who is the enemy and who is a good man. The general is very aware of that. Security in Long Cheng is very risky now.

NHIA "JUDY" VANG, former field liaison officer (FLO), MR2, Laos

Because of the shaky security, Jerry and us know we have to play a trick to get VP safely out of Long Cheng. It is a very dangerous situation. For sure, the last flight will be on the morning of May 14.

DANIEL C. ARNOLD, former chief of station, CIA

VP and Jerry had to leave at the same time because all hell was going to break loose in Long Cheng when they left. That's why a calm, cool professional who could be trusted had to be there in the final stage—someone who would be cool in a very, very stressful situation. It was a gamble we had to take. All of this took place very quickly because of the events and forces that were forcing the issue.

KEN HESSEL, former smokejumper; former Continental Air Services (CASI) Air Operations, MR3, Laos

Jerry was *fearless*. Would take on anybody or anything, but was always *smart* about it. And cool. He'd get in a situation. He'd assess it and stay calm. I believe if he hadn't been there when VP left Long Cheng in '75, and doin' the things that he did at that time, they'd probably be dead right there.

CHU VANG, son of General Vang Pao

On the morning of May 14, VP is quiet. He gets quiet when he is depressed. Even though he knows that Jerry did everything he could possibly do, VP isn't happy. The Americans did not stay to back up the Hmong and back up VP. The Americans all pull out except for Jerry. When I meet VP that morning, he and Jerry already made a decision that this is the final day.

JACK KNOTTS, former Bird Air Jet Ranger helicopter pilot, Laos

In my estimation what Jerry's plan is on May 14 is to have the C-130 make one or two runs, preferably one, and the C-46s to make one run. Dave Kouba in his Porter and I in the chopper would get up to Long Cheng, get VP and Jerry out, and the whole evacuation would be called off. Those people who were led to believe that they were

Hmong people running to board a C-130 on the final day of the evacuation of Long Cheng, May 14, 1975. Chee Yang collection.

going to be evacked—and there were thousands of them on that ramp, it was just a sea of humanity—they were just going to be left.

CHU VANG, son of General Vang Pao

On the morning of May 14, thirty of Vang Nou's guards are still on duty at VP's house, still securing the area inside the fence. I go inside the house, but I can't find VP. Vang Nou says that VP is with Jerry at Jerry's office, up at the Sky compound. Captain Vang Nou and I leave the house, and all of his men are still on guard.

At the Sky office we walk inside, and VP tells me and Vang Nou to go back to the house and get his briefcase, then drive to the market road and wait there. So Vang Nou and I drive back down to the house. It's less than half an hour since we left, but now I see new guards at the gate and at the house. The new gate guard asks very politely, "Where is the general? Is he coming back here?" Very quietly I ask Vang Nou, "Who are these people?" He says, "Keep cool. Pretend that you don't notice anything different."

I go quickly into the house to grab my dad's briefcase, nothing more. We act very normal so the new soldiers won't know we are leaving. When we drive out of the yard Vang Nou tells me, "None of those soldiers belong to me." He is upset because all of his troops are gone. I don't think those new guards are from the Long Cheng area. They are very young Hmong guys sent to catch VP. I hate to call them "assassins," but that is the way I see it.

Vang Nou and I park on the market road, and I see my dad run down the hill from Sky. He says he already knows about the assassins at the house. That is why Jerry didn't want him to go there. VP tells me to drive up the hill out of town to the fishing pond. He grabs my hat to cover part of his face so he won't be recognized. That area is isolated and anything can happen. The Pathet Lao might already have moved into that area. The only ones they are looking for are VP and Jerry.

We get to the fishing pond, and a small American helicopter lands beside the jeep. The helicopter picks us up and flies us up to the village of Phou Khang, very close, right on top of the mountain. The pilot drops us off, then leaves.

JACK KNOTTS, former Bird Air Jet Ranger helicopter pilot, Laos

I drop VP off at Site 337, Phou Khang, then I go back to get Jerry. I land in the little saddle behind the king's house. I sit there and wait, and it's a nervous situation. Finally Jerry comes around the corner in his Ford Bronco and parks. But he won't get in the chopper. He doesn't want to leave yet! He gets his briefcase out and then he starts talking on the radio. He messes around and messes around and finally—and this is a very bad thing for Jerry because he's been there so long—he salutes. He comes to attention, just like he is saluting the jeep. But he is really saluting ten or fifteen years of hard work that turned into nothing. He salutes the jeep, he turns around and walks over and gets in the chopper.

I edge off, and there is a gaggle of soldiers walking out that road. Just as we lift off, we haven't really started flying yet, two of the soldiers drop their M-16s off their shoulders and take ahold of the lever and throw a round into the chamber. Well, my heart jumps into my mouth. I think they're gonna let us have it, but they don't. I head to Site 337 to pick up VP. Then I meet up with Dave Kouba in his Porter, and we both land at 113, Moung Cha. We transfer Jerry and VP to Dave's Porter, and Dave takes off. He takes Jerry, VP, and his group across the Mekong and down to Udorn, Thailand. I am well aware of what is happening in a historical angle. I am saddened for this thing, but my thoughts are to carry on.

Laos, Part IV: Uprooted

S EVERAL newspaper articles; difficulties for Hmong refugees in Thailand; exodus from Laos continues; a secret memo from Henry A. Kissinger, U.S. secretary of state; refugee resettlement to the United States begins; Lao dirt; more letters; new year letter from Jerry Daniels to the Hmong refugees in Thailand.

English-language *BANGKOK POST*, June 2, 1975

PATHET LAO SHOOT FLEEING MEOS

Vientiane (Reuters)—Pathet Lao police have begun using armed force to keep Meo [Hmong] hilltribes people from fleeing to Thailand. . . .

Eight hilltribesmen were killed [and about 30 wounded] by Pathet Lao police, a US government official reported in Bangkok, and thousands of other Meo people have been turned back at gunpoint in what appears to be the first violent social upheaval of Laos' inexorable postwar drift toward Communism. . . .

The eight Meos were shot as . . . [the] hill people ignored a police order and tried to cross [Hin Heup] bridge over a small stream 35 miles north of Vientiane, the government source said.

The US official in Bangkok, an expert in Lao affairs, said as many as 150,000 tribesmen are trying to make the exodus. . . .

The group fired on by the Pathet Lao police Friday were reported going to join Vang Pao [in Thailand]. "We have been with Vang Pao for 20 years, and he is the only one we believe," one would-be escapee was reported as saying.

GEU VANG, former colonel, SGU Army, MR2, Laos

By the beginning of June a terrible number of refugees are coming across the river and the Thai officials start to complain. Jerry is so busy on the General Vang Pao issue and the refugee issue, and he has so much pressure from the Thai officials. The Thai are not happy to Jerry and not happy to us Hmong, too. They don't want our people in Thailand. The situation is very hard to control.

Letter to LARRY WOODSON, former USAID Laos Refugee Relief Program, from Jerry Daniels, June 22, 1975

Larry,

Needless to fucking say I have been left here [in Thailand] holding the proverbial bag. Everyone along the line, regardless of which government(s) I deal with or Volags or UN etc. etc., all now say Muong [Hmong] Who? I will also never forgive the cocksucking religious organizations as they have not (nor ever did) a fucking thing when the going got rough. I'm a bitter weed but will hang in there to help the monkey folk. Unless things get out of hand I should be able to remain around here for another year or so anyway. . . . La de fucking Da.

I have been beer soaked for numerous days and find it mighty pleasing. . . . (As you know, I was never in favor they move, but since they did and will continue, as will many Lao to come, there is an unavoidable issue to deal with.)

. . . As you most likely can assume from above I have lost faith in most of mankind. Once resettlement issue of Monkey's is determined, I'm stacking my arms and retire on my gold fields north of Butte Mont.

PEACE

Jerry

Excerpt from _WASHINGTON EVENING STAR_, Washington, DC, October 6, 1975

WAR LEGEND BECOMES A GHOST
BY HENRY S. BRADSHER

. . . When the end came in Laos last spring, the war lost and the Communist Pathet Lao in control, Vang Pao and his top officers escaped to Udorn the center in Thailand for CIA operations into Laos. But he was too legendary a figure for Laos to rest easy as long as he was just across the Mekong River, and Thailand wanted him to move on so it could try to improve relations with Laos.

The Thai prime minister, Kukrit Pramoj, gave Vang Pao a farewell dinner last June 18 and the Meo general flew off to Paris and obscurity.

Under cover of this obscurity, or even secrecy, he came back to the United States . . . at the age of 46 to settle down . . . in Montana.

Excerpt from _RAVALLI REPUBLIC_, Hamilton, Montana, June 8, 1976

LAOTIAN SECRET ARMY CHIEF RETIRES NEAR CORVALLIS
BY CHERYL YOUNG

After more than 4000 years, a wandering people has found itself at home in the Bitter Root Valley. Looking at [Vang Pao] now in the peaceful early summer of the Bitter Root, listening to him talk of plans for a small hog operation to feed his family, it is somehow hard to imagine that this man was head of the entire secret army of the Central Intelligence Agency (CIA) in Laos until 1975.

English-language *BANGKOK POST*, September 5, 1975

SIX LAO RIGHTISTS ON DEATH LIST

Six former rightist leaders who fled Laos after the Pathet Lao takeover were sentenced to death yesterday by the central supreme court of Laos, Vientiane Radio reported. Among those sentenced to death in absentia were Meo tribal leader Gen Vang Pao.

RANDOLPH "TOBY" SCOTT, former smokejumper; former Continental Air Services (CASI) loadmaster, Laos

I tell you, the way we did the Hmong, I tell you that was the sorriest I've ever heard of anybody. We never did win a damned war. Every damn war the CIA ever got into they lost the damned thing, you know it? It just really pissed us off because we could see that we could've won that war. We could've done something. But they tell you no and tie your hands behind your back. Well, it made me sick to see how everything operated over there.

I never could figure out—you know, we worked for the ol' CIA but, my God, they never would stick with anything, you know? If it got tough they just pulled their damn tail down and took off. Boy, Jerry was madder than hell about that. It was a sad deal. Jerry was really pissed. Really disgusted. Damn. I mean Vang Pao and the Hmong were the only true fighters we ever found in Southeast Asia, and we just turned our backs and ran. It was just terrible.

SHUR V. VANGYI, former Ministry of Economy, Royal Lao Government; former executive director, Lao Family Community Inc., Santa Ana, California

It was mid-June 1975 when General Vang Pao left the Nam Phong refugee camp in Thailand. Due to political pressure from the Thai government, he left Thailand and went to the U.S. [See Map 1 on page 33.]

In June the Hmong and Lao refugees in Nam Phong and Nong Khai camps as well as other camps did not have enough food to eat because there were new refugees coming into those camps every day. At that time, probably I spoke more English than any other person in the Nam Phong camp. I had been educated in the U.S. as a high school exchange student in Iowa and Michigan from '64 until I graduated in June 1966. In 1971 I graduated from the University of Hawaii with a B.A. in marketing. Then I went back to Laos and worked for the Lao government as a deputy director for trade in the Ministry of Economy. When Yang Dao returned from his studies in

France he also worked for the Lao government. While we were working in Vientiane, we were both advisors to VP.

After we fled Laos, Dr. Yang Dao lived in the Nam Phong camp as well. Because I spoke English and Yang Dao spoke French, we were the ones that often went out to make contact with officials in Bangkok. So on a day at the end of June, not long after General Vang Pao left Thailand, Yang Dao and I went by ourselves by bus from the Nam Phong camp to the U.N. headquarters in metro Bangkok. We went to ask for more food and clothing for the refugees; about 30,000 people lived in the camp at that time. We met with several U.N. staff. They said, "Okay, now that we know there are more refugees coming in, we will provide more food, more support." And they did.

On August 4, 1975, Yang Dao and I went back to Bangkok to meet with U.S. Embassy staff because we had heard that many ethnic Lao, lowland Lao, had left the refugee camps in Thailand for resettlement in the U.S., but no Hmong had left. So we got quite mad and went to the U.S. Embassy and talked to one officer in the refugee program. We said, "The Hmong were the primary group recruited to assist the American CIA. The Lao group, of course they helped too, but the Hmong are the number-one priority for being the foot soldiers for the U.S. Now the Lao are going to the U.S. and the Hmong are not? Why?" He said, "Well, I don't work for the Hmong. I only know the ethnic Lao and I work for the Lao. That's why the refugee program is for Lao."

In Laos that man had worked with the Lao government for the lowland group in the southern part of Laos—Vientiane, Pakse, Savannakhet, Attopeu, Saravane. In Thailand he took care of only the lowland Lao refugees, the southern people, and he said he knows nothing about the northern people, the Hmong. We said, "Why do you say that you don't know the Hmong? The refugee program should be for everyone who assisted the U.S. fight against communism in Indochina, particularly in Laos, and Hmong are the Number One group that was recruited by the CIA." About the Hmong he said again, "Well, I don't know them. That's why I only help resettle the Lao from the southern part." He said, "You can ask other officers here to see if they can help you." Then we went to a higher officer. Yang Dao and I discussed our concerns and he said, "Okay, we will look into the Hmong situation."

After that meeting we returned to Nam Phong the same day. But Yang Dao and I are not happy because the first Embassy staffer said he didn't work for the Hmong. Because of that problem, Yang Dao and I talked about Jerry. That Jerry worked for the Hmong and lived with us for so long in Laos. We knew the only person that could help the Hmong was Jerry. But we didn't know where Jerry was.

**Excerpt from *WASHINGTON EVENING STAR*, Washington, DC,
October 6, 1975**

END OF WAR LEAVES TOUGH MEO TRIBESMEN
IN DESTITUTION
BY HENRY S. BRADSHER

. . . It was a most irregular sort of army. . . . But when it was marshaled together
and dropped down by U.S. helicopter or small, short-field airplanes, the secret army
was devastatingly effective. Its men fought with discipline and bravery for their
American controllers. They repeatedly turned back offensives of NVA divisions with
guerrilla strikes or savage frontal combat.

. . . The United States so far has provided $1.3 million in cash and $370,000 worth
of rice. Ford's new allocation will include another $4 million for the Meo refugees in
Thailand plus $2.75 million to resettle in the United States between 3,000 and 3,400
Lao and Meo refugees—mostly Lao, who might adjust more readily here than the
hilltribesmen.

**"GLASSMAN" YANG SEE, former liaison between Jerry Daniels/Sky and
General Vang Pao/MR2 staff, Laos**

The first group of Hmong people who came to the United States in early 1976 were
Category 1—the field liaison officers, forward air guides, and other important service groups, who back in Laos worked for and were directly paid by the U.S. government. Because of Washington's failure to recognize the Hmong as political refugees,
as victims of the secret war, it was very difficult to convince the people in the United
States Congress about the status of Hmong refugees in Thailand. We had to use the
FLOs and FAGs as bullets to pierce through the wall of unawareness and irresponsi-
bility of the Washington politicians in order to urge them to consider and appropriate funding for the mass of Hmong refugees.

Washington politicians' rejection of the Hmong was caused by countless mislead-
ing reports that the Hmong were similar to stone-age people. So our plan was to fight
for funding for these few English-speaking Hmong who had performed important
and wonderful jobs for the U.S. government back in Laos. These few would come to
the U.S., get jobs right away, and reach a minimum level of self-sufficiency in just a
short time.

Jerry "Hog" Daniels came from duty in Thailand to conduct nationwide surveys
and write reports for the State Department refugee program on how these initial
Hmong were doing. He showed that the Hmong performance was great, that the first
Hmong refugees who came to the U.S. demonstrated endurance, hard work, self-
sacrifice, risk taking, and dedication. Therefore, resettlement funding for the Hmong
people could increase, and eventually thousands of Hmong could come to the promised land of America.

SHUR V. VANGYI, former Ministry of Economy, Royal Lao Government; former executive director, Lao Family Community Inc., Santa Ana, California

Quite a few months after Yang Dao and I met with U.S. Embassy staff we found out that Jerry was in charge of the new Hmong refugee program. Probably it was the end of '75 or early '76. Soon after that I was talking with Vang Xeng, a relative of mine. We were both living in Nam Phong camp. A lot of new Hmong refugees still were coming from Laos to Thailand every day. Vang Xeng said, "Since Hmong will be going to the U.S., for those who go first, what about the Hmong group soul, the *Hmoob cov plig*?" We talked about the Hmong group soul, the soul of all the Hmong that would go to the U.S. We talked about that because eventually half of the Hmong would stay in Laos and half would go to America. For the Hmong who go, if the Hmong soul doesn't go with them they may get sick, they may die, because they are missing the people and missing the land they left behind. They need a way to connect with them. Those who go need to take the soul with them so in the future they will eat well, live well, progress.

Because of this situation, Vang Xeng thought about dirt because dirt is related to soul. Dirt is what you stand on where you live. Your soul is tied to your home, your land, and the area around your house as well. Hmong believe everybody has multiple souls. When I step outside my house and I will go far away, my wife takes a pinch of dirt from just outside the door and puts it on top of my head and says: "Please, go well and bring all your souls back. This dirt will keep your soul well here at home. All souls that travel, don't get lost! This is your place. Come back safely." That ritual is called *av tuav plig*, "dirt that holds the soul." *Av* is dirt. *Tuav* is hold. *Plig* is soul.

Also, when a Hmong person dies, in the funeral ceremony they talk about dirt. The funeral chant shows the dead person the way to go back to where he was born. In the chant they talk about the dirt where that person's placenta was buried at birth—under the bed for a girl, or at the main post in the house for a boy.

So Vang Xeng and I wanted to get dirt from Laos because dirt represents the soul when you leave the land. Some soil must go with the refugees to America so there is a connection. Then maybe the people will know how to come and go, back and forth, helping each other. That was the reason for the dirt.

Then Vang Xeng and I talked about who will be the person to take the dirt to the U.S. Who is the person involved with the Hmong, who knows the Hmong soul? Vang Xeng said, "That would be Jerry. Jerry has been with the Hmong for such a long time, he's part of the Hmong." We agreed that Jerry was the right person to contact. Xeng said, "I can get the dirt from Laos, but first I have to know if Jerry will accept it." We didn't mention this plan to anybody else because it was a secret.

A week or so later I approached Jerry. I had not seen him in Thailand until the day I went to meet him at his office in Udorn. I was alone when I talked to him. I told him the story about me and Yang Dao meeting with the U.S. Embassy staffer in the refugee program who said he did not recognize the Hmong people, did not serve the Hmong people. I said, "Jerry, you are the only American who knows the Hmong people. You are the one who worked directly with General Vang Pao in Long Cheng. You are the core person who recognizes Hmong, loves Hmong. You lived with the Hmong, ate Hmong food, slaughtered a few Hmong chickens. After our experience with the Embassy staff down in Bangkok, you are the right one to deal with the Hmong. You are the one who can say correctly yes or no for the Hmong refugees to go to the U.S. Stay with the Hmong and do your best to help those who come to you. Take them with you to the U.S."

In that meeting I also said, "Jerry, I have a favor to ask you." I talked to Jerry, "The love that you give the Hmong is so deep. Now Hmong and Lao refugees are going to the U.S. Some dirt from Laos must go along with the people. Can you take some dirt from Laos and give it to VP?" Jerry said, "Okay, I will accept it. But who will get me the dirt?" I told him, "No problem. Someone will get that for you, as long as you accept it."

I said, "Jerry, this is a secret mission. We should not mention it to more than three people: you, me, and the person who will get the dirt. The dirt is not supposed to be revealed to anyone else." Jerry knew that dirt was for the Hmong and Lao refugees in the U.S. He knew that in our minds and our hearts, that Lao dirt holds the Hmong soul. "Be careful when you put the name tag on it. If someone reads 'Hmong soul,' they will not accept it. Just write 'Lao dirt.' Please use the government seal and label it: 'Lao Dirt. Do Not Open, Property of U.S. Embassy.' Jerry agreed and said, "I'll take care of it. If I can carry it myself, I will. If not, I will ship it and nobody will open it." I left feeling much happier.

After I talked with Jerry I went back to the camp, and right away I talked with Vang Xeng. I said that Jerry agreed and we should get some dirt to him. Vang Xeng was a very good person to rely on. Since he was a former police officer in Laos he knew how to get around and follow through. Vang Xeng said, "Uncle, I will do it." At that time the situation was still quite flexible for Hmong to sneak in and out, crossing the border to Laos. I asked Xeng, "Can we get the dirt from Long Cheng?" He said, "No, impossible. It's too dangerous to go back there. But we can get it from nearby." After that I never asked to see the dirt because I had no doubt about Vang Xeng's capability. In less than a week he got the dirt from Laos and delivered it directly to Jerry.

About two weeks after the first time I talked to Vang Xeng, I talked to Xeng again, just the two of us. He said, "Uncle, I got it. I delivered it and Jerry accepted it." Xeng said the dirt filled only part of a rice bag—"enough to carry" were his words. Xeng delivered the bag of dirt to Jerry's hands. This time I asked him, "Where did you get the dirt?" He said, "I got it from a Hmong observation and rescue team that came back from the town at Kilometer 52, K52." We Hmong had teams who went back and forth to pick up relatives and other people inside Laos, then lead them to Thailand. He said, "At K52 there are many Hmong who were at Hin Heup bridge." Hin Heup bridge is the historical site where there was a bloody shooting of unarmed Hmong civilians on May 28, 1975, two weeks after General Vang Pao left Laos.

Lyteck[1] was at the bridge on the day of the shooting. Hundreds of Hmong families were there: men, women, and children. Lyteck said the Hmong could not cross the bridge to follow Vang Pao to Thailand. He said, "Now I am replacing Vang Pao as the Hmong leader! You can't leave!" When the civilians tried to cross, he told the Pathet Lao soldiers to shoot them. Half of the people rushed forward, crossed the bridge and got to Vientiane, then crossed the Mekong River to Thailand. For the other half, some died at the bridge, some were wounded, and the rest ran back to the villages and into the jungle and started to fight against the Lao communist government from that day on.

The Hin Heup bridge was where the Hmong people were split. Vang Xeng specifically mentioned Lyteck and said, "Uncle, don't worry. I got what we wanted. I got the real Hmong dirt. Dirt from the end of the Hin Heup bridge where Hmong were shot." Xeng said that dirt represented not only those who died at Hin Heup, it represented all the Hmong who got caught in between, one side escaping, and the other side so afraid that they fled into the forest to take up guns and fight. Xeng was very sure that we must get the dirt from the Hin Heup bridge because that was the point where the Hmong soul was split.

English-language BANGKOK POST SUNDAY MAGAZINE, August 17, 1975

SIX WEEKS DELAY THAT MEANT DEATH FOR 200 MEOS
BY A SPECIAL CORRESPONDENT

Hundreds of Meo hilltribe refugees who survived a death march out of Pathet Lao-controlled Laos have died because of a six-week delay by the Thai Government in seeking humanitarian assistance from the United Nations. . . .

The mass evacuation of the tribesmen from their mountain settlements in Sayaboury, Luang Prabang and Xieng Khouang Provinces was clearly precipitated by the flight of their leader, General Vang Pao, from his Military Region II headquarters at Long Cheng. . . .

Along with Vang Pao went the hopes of his battered troops who had been supported by the CIA and USAID for the past 25 years in a bitter struggle against North Vietnamese and Pathet Lao forces. . . .

More than 12,000 Meo reached Nan's mountain frontier in early June. Many of the refugees were in serious condition, suffering from severe malnutrition, malarial fever and acute gastrointestinal disorders. By mid-July, the death toll among the Nan refugees had reached 150—and was climbing daily. . . .

When it became obvious the refugees were prepared to die [in Thailand] rather than return to Laos, Thai officials began to dole out 25 grams [less than one ounce] of rice a day to each refugee. Those with sufficient strength scoured the water-logged camps for rats, snakes, insects and edible leaves to supplement the meagre ration.

As one Thai official in charge of refugee affairs in Nan explained: "Thailand doesn't want to be accused of fattening up these Meo to go back and cause trouble in Laos."

Declassified secret memorandum from HENRY A. KISSINGER, the White House, Washington, DC, August 5, 1975

FOR: SECRETARY OF DEFENSE
DEPUTY SECRETARY OF STATE
DIRECTOR OF CENTRAL INTELLIGENCE

As a result of Pathet Lao actions to gain complete control of the Provisional Government of National Union in Laos, approximately 23,000 Meo tribesmen have been forced to seek refuge in Thailand. There is every reason to believe that these Meo refugees will desire to remain in Thailand as long as the Communists control Laos.

Spokesmen for the Royal Thai Government have indicated Thai willingness in principle to permit the Meo to remain in Thailand if adequate financial assistance is provided by the United States.

It is requested that a working group comprising representatives of the addressees, and under the chairmanship of the representative of the Department of State, on a priority basis develop a plan for the permanent resettlement of the Meo refugees in Thailand. Knowledge of this plan should be limited to a strictly need-to-know basis. This plan should be forwarded for the President's review no later than August 15, 1975.

Excerpt from English-language *BANGKOK POST*, November 11, 1975

NAN GOVERNOR URGES RETURN OF REFUGEES
BY SUTHEP CHAVIWAN

(Nan)—The presence of refugees from Laos in Nan [Province, Thailand] has created grave problems to provincial authorities and although [the Meo/Hmong] prefer to settle here it is vital to push them back [to Laos] according to the Governor: "We already have problems with our own local hilltribes and we don't want more of these Meo refugees."

Letter to LARRY WOODSON, former USAID Laos Refugee Relief Program, from Jerry Daniels, November 19, 1975

Rumbucket,

Received your ranchbum's music tape. Mighty pleasin, but would rather be listening to it somewhere at the top of Phou Bia [mountain in Laos] than here in shitsville Udorn.

. . . Don't know yet how much longer I'll be around, my people want me to push on forever, but the locals have me branded as a monkey lover. . . . Therefore come visa time they may conveniently lose their chopping stamp when my passport comes into view. . . . Fuck their tits they give me the shits. I think by that time I will have done just about all I can anyway as far as initial relief, resettlement here, and U.S.

immigration opportunities. All of which I am not satisfied with but can say I never shirked and did all I could. (From zero to over 1,500 monkeys being given chance for U.S. parole; initial relief for the Nong Khai and Nan people which was fought by all governments for some time; different resettlement areas here which I am not at all satisfied with but better than being forced back to their homeland immediately; severance pay for USAID's monkeys from MR-II who were just left neatly dangling; plus I have been able to help out on quite a few individual U.S. parole cases; money conversions for those stuck with KIP [Laotian money] etc)

Hope that some day we get a chance to have a few nectors together and I'll relate the stories of the real men who remained here in a beer soaked haze.

. . . Today marks day 20 of a dry, wasn't bad until the last few days which have seen me making frequent glances towards me teepee.

Npua [Hog]

Excerpt from English-language *BANGKOK POST*, December 16, 1975

PATHET LAO BATTLE MEOS

(Vientiane, Laos—AP) Pathet Lao officials say they have recently begun operations in the rugged terrain north of [Vientiane] to wipe out bands of Meo tribesmen who have resisted their control. . . .

Letter to Jerry Daniels from a HMONG MAN IN A REFUGEE CAMP in Thailand, March 25, 1976

Jerry, If possible may you please let me to borrow your some money, one or two thousand baht for to buy some clothes for my family. If I have opportunity to go to USA and to start my new life, I will send back to you later again. And I will not forget your pity to me all my life.

Letter to Jerry Daniels from a HMONG MAN IN THE UNITED STATES, May 26, 1976

Dear Mr. Jerry: Would you please help me? . . . If possible I would like you please pay $200 to my older brother in refugee camp NongKhay. How much please let's me know I will sure that I'll pay for your mother in U S A.

Excerpt from a letter to LOUISE DANIELS from Jerry Daniels, April 23, 1976

Louise, please try and discourage anyone from having me pass funds [to their relatives]. I like to help, but am only allowed [to] cash so many checks (or amounts) and just cannot use that entire privledge for paying to others. And I frankly do not want to ask for special considerations.

Letter to Jerry Daniels from a HMONG REFUGEE IN THE UNITED STATES, 1976

Dear Jerry, My family we all are trust you. You only person that understand me better. Jerry try to hold my hand. Don't throw me away before I be able to stand with my feet. Jerry at present time I don't know. I don't have any hope in the future. Please help. Give me some idea. I need help on job that will help me in the future. Don't sad, Don't mad. Many people are looking at you. Special my family we need your help. Without you we zero.

Letter to Jerry Daniels from a HMONG REFUGEE IN THE UNITED STATES, February 24, 1976

Dear Hog,
Please help me if you could. . . . I like to ask a money from you $1500 to buy a use car. I'll pay you back in about 3 or 5 months. If you will help me a couple hundreds or whatever I'm very appreciate. The reason that I have to buy a car is [in addition to myself] my wife and my brother got a job. . . .

Letter of response from JERRY DANIELS, May 1, 1976

About your request for help in obtaining a car, I recognize your need and sound reasoning behind this request, however would like to wait until I know for sure exactly when I will be leaving here before assisting in that effort. . . . Whether I stay or not has a direct effect on how I manage my own finances, therefore I must ask you to wait until I know better at which time I will advise you what I can do.
Best regards,
Hog

Excerpt from a letter to LOUISE DANIELS from Jerry Daniels, March 25, 1976

You would really be sad at my rakishness. The other day I was down to 155 Lubs, yes 155. Sticking with one meal per day. Surprisingly no agony. Am busy which takes the mind off food. . . .

SHUR V. VANGYI, former Ministry of Economy, Royal Lao Government; former executive director, Lao Family Community Inc., Santa Ana, California

At the end of February 1976, about three months after I talked to Vang Xeng, I talked to Jerry again. By that time VP was already living at his ranch in Montana. At our first meeting, Jerry and I discussed the dirt and the reason why the dirt must go to

VP. Jerry had said, "As long as you find someone to get the dirt to me, I promise you I will accept it and do what you want." At the second meeting he said, "I got the dirt and I put it in my closet in Bangkok where I will remember it. I put a tag on it that says: *Lao dirt*. It is protected by the U.S. Embassy's security code, and I promise you I will get it to the U.S. I will send it to Missoula, Montana, since VP lives near there, nearby my family. Then I will get it to VP. From there it will go to the Hmong whenever you are ready to use it."

The dirt will go to the main post, the main person, which is VP. Our purpose is to follow VP. The Hmong that go to the U.S. belong to VP so we need to send all the souls for him to hold.

I cried, you know, when I talked to Jerry the second time. It was quite emotional for me and I cried. First, sadness because we fought so hard for our country, why do we have to leave it? Second, happiness that we got our dirt, the Hmong soul, and it will go with us to America. I cried from both sadness and happiness that day. After that second meeting I had no more communication with Jerry.

MACALAN THOMPSON, former USAID Laos Refugee Relief Program; former Refugee Program, U.S. Embassy, Bangkok, Thailand

In Laos I had worked for USAID mostly in the north at Luang Prabang, Nam Bac, and northwest at Ban Houei Sai, Hong Sa, Xieng Lom. I departed Vientiane to Bangkok in June '75. In early August '75 I signed up with the U.S. State Department to go up to Udorn and get a refugee program started for the Lao, the Highlanders, and Thai Dam—all from Laos. That's when I ran into Jerry again. He was staying upstairs at JLD, Joint Liaison Detachment, at Udorn, and tripping down to the Nam Phong refugee camp often to meet with Hmong leaders of the several thousand Hmong who were ensconced at the old Nam Phong air base.

Of course Jerry and I had a few beers and compared stories and where-do-we-go-from-here type ideas. His comments were always positive and progressive.

CHA MOUA, Hmong friend; Hmong funeral organizer

Some months after we lost Laos, Jerry came to the U.S. When he came to Montana the first time after Laos was gone, I remember we talked a lot about Hmong refugee resettlement. He said, "Cha, I feel so sorry that everything fell apart. But it is going to be better in the future for your Hmong people." He knows it's bad but he also thinks it might be a good idea that the Hmong will have a chance to come to the United States to get a better education and to prepare ourselves for the next generation. He is a guy that pushes for positive future development. He doesn't concentrate on what happened in the past. Past is past. He is a guy that does more planning for the future and he was absolutely right.

Excerpts from a New Year letter written by Jerry Daniels to the HMONG PEOPLE in the Nam Phong refugee camp, Thailand, December 31, 1975, seven months after the fall of the Royal Lao Government to communist forces.[2]

Please allow me this opportunity to wish all of you the best of luck and the happiest New Years for 1976. While to many of you the future looks bleak and discouraging, I am confident the Hmong people, provided with the adequate resources, can and will start a new and interesting life this year. . . . I believe the future life seeds to be planted this year during Hmong resettlement and readjustment to the changing times, should not scatter you in mind and heart, but rather should result in better educating and preparing your future generations on how to best cope with the ever changing world situations as they apply to the Hmong. This is not accomplished by striving for the same old things of yesteryear, or caring only about your individual needs. But rather by collectively looking ahead, and in addition to maintaining your same basic traditional ways of life, you also expand horizons through further education, travel, acquiring new skills and interest etc. . . . By following that road which expands wisdom and following that road only can the proud Hmong name and heritage survive with dignity. . . .

I hope you all believe me when I say that your welfare has always been, is now, and will continue to be of the highest priority interest for me and my fellow U.S.A. co-workers. I still remember that I and perhaps other Americans who are representatives of the United States government, have promised you, the Hmong People, that you fight for us, if we win, things will be fine. But if we lose, we will take care of you. . . .

Admittedly we may not always assist you as much as we would like, however, when we fall short it certainly is not because of forgetting or not trying, two things that none of us who have lived with you will ever be guilty of for the remainder of our days.

Again Happy New Year, and the very best of luck for all of the Hmong, not only this year but for many thousands to come.

Warmest Regards,

Jerry

Mrs. PAT DONTIGNY, former Missoula County public health nurse

When the Hmong talked about Jerry's death it was as a great loss because he had helped them so much over there and helped to get as many as he could over here. He had said, "If we lose this war, we will take care of you." The Hmong talked about that a lot. Not specifically that Jerry had promised that, although he did, but there was a lot of bitterness in general: "Your government said that if we got here you would take care of us." The CIA and U.S. government promised the people this in Laos when they got the Hmong to fight the war for them. A lot of the Hmong felt that the U.S. government had let them down.

Excerpt from the English-language *BANGKOK POST*, **December 4, 1975**

AMERICA'S LOST CAUSE IN THE LAO "DOMINO"
BY LEON DANIEL

Hong Kong (UPI)—. . . The United States never really lifted its veil of secrecy from the war it masterminded unsuccessfully to save Laos from communism.

Laos was a victim of its strategic location . . . [and] American B-52s bombed hell out of Laos. . . . At enormous expense, the United States equipped and directed in Laos an army of Meo tribesmen, tough little mountain men who fought bravely in the lost cause. . . .

The United States never officially admitted that Americans fought in Laos. Some did. A few died. They fought well too, but in a cause that their government never really officially acknowledged.

Coming Together

FRIENDS prepare to go to the funeral for Jerry Daniels; final preparations are made for the opening day of the three-day traditional Hmong funeral ceremony; comments by the funeral organizers; flowers, wreaths, and guests arrive.

JON FOLAND, Missoula crony; former smokejumper

My wife and I were at Clark Canyon when we heard Hog died. We'd gone there to meet the Olsens and fish. General was there; Elmer, too. My wife and I were pretty much round-mouthed like everybody else. Everybody assumed that they finally got him. Hog had a bunch of enemies, but he didn't let that bother him a bit. He never talked about them much other than making jokes. And I think the commies still had a price on him. At least they did when he was working in Laos; I know that. Hardly anybody believed his death was accidental. The people closest to him, well, they just didn't *want* to believe that he could die accidentally. He should have died a thousand deaths just bein' common drunk, anyway.

We heard about Hog right there at Clark Canyon. Instead of going back home to LaGrande, Oregon, my wife and I went from Clark Canyon to Missoula for the three days of his funeral.

Mrs. CAROL LEVITON WETTERHAHN, former Highland Section chief, JVA, Thailand

Before I went to Missoula, I *knew* there would be a lot of Hmong there, and I guessed it was going to be a Hmong funeral. One of the reasons I went to the funeral was to be supportive towards the Hmong. "Pop" Buell[1] had passed away a year earlier; now Jerry had passed away, and the Hmong community in the U.S. might feel deserted. They needed to know that there were people still here for them. Just to say, "We're here. We want you to know you're not forgotten. Jerry's gone, Pop's gone, but there are still people around who worked in the refugee programs and who are advocates for the Hmong." I think that was one of the reasons, besides the mourning of Jerry and *wanting* to mourn and wanting to be a part of the mourning experience. But the fact that all his old buddies showed up, that surprised me. So many people came, probably for the same reasons that I came. They liked him. They felt the loss.

When we worked together in Thailand, on occasion Jerry would talk about how someone from his group died. It had been a much bigger circle, and their friends were dying in such unusual ways and dying before their time. Then Jerry would go on a binge. It was because so-and-so died in Angola or somewhere. I had heard stories directly from him about his years in Laos, and it was interesting to meet some of these people like Burr Smith, "Mr. Clean." You hear Mr. Clean stories and you have the sense that he's a larger-than-life action hero. Then you meet him, and he's just a nice guy. It was interesting, but on the other hand it was odd because now Jerry was dead. And here's this whole circle of people. So many friends, so many peers he knew from his earlier days in Laos. And there were a lot of people there who were his friends from before he even went to Laos. Friends of his from Montana, smokejumpers, whatever, before he wound up overseas. For the rest of us, that was his life over there, Laos or the refugee program in Thailand.

And meeting Jerry's mom, of course, was memorable. What a woman. And meeting Lucky. I'd heard *so* much about him, and he just totally impressed me as a person. And seeing Vang Pao there. Observing him and watching people cater to him. I remember that.

"LUCKY" LUE YANG, former field liaison officer (FLO), MR2, Laos; Hmong funeral organizer

To me, Jerry was a one-of-a-kind. We had a lot of good times together and a lot of bad times together. One time Jerry and Snowball and I had a race to see who could get up Phou Bia mountain first. Phou Bia may be the tallest mountain in Laos, and most of the time it is cloudy way up on top.

The three of us agreed that we will compete to race up Phou Bia. I carried very little with me, but Jerry carried his regular pack. I mean a *big* pack he carried! It had his sleeping bag and *everything* in there. Big! We started so early and we followed each other *all* day, I mean continuously. We had a little tiny trail that went up and Up and UP! and UP! and *UP!* If you wanted to take a break, when you stopped you had to sit with your back against the mountain and put your foot against a tree in front to brace yourself because it was that steep!

Hmong soldiers walk *very* fast, all day long. Very few Americans can keep up. But Jerry, we could hardly keep up with him, I tell you! I can't believe it! When we started I felt that I was one of the strongest young men in those days. But at the end of the day I was so tired that I didn't want to walk any more steps. I kept going, but in my mind I said, *I can't. I give up.*

Jerry kept going. He was first, and Snowball was second. I was the *last* guy, at least a mile behind. They sent a couple of little soldiers to come out and help me. I was so tired, but we finally got up there just before dark. That was one night I will never forget. We stayed there, and in the morning the helicopter came to pick us up and take us to other outposts.

After we left Laos, Jerry and I still worked together in Thailand from May '75 until I left in June '76. In Thailand I worked for Joint Voluntary Agency [JVA] with

Jerry and Mac Thompson and John Tucker. Mac was an office person, but me and Jerry liked to go out in the field a lot. That year we were really working hard in the refugee program. All we had was a manual typewriter and we had to interview people, family by family, and do all these applications. It was a lot of writing, a lot of translating. Jerry understands a *lot* of Hmong. When they speak Hmong, he knows what they say. But he doesn't speak much.

After I resettled to the U.S., Jerry came back from Thailand in early December 1976. He made a special trip to see me and my family in the city of Greenfield, Indiana. In Indiana we have no sponsor; we have nobody. We lived in a duplex in very bad shape. When Jerry comes he looks around and says, "No, Lucky. You're not going to live like this." He said, "You don't stay here in Indiana." He wrote a check to me and said, "Here is the money. You pay for your bus tickets and you take your family to Missoula, Montana. I'll see you there." The next day he departed from Indiana to DC. Right after that I buy the bus tickets and my family moves to Missoula.

Yeah, we had a lot of good times together and we had a lot of bad times together. I was so sad when Jerry died. I cried for days. Jerry was more than a brother to me. More than a brother. When he died, part of me died, too, for a long, long time.

•

Once Jerry's funeral started there were so many people and we were so busy taking care of the ceremony. It was not just me and Moua Cha who organized the whole thing, but we were the ones who acted as really close family. Me and Moua Cha acted as Jerry's brothers. So according to Hmong culture everything was up to us to do. In addition to organizing the ceremony we had to make sure we had food for all the guests to eat. A lot of the cooking was done at my house because the funeral home was only about a block from my place. All of the Hmong ladies cooked. We cooked at Moua Chou's house and also at Vang Pao's house on South Avenue in Missoula.

General Vang Pao was involved with Jerry's funeral, too. He was there as the leader of our Hmong people. The general was there to be with the American guests. He was there to show the Americans that Jerry was one of the most important people to us. He knew Jerry was our best friend, the best friend of the Hmong people.

TOU-FU VANG, former lieutenant colonel, Royal Lao Army (FAR), Laos

General Vang Pao considered Jerry to be his close friend, more as his younger brother. With Jerry the general could talk openly about anything—military and civilian secrets and issues—*anything*. The general was probably counting very much on his close friend Jerry, but now his friend was leaving him.

RANDOLPH "TOBY" SCOTT, former smokejumper; former Continental Air Services (CASI) loadmaster, Laos

Vang Pao was there. Oh, you bet. I didn't know Vang Pao real well, but I always thought the world of him. I know there were people who bad-mouthed him. But I really believe that that guy, the main thing that he was wantin' was to kick the hell out of those damn North Vietnamese and turn that Lao country back over to the people. And I agreed with that. I didn't care how he did it. He probably did some things that weren't supposed to be done that way, but he did it the best way that he knew how. And I'll guarantee you he was the only leader I ever saw over there that got results. Sometimes they were pretty crude, but I guarantee you they were effective.

I'll tell you I've got as much respect for that man as anybody I've ever met in my life. And I know how he did things. I watched him when he was in action. There's no way he could bullshit his way and do the job that he did. He really cared. Don't let somebody tell you a bunch of lies because I *saw* it. And Jerry—I guarantee you he wouldn't have fooled Jerry if he was a phony. Jerry Daniels thought a lot of Vang Pao. And a lot more Americans did, too. That guy was fightin' wars for thirty years!

> TRADITIONAL HMONG FUNERAL CEREMONY—DAY ONE
> SATURDAY, MAY 8, 1982
> "OPENING DAY OF THE FUNERAL" [*HNUB PIB COJ LO UA DAB QHUA*]

Preparation Section:
"To wash and dress the deceased" [*tu zam*]

In Hmong tradition all metal is removed from in or on the body before it is prepared for the funeral. After that, family members wash the face and hands of the deceased, then dress the body in special Hmong funeral clothes called "elder clothes" [*tsoos laus*].[2] The elder clothes are worn under a long funeral coat [*tsho tshaj sab*]. In the old days the funeral coat was plain, but now in America the women trim the coat with Hmong embroidery [*paj ntaub*]. Also two long sashes, one pink, one green, are tied around the waist. For Jerry, the Hmong would have put the long funeral coat over his American suit if his casket had not been sealed.

During the preparation section the kheng players set up their musical instruments. Traditionally three or four kheng players are invited, but other players are welcome to play if they want. Also the drummer [*txiv nruas*] sets up the funeral drum [*lub nruas*]. In Laos the funeral ceremony is done at home, and the large, heavy wooden funeral drum is braced against the main post in the house [*ncej tas*]. A wood leg extends out from the main post at about forty-five degrees to add support. That is called the "drum leg" [*ncej nruas*]. The drum is lashed to the posts and hangs horizontally at chest height. The drummer stands in front of the drum to play it. In an American funeral home there is no main post so two-by-fours are lashed together to form a tripod eight feet tall. In the middle of the tripod hangs the drum.

The Hmong drum is used only for funerals. There are special families of drum keepers who take care of a drum, one generation after another.[3] One story told about the Hmong funeral drum is that when a person dies, the drum starts tapping on its own. When the drum starts tapping, the owner knows that someone will come and ask to use the drum.

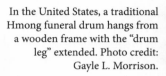
In the United States, a traditional Hmong funeral drum hangs from a wooden frame with the "drum leg" extended. Photo credit: Gayle L. Morrison.

In Missoula the Hmong don't have a drum-keeping family, so for Jerry's funeral they improvise and use a large plastic bucket. Heavy black plastic is stretched across the top of the bucket and tied down tightly. Two pieces of wood are cut and rounded off at the ends to make two drumsticks. For Hmong, it doesn't matter what is used as long as it creates the proper drum sound to perform the ceremony.

During the preparation phase a narrow strip of red cloth is tied around the wrist of each of the main participants.[4] This "spirit cloth" keeps each participant's soul safe from harmful spirits that may appear during a funeral.

Also in preparation for the funeral ceremony, a short stool and a small table are placed next to the head of the coffin. The area around the coffin is decorated, and any flowers that have arrived are arranged. Generally this preparation takes less than one hour. For Jerry's funeral, the preparation is even shorter because there is no body to dress.

•

Late on Saturday afternoon, the same day Jerry's casket arrives in Missoula, the casket is rolled into the service room not long before the funeral ceremony starts. According to Hmong tradition it is placed in the front of the room with the foot of the casket facing out into the room, perpendicular to the front wall.[5] That is the proper orientation for the deceased at the start of a funeral.

Word is sent out to all the Hmong people; by 4:30 p.m. they start to arrive. According to the records, in 1982 there are 840 Hmong refugees living in the Missoula area. Most of them are relatives of General Vang Pao. There is also a large group of Moua families who came originally from Sam Neua Province in northern Laos. Approximately 120 to 150 Hmong families live in the town of Missoula; six families live south of Missoula in the Bitterroot Valley. At least one member from each family comes to represent their family because everyone wants the chance to see Jerry and pay their respects to him.

In attendance are also quite a few Hmong from twelve different states, including Minnesota, Rhode Island, and California. They come on their own behalf and as representatives from almost every area of the United States where Hmong live. Some drive, others fly. For the first two days of the funeral, Saturday and Sunday, it's mostly Hmong people who show up at the funeral home.

CHA MOUA, Hmong friend; Hmong funeral organizer

Shortly after the casket arrived, the flowers started to arrive. We made a special wreath of flowers in a big heart shape and put Jerry's picture inside. That wreath was from his Hmong associates: the field liaison officers and the forward air guides, the FLOs and the FAGs. I put that wreath right beside the head of the coffin. Also I wrote a memory letter to Jerry, and I posted it above that wreath. The wreath and paper were on a stand in front of his coffin throughout the funeral for everyone to read.

IN MEMORY

From 1961 until the Communist take over of Laos, our friend Jerry Daniels, dedicated his every ounce of energy towards helping the Hmong, the Free People of Laos, improve the quality of our lives. Jerry gladly accepted life in our rural villages in order to better understand our problems, aspirations and dreams. Jerry shared with us the dream that one day life would return to normal and the Hmong people would be able to once again enjoy the beauty and serenity of the high mountains of Laos.

Sadly, the dream was not to be. In 1975, the anti-Communist government of Laos fell to the invaders and the Hmong people along with our American friend had to flee for our lives to seek refuge in Thailand.

Jerry continued to serve the people he loved as a State Department Official at the American Embassy in Bangkok. Jerry saw to it that the Hmong were given the opportunity to come to the U.S. to begin a new life. We have the courage to meet the challenges which we must face because our friend Jerry taught us well. Jerry was not only our mentor, but our friend as well. He dedicated more than twenty years of his life to us and we grew to know him well. Not only in name but in spirit, too. I guess we love Jerry so much because we always knew that he honestly cared.

"Glassman" Yang See was the liaison between Hog Daniels/Sky and General Vang Pao/SGU Army in MR2, Laos. The funeral wreath is from all of the field liaison officers and forward air guides who worked with Daniels in Laos. Photo credit: Bob Johnson.

Jerry's life came to a premature end in Bangkok, still serving the people he had grown to love. We all owe Jerry a lot and will miss him very much. Each of us in our own way will wish our friend a sad farewell.

So, until we meet again—goodbye old friend.

JON FOLAND, Missoula crony; former smokejumper

I remember helping to order a wreath from the cronies. We went some place right there in town, and I ordered an Oly can to be put on the wreath. That can was the real thing. We drank the beer, then handed the florist the can and said, "Use this." That didn't faze the florist a bit; he didn't bat an eye.

Mrs. NORMA HUGHES, wife of Charley Hughes; Ovando rancher; friend of the Daniels family

Charley and I wanted to do something, and I asked Louise if they'd like a blanket of evergreens to put on top of Jerry's casket. And, being nice to me, she said yes. I made that wreath myself, but it wasn't any great shakes or anything, no big feat. Just go around and pick out all the evergreen types that we have here: lodgepole, spruce, white fir, juniper. I went over to Louise's property to get those limbs for Jerry. I felt that evergreens from their own land would be more appropriate than our trees, even though our property is next to theirs. Then I put the limbs together with chicken wire and made it into a big blanket.

THOMAS J. "T. J." THOMPSON, former smokejumper; former air delivery specialist, MR2, Laos

There were a lot of people that came in for Jerry's funeral, and they are lookin' at us like, "Who in the hell are *those* people?" and we wondered, "Who are *these* people?" Of course we met and got acquainted. And we talked with the Hmong. Lucky and I had served on the PDJ together and at Long Cheng. Several of the Hmong I knew by sight, a few by name. But a lot of them that came there to the funeral were refugees that I didn't work with and didn't recognize. Because we, meaning the Agency, weren't in the refugee business at that time. We also met people Jerry worked with after 1975 in the refugee program.

Mrs. CAROL LEVITON WETTERHAHN, former Highland Section chief, JVA, Thailand

I remember an alone time in the funeral home. If there were one or two other people there, I wasn't aware of them. I remember just being there and kind of being able to have a private conversation with Jerry. And I was still angry. I don't remember what I said but I can imagine it was, "How could you be so stupid?! How could you let that happen to you?" Something like that, you know? When we worked together in the refugee program in Thailand I always lectured him so that would have been typical.

KEN HESSEL, former smokejumper; former Continental Air Services (CASI) Air Operations, MR3, Laos

You know the old picture of the Indian sittin' on his horse on a mountain with the horse's head hanging down? Toby and I looked all over town for that picture, and he finally found a black-and-white print of it, good-sized, about eighteen by twenty-four inches. We put it inside a horseshoe-shaped flower arrangement that was from "Jerry's friends." We put that up at the funeral home. That picture was kind of the way a lot of us thought about that whole thing: End of the Trail. Kind of a sad thing, you know. Jerry had all that fire for the life that he led up to that point and then it was wiped out. Just a sad ending to a hell of a good man. And that picture displayed it better than anything else we could think of.

Refugee Program, Thailand
(1976–82)

FORMER coworkers from the refugee program remember time spent with Jerry Daniels; letters from Daniels to his mother; the question of alcoholism; political screening techniques; work ethic; relationship with Hmong interpreters; changes in Hmong attitudes toward resettlement; General Vang Pao and the resistance; Daniels and a young Hmong refugee fly to the United States. [See Map 1 on page 33.]

BOB JOHNSON, former Highland Section chief, JVA, Thailand; regional director, International Rescue Committee (IRC), Seattle

On the first afternoon while the Hmong got ready to start their ceremony, I went to the local Safeway and loaded up the trunk of my rental car with as much ice and beer as I could put in the empty tire well. It was *full* of beer and ice that I kept refilling. I drove around dripping water from the trunk for three days, but it worked pretty well.

I parked out back at the funeral home so those who got "parched" had a steady supply of cold beer during the ceremony. There were always some Americans around at the funeral home. While the Hmong were doing their thing, we'd sit around telling stories since quite a few of us had worked with Jerry in the refugee program in Thailand after 1975.

Mrs. CAROL LEVITON WETTERHAHN, former Highland Section chief, JVA, Thailand

Jerry was a U.S. government employee on loan to the State Department, Bureau of Refugee Affairs. He was the ethnic affairs officer for the Highland Lao refugee program, which was mostly Hmong. As EAO, Jerry had to verify all the military battles. I don't think there was anyone else who had the kind of Highland Lao background with the military that Jerry had. If he couldn't verify them, he'd do some cases over and over and over.

THOMAS TONG VANG, former Hmong interpreter for JVA, Thailand

Bill Sage recruited me as an interpreter to work with Jerry B. Daniels. One day we interpreters were talking with Jerry and we said, "Were you in Long Cheng?" He said, "Yes, I was in Long Cheng. Vang Pao and I were good friends." "Were you a *good* friend, or just an eating friend?" There are Lao terms *puen kin* and *puen tai*. *Puen kin* are eating friends; they show up at dinner parties. They are people who become friends as long as they get benefits from you or as long as you have money to spend, and they disappear if you get in trouble or lose your money. "Are you a *puen kin* or a *puen tai*?" We knew that he was joking when he said, "Oh, I'm *puen kin* only!" We said, "Are you sure? *Puen kin* only? You're not a good friend?" Then he said, "No, no, no. I'm not *puen kin*. I just make a joke. I'm a real *puen tai*." When he says *I am puen tai*, he's serious. "I am Vang Pao's *real* friend. That's why we left Laos together."

In my simple words, *puen tai* means that we share one life. If I die, you die. If you die, I die. We will die together or live together. It doesn't matter how miserable life is, if you encounter a problem, we will share it until the last day of our life. That's the meaning in Lao. Jerry said, "I would be willing to sacrifice everything for him, and I believe he would do the same thing for me. Otherwise, I would go home and I won't come back here."

Then Jerry said, "When the communists came to Long Cheng in '75, maybe Vang Pao would be killed if he stayed, so we had to leave the country. That's why we interview your Hmong people, those who have served and done things for the U.S. We will see if we can help them out. I know the situation in Laos is bad and people are killing each other. I will stay here in Thailand to handle the Hmong." That's what he said.

Mrs. CAROL LEVITON WETTERHAHN, former Highland Section chief, JVA, Thailand

I worked in the Hmong camps with Jerry in 1979 to '80. I think those might have been the most intense years for the Hmong refugee program—intense in terms of how the program got beefed up. Ban Vinai was the largest of the Hmong refugee camps. There were so many Hmong being processed out of Ban Vinai and the other camps in 1979. It was work, work, work.

When we worked in the camps, we'd start in the morning and pretty much go all day; then we would work at night by flashlight. We didn't have electricity. It was very primitive. Little wooden desks, little wooden tables, either outside under a porchlike structure or inside a thatched hut. When we stayed in the Ban Vinai camp, we would work until ten, ten-thirty, eleven o'clock at night. Then start again the next morning. It wasn't like that every night, but it was often, because our interview team of JVA American caseworkers and Lao-Hmong and Thai-Hmong interpreters was preparing cases for the immigration officers. In 1979 it was very competitive. There was a quota of refugee approvals each month. Whatever camp had the cases ready in time, they got the numbers.

I've got to say, our interview team was pretty good in Ban Vinai. We hustled. "Let's

JVA interview team and Hmong interpreters at work in Ban Vinai refugee camp, Thailand, 1979. Carol Leviton Wetterhahn at far right. Carol Leviton Wetterhahn collection.

get these Hmong through the window *now*, while we have a chance." And in '79 Immigration and Naturalization Service, INS, had opened up all the categories. Cat 4 was anybody who qualified as a refugee could go to the U.S. In '79 it was a factory, really! We had *huge* numbers that we could finally take so it was a very intense situation with a lot more time spent in camp.

I was a very conscientious caseworker. And the people that I trained, they had to be interested in this group to figure out a way to get the story right or the case was going to be rejected: "Come on, let's get it right so it will get through the system. Make sure those guys are really brothers. Make sure those are really their kids." It's a kind of job where you have to be thorough and you have to be good because the case files are going from you to INS. If you haven't been thorough, if you haven't worked this case and made an argument for this case, it was going to get rejected. These were big, complicated families and histories to deal with. And I would say that the INS officers did not like the Hmong at all.

JIM SCHILL, former USAID Laos Refugee Relief Program; former Department of State, Bureau for Refugee Programs

In '77 and '78 there was a *tremendous* amount of friction between the INS and State Department people because we at State wanted to *move* refugees and they at INS wanted to adjudicate each case on its own merits, in writing. We were trying to move 4,000 to 5,000 cases per month. For three INS officers that's more than 1,000 cases each—per month. Then you divide that out by thirty days and you're *moving*, man, you're *moving!*

Excerpt from an audiotaped letter to LOUISE DANIELS from Jerry Daniels, October 20–25, 1977, Udorn and Nong Khai, Thailand

I thought it might behoove you to know some of my responsibilities here in case there are questions as far as the Hmong folk go. It takes a little while to explain it.

Beginning this year the volunteer agencies [volags] all united and presented a package to the State Department offering personnel, Americans, that would come out to represent all of the volunteer agencies [as Joint Voluntary Agency, JVA]. They're composed almost solely of former Peace Corps volunteers, young people that know Thai. They come out [to the camps] in teams to prescreen the refugees. Any refugee who thinks he may be qualified and has an interest in going to the States is free to darken the doors and provide all of their bio data, biographical information, and the reasons why they think they are eligible. We're probably through around 50 percent of the entire refugee population, which is nearing around 90,000 in the camps now, and some of the Hmong camps are running as high as 80 to 90 percent registering.

On this prescreening deal I'm favorably impressed. The [JVA teams] are not out trying to preclude people. However, I do think they have a basic concept that is a little more focused on assimibility in the U.S. rather than association, because assimibility would lower costs and it's easier to resettle those type of people. Whereas Immigrations and people like myself feel more oriented towards selecting those who have been associated [with the United States] because to be a bit facetious, we're not necessarily looking for a gene pool. If we were looking to add doctors and people like that we could go to other countries. We're here, we believe, for those who worked with us before and stuck their necks out.

Anyway, to put a safety in this so that volags are not controlling it all, the State Department has set up a mechanism they call ethnic affairs officers. That is a person who, by job description anyway, has extensive background and relationships with a particular ethnic group. There's one for the Vietnamese and one for the Khmer, one for the Lao and one for the Hmong people or Hilltribes. And I'm the one for the hilltribe-types.

The hilltribe-types are composed in about seven or eight different camps to the tune of about 48,000 huckleberries. The bio data that's collected by the prescreening team is put in a nice packet that goes to the ethnic affairs officer. My job is to look at 5,000 heads-of-family packets and determine who is qualified, and put my name in blood that they're qualified. Then in blows Immigrations and we sit down together and I present the case. From there I hope it's more like a rubber stamp for those that I qualify.

I have good rapport with Immigrations people. And I feel pretty well assured that those I verify and recommend, the vast majority will hack the act. So I'm fairly well satisfied with the whole thing. There are some pretty thorny problems with the polygamists, but it's interesting. Just push on. Do to do.

RANDOLPH "TOBY" SCOTT, former smokejumper; former Continental Air Services (CASI) loadmaster, Laos

Oh, I'm sure when Jerry was working in the refugee program in Thailand he was working for the CIA with State cover. He never did tell me any different. Hell, he kept hangin' around because there was no one else to do what he did. He could speak the language, he knew the people, knew the area and knew the background. He was the only one.

Mrs. CAROL LEVITON WETTERHAHN, former Highland Section chief, JVA, Thailand

The JVA team would go up to the camp with a couple of boxes of files, interview all those people, do the work we had, then we'd go back down to Bangkok. So there'd be a couple weeks working in the office, then a couple weeks working in camp. I don't think Jerry liked being in the JVA office in Bangkok. He'd come into the office, never look at anybody, and was very businesslike. And he didn't have as much paperwork to do in the office as we did. Most of his work was in the field, so he could come and go as he wanted to. He was the expert on the Hmong and whatever he said goes.

Letter to KEN HESSEL, former smokejumper; former Continental Air Services (CASI) Air Operations, MR3, Laos, from Jerry Daniels, March 21, 1979

Stone Face,
. . . I spend about 80% of my time up-country which I much prefer, and when in Bangkok seldome get around much—Just work and get the fuck out.

Doing a lot of traveling here and really busy, but enjoy it, little paper work except for just the slam bam ops type, and plenty of slaves & secretaries to handle the peasant labor. People are good to work with, except they take it with little humor when my moccasins are slipped on. Even frown on the old disappearance act, although I keep them abreast of my runaways from various skidrow hotels. . . . I must say I have gone native regards the pitutsies.

Peace
Hog

Ms. BERTA J. ROMERO, former JVA caseworker, Thailand

There were rumors that Jerry was an alcoholic and that after each camp visit he would return to Bangkok and hit the bottle. Even with these rumors I saw the opposite in the refugee camp. He never drank after work. This I know because our team would get together for dinner and drinks to unwind and discuss the day's work and prepare for the next day. Jerry was very disciplined and refused to drink while he was up-country working. He was determined to stay physically fit. We would often meet at six o'clock in the morning to go jogging.

BOB JOHNSON, former Highland Section chief, JVA, Thailand; regional director, International Rescue Committee (IRC), Seattle

Jerry and I worked together quite a bit when I was at JVA. And in Bangkok we lived a block apart so I saw him. Actually, I ran in the morning and he ran in the evenings. The joke was, he was sleeping in while I was running. Then I would sit on the front porch of my place, and he would run by and I'd wave at him with a gin and tonic in my hand.

The last time I saw Jerry would have been in late 1980, right before I came back to Seattle. He was getting ready to go on his great Everest safari. Jerry wanted to go to the Everest base camp and eventually did, by himself with a sherpa guide.

Jerry Daniels on his "Himalayan adventure," November 1980. Daniels trekked to the summit of Kala Pattar, 18,192 feet, with a sherpa and a porter. Behind him is Mount Everest (left) and Nuptse (right). Daniels family collection. Used with permission.

DOUG VINCENT, former JVA caseworker, Thailand

He was an interesting man. Jerry would have to go back to Washington, DC, every two years or so, and before he went he would always wonder if he would be able to come back to Thailand. I remember that he used to go out and run like ten to twelve miles a night when we were in Nan because he had to go back and pass a physical test of some sort. He would do like a hundred push-ups and sit-ups as well, but he also smoked—menthol cigarettes because they weren't supposed to be as bad for you. He smoked only at night before bed while reading a western novel.

JON FOLAND, Missoula crony; former smokejumper

Western novels and country music. When Hog was in Laos I'd send him care packages of cassette tapes of country music, ranchbum music. He loved the cryin', lyin', cheatin', dyin', poor-boy-gone-wrong-movin'-right-along songs. He just loved any old country shitkicker music, old '50s-era stuff especially. After Laos was lost in '75 and he was working in Thailand, I asked him, "How about those cassettes? Did you salvage any of that music?" He said, "Hell, no. All that stuff was up at Long Cheng. You can just bet some nice little yellow hands are wrapped around those fine cryin'-and-dyin' tapes."

Mrs. CAROL LEVITON WETTERHAHN, former Highland Section chief, JVA, Thailand

I don't think when Jerry first started in the refugee program that he expected he was going to be there as long as he was. My guess is that he hung on and stayed with it because he felt some responsibility. I think he wanted to stay and see it through, see that the people weren't left on their own. Maybe he felt that our country screwed those people over a little bit so he wanted to do something to make up for it by trying to help in the aftermath of the war. Some coworkers said, "He's been at it too long. He needs a break. He needs a change. His life is out of focus."

MIKE OEHLERICH, former smokejumper; former Air America loadmaster, Laos

My last meeting with Jerry would have been when he was on home leave in 1980 because I'd already been sober for over a year. Daniels was in Missoula, and we met at the Ox and talked. I'd gotten out of the treatment center, and I tried to explain that there are certain things you go through as an alcoholic.

Daniels had a few comments to make to me, that it didn't seem like I was doing anything with my life. Possibly I wasn't challenging myself enough, and maybe getting away from drinking had something to do with that. I didn't think that was true, but I did know I was an alcoholic, and I had to get ahold of it or I was toast. So I was firing back a little, saying I wasn't drinkin' with the boys anymore or running amok in the jungle like he was. I was interested in raising kids and having a family, and I was wonderin' when in hell he was ever going to get around to that—and whether he thought it was important or not, you know? His response was, "I haven't lost my perspective." That "perspective" was in reference to the big picture: What are you going to do with your life? Are you still in Phase One when you should be in Phase Two or Three by now? Where are your goals and what are you after?

His "perspective" had come up quite a few times before, and I thought it was losing its meaning. I think the perspective conversations started when he was doing the refugee camp stuff. Everything prior to that was just wild, raucous, riotous living in between hard work. Just like ranch bums do. You work hard all week hayin', then you go to town and you party hard. That's just the way it is. And that's the way it was when he was up-country as an advisor. He was hardcore working and doing a good job. Then he'd go to town and he'd party hard, just as hard as he worked.

Jerry was the one that brought up "perspective" the most often, even when it wasn't being questioned. But he was never defensive about anything. No, because nothing had any reverence to him. When you talked about stuff like that, he interjected all kinds of totally irreverent, nasty talk. If you've seen the worst boy movies ever made where they talk rotten talk, that kind of talk was flowing through the conversations all the time. You'd never think we were ever talking about anything serious. So I don't think he was defensive. But he was attacking me about not doing anything. Saying that I'm just here in Montana not trying to change the world. I'm just mowing my damn lawn and trying to raise two snot-nosed kids. Just like John Doe or any other average person. Oh, we could get into it. He was probably right, and I was probably right. We were both right to some extent.

Of course we ended it on a friendly note down at the Ox. Oh, hell, there was never anything else. But with his drinking, at first he was always in control. He'd say, "I'm gonna shut it off on this date," and he'd do it. Later on, no. *His* hard-and-fast rules were stretched out and getting broken. His difficulty over separating himself from the booze was progressively gettin' worse every time he came home.

Mrs. CAROL LEVITON WETTERHAHN, former Highland Section chief, JVA, Thailand

As I recall, Jerry'd either be drinking or he wouldn't be drinking. He never talked about feeling that he'd lost focus or perspective. What I remember him saying was that he was going to do this refugee program and then his plan was to go back to Montana and live on his land. He invested in Krugerrands, and he invested in land. He didn't plan to stay in Bangkok forever, working. And the refugee resettlement program was going to close eventually. It was *always* going to close.

THOMAS TONG VANG, former Hmong interpreter for JVA, Thailand

People wanted to go to the U.S. badly. Many people tried to cheat. Some lied to Jerry that they were soldiers. Some of the people who smoked opium lied to him and told him that they were clean. Some had more than one wife and they said they don't have more than one wife. But Jerry finds out the truth.

Jerry tells us to tell them there is a computer that will catch any information that they didn't give to him. Jerry said to the people, "If you lie to me and you smoke opium, the computer will catch it. If you have more than one wife and you tell me you don't have more than one wife, the computer will catch it. So tell me exactly right now so I can try to do good for you." All of us, the interpreters, we asked, "What's a computer?" Nobody knows what that is. Jerry just said, "It's a *computer*!" All of this made people shake. Including us! Some of those cheater people came to interview shaking. They asked, "What's a computer?" We said, "We don't know what's a computer. We never heard of that but don't lie because the computer will catch it!"

Many times we asked Jerry, "What's a computer?" Jerry didn't want to tell us anything. Many times he just said, "It's a *computer*! It's from the air. You never see it but it sees you. It knows if you lie when you talk to me. The computer will catch that information and tell people in the States that you lied to me and you will be punished." We thought the computer was a ghost, something in the air, and when you fly in the airplane the computer will scan you and when you go through the scan it will tell people in the States, "These people lied."

When Jerry talked about the computer, people realized they'd better be honest. Including us! We interpreters had to translate *exactly* what the people told us to tell Jerry and the INS. We said, "Be honest, because something will catch any lie. I don't

Jerry Daniels reviewing interview files at the Nong Khai refugee camp, November 1977. Daniels family collection. Used with permission.

know exactly how but somehow it will show when you go to America. Maybe the ghost will see it and tell them." So that worked for everyone!

When I came to the U.S., the first time I saw a real computer I said, "Oh, *that's* a computer? I am not afraid of a computer anymore!" And now I work with one every day.

NENG VANG, former lieutenant colonel, SGU Army, MR2, Laos; former Hmong chief of Ban Vinai refugee camp, Thailand

Jerry interviewed people who were soldiers, who were orphans, who were widows. For the political interviews, Jerry was quite good at figuring out who was a soldier or not because he was involved in the war. He might ask ten questions to see if they gave a consistent answer.

Jerry also played a picture game with the soldiers because he had pictures of all the commanders. If I was a soldier in an interview I would say I belonged to this battalion and this commander. Jerry would pull out three or four pictures of commanders and say, "Okay, you say you are this battalion, this commander. Pick your commander." If I pick the right commander that fits with the right battalion, that is a yes. But if I pick the wrong one, Jerry knows I am lying. If he knew they were not soldiers they were not approved. A few people failed his picture game, but the majority passed.

Excerpt from an audiotaped letter to LOUISE DANIELS from Jerry Daniels, October 20–25, 1977, Udorn and Nong Khai, Thailand

In the verification process, if I'm going to present the people with my name signed in blood, anyone who is questionable I'd rather see with my own eyes before I present them, and have a little more time rather than whipping right through and passing them onto Immigrations. I'll try to see as many as I can. I'll be spending a lot of time in the camps talking to them and weeding them out. I will do what I can do, but no skullduggery can be involved. I have to go within the confines of the law.

THOMAS TONG VANG, former Hmong interpreter for JVA, Thailand

I know that Jerry was a very good man. I worked with him for so long. I know he didn't discriminate. Some people got mad at him when they didn't get approved to come to the States, but I say he was very fair.

There were many reasons why a case couldn't get approved. For example, back in Laos, because the war was going on, many men had quite a few wives, especially the commanders, colonels. Many of them got mad at him and a few of them didn't have the chance to come to the U.S. because of Jerry. But he was straightforward in explaining the rules through us, the interpreters. He'd say, "I like you, but this is policy. You either have one wife or you don't go to America." They said, "How can I throw away my other wife?" He said, "I don't know what you are going to do, but think about it because America will only accept one wife for each man."

One time, one of the colonels gave Jerry 10,000 *baht* [Thai money], just to buy him out. Jerry got *so* mad! Jerry said, "You give me money?! That means you kill me! I won't take money!" He got so mad. They have a dispute, an argument. He said, "You take your money back and go home. I am not going to send you to America. That's it." That day Jerry just stopped working and went back to Bangkok.

JACK TUPPER DANIELS, brother of Jerry Daniels

My wife and I went into the refugee camps in Thailand with Jerry when we visited him in 1979. The people just mobbed him. Some of them tried to bribe him to get a relative to the U.S. "I'll give you my only chicken to get my uncle out." Everybody in the place wanted him to do a favor for them! It was so sad, because they were so desperate. As Jerry explained it to me, if a man got killed, then his children became the children of his brother. Immigration would ask Jerry who was authorized to legally immigrate to the United States. He'd say, "This child belongs to this man." And they'd say, "Yeah, but this man's not the *father*." Jerry would say, "In his culture he *is* the father." He had many, many cases like that.

Mrs. CAROL LEVITON WETTERHAHN, former Highland Section chief, JVA, Thailand

The Hmong treated Jerry with respect. People always asked, "Is Jerry coming? When's Jerry coming?" But it was basically because, *Hey, I want to get on with my life.* They wanted to talk about their case, but they knew to give him some distance.

Jerry was no "Pop" Buell. I mean, when "Pop" Buell walked into camp it was like the messiah arrived. People would come out and gather around him. Probably when he was in Laos, in his job with USAID, he was always *giving* people things. When "Pop" came it was, "Here's some rice and here's a cooking pot." He was giving stuff out, right? So the refugees, the people, were always happy to see him, whereas everybody kept a little distance with Jerry. And Jerry didn't reach out. He had an invisible wall around him.

Here's an example of what I'm talking about. Colonel Moua Sue had a section, like a row house, in Ban Vinai. It was called "Moua Sue's house." That's where the JVA team stayed and where Jerry stayed. The rest of us shared a few rooms, but Jerry always got his own room. And he had his people who were like a little security group—his devoted Hmong gofers that did his bidding. Anyway, in camp the shower stall was outside of this row house where we stayed. There was a path that went past the house and up to the shower. When you shower there, even though you're inside a closed wooden fence, you're not naked. You're still wearing a sarong. I remember trying to get up early, before it got light out, to go take my shower because that's your personal time. I'd shower and be thinking about my day, then I'd come out of the shower and there were all these people lined up out there who wanted to talk to me. "I want to talk to you about my case! I want to talk to you about my case!" Lined up outside the shower!

We all worked a long day interviewing. You just wanted to be able to have your cup of coffee and your breakfast first. Organize your thoughts, wake up before you have to stand there in your dripping wet sarong answering people's questions. After a few mornings of this I talked to Moua Sue and said, "No more of this, please. Tell the people to go away." And they would, for a while. But when Jerry took a shower, nobody, *nobody* lined up to talk to him outside the shower. Jerry had a kind of mystique, and everybody kept their distance a little bit.

THOMAS TONG VANG, former Hmong interpreter for JVA, Thailand

When I worked as an interpreter, at first I didn't know Jerry because he was a serious person. In late 1978 we got acquainted so well, then he took us to places in Bangkok to socialize. Not only me, but four or five of us Hmong interpreters would all go together. And sometimes "Tan Pop," "Pop" Buell, went with us, too. We all went together to the bar to drink. By then Jerry was more relaxed with us and we could make jokes.

At first we didn't know that Jerry understood the Hmong language. But when we went out and chatted and socialized, when we spoke Hmong he reacted so we knew

Daniels stops on his way to Ban Vinai to talk with Thai boys on the Mekong River Road, 1980. Photo credit: Bob Johnson.

he understood what we said. We said, "Oh, you know Hmong!" He said, "No, no I don't." We said, "Yeah, you do," but he didn't want to speak a word. When we talked among ourselves we teased and said, "Oh, be careful! Don't forget he understands Hmong!" Jerry seemed to like us as if we were his own children. When we went with him to the camps, he treated us just like a Hmong person treats another Hmong.

NENG VANG, former lieutenant colonel, SGU Army, MR2, Laos; former Hmong chief of Ban Vinai refugee camp, Thailand

Jerry came to Ban Vinai camp a lot. He repeatedly talked to me about the current living situation and the future of the Hmong. He wanted me to understand that there was only one choice that we Hmong could make: "Go to America." Always the only way to go forward was to go to America where Hmong children could be educated and have a brighter future. Jerry never talked about going back to Laos and never talked about supporting the resistance in Laos. No, no. He never talked about that. He always asked me, "Neng, are you ready to go to the U.S.?" I said I was going to go but not yet.

Jerry never supported the resistance movement, but I wasn't angry or disappointed with him. He had always been a truthful man about the national interest of the United States government. He never lied to me. Whatever the situation was, he was straightforward and honest about it. I respected and trusted Jerry because of that.

BEE VANG, former Hmong T-28 pilot, Laos

One time in Ban Vinai camp Jerry came to talk to me. Only him and me. He says, "Vang Bee, I know you well. You worked for me, you worked for the U.S. government. I need you to go to the United States." He tells me *everything* about the United States government policy. He says, "We can do *nothing* for your country right now. Maybe in thirty years my government will turn to think about Asia and what they can do for your government. For the next thirty years if you go to my country you can go to high school and get some diploma. Then you will have money! Good! Then you come back, no problem. But now the U.S. has *nothing* to support you." Then he said, "Okay, you don't want to go to my country now, but I will give you a refugee approval number. When you are ready to go you talk to me." And he walked out.

Oh! Jerry was very good to me. He told me the U.S. policy, the true story. And he was right.

Excerpt from an audiotaped letter to LOUISE DANIELS from Jerry Daniels, October 20–25, 1977, Udorn and Nong Khai, Thailand

Don't think I clarified my thinking on the contrary opinions of the Hmong people staying here, or Vang Pao wanting [them] to stay, or me representing those who are going. I've tried to walk the line on that. I don't want to undercut him so I think

Hmong girls on their way to school, Ban Vinai refugee camp, 1979. Carol Leviton Wetterhahn collection.

I've handled it fair enough, explaining the whole picture without stampeding people to go and telling them it's futile to push on [here] because that would sort of down VP's ideas.

Except for family reunification he's not too much in favor of this [resettlement] program. It's the old dream, and he thinks with his heart more than his brain-ball that he'd like to have them stay [in the refugee camps] and there would be an opportunity to go back [to Laos] and all that good stuff in the future. Maybe there will be, but it will probably be 100 years. I have not blatantly gone around trying to oppose his theory. I explain all the true facts as I see them and the way he feels about it, and they can make their own choice. I leave it up to them because I think it would be doing a disservice to people to say, "Stay here and everything will be all right."

THOMAS TONG VANG, former Hmong interpreter for JVA, Thailand

The first wave of Hmong refugees to the U.S. were USAID employees or those that worked with the military or the U.S. government. That was Category 1. And my family was not that. I was not a soldier, and my father was not a soldier. After I got the interpreter position with the U.S. Embassy Refugee Section I asked Jerry every day, "I know I was not a soldier and my father was not a soldier, but a lot of my friends already left for the States. I want to go, too. Please give us a chance." Jerry said, "No, no, no. Just wait. There are many people like you. I don't have time to talk about that now. You just work until I tell you something." He said, "Don't worry! Let's *work*!"

I worked as an interpreter, then in March '79 suddenly Jerry said, "If you want to go to the States, *Go!* You were not a soldier, but that's okay. Category 1, 2, and 3 are already gone. You are in Category 4." Four was not military, not USAID. I took my father, mother, brothers and sisters, my wife, and two children. I think my whole group was ten people. When Jerry said *Go!*, we swear and we *GO!*

DOUG VINCENT, former JVA caseworker, Thailand

I started as a JVA caseworker in September 1979, and it was about this time that the Hmong were refusing—yes, refusing—to go to the U.S. I was sent to Ban Vinai to work, and I fell in love with them from the first day. I think it was their attitude that attracted me to them. The Hmong really didn't care that the U.S. wanted them to be refugees to America; they wanted U.S. military aid to go back to Laos to fight, and I found that very interesting.

TOU-FU VANG, former lieutenant colonel, Royal Lao Army (FAR), Laos

I was living in the U.S. by then, but I know there were *thousands* of resistance troops still fighting in the jungle in Laos against the communist Lao government troops. The resistance leaders in jungle positions inside Laos called on their radios to our people in Thailand. They were asking for help and what to do. Then those people in Thailand passed the messages along to General Vang Pao by telephone. They called the general all the time, so his head was always full of civilian and military work. And politics, too.

SHUR V. VANGYI, former Ministry of Economy, Royal Lao Government; former executive director, Lao Family Community Inc., Santa Ana, California

For many years after I came to the U.S. I worked closely with General Vang Pao. During that time I was thinking, *How come people keep calling VP?* Every single word, every request, complaint, or report went to VP. From Laos they cried on cassette tapes, letters, telephone calls, "VP, come back to Laos and help us, save us, please!" From 1975 on, our people in Laos were begging for VP's help. They wanted to resist the communist government and have VP bring back American assistance to help them save the country from communism. VP had a whole big bag of those cassettes, those crying tapes.

DOUG VINCENT, former JVA caseworker, Thailand

I was in Ban Vinai for three months solid, October 1 to December 30, 1979. We worked Saturdays, Thanksgiving and Christmas both. During that time I got to know Jerry a lot better and we became friends. He told me stories from Laos about the Hmong and the war. He told them in a matter-of-fact way without a lot of comment on the rightness or wrongness of the war.

Anyhow, we were interviewing and INS was approving maybe 2,000 Hmong a month for those three months. But when the buses went in January to pick up an expected 5,000-plus Hmong to take them off to the U.S., maybe thirty got on. Everybody else was a "no-show for movement," as it was called. I thought it was funny as hell. I guess the Hmong leadership in the U.S., meaning VP, decided that if they all left Thailand it would have killed the resistance in Laos and the Hmong story may have ended there, so they refused to go.

Excerpt from *THE SPOKESMAN REVIEW*, Spokane, Washington, November 9, 1980

LAOTIAN LEADER TENDS FARM—AND A PEOPLE EXILED IN U.S.

Woodside, Mont.—. . . During the first years of his people's resettlement in the United States, the phone at [Vang Pao's] home would ring 40 or 50 times each day with calls from Hmong who turned to him for help with some problem. Until two years ago he accepted collect phone calls from Hmong refugees anywhere in the country. . . .

"I need to help my people," he says in his fractured English, "because only myself who order anybody to fight during the Vietnam War to help United States. Today everybody lose their country. They lose their parents in Laos and some in Thailand. Many die in the jungle.

"If I wash my hands and do nothing to help, this is bad. I cannot do this. Because I am a political man, I need to see my people at any time to help them. If it good reason or bad reason or hard reason, no problem.

"Any reason, I have to help . . . because I am leader. I cannot say, 'I have no power; I am not General today.' I cannot do this to them."

And so to 30,000 Hmong in this country and many thousands more outside it, he remains their father, their leader.

SHUR V. VANGYI, former Ministry of Economy, Royal Lao Government; former executive director, Lao Family Community Inc., Santa Ana, California

The Hmong community depended on General Vang Pao for everything. I started thinking, *Maybe because of that Lao dirt, all the souls of the Hmong are following VP.*

The dirt connects all of us over there to here. So for many years it seemed to me that maybe the Lao dirt from Hin Heup would be the soul door, the portal that would open and give the opportunity to General Vang Pao to return to power in Laos. But then what happened to that dirt?

Excerpt from an audiotaped letter to LOUISE DANIELS from Jerry Daniels, October 20–25, 1977, Udorn and Nong Khai, Thailand

Unfortunately, as you know, the Thais don't like the Hmong, and they've already proclaimed that they feel that most of the Hmong are economic and not political type [refugees], which is just to the contrary. The Hmong are the *only* ones probably. . . . The Thai Ministry of Interior will take a tough stance, as much as I don't think they should. They should look at [the Hmong] as an asset, not a liability, but they don't.

Excerpt from a letter to LOUISE DANIELS from Jerry Daniels, March 9, 1981

The Thais are becoming very obnoxious over the fact that Hmong are not moving to other countries. Don't know what will happen but Hmong will be told (threatened) with forced return to Laos (unarmed needless to say) then they'll probably get scared and either flee into the jungle here or reluctantly opt for the U.S. Hope we can come up with resettlement here [in Thailand], but doubtful. The number of Hmong actually going to U.S. now is just about zero. We don't even plan to interview them for several more months.

Currently my plans are to leave here 28 March and spend several days in Manila. I will have until late May to be in the U.S. Most of the time I'll probably hunker in Missoula. I will provide a warning now that this time I just plain will not get involved in refugee matters. If people of any caliber want to speak with me tell them my time is already fully committed. If they have a request—put it in writing and I'll look at it upon my return to work in late May. I will visit VP some time early on, but do also have numerous personal things to do. I will probably stay at the General's [Kurt Olsen] or a motel. Looking forward to the visit.

Later,

Jerry

DOUG VINCENT, former JVA caseworker, Thailand

By 1981 to '82, because the Hmong refused to budge, Jerry's job was in jeopardy as he remained in Thailand on loan to the refugee section. With the Hmong being recalcitrant, he really didn't have as much to do. Do you remember from the book *Bohica* that he supposedly was off running around southern Laos looking for, and supposedly finding, American POWs in late 1981? No. He was in Bangkok worrying about his job and the possibility of having to go to either Afghanistan or Nicaragua.

Excerpt from an audiotaped letter to LOUISE DANIELS from Jerry Daniels, November 1 and 2, 1981

The Hmong who are here don't want to go to third countries. Or if they do, they're ineligible. They're minors with parents in camp. Or wives with relatives in the States and wherever they want to go the husband doesn't. Young married couples, maybe the guy's married to a girl whose parents don't want to go or won't let him go, even though he wants to. The final line is that when we send our teams in there hardly anybody comes. We've got people in camp who can prescreen fifteen to twenty families a day, and they're doing two and three and four [prescreen interviews]. It's just not cost efficient. Working for the U.S. people, I can't do 'er in good conscience.

For all intents and purposes, there's not any compelling reason to even *go* to the highlander camps with the exception that the Thai Ministry of the Interior and a few others believe that we are "neglecting" them. They keep harping on us and so really, just to show the flag, we go up. Sit there like a nice ticket office for an airline, a nice travel agency.

I know you hear a different story there [in the U.S.] but that's the way she is. Just two great things. They believe they can go back [to a free Laos] any month now, any day. Or that the resettlement in the States is so awful, with sponsors raping wives, airplanes crashing, all sorts of stuff, that they just aren't going to risk it.

The thing that gets to us is that—it's admirable, kind of a love/hate deal—you just get angry at the fact that these people, the Bitterroot Man [General Vang Pao], cling to all these great stories for six years now and they are *so* misinformed. Every month is *it*, and actually it's just pathetic. Pathetic and admirable that they want to continue on. But then you look at the realistic side and you really feel like you should try and do something. It's so stupid, people pushing on with this dream world, running around the country with great meetings and they're going to go back [to Laos] tomorrow.

CHAO YANG, former student from Moung Cha, Xiengkhouang Province, Laos

I escaped to Thailand from Laos at the end of March in 1979. The first person I see in Ban Vinai camp is Jerry. I recognized him and I knew he was with my father during the war.

In Ban Vinai somehow I had two sisters. They were my father's brother's wives. Those two sisters stayed with me. The three of us went to interview with Jerry to go to the United States. After the interview I gave him the picture of my father and he said, "Oh! You were in Moung Cha?" I said, "Yes, I was there." He said, "Well, for the interview we have to do like the rules say, but I think you can go to the United States." Then I started to study English every day in Vinai camp.

Now we go to November 1979. Jerry came back and he said, "The whole screening, X-rays, everything has been done. What do you want to do?" I said, "My two sisters got remarried. They don't want to go so I will go by myself." He said, "How are you going to set up your life over there?" I said, "I have some cousins in San Diego. Hopefully when I get there I will stay with them and I can find better things to do." I wasn't familiar with the United States at all so I didn't know what San Diego meant. He said, "I *hope* so! You are the only one now."

After one night Jerry called me over the camp loudspeaker. He said, "Come to the office of the Thai MOI [Ministry of Interior]. I want to talk to you." I went there and he said, "Now I want to hear what happened to your dad." He started asking me questions from the beginning all the way to the end. Then he said, "I'm kind of sad that your dad didn't make it." I said, "Me, too. He didn't make it, but hopefully I can make it to the United States." Jerry said, "You will make it. You will get to Bangkok on January 25. You won't stay there long. As soon as you get there you call me at this telephone number."

When I got to Bangkok I went to Krung Tep camp. I went to the office and I called Jerry. He said, "Oh! You got there? I'll be there tomorrow morning and I'll make sure you get on the bus because I'm going back to the United States, too. We will fly in the morning." I am ready *anytime*! I didn't have much with me. Two sets of pants and shirts, a blanket, my English books, a dictionary, and about two hundred Thai *baht*.

The next morning at four o'clock AM they talk on the loudspeaker and wake up *everybody*! They tell us we have one hour to prepare to leave. That morning Jerry didn't come, so I had to go on the bus with the other refugee people. They are all Hmong people, but I don't know any of them.

When the bus got to the airport Jerry was there. He said, "Oh! Too much traffic! I can't come get you because there was a traffic delay." Then Jerry said, "Now we fly to the United States." Jerry and I got into the same airplane at the Bangkok airport. There were both regular passengers and refugees on that plane. I think there were forty-five people in our refugee group when we left Bangkok.

We flew all that day and got to Hong Kong. Then the sun set. He said, "We stay here for about thirty minutes. Then we will continue on to Tokyo." I asked, "Is that in the U.S.A.?" He said, "Nooooooo. Not that fast, son. That's in Japan!" He speaks some Lao and I speak some Lao; we speak some Hmong and we speak some English. All mixed together!

When the flight boarded to leave Hong Kong, now it was about fifteen refugee people that go with us on that airplane to Japan. The others disappeared. I asked Jerry, "Where are they?" He said, "Well, they went to a different country. Canada or Australia or some other place." After we take off from Hong Kong, Jerry tells me about the United States and how is the life there and what the refugees who came before are doing. He explained that and I got the idea. He said that when I get to the United States I will do the same way that the other refugees did.

When we stop in Japan it's about three o'clock AM. The next time we see the sun I have a question for Jerry: "How far are we flying?!" Jerry said, "You can see that sun for three hours, then the sun is going to go down." I said, "How can it go down so fast, Jerry?" He said, "I don't know. I have the same question as you do. Every time I come this way it's like that. I don't know why!" Three hours later the sun goes down again. In my life I never saw the sun stay up so little!

It was still dark when finally they said, "Safety belts. We are going to go *down*. Now we are in San Francisco, U.S.A." I look out of the window. I see lights everywhere. It looks real pretty. I can't imagine it! To me it looks like heaven. All the lights look like the stars in the sky. I say, "Oh! That's San Francisco!" I am not scared by the size of the city. I have no feeling about that because I don't know anything about it.

When we got to San Francisco, Jerry said, "I'm going to go on to Montana. We will leave each other here. You go on to San Diego. Here's my address and telephone number. I will stay there for a week. Keep in touch. Write me a letter." That's the last time I saw him.

KEITH "SKID" WOLFERMAN, smokejumper; friend Deeder and Farrett Daniels

I don't know, but I think Jerry probably felt really let down by the way things ended in Laos and what happened to the Hmong. Especially when you put that much time into government service and you feel that the government has done a great disservice to people that you've grown really close to. It used to piss off Farrett and Deeder [nephews of Jerry Daniels], and in time myself, too—when we'd hear somebody shooting their mouth off about, "Oh, the refugees get the government handouts," and they'd treat the Hmong as second-class citizens. *We* were always saying, "Hey, Jerry told us the real deal. We know what hard workers these guys are." And as I put together the bits and pieces about the Hmong through what I was able to research, we hosed those people! We hosed those people so bad we'll *never* be able to pay back the debt that we owe them. So for Jerry, I think dying is better than him saying, "Everything I stood for and worked for in my whole adult life ended up being a failure." That's *my* feeling about that kind of person, that personality.

The way I see it, he never did throw up his hands and just walk away. He did everything he could to help the Hmong people out after the fact. I think that has always been important to the Daniels family, to know that he stayed true to what he believed in right to the very end. He was doing something that was making a difference in those people's lives. He didn't grow old or weak or ineffectual. He died in the prime of his life, working his ass off for something that was important to him.

Condolences and Rumors

MONEY contributions and condolence letters; eight Midwest representatives; Hmong friends want to open the casket; rumors circulate.

Traditional Hmong funerals typically go on for many days, especially for an elder or a revered person. As a consequence they can be expensive. This is understood within the Hmong community, and monetary contributions are made directly to the family. Those attending the funeral make their contribution in person. If someone lives far away and cannot attend, they put money in the mail and send it straight to the family. For the funeral of Jerry Daniels, money is sent to Louise, Jerry's mother.

The family ritualist [txiv cuab tsav] acts on behalf of the host family group [xyom cuab]. The family ritualist assigns an immediate family member to receive cash donations from guests.[1] Jerry's mother, Louise, receives all of the money contributed by the Hmong community and by some Americans. Louise decides not to use the money to pay for Jerry's funeral expenses. Instead, she later honors Jerry by giving that money to open a charity to help the Hmong.

Maybe seventy Hmong people are at the funeral home to start the ceremony on Saturday afternoon. Everyone feels very sad, and most of the Hmong walking into the funeral home go straight to the casket to see Jerry's face. When they cannot see him, they are so disappointed and frustrated. Everybody is crying and asking, "How can we know if it's Jerry in there? How can we know if there's even a person in there? It might be somebody or something else." Cha Moua and "Lucky" Lue Yang try to calm them. They say, "No matter what, we have to accept it. Time is critical, and no questions can be asked right now." The casket is there, and the people are asked to believe Jerry's body is inside in order to complete all the traditional funeral rituals.

Condolence letter from the HMONG NATURAL ASSOCIATION, Marion, North Carolina, May 7, 1982

Dear Mrs. Daniels,

The Hmong Natural Association of North Carolina wishes to express its extreme sorrow upon the death of your son, Jerry B. Daniels.

Jerry Daniels was a very great friend to the Hmong People and will be deeply missed by all of us.

Please accept the enclosed gift which has been donated by all the Hmong people in North Carolina to show their deep affection for your son. We hope you will find comfort, during this time of sorrow, in the knowledge that Jerry was revered by so many.

Sincerely,

Kue Chaw, "Bison"[2]

Director

Hmong Natural Association of North Carolina

IN MEMORIUM: JERRY B. DANIELS

1. Kue Chaw, "Bison"	$100.00
2. Lo Ma, "Swamp Rat"	20.00
3. Va Xiong	10.00
4. Nhia Yee Yang	10.00
5. Kue Chou	10.00
6. Wang Sao Yang	5.00
7. Lao Va Yang	5.00
8. Pang Xu Yang	5.00
9. Long Yang	5.00
10. Chao Lor	5.00
11. Chue Moua	5.00
12. Xang Thao	5.00
13. Lee Geu	5.00
14. Chia Yang	5.00
15. Chia Lee	5.00
16. Vang Lo	5.00
17. Xang Lee	5.00
18. Cheu Vang	5.00
19. Pao Vang	5.00
20. Ying Moua	5.00
21. Lee Gee	5.00
22. Chang Houa	5.00
23. Eng Yang	5.00
24. Soua Xiong	4.00
25. Youa Pao Yang	3.00
26. Chia Kee Yang	3.00
27. Nhia Xoua Yang	3.00

28. Ria Moua	3.00
29. Yia Yang	3.00
30. Xiong Vang	3.00
31. Lee Vang	3.00
32. Srichane Suwandee	3.00
33. Doua V. Lor	3.00
34. Doua Xiong	2.00
35. Yia Thao	2.00
36. Fue Lee	2.00
37. Thai Lor	2.00
38. Ko Vue	2.00
39. Long Lee	2.00
40. Ben Vue	2.00
41. Cher Vang Yang	2.00
42. Phay Thong Savath	2.00
43. See Yang	2.00
44. Lue Vang	1.50
45. Yee Yang	1.00
46. Koua Moua	1.00
47. Nou Chue Vang	1.00
48. Seng Vang	1.00
49. Chue Vang	1.00
50. Chang Yang	1.00
51. Kia Hue Vang	1.00
52. Leng Vang	1.00
53. Mang Vang	1.00
54. Chong Mong Vang	1.00
55. Yong Kong Vang	1.00
56. Nhia Pao Yang	1.00

Condolence letter from the HMONG IN SEATTLE, WASHINGTON

Mr. Daniels's family,

We feel very sorry about Mr. Daniels. All of us know that he is a very good person and he worked for us since the United States start taking refugee people to come over to the U.S. We feel really sad when we have heard that he died. What we will say for him is to say thank you for everything he has done for us in the past. Even he died or alive we never and ever forgotten his help and kindness done.

Would you please say good bye to Jerry for us, and tell Jerry that all of us love him. Please say good luck to him for us. Please let him know that the refugee people he had help to the U.S. want to die replace Jerry and let him stay but impossible, they said.

Please say good bye to Jerry for us. Thank you.

Wa Thao for the Northern Hmong in Seattle

Condolence letter from the LAO AND HMONG IN MICHIGAN

Ms. Louise Daniels
This is contribute donation from Lao and Hmong refugee in State of Michigan, to our best friend Jerry B. Daniels's family. 5-7-82
All Lao and Hmong refugee in State of Michigan.

Excerpt from a condolence letter from ADULT HMONG REFUGEE STUDENTS IN ST. PAUL, MINNESOTA, November 19, 1982

Dear Louise:
We are sorry to see Jerry's passed away from us. With the love and care about him, we, the students of English as a Second Language at Lao Family Community in Minnesota are happy to give $13.25 as contribution to Jerry's funeral. Please accept our gift for him.

There is nothing in this world would be like him. We knew that his life was for all of us. He loved us all.

JACK TUPPER DANIELS, brother of Jerry Daniels

The letters that the Hmong sent to my mother were just unbelievable. All of them sent donations. Small sums. They'd send five dollars in an envelope. I remember that there was a letter from North Carolina where there was a large group of Hmong. They said they couldn't make it to the funeral. They were so sorry they couldn't make it, but they sent an envelope with money in it. It represented all the families and they gave whatever they had. There were lots of those kinds of letters with donations. Just small amounts of money. It was just unbelievable.

GEU VANG, former colonel, SGU Army, MR2, Laos

The eight of us from the Midwest arrive at the funeral home where we see the casket. That casket looked so strange. It was long enough, but narrow at the feet. The authorities said no one can open the casket to identify Jerry. That small casket made many people think that it was not Jerry's body inside. That Jerry did not die. For myself, I am pretty sure that maybe it is him, not another person, but many people talk about that: "Jerry is not dead. He is alive someplace else." Maybe he had a new place to go to, maybe a new assignment from the CIA.

TOU-FU VANG, former lieutenant colonel, Royal Lao Army (FAR), Laos

I was thinking to myself that Jerry may have gone to work in Cambodia or the new country of New Guinea because these were the two trouble spots in Asia at that time. So maybe he just pretended to be dead. Maybe this is just a trick, a camouflage.

Group photo of the Midwest representatives and others outside of the Mountain View Mortuary, Missoula. Back row (left to right): Lieutenant Tou Ly (FAG), Lieutenant Colonel Tou-Fu Vang, Jerry Connor, Colonel Geu Vang, Burr ("Mr. Clean") Smith, "Snowball" Chou Thao (FLO), unknown, Tsucheng Vang (Sing Vang, FAG). Front row (left to right): Pilot John Xiong Yang, "Judy" Nhia Vang (FLO), Kao Vang, "Snoopy" Shoua Vang (FLO), and Mouasu Bliaya. Mouasu Bliaya collection.

CHU VANG, son of General Vang Pao

People who knew Jerry, they really want to see him. Even though it's so many days before they find his body, if you know him for so long, you can tell if it's him. The funeral home will not let us open it. But still, still, we still want to open it.

Even if most people accept that Jerry's dead, the point is that we are not sure how he died or if the body we received was his. Those are two different questions right there. Since we cannot see the body, the real cause of his death is unknown. There could be a reason why they don't want people to investigate and do some research on what caused his death. Maybe it was not an accident. Maybe somebody has to cover up. Maybe that's the reason why we could not have the authorization to open the box to find out the truth, you know? So we have all kinds of questions. We don't have the authority to open the casket. The casket is too small. The weight is too light. All kinds of things like that make us believe that might not be him.

BOB JOHNSON, former Highland Section chief for JVA, Thailand; regional director, International Rescue Committee (IRC), Seattle

The Hmong were talking about big conspiracy theories. There were all sorts of rumors that he wasn't really in there—that he'd gone back to Laos to lead the resistance or that he was killed and this whole story about asphyxiation was just a cover-up. There were all sorts of theories flying.

GEU VANG, former colonel, SGU Army, MR2, Laos

Both the Lao communists and the Thai didn't want Jerry to stay in Thailand. The communist government in Laos wanted to cut the Hmong to the root. They didn't want us to come to the United States and have a better life than they have. They killed many Hmong civilians who tried to escape that country. You can say they really wanted to revenge, to kill every one of us. So anyone helping the process of Hmong survival was the enemy. If Jerry did not stop work and go back to the United States, then the only way was to assassinate him. Because if he stayed in Thailand, the Hmong people would keep having hope: "If Jerry's still here, it's like General Vang Pao is still here, too." A lot of people believed that.

NENG VANG, former lieutenant colonel, SGU Army, MR2, Laos; former Hmong chief of Ban Vinai refugee camp, Thailand

I don't think the communist Lao government would hire somebody to kill Jerry. The Lao government is happy that Jerry is taking the Hmong people to America. Send the Hmong away! Get rid of them! Make the Hmong disappear from Thailand quickly!

Mrs. CAROL LEVITON WETTERHAHN, former Highland Section chief, JVA, Thailand

Was it an accident? Was it murder? And if it was murder, why and who? Or was it staged? Did he need to go underground? Those were the kinds of things people were looking at. Somebody even mentioned suicide, but I just dismissed that.

GEU VANG, former colonel, SGU Army, MR2, Laos

I think 10 percent he was killed, 10 percent he died like they said, but 80 percent I believe he suicides. Because the refugee law discriminates against the Hmong, and Jerry knows that. In 1975 the United States pulls back from Vietnam *suddenly*. And from Laos *suddenly*. Places like Bouamlong, Lima Site 32, and Moung Mok, Lima Site 46, are so isolated, so far from the Lao border with Thailand. Ten thousand people—soldiers and their families—lived at each site, and we don't have time to pick them up. Those people are left behind. They try to escape, escape, but it can take *years.* In 1980, '81, '82, and so on there are still many of those *political* refugees coming out of Laos.

The U.S. government pressures Jerry, "You bring a lot of Hmong refugees to this country. They come and depend on public assistance." The U.S. government has to do something about this so they start to close down the refugee program and they pressure Jerry to return to the United States. I think Jerry was unhappy about that because he knows the situation in Laos. That's one thing.

Second thing, Jerry stayed with the Hmong for more than twenty years and he was content with the people. He loves the people and doesn't want to abandon them. And the Hmong people respect him like a father. If people love you and you have to abandon them because of pressure, you feel guilty. But if he suicides there is no guilty feeling for him. Eighty percent I believe he suicides.

JIM SCHILL, former USAID Laos Refugee Relief Program; former Department of State, Bureau for Refugee Programs

I personally discounted both suicide and foul play after I had the opportunity to speak with some of the officers who received the investigative reports on Hog's death. But it makes good reading to think someone or some organization did him in.

SHUR V. VANGYI, former Ministry of Economy, Royal Lao Government; former executive director, Lao Family Community Inc., Santa Ana, California

At the funeral home, that is the time we want to see his face, to put our hand behind his head to cradle it, raise his head up a little and say to him, "Jerry, you have gone in peace. But don't forget us. Open your eyes to see that we are still alive in America." Everybody wants that. When we can see his face and say such words to him; after that, that's it. After that, no more disturbance.

JACK TUPPER DANIELS, brother of Jerry Daniels

I don't know how many times I went in and out of the funeral home. Since there was never a body to view, it just wasn't that emotional for me. But I recall that the Hmong had a low table that was used for different ceremonies. They'd fill little shot glasses. People would gather and drink. And there was always one for Jerry that nobody else drank. They had a picture of him, and flowers, and the casket at the front of the room. And they had this guy who played a flute-type thing and another guy beating a drum.

I don't know what was going on. People explained what they were doing, but to me it just seemed like the same thing going on and on. And that was perfectly fine with me because this was a Hmong funeral and the Hmong were Jerry's family. I mean, the guy was forty-one years old and he only lived with us for sixteen of them. He lived with the Hmong for twenty-five of them. That's a whole lot of years.

The only concern I remember is that the funeral home people were not accustomed to the long duration of the ceremony. They weren't particularly excited that this thing was going to go on for three days.

GEU VANG, former colonel, SGU Army, MR2, Laos

The eight of us from the Midwest left late on Saturday night. We were not able to stay until the burial on Monday. We had a long drive back to Minnesota, and we had to get back to go to work on Monday. We left Jerry's funeral with so many questions, but no one can answer them.

Funeral Chant Phases 1, 2, 3, 4, 5: "Showing the Way"

INSTRUCTIONAL section [*qhuab ke*] of the funeral ceremony begins; drinking stories; poem about the creation of water; re-membering Daniels. The creation of people, crops, and death; the rooster as guide for Jerry Daniels; release from house spirits; the need for spirit money; city thank-yous; reclaiming the "birth shirt."

HMONG CEREMONY CONTINUED

Instructional section: "Showing the Way" [*qhuab ke*]

After Jerry's casket arrives in Missoula on Saturday, May 8, his funeral begins about five o'clock PM. That's when Kia Moua Thao starts to perform the Hmong funeral chant [*qhuab ke*]. In his duty as soul guider [*txiv qhuab ke*] he will "show the way" by chanting step-by-step verbal instructions that will guide Jerry's spirit on a journey to find his ancestors.[1] There are seven phases in the Hmong funeral chant. To complete the seven phases usually takes two to three hours.

Funeral chant phase 1

Kia Moua Thao, as the soul guider, sits on a short stool near the head of Jerry's coffin. Kia Moua knew Jerry personally, so he will talk to Jerry's spirit by name. He will speak to him in Hmong language because he knows Jerry understands it quite well. When Kia Moua instructs Jerry's spirit, sometimes his voice sounds like normal speaking and sometimes more like a monk's tonal chant. Kia Moua begins by asking Jerry's spirit,

> Are you really dead, or not? If you are not really dead, wake up and work around in the house. But if you really died, then accept these bamboo pieces [*txhib ntawg*].[2]

A short piece of bamboo has been split lengthwise into two pieces. Using the two bamboo pieces is the only way the soul guider can communicate with the dead. The soul guider tosses the split bamboo pieces onto the small table in front of him. If one face is up, "open," and the other face is down, "closed," that means

Jerry's spirit acknowledges the message, accepts being dead, and agrees to leave this world.

After Jerry accepts that he is dead, the soul guider pours him one drink. Pure whiskey [cawv] is traditional, but any kind of liquor can be used, even wine or beer. At the small table near the head of the coffin the soul guider pours Jerry about half a cup of drink and says, "I will give you three drinks and then I will wash your face." Again he drops the two pieces of bamboo onto the small table. If Jerry refuses to accept his drink—signified by both bamboo faces being open or both closed—the soul guider soothes his spirit: "Don't feel angry or sad. This is the way of our ancestors. You accept this drink, then you get it." If Jerry keeps refusing, the soul guider will continue talking to him, urging him to take the drink. "Jerry! Come and get your drink! Accept this drink then you get it!" He will talk to him until one side of the bamboo is open and one side is closed. When Jerry accepts the first drink the soul guider says,

> Eat, only you eat. Drink, only you drink.
> If you cannot finish your food, put it into the gourd.
> If you cannot finish your drink, pour it into the bottle.
> If you cannot finish your food, don't let other spirits eat it.
> If you cannot finish your drink, don't let other spirits drink it.
> If you cannot finish your food, you must carry it.
> If you cannot finish your drink, you have to take it with you.
> You have to take it so you can give it to your grandpa
>   and grandma [the ancestors] so they can eat and drink.
> You are going to start a new life so you can eat and drink later, too.[3]

Then Kia Moua pours a little bit of Jerry's drink from the drinking cup into a big empty receiving bottle. When the first drink is done, a second and third drink are given in the same way.[4] Jerry's spirit must accept all three drinks. A few of the guests who knew Jerry well believed that he would like this ritual because he liked to drink a *lot*!

FARRETT DANIELS, nephew of Jerry Daniels; son of Kent Daniels

Jerry had a block of wood, and before he'd go into a bar—a "nectar parlor"—he'd stick the wood underneath the gas pedal. Then he and his cronies'd go into the bar to get drunk. They'd go drinkin' and after a while he'd say, "I'm goin' now." They'd all pile into the car. Jerry'd be drivin', and he had it floored. He didn't have to drive fast, he just had to have his foot on the gas pedal all the way to the floor all the time. He'd think he was just rooster-tailin' down the road. He'd only be going fifteen miles an hour, but as long as he had the pedal floored, he was happy. It's not like he didn't know what he was doing when he was sober. He was smart enough to know what to do before he got drunk.

MIKE OEHLERICH, former smokejumper; former Air America loadmaster, Laos

The way I remember it, Daniels was on home leave from working overseas. We were stayin' at Taber's ranch in Shawmut, Montana, and it was the middle of winter. Fifteen miles from Shawmut and Ryegate was Harlowton with a population of two to three thousand people. We went to a bar out on the west edge of Harlowton. Kind of a dance hall place and me, Taber, and Daniels'd be dancin' and drinkin'. Not much dancin', mostly drinkin'.

We milled around talking to guys until we were leavin'. We're clearin' out of the parking lot, and all of a sudden we can't find Daniels. We wondered where he had disappeared to because it was something like ten below, very cold, and the wind was blowing about twenty miles an hour. This is not one of those deals where you're going to find anybody walking very far. It's colder than hell and it's been cold for a while and there's snowbanks all around. We drive into town, drive around, look all over hell and there's no Daniels.

We finally got too tired and drove back to the ranch. Was I worried about him? Well, we just didn't use words like "worry." It's just inappropriate. We were speculative. Wondered what the hell happened. Wondered if he was dead, but not worried. Like I said, that would be inappropriate.

The next morning we still didn't hear anything from Daniels, so about one o'clock we drove out to the bar again. We circled around the bar parking lot and slowly drove back into town. We were definitely looking in the barrow pit, the ditch along the road. I expected to see a frozen hand sticking out of a snowbank there. So it wasn't like I thought he was in a safe place, but we didn't see him.

I don't know how in the hell we finally found him, but it turned out that he had gone into the Troy Motel, a half mile or more out of Harlowton. Daniels didn't have any money with him, but that guy at the Troy Motel was a good ol' guy. When Daniels stumbled in there he just gave him a room. Daniels was probably on his last legs after he walked all the way there. I told him I figured we'd find his hand stickin' out of a snowbank. He could have died very easily that night, but he didn't. We were doin' a lot of crazy things in those days. Nothing fazed any of us.

LEE "TERRIBLE TORGY" TORGRIMSON, grade school friend; Missoula crony

We'd be at the Flame Lounge for hours and hours and hours drinkin' beer. You could always tell when Jerry got drunk because his complexion would get really dark, almost black. In high school we called him "Black Man" or "Black Meat" when he'd get drunk. He'd get black, and he'd start swerving when he'd walk.

At the Flame the can was way at the back of the bar. One night we see him staggering back there. An hour later he's still gone. Someone says, "Where the hell did that damn Daniels go?" Everybody starts searching for him. We finally figure out that he is sittin' in the can. He locked himself in the stall and he's sleeping on the toilet with his feet up against the stall door so you couldn't see anyone was in there!

That was the first time. From then on, anytime he got drunk and he'd disappear, we'd know he was back there in the toilet sleeping. He was famous for it! Hell, it might be half an hour or an hour. Everybody's asking, "Where in the hell is that goddamn Daniels?" We'd have to go in there and get his ass out. "Get outta here, goddamn it! Let's do some drinkin'!" Then we'd all start again.

THOMAS C. "SHEP" JOHNSON, former smokejumper; former air delivery specialist, MR2, Laos

One time Jerry and I took my hay truck and went up from Marana to get a load of hay in Casa Grande, Arizona. That was my little moonlight job. I'd pick up a load and sell that hay to anybody that had a horse, including Gar. But anyway, when we got to Casa Grande that damn farmer had sold my hay. So Jerry and I just kind of looked at each other and looked at our options. The hay was gone. Well, there's nothing else to do but go into the Birdcage in Casa Grande. Have a few beers, you know.

So we go into the Birdcage, a pretty uppity-up place, but then somehow we're back in my hay truck, drivin' around, and we end up in a bar on the other side of the tracks where all the Indians went. Well, after a while these Indians wanted to go out to the reservation. The next thing I know, Jerry's loadin' all these Indians on the back of my hay truck and we're headed out. Oh, shit, we was all drunk. Daniels is drivin'. And I'm ridin' in the back with the Indians! But anyway, we went on out to the Papago Indian Reservation. Of course, they don't have any liquor on those reservations. Well, that was bad.

It was probably midnight or one o'clock when we got there, and Jerry got pretty vocal and started cussin' at this one Indian, arguin' back and forth. They were mad at Jerry because he was cussin' them out. And one big fat Indian got ahold of me and sat right on my chest and hell, I didn't know what he was goin' to do next. That big guy must've weighed between 300 to 400 pounds. Well, Jerry took off runnin' through the desert and up to the hills or I think the Indians might've scalped him. Hell, I would've took off, too, if I hadn't've got caught! I thought maybe that Indian was goin' to cut my throat, but he finally let me up. He left and I got back in the truck and went to sleep. About three or four in the morning here comes Jerry. He says, "Let's get the hell out of here." I didn't want to go. I wanted to stay there because it was dark, and I didn't know how to get out of there.

Jerry takes off drivin' across the desert. I guess he had the headlights on, but there's no road or nothin'. He just drives through the desert so the cactus strip all the clearance lights off my truck. Then one wheel falls into a mine hole, a diggin' prospector hole. It was lucky it was just one wheel. And I says, "God!" to Jerry. I says, "Well, you're gonna have to walk into Casa Grande. You got us into it, you get us out." So he takes off walkin' to Casa Grande to get the wrecker. That's about thirty-five miles.

I went back to sleep. Daylight come. You could look down there and see the Indian village. That truck wasn't even half a mile from where we started. Well, I had to do somethin'. So I walked down to the village there to see if I couldn't borrow a shovel. I wasn't worried. All the Indians that were drunk were still asleep. I got a shovel.

Damn, it was startin' to get hot, and I didn't know if Daniels was gonna get back or not. So I started diggin' on that thing, and I might remind you that the damn shovel might have had a damn cornstalk for a handle it was so limber, you know. Well, I got to rockin' that truck back and forth, and damned if I didn't put it in reverse and I backed right out of there. I drove down to the village, returned the shovel, and got on the road, a paved road. As I'm drivin' toward town I see all these bottles busted in the road here, there, everywhere. There's whiskey bottles, wine bottles. It looked like the kind of thing that Daniels might do because he was pissed off at the Indians. I figured everywhere Jerry'd see a bottle at the side of the road he'd get it and just throw it down. He was hopin' an Indian would run over them and get a flat tire.

So anyway, I see this object off in the distance. I thought it was a damn buzzard sittin' in the road. I look closer—and it's Daniels. Layin' right across the center stripe. Right across the middle of the road with his chin on his arm. I pull up and says, "Jerry, how in the hell did you know it was me and not some damn drunk Indian that was drivin'? Hell, they'd have run right over the top of you!" He says, "Oh, I knew that was you! I knew it was you!"

Anyway, we took off. Went on into Tucson where I lived. Jerry walks up to my wife and he says, "Shep was a straight arrow last night. A straight arrow!" We was on the Indian reservation all night so that was the proper term. Well, she was madder than hell.

Jerry and I decided the fat's in the fire. There's only one thing to do now. So we went to Nogales, Mexico. Tucson to Nogales is about eighty miles. We went down there and had a few more beers, after which I kind of slept on some steps while Jerry went across the street and ate some tacos. Then we went on down to the B-29 Bar to wash the tacos down. We're sittin' up there at the bar, and this Mexican, he's shinin' that marble floor with a buffer and it just shines. In Mexico a lot of bars got a little trough that runs under the bar. I don't know what it's for. Maybe to spit into or somethin', a spit trench. But Jerry must've got a bad taco because about that time he got to feelin' sick. Jerry eyed that trough and he went—*URGHH*! Just laid it all along that trough, all over. That Mexican that was buffin' that floor, he looked at Daniels and just shook his head. Ha! About then we decided we'd better get out of Nogales.

KENT "DAN THE ANIMAL MAN" DANIELS, brother of Jerry Daniels

Jerry and I were both driving by the time we were fourteen. Jerry was fourteen and I was sixteen when he drank a six-pack between Helmville and Missoula. I was the driver, and I probably bought the beer, too.

See, in Helmville nobody cared. There was a constable that lived there. He'd say, "Well, I don't know if you're old enough to buy beer but you're big enough." If you didn't get in trouble, out there nobody cared. And in Helmville all you could do if you got drunk was run off the road into the ditch. Nobody got hurt. The next guy

The Blackfoot Valley as seen from Marcum Mountain. The small towns of Ovando and Helmville are located here. The Daniels family lived in Helmville from 1951 to 1953. Photo credit: Gayle L. Morrison.

along would pick you up, pull you out of the ditch if he had the gear. Nobody ever reported nothing because it wasn't necessary in those days.

It was the same thing on skid row in Missoula. Jerry and I'd go down there when we were sixteen and eighteen years old. That was a good skid row back then. Bums were a profession! One bartender said to us, "You guys don't ever stir up trouble. So if the cops come in the front door just sit quiet, then act like you're goin' to the can and out the back door you go." And that's what we did.

I didn't see Jerry overseas, but when they'd go on R and R I heard he was a beauty. There're some dandy stories there from what I understand.

PRACHUAP YANGSA-NGOBSUK, former Thai-Hmong interpreter, JVA, Thailand

Since the beginning of my employment as a translator with JVA in 1980, I worked closely with Jerry. What I know from working with him is that once he takes a break then he will go somewhere and drink nonstop for three to seven days, day and night and no food! At the same time, if he concentrates on work, he will work nonstop, no weekends, for three to four months. When he concentrated on business, he will not touch any alcohol for months until he takes leave or meets friends. However, when he drinks, no one can stop him. To me, that was just his normal schedule.

DOUG VINCENT, former JVA caseworker, Thailand

Jerry would drink only two to three times a year, but when he did it lasted for a few days. I joined him on a few forays myself since I, too, had the predilection towards strong drink. I always thought he "pulled the moccasins on" because of past ghosts, meaning that I think that the war had a lot to do with it. I remember him telling me once of a time when he was in Laos and they were getting rocketed. He didn't get a scratch, but some young Hmong kid of about fourteen or so was hit. He was still alive but bleeding badly so Jerry grabbed him, threw him on his back, and ran. Later when he let him slide off, the kid had died. When he told me, it struck me that this event really had an impact on him. So later on when I thought about his drinking sprees, I always thought that he was trying to exorcise the ghosts. Maybe the pressure and toll from the war built up so that he needed relief and he did it this way. His way of coping, since he was supposed to be a "man's man."

BOB JOHNSON, former Highland Section chief for JVA, Thailand; regional director, International Rescue Committee (IRC), Seattle

In Thailand, which beer you drank was a great bone of contention. Mac Thompson was a dedicated Singha guy, but there weren't a whole lot of Singha people because it was pretty hard core. Singha was what you got up-country when you couldn't get anything else. Jerry and I had a couple of sessions with warm Singha at Ban Vinai that aren't a real pleasant memory. Cold it was okay, but you still got the "Singha headache" after you stopped drinking. The label on Singhas you got in the States said, "Warning, Made with Formaldehyde." Because Thailand was a warm production area and stuff would ferment and the bacteria would make it bad if you didn't put a little formaldehyde in. Drink enough Singha and it would probably preserve you after death!

Did you hear about the memorial stairs at Ban Vinai? Jerry and I were at Ban Vinai, drinking warm Singha, talking. Jerry says, "Whatever you do, don't throw the bottles away." I said, "What do you mean?" He said, "Well, we use them." He showed me that the Hmong took the bottles, installed them upside down in the dirt, and built stairs which were pretty substantial. They were packed in there perfectly and particularly in the rainy season that was a major improvement. It was quite impressive! So in a way, drinking beer was contributing to the architectural substance of the building, which is a good way of rationalizing almost any amount of beer drinking. After Jerry died we referred to them as the "memorial stairs." That was in his honor since he had contributed a lot of material to the project over the years.

After Jerry has accepted his three drinks the soul guider sings a poem that tells him how water was created. The Creator-God [*Yawm Saub*] is the one who lives up-in-the-sky and knows everything. The poem reads,

> *Once upon a time, the sky was dry for seven years,*
> *the earth was parched for seven years.*
> *There was no water anywhere,*
> *so the Creator-God sent a message to Thunder.*
> *Thunder shouted, rain poured down,*
> *then water came rushing from under the rock.*
> *Nowadays, your cousins bring water,*
> *water boiled to warm it, to wash your face clean and soft*
> *so you can go to your ancestors' country.*
> *Thunder shouted, rain poured down,*
> *then water came rushing from under the log.*
> *Nowadays, your cousins bring water,*
> *water heated to warm it, to wash your face clean and bright*
> *so you can go to your ancestors' city.*[5]

After singing this poem the soul guider says to Jerry's spirit, "Now I will give you three drinks and warm water to wash your face. You accept it, then you get it." He tosses the two bamboo pieces onto the table again. After Jerry has accepted each of his drinks and the water, the soul guider performs "wash face, wash hands" [*rau dej ntxuav muag*]. He holds a new white washcloth that he dampens with warm water. If the coffin was open he would really wash the face and hands of the deceased. But Jerry's casket cannot be opened, so Kia Moua just introduces what he gives him: "This is your washcloth and warm water to wash your face so your face is clean and soft when you go to meet your ancestors." That's all that can be done.

After "wash face, wash hands," the soul guider introduces to Jerry's spirit one scoop of freshly cooked rice and one boiled egg. This is the "egg breakfast" [*noj qe tshai*]. It's not a real meal, more like a snack for the spirit. The food is introduced to Jerry, he accepts it, then it's put into a box where all his food and meals will be placed. In Laos a gourd would be used to hold the food, but for Jerry's funeral a cardboard box is used.

> *You can no longer talk with men*
> *You have glided into the Beyond, you can talk with spirits.*
> *Let your feet glide and follow the spirits.*[6]

DEEDER DANIELS, nephew of Jerry Daniels; son of Kent Daniels

As a kid, I knew that Laos was part of the Vietnam War, but I did not know where Vietnam was. As far as actually spinnin' a globe and going there—no, I did not know where it was. I knew it was a war on television and at the end of the day they ran the names of the people killed and I'd hold my breath when they went by 'cause I knew Jerry was over there. I watched to see his name! There was a war goin' on and it's like, *Well, if I see his name that's not a good thing.* So I wasn't watching to *see* it. I was watching to make sure I *didn't* see it. As long as you don't see his name it's all good. I would have been around ten years old, so, "Okay, good! Now let's go play!" But when I mentioned to somebody that I watched for Jerry's name they told me, "He's not in the war you hear about on television; he's there in another war. His name's not going to be on the TV even if he's over there somewhere." After that I thought, *Well then, that's no help, so I'm gonna quit watching TV because the news sucks and it's not telling me what I need to know.*

That's one of those things that I learned early. Instead of having it drilled into my head that TV isn't real, I learned that in a pretty basic way: *He's over there, but you're not going to see his name on the TV if something happens to him.* When I found out he's not going to be on that screen it's like, *Okay, can't care, it's just TV.* It's a television war.

JACK TUPPER DANIELS, brother of Jerry Daniels

After Jerry started working in the refugee camps he came back to the States periodically. On one of his visits I was still teaching exercise physiology and coaching track and field athletes at the University of Texas at Austin. We went up to Dallas and visited with a group of Hmong, ten or twelve of the elders. I remember him telling me he had to spend most of his energy trying to convince them that they weren't going to go back to Laos. "You're not going back. That's all there is to it. Now you're in the United States. Learn English. Get a job, or go to school if you're young. Give up the idea that you're going back to Laos. Vang Pao's not going to go back and take over Laos." He didn't even say, "Maybe someday when peace reigns." He said, "You're outta there. Your new home's here. Do the best you can." He said that was the hardest thing, to try to convince the older Hmong. Because many of them really believed that VP was going to lead them back.

HMONG CEREMONY CONTINUED

Funeral chant phase 2

The soul guider talks to Jerry's spirit and says, "Jerry, I'll give you another three drinks, then if you will listen I will tell you a poem about how the world began." Kia Moua pours the liquor into Jerry's cup then he drops the split bamboo pieces on the table until Jerry accepts his drinks. Then the soul guider sings a poem about how long ago Creator-God sent a flood that was survived only by a brother and sister. He tells how the earth eventually became repopulated with people and crops, and the people lived forever. The poem also tells how humans and animals were cursed by Miss Toad so they will get sick and die and have to leave their loved ones behind. This is the way death came to earth.[7] At the end of the story about how the earth was created and why people must die, the soul guider says to Jerry's spirit: "This is the way of the ancestors. Don't feel sad or unhappy."

Now that people must die, the soul guider sings a short poem about how bamboo was created to make the split bamboo pieces [txhib ntawg] he uses to communicate with the spirit of the deceased. The poem tells how long ago there was no bamboo and no trees on earth. Two boys ask Sparrow to go get bamboo and tree seeds from the barn of the Evil Spirit [Ntxwj Nyoog]. Sparrow gets the seed, and the boys lay it down on the dry ground. Seven years pass, but no rain has fallen and nothing has sprouted. The two boys have no success, so they go to talk to Creator-God, and Creator-God talks to Thunder.

> Lord Thunder growled, thunder water rain water
> came rushing out from everywhere.
> Lady Thunder growled, thunder water rain water
> came rushing out from everywhere.
> The bamboo seeds began to grow, the tree seeds put out shoots.[8]

Water pours down from the skies and the seeds sprout. Three shoots of bamboo come up. One is eaten by a rat [nas kos] that lives underground and only eats bamboo. The second one is cut down by a Chinaman to make the large flat basket used to winnow rice [lub vab]. Now only one bamboo shoot is left. The third bamboo is cut and split into two halves to make the bamboo pieces that the soul guider uses to communicate with the dead.

Next the soul guider sings a poem about the two tree seeds that grow. One tree seed produces the wood that's used to make a coffin [lub txab tuag].[9]

> The tree seeds didn't come to much, the tree seeds gave two trees.
> One belonged to a Chinaman. The Chinaman cut it to make a boat.
> The other is yours, dead man.
> Its top was cut off and it was split in two to make your four-sided house,
> dead man.[10]

Funeral chant phase 3

The soul guider pours three more drinks for Jerry. After Jerry accepts each of them, the soul guider tells Jerry that his body has passed away and, according to the Hmong system, today his spirit-soul [plig] will go on a journey back to his ancestors.

Kia Moua talks about the rooster that is going to be Jerry's guide. He sings a

Khoua Ker Xiong was the funeral coordinator [*kav xwm*] for the funeral for Jerry Daniels, May 1982. Photo credit: Mouasu Bliaya.

poem about how the rooster was created. A live rooster [*qaib taw kev*] is brought into the funeral home and introduced to Jerry's spirit: "Here is your guide. Rooster will guide you to your ancestors."[11]

CHA MOUA, Hmong friend; Hmong funeral organizer

A live rooster is in a box we put at the head of the coffin. That rooster is very important. After Kia Moua finishes introducing the rooster to Jerry, we take the box outside. We go to my truck and kill the rooster, break his neck. Then we cut a little hole under the wing and pull out the liver, *only* the liver. We use a cigarette lighter to heat the liver a little bit. Just heat it enough to make it smell like cooking. Then we take the cooked liver inside and give it to Kia Moua for Jerry's spirit.

For the body of the dead rooster, we put it in a brown paper bag, wrap it up securely, and put it back into the box. Then the box is returned to sit next to the head of the casket. That is how we sneak the rooster back in. For this animal part, Hmong tradition is not outside the law, but some of it is unusual for Americans so we don't tell them what we are doing.

HMONG CEREMONY CONTINUED

Three more drinks are poured and accepted, then the soul guider gives the rooster's cooked liver to Jerry's spirit to eat. Jerry's spirit needs to eat the liver so he can understand the spirit language that the rooster speaks. The rooster-brain must become part of his mind.

After Jerry's spirit and the spirit of the rooster combine to be one mind, the soul guider says, "Jerry, your rooster will walk ahead of you and you will follow your rooster. If your rooster shakes his feathers, you shake your clothes. If your rooster shakes his body and legs, you shake your shoes. If the day gets hot, you hide under the rooster's wing for shade. Follow your rooster to the ancestors."

Funeral chant phase 4

The soul guider will begin the long journey to the ancestors starting from Jerry's house. Before they can travel, Jerry's spirit must be released by each of the house spirits [dab vaj dab tsev].[12] For Hmong, the house spirits guard and protect everyone who lives in the house. Each of the house spirits must be informed of a death so that the spirit of the deceased will be released and free to go. Usually the first house spirit is the Bed Spirit [Dab Rooj Txaj], the bed of the deceased. That poem instructs the deceased, "Now that your rooster is walking ahead and you are walking behind, when you get to the bedroom door the Bed Spirit is going to say:

> You are a person who belongs to this household.
> Every day you walk about, flexing your body, moving about.
> Today, why are you lavishly dressed, lying across the middle of the floor?
> In the old days, you moved about, shifting your poise, full of energy.
> How is it that you are now so richly adorned, sleeping on the ground,
>   occupying the length of the floor?
> Why do you not stay and prepare the harvest for the arrival of brothers
>   and cousins?
> Or raise animals, expecting visits of other relatives?
> You are a person of this household.
> Why are you brilliantly dressed and taking leave, for what purpose?[13]

The soul guider continues, "The Bed Spirit will say to you, 'You will leave this bed with nobody to sleep here. You will not come back so we won't allow you to go.'" The soul guider instructs Jerry's spirit to answer:

> I am a member of this household, a person of this family.
> But the Evil Spirit [Ntxwj Nyoog] is unkind; he has unleashed the fruit
>   of death onto the earth, scattering it on the far side of the
>   mountain.
> Unaware of it, I have picked it up to eat.

Sickness has swept over me, engulfing the essence of my liver;
Chills spread slowly, invading the vessels of my heart. . . .
As the pillars of life collapse, my veins weaken and wither.
When the columns of life crumble, my veins and vessels sever.
My flesh disintegrates, melting away like honey and bee wax;
My bones decay, becoming as fragile and brittle as the stalks of dry
  hemp.
In this way, the road has opened up for me to be on the way.[14]

The soul guider continues the response to the Bed Spirit: "I cannot be alive any more. Today I dress up because I go to my ancestors." After that, the Bed Spirit knows that the person is dead and dressed to go. With that, he is released by the Bed Spirit.

They go from the Bed Spirit to the spirit of the main or center post in the house. The same song is sung to the Main Post Spirit [*Dab Ncej Tas*], then to the Altar Spirit [*Dab Xwm Kab*], which is the main house spirit. After he is released by the Main Post Spirit and Altar Spirit, the soul guider and Jerry's spirit move to the Spirit of the Left Side Door [*Dab Rooj Txuas*] to be released, then to the two Hearth Spirits,[15] then to the south side door. As with the other house spirits, Jerry is instructed on what to say in order to be released by the Spirit of the South Side Door [*Dab Rooj Tag*]. The last house spirit is always the South Side Door Spirit because that is the door the soul guider and Jerry's spirit will use to leave the house. Kia Moua informs Jerry that all the house spirits recognize that he has died and they have released him.

Kia Moua directs Jerry's spirit to go out the south side door. Now outside, the soul guider instructs Jerry's spirit that when he is stopped by the Village or Area Spirit [*Dab Teb Dab Chaws*], again he must say that he has died so he can be released. Then the soul guider says, "Now we are going to take you on a journey back to your ancestors. This is the way of the ancestors. Don't feel sad or unhappy."

Funeral chant phase 5

Three drinks are poured by the soul guider and accepted by Jerry. Then they start to travel. In this phase, paper spirit money [*xav txheej*] is given to Jerry for his journey.[16] For Hmong who die in Laos, most spirits simply walk back to their home village so there are not many expenses. But Jerry is an international traveler and he needs to travel first class. In order for his spirit to travel, he will need lots of gold and silver spirit money to pay for his tickets, visas, and permits. The soul guider already prepared everything he will need to give to the spirit of the deceased. He has enough spirit money and all the right tools. If he is not prepared, Jerry's spirit may make him ill.[17]

To begin the journey to the ancestors, the soul guider and Jerry's spirit will start in the city where Jerry died: Bangkok, Thailand. Before Jerry's spirit can leave that city he needs to say "Thank you" for all the city resources he used in the past [*ua tsaug teb ua tsaug chaws*]. To say "Thank you" he gives spirit money to the city spirit of Bangkok.

The soul guider has a helper who sits beside him. The helper's job is to burn the paper spirit money at each stop. Burning the paper money is how it is sent to the spirit world. Each place they stop, paper money is lit from a candle one piece at a time. Then the money is dropped on a tray to burn. They burn the spirit money so Jerry can use it to say "Thank you" to the Bangkok Spirit. Then the soul guider says to Jerry's spirit: "You are finished here. Now that you said "Thank you" to the guardian of Bangkok, next you go back to the town of Missoula. When you get to Missoula, you have to say thanks to the Missoula Spirit because you lived there in the past. When you were alive you used the firewood, you drank the water, you used the land for farming, you hunted and gathered in the forests. Now your mission is done. You are dressed in good clothes and you are going back to your ancestors. Give money to the Missoula Spirit to say "Thank you" and pay for all the resources you used in the past. Then you can go on." The soul guider's helper burns more spirit money for Jerry to use at that stop. Then they continue on, traveling backward in time, step by step.

After Jerry has thanked the Bangkok Spirit and the Missoula Spirit, he goes back to Thailand again. This time the soul guider says "Thailand" in general because Jerry was working in the refugee program throughout the whole country. He is instructed to thank Thailand, then they go back to Laos where Jerry stops at each of his three main posts to say "Thank you" and give money: the capital city of Vientiane, and the outposts of Long Cheng and Na Khang. Jerry makes three stops in Laos before he goes back to the United States. He lands and says thanks in Missoula where he grew up. Then he goes back to San Carlos, California, then to Washington State where he was a little boy, and finally to Palo Alto, California, where he was born. California is where his journey on earth will end. After Jerry has said "Thank you" to the Palo Alto Spirit, he has paid his debts and said his thank-yous to all of the city spirits where he lived. Now he needs special clothing to wear on the next leg of his journey.

At his birth town Jerry's spirit finds his "birth shirt" [*lub tsho menyuam*]. The birth shirt is the placenta that he wore when he arrived in this life. Each person is born wearing that gown. When someone dies and goes back to the ancestors to be reborn as a human, that person needs to wear that gown again.[18]

> *Sho, hey! You are leaving for good.*
> *Your mother and father hid your satin garment . . .*
> *You will go searching over the ground*
> *From the pillar to the bed, from the bed to the pillar*
> *And you will find your satin shirt and put it on.*[19]

Putting on his birth shirt is the end of Jerry's travel journey on earth. Now his way is completely cleared, and the soul guider is ready to send him up-in-the-sky.

A Way of Life

EARLY childhood of Jerry Daniels; the move to Helmville, Montana; Missoula County High School; Death 'o Dirt; college graduation party. Memories about hunting and fishing trips with Daniels including antelope, black bear, rabbit, porcupine, squirrel, coyote, grouse, goose, pigeon, dove, trout, walleyes, perch, pike, paddlefish and grouper. [See Map 5 on page 307.]

JACK TUPPER DANIELS, brother of Jerry Daniels

We always called them "Louise" and "Bob." We never called them "Mother" and "Father." Never ever. Bob and Louise met and married when Bob was twenty-four; Louise was only fourteen but she had graduated from high school. Louise always said she

Jerry Daniels and brother Kent Daniels with young sparrow hawks that belonged to their oldest brother Danny. San Carlos, California. Daniels family collection. Used with permission.

got out of school early because she *hated* school so much. She was *bright* but she hated school.

Louise and Bob had Danny and me in Michigan, one year apart. Danny and I did everything together. Kent and Jerry came along six and eight years later. They were both born in California. And Kent and Jerry did everything together. They were very close.

Then we inherited land in Montana from our great uncle, Gordon Tupper. One hundred sixty acres with a thirty-acre lake and a pond. My uncle had homesteaded the land and built a log cabin, two barns, a root cellar, and a little shed. In the summer of 1947 our whole family visited the property for the first time, and we spent a few days there.

Mrs. NORMA HUGHES, wife of Charley Hughes; Ovando rancher; friend of the Daniels family

The first time I saw the Daniels family was probably the first day they were in the area. My sister Irene and I were high school age. We were haying out at Ed Geary's place, out at Kleinschmidt Flat. Of course, everything was done with horses in those

Louise Daniels with the family's woody near Helmville, Montana, 1950. Daniels family collection. Used with permission.

Kent (fifteen-inch, one-pound sucker), Jerry (sucker), and Jack (eight-and-one-quarter-inch trout) show off their catches from the Blackfoot River, Montana, August 1950. Daniels family collection. Used with permission.

days. My sister was probably running the dump rake with a team and I was on either a mowing machine or a bull rake. That day this station wagon with a California license plate drove out into the meadow where we were haying. In 1947 in Montana you really paid attention when you saw an out-of-state license plate. Oh, they were a novelty. You looked at 'em: "Who's showing up?" That car was a maroon-colored station wagon that had real wooden panels on the sides. Well, it was Louise and Bob and the kids in that station wagon. Jerry and Kent and Jack and Danny. Danny was more my age. They drove right out in the field, and it was Ed Geary that told Louise how to get up to her Uncle Gordon's property.

KENT "DAN THE ANIMAL MAN" DANIELS, brother of Jerry Daniels

We went back to Montana a second time in the summer of 1950 and pitched a big tent on our land. We had a great time. At the end of the summer we went back to California, then we moved to the little town of Helmville, Montana, in March '51. The day we arrived they had to get a tractor to plow the snow out so we could get to the house. They'd just had a big blue blizzard two days before we got there. Jerry and

I cried. "Oh, Montana is nothing but snow!" It was deep, and we didn't think it would ever end.

In Helmville we were living in a ghetto house: one bedroom, a front room, a little kitchen with a wood stove, and an outdoor shitter. That house was a cold huckleberry with linoleum floors. There was no indoor running water, and we had to go out thirty or forty feet to an old hand pump. For bathing we used a galvanized washtub; probably that was pretty standard back then.

We moved to Montana in the middle of the school year. There was a two-room schoolhouse for all eight grades, a double-decker, but they didn't have enough kids so we just used one room. Maybe eleven kids total. It was a very strict, very good school. Jerry and I were used to taking care of each other. I hate being cold, so on school mornings Jerry'd get up and start the fire. He'd fix breakfast—hard-boiled eggs and toast or cold cereal. Then we had to run down a quarter of a mile to school. To me it felt like four miles uphill both ways. It was a cold huckleberry if you walked it and didn't run.

Jerry and Kent Daniels experience their first winter in Helmville, Montana, 1951. Daniels family collection. Used with permission.

JACK TUPPER DANIELS, brother of Jerry Daniels

Bob opened a restaurant in Helmville. Well, you're not going to make any money in a town with fifty-five people. The farmers would come in on Saturday and have dinner and that was about it. Frankly, I felt sorry for my dad. To me as a college student at the University of Montana, it was an exciting move. Montana was new, and I got to hunt and fish. But I felt sorry for my dad because he had a really good job in San Francisco with the U.S. Army Signal Corps. To leave that for *no* job in Montana? I think that must have been tough on him. Although all of our lives would have been very different if we hadn't moved to Montana.

Ronald L. "Bob" Daniels. Daniels family collection. Used with permission.

BOB WHALEY, former smokejumper; lieutenant colonel, USMC (retired)

I worked up there in Helmville for the highway department in the summer of 1952. I remember those days very fondly. The Daniels ran the cafe. Louise worked long, hard hours in that cafe. She was gregarious and sweet and just couldn't do enough for the boys, the road crews. She was up early to cook breakfast starting at about six-thirty or seven o'clock in the morning and open at night until about nine o'clock for dinner. It was a long day for her, and she didn't miss work once. I had respect for that family, especially Louise.

In 1952 Jerry was just a kid. I'd see him at the cafe. See him in the bars. There were two bars in Helmville: Ellsworth's and McCormick's. Kids could go into bars in those days. That's where people met to socialize. There was no stigma to it, and really there was no other place to meet in the evening. It was a nice, good environment. They were *all* nice people in Helmville. Down to earth. Just the kind of people you like to be around.

KENT "DAN THE ANIMAL MAN" DANIELS, brother of Jerry Daniels

For many summers starting when I was twelve years old, I hayed. I started out running the winch for the Beaverslide stacker for loose hay. At twelve Jerry started to run the winch. Then in '53 when I graduated from eighth grade we moved to Missoula. Every summer Jerry and I continued going back to Helmville to hay even after we moved. We had a good reputation for working in that valley.

Jerry Daniels about twelve years old. Daniels family collection. Used with permission.

Ms. MYRA L. SHULTS, high school friend of Jerry Daniels

I knew Jerry since we were juniors at Missoula County High School. Back then, in the '50s, girls didn't hang around in the same crowd as the guys. Girls hung around with other girls, and boys hung around with other boys. The group of boys that Jerry hung out with was mostly interested in sports, hunting, fishing, outdoor kinds of things. All very mountain-mannish. I mean, what else can you call it? Back in the '50s, boys and girls had their different roles. Mostly girls didn't even do sports in the '50s, you know?

Jerry had all guys as his high school friends, and the things they did didn't include women. Those boys didn't date and didn't have girlfriends. I would say that they lived in a state of arrested adolescence. They were not troublemakers in high school. Absolutely not. But they were thrill seekers. I think those boys would do things that were on the edge of being delinquent just to see if they could get away with it.

KENT "DAN THE ANIMAL MAN" DANIELS, brother of Jerry Daniels

Jerry and some of the other fellas went over to Anaconda to the high school basketball tournament. Anaconda's 100, 110 miles from Missoula. Of course they were drinking. Jerry had a '54 Ford, four-door, maroon. That car had some pretty good pipes on it. That was before the freeways were in, so on the way back Jerry raps those pipes off going down Highway 10 through Deer Lodge. They drew attention to themselves. Deer Lodge didn't have a police department, so it was the deputy sheriff that gathered 'em up and put Jerry and his cronies in jail. I don't know what the charge was—disturbing the peace, speeding—it could have been anything. Enough to get thrown in jail.

The sheriff is inside with the boys, and his deputy is outside. Pretty soon the deputy comes in and says, "Look what I found under the seat of his car." It was a .38, loaded, of course. The sheriff says, "Oh, don't worry about it. He's a Daniels. I know they've been poaching up in that Helmville country. I always wanted to catch them poaching and I never did. But they wouldn't hurt anybody with that so just put it back." Ha! I thought that was kinda neat. It was just the reputation we had. That sheriff knew we weren't carrying guns to shoot people, so he assumed we were carrying guns to poach with. But we just didn't do that much poaching. I'm not saying we didn't do *any*. But you don't poach with a .38. You poach with a .22 because you don't want to make noise.

Ms. MYRA L. SHULTS, high school friend of Jerry Daniels

Jerry wasn't soft, and there was nothing soft about the way he was brought up. No comforts. I think that Jerry was just hardened by his existence. He got by with the very minimum amount of material things. The things that were important to kids that were part of the establishment simply weren't important to Kent and Jerry. Probably having a good rifle and a good fly rod were what was important to them, not the sort of fluffy stuff that other kids thought was important. *They* didn't care if we all thought we had to have Jantzen sweaters. That was the last thing in the world *they* wanted. They had different values.

Jerry wasn't used to comforts. I think that's why later Jerry could go to Asia and he could live with the Hmong and he could find a fit. It wasn't a big culture shock for Jerry because he wasn't used to having life easy.

KENT "DAN THE ANIMAL MAN" DANIELS, brother of Jerry Daniels

Jerry and I bought a cleaning business for $5,000 when we were in high school. We didn't come up with any big pile of money to buy it, maybe $1,000. Death 'o Dirt was the motto before we bought the business. That motto was printed on the side of a hearse: "Death to Dirt." The hearse was the original business vehicle that carried the cleaning equipment. Jerry and I didn't have the hearse. We had a van, kind of a pukish yellow.

Death 'o Dirt cleaned the old city hall, and Louise knew all the cops down there. One night the cops called and asked if we'd do a clean-up job for a suicide. A high school kid shot himself, and nobody else wanted to clean it up. Jerry and I said, "Yep, we might as well."

We drove up to the house in the Death 'o Dirt wagon. The family wasn't home, but the cops met us there. This suicide happened in the kid's bedroom. The cops told Jerry and I, "The family's requested that if you can't clean it, throw it away." Like the mattress and the bed clothing. They said, "When you get done give us a call, and we'll escort you out to the dump and get rid of whatever stuff you have to throw away."

The cops left, and we pussyfooted around in there. We were kind of unsure at first. Of course the body was gone, but it was clear that the kid was layin' in bed when he stuck a rifle barrel under his chin chopper and pulled the trigger. The guy's head was completely gone from the bottom of his ears to the top and it was just everywhere. Blood and brains were still moist on all four walls and the ceiling. We'd been around animal guts and stuff like that, but when you correlate it with a human there's a difference. We were tentative at first, pokin' around, somewhat respectful. Should we be gentle with this stuff? We dabbed at spots and that didn't work. Eventually we had to get in there and really do some scrubbing. Then it just sort of eased into the fact that, well, he's a goner. He shot himself; he's dead. So we commenced to clean it up. The more you worked with him, the different chunks and parts, the more it was just another cleanup job. We grannied in there for quite awhile until we had it all pretty well done. I think it was one or two o'clock in the morning when we called the cops. We had the Death 'o Dirt wagon loaded with a bunch of stuff rolled up in rugs. The cops came out and looked the room over and said, "Well, I can't see how the parents could complain about this."

The dump at that time was south of town. We probably had a five-car escort: a couple of city police, a couple of county sheriffs, and a highway patrolman. No sirens but red lights flashing, and Jerry and I thought, *Oh, this is groovier than hell!* We got to this big iron gate. The gate's locked. The cops were flashin' their lights on this old guy's trailer house that runs the dump. The old guy came out and said, "We're not open!" Cop said, "Yes, you are." Old guy said, "No, we don't open 'til seven o'clock." Cop said, "You just let these guys in there and let them dump whatever they want to dump and don't you look at it." So that's what we did. When we came back out the cops were still there. I guess their shift was over, and someone mentioned that we could go for coffee.

We drove to Bug's Bar-B-Q, an all-nighter cafe that had great pies. All the cops and Jerry and I went in there to have coffee. Most of the cops were smokin'. I guess I was smokin', too. They offered Jerry a cigarette and he said no, then reached into his breast pocket and pulled out rum-soaked Crooks cigars. He was about sixteen and the cops never batted an eye. Then the cops started tellin' stories about different suicides they'd been on. All of them had been involved with suicides at some time, and now *we'd* been involved so they were telling different suicide stories.

Jerry and I probably talked about that some for the next couple of days, but I never had any bad dreams about it, and I don't think Jerry did either.

LEE "TERRIBLE TORGY" TORGRIMSON, grade school friend; Missoula crony

I'd been friends with Jerry since grade school but didn't see him after we graduated from high school. Then in the summer of '63 me, Jerry, Brent Russell, and Larrae Rocheleau started huntin' and fishin' and dinkin' around together. Then in '65, '66, '67, we started hanging out in the Flame Lounge on West Main Street, and that's when Jerry met the General—Kurt "General" Olsen. By the early '70s when Jerry came back on home leave, he stayed with General and his dad, the Old Man. He was real close with both of them. Jerry had a queen-size bed downstairs. He kept his clothes, guns, maps, his boat—everything there at General's place.

KURT "GENERAL" OLSEN, Missoula crony

Up there in that bar, the Flame Lounge, is where we used to hang out with Jerry. Right away I started runnin' around with him. We lived together and done everything together when he was here. When Jerry'd come home from overseas, we never knew when he was going to show up. Didn't know, didn't care. Jerry had a key to the house. He'd just unlock the door if he wanted in. He had the run of it. He was probably at the house fifteen years or more, off and on. I pretty much knew Jerry as well as anybody.

Jerry, he loved my dad, Elmer. He called him Old Man; we all did. Jerry'd say, "Old Man, when I retire you and me are goin' down to Mexico." The Old Man, he just fit right in. Sometimes Jerry'd come in and the Old Man would be sittin' there in a chair. Jerry would act like he'd tripped and just slide by him like he was drunk. The Old Man'd look over at me and say, "Well, there he is. Drunk again." They were close. The Old Man thought of him as one of his own sons.

Jerry had a bedroom downstairs. He called it the "drunk man's bed." He'd go down there and crash. My bedroom was down there, too, and there was a lot of nights I'd like to have shot Jerry. He'd stay out at the bars until they closed, and then he'd come downstairs and bug me and I had to go to work. He'd just sit on the bed and jabber. Just jabber about everything, like a guy who's been in the bar too long jabbers about, and I couldn't go to sleep. I'd say, "Get outta here! I gotta go to work in the morning!" He'd say, "Aw, you can just have *one* with me." He wanted me to drink a beer with him. I'd run him out, but he was hard to run out, too. That happened more than once.

RANDALL "PETERBILT" OLSEN, Missoula crony; brother of Kurt "General" Olsen

Jerry'd come in and sit on your bed, all stewed up, and start talkin' to you. "Aw, come on. You can just have *one*, can't ya?" You'd go, "Goddamn it, Jerry. Leave me alone!" Then he'd say, "It's the heir of the mustard seed around here." He'd get up and out he'd go.

LOY "RINGMAN" OLSEN, Missoula crony; brother of Kurt "General" Olsen

With Jerry it was "the heir of the mustard seed" and "the mustard seed footlocker." That started because my wife, Kathy, and I wore little mustard seed necklaces that have a Bible verse on the back, Matthew 17:20. Well, Jerry got onto that and he'd always talk about the mustard seed. Then he got onto the heir of the mustard seed. Then he'd go into the mustard seed footlocker. The footlocker was where the women kept all the men's nuts. If somebody'd go out and get drunk and not come home that night, his theory was the guy broke into the mustard seed footlocker and got his nuts back and had them for a day to use before the women tracked him down and jerked 'em off and put 'em back in the footlocker! He was *constantly* sayin', "You're in the mustard seed footlocker."

Mrs. KATHY G. OLSEN, wife of Loy "Ringman" Olsen

Jerry really liked oysters, and one of the famous things about the Flame Lounge was that they would serve raw oysters on the half shell. They were arranged in a bowl on ice. They'd spoon the oysters out of that little shell, put a little Tabasco sauce on it, and down the throat. Eat it whole. Jerry and all of them did that. I have a recipe for oyster dressing that I still make for Thanksgiving. The recipe card has Jerry Daniels' name on the top as having given it to me. I don't know where he got it or if it was an old family recipe that he passed on to me, or what, but here it is.

OYSTER DRESSING

1 sack prepared dressing mix

1/2–3/4 cup chopped onion

1 cup chopped celery

several tablespoons chopped parsley (or flakes)

1/2 cup melted butter

several squirts lemon juice

1 can of chopped olives

2–3 teaspoons sage

2 eggs

1 3 oz. can of sliced mushrooms

1 8 oz. can of Blue Plate oysters

several shakes of paprika

several shakes of salt and black pepper

giblets boiled and chopped

Add the water from the mushrooms and oysters to the giblet water. Add eggs to this broth and stir well. In another bowl, mix together all other ingredients for dressing. Pour broth into the dressing mix until it's the proper moisture and taste.

TED O. "LITTLE O" LYMPUS, high school and college friend

Jerry and I both went to Missoula County High School and then we both ended up at the University of Montana. I graduated from the U in '66. We'd laugh about how it

The Montana legislature established the university system in 1893. Daniels graduated from the University of Montana in Missoula, June 1969. Photo credit: Gayle L. Morrison.

took me six years to get my undergraduate degree, and Jerry'd say, "Well, it took me nine!"

Jerry graduated in June 1969, and in the spring of '69 he started planning for his graduation party. Jerry'd bought twenty-seven acres of property up at Nine Mile, out west of Missoula. It was undeveloped land, not thickly timbered, with open spots and a creek that ran nearby. He was going to have a big graduation party there, and it became a major event.

Jerry had several of us helping him with the planning. We'd meet down at the Flame. That was our hangout, and preparing for that party was a big deal for us. Getting the pig was major. The day of the party came, and a bunch of us had to go up to the property early and get the fire going in the pit, get the pig set up on the spit, and then get the pig cooking because it was a pretty good-sized porker. Somebody had to sit there with a beer in one hand and the manual crank in the other hand turning that pig.

MIKE OEHLERICH, former smokejumper; former Air America loadmaster, Laos

In June '69 I was up in Alaska jumpin' fires on a booster crew so I had to miss Daniels' Nine Mile party. But I had four or five pigs I'd raised, and Jerry and I had already talked about him using one of my pigs for the party. I was already gone when he came and got my pig and took it down to the local butcher. Jerry said he wanted to put that pig on a spit and roast it whole, so he just wanted the lower end of it gutted. Well, that butcher was drunk and had butchered so many pigs the same old way that he just couldn't get it in his head. He automatically split the carcass in half. Two halves of a hog, so Jerry couldn't put it on the spit. Jerry went and got another pig from me and took that son-of-a-bitch pig down and told the guy to keep it whole, just gut the lower end. And the guy did the same thing again! He split it in half. Jerry just couldn't get the guy to do it right. Took two pigs to him and he screwed them both up. Finally Jerry just wired up the second pig and cooked it on the spit that way.

TED O. "LITTLE O" LYMPUS, high school and college friend

This was "Jerry's party," and he paid for everything. Most of us were going to school, just struggling along. But Jerry'd been working overseas, and he'd saved up $1,200 just for his graduation party. Even so, he was very frugal. He didn't throw money around.

Excerpt from an audiotaped letter to LOUISE DANIELS from Jerry Daniels, Long Cheng, Laos, May 1973

The high price of beef has finally come over here. It's being felt, and I don't like to pay it. So Burr Smith and I—he's another guy who works up here and has been a friend of mine for a long time—we're going to buy a cow and a freezer and get one of the restaurants around here to cook our food for us and try to cheat it. Because we can probably get a cow for 100,000 *kip*, eighty dollars, something like that. Anyway, try to cheat it a little bit.

LEE "TERRIBLE TORGY" TORGRIMSON, grade school friend; Missoula crony

At Jerry's pig feast there was a great big stock tank full of ice and about a thousand dollars worth of booze and beer, there was. He also had two or three sixteen-gallon kegs, and I think he bought a couple of cases of champagne, too. There were thirty or forty people there, in and out. People sittin' around, shootin' the bull, drinkin', talkin', havin' a good time.

LOY "RINGMAN" OLSEN, Missoula crony; brother of Kurt "General" Olsen

Champagne was *typical*. Right in the horse trough. That was Jerry. I just didn't know it was his college graduation party until now!

The college graduation party of Jerry Daniels at Nine Mile. Ted O. "Little O" Lympus (standing), Jerry Daniels, and Lee "Terrible Torgy" Torgrimson with son Craig, June 1969. Lee Torgrimson collection.

TED O. "LITTLE O" LYMPUS, high school and college friend

We drank and ate the whole pig: eyes, ears, snout, everything. Jerry told us that the jowls and the brains were supposed to be the best part of the pig to eat. Probably it's something he picked up in Laos. Or else he just made it up! Eating the brains was this major event, which Jerry demonstrated. "Jerry the Graduate." How to eat the pig brains, the headcheese. I'd say Jerry's graduation party was a great success. Oh, it was a *resounding* success.

Mrs. PATSY SKELTON LYMPUS, wife of Ted O. "Little O" Lympus

That party went on for three days! We had a big fire going and people came and went. Some had sleeping bags, some slept in cars, some out on the ground. Julie Daniels had her guitar and we'd sing, talk, party. We laughed and laughed and had a great time. Back then we were all so close. Then Jerry went back overseas, and we didn't see as much of him after that.

LEE "TERRIBLE TORGY" TORGRIMSON, grade school friend; Missoula crony

When Jerry'd come back on home leave, before we'd do anything, we'd sit there at the Flame drinkin' and he'd go through his whorehouse escapades. Whorehouse escapades was one of Jerry's favorite topics. It was always good, always entertaining. Then we'd move on to what *we'd* been doing here—what's goin' on around town, what's goin' on with Animal Man and with friends. Then we'd start thinking about where we'd go fishin'.

Almost every time Jerry came to town we went down to Clark Canyon, which is just south of Dillon, Montana. It was usually from May through July when we went there—General, Jerry, and I. Jerry had a green Ford pickup, and we'd put a boat rack on top of that truck and haul his boat there, a fourteen-foot motorboat. Usually on the first night we'd drink and drive all the way down there. We'd stop at Dillon to take a shot at the bars. Eat a big breakfast at two or three o'clock in the morning, then drive on down to Clark Canyon, which is about another twenty miles. We'd hit the sack, then be up at seven or so. Always took potatoes and meat with us for breakfast. I'd buy an extra chunk of pork sausage in the restaurant at Dillon. We'd have that pork sausage with onions and potatoes for breakfast. Oh, they were wonderful! *Wonderful!*

On fishing trips we did a lot of fishin'. We'd fish for *hours*. Rainbows, mostly. Anywhere from two to six pounds. We'd usually go out at seven and fish until eleven or twelve noon. Come in for a couple of hours and eat sandwiches. Big chunks of hard salami we used to call horse cock. "Have a horse cock sandwich!" Then we'd go out again. We'd fish all day then come back in and have dinner. For dinner we always ate a bunch of fish. And that fish was so good. Oh, it was *so good!* We had a big fish fry every night, or if we didn't have fish we'd have those split cans of Chinese food made by La Choy, the noodles and sauce. It was easy and it wouldn't spoil. I always cooked.

I'd throw it in the frying pan and Tabasco it up to add some flavor, but usually we had fish. Come in for dinner, then go out for another hour or two before it got dark. Morning and evening fishing was usually the best.

Daniels fishing at Clark Canyon Dam. Daniels family collection. Used with permission.

We didn't drink much while we were fishin', but at the end of the day we'd sit around the fire and drink and bullshit about anything and everything and wait for the sun to go down. About ten o'clock it'd be dark, and we'd jump in the truck and go rootin' around, rabbit huntin'. Not huntin' with our guns, but with Jerry's green truck. At Clark Canyon it's great big open fields. Jackrabbits all over the place. And rocks all over the place. And not just rocks, huge *boulders*! How the hell we didn't run into any of those boulders is beyond me, because they're all over the place and we used to *tear* around there. We'd be chasin' rabbits out in the fields, out in the sagebrush. Jerry'd try and run 'em down, and all night we'd be drinkin' and knockin' over giant sagebrush, tryin' to run over those jackrabbits. They'd hide in the sagebrush, and we'd smack 'em. We'd just laugh and do it again the next night! Just trashin' around the country-side. If the radio was on, western music was what we'd listen to. Jerry was real big into Patsy Cline and Hank Williams, Jr. He loved Patsy Cline even in high school. We just had great times.

KURT "GENERAL" OLSEN, Missoula crony

When Jerry came home, we went bear huntin', too. We went black bear huntin' at Cache Saddle in Idaho, up along that Montana-Idaho border. It was a pack trip, just me and Jerry and two horses. We got up in there and it got late on the third day and he shot a bear and it started rainin'. So we built a little kind of a lean-to out of pine boughs and old logs. We spent the night in there. It was rainin' like hell and that damn thing started leakin'. Heavy rain all night, and we got wetter and colder than hell in our sleeping bags. I remember that.

The next morning we wake up. We was high up and it was misty, foggy in the morning, and it was cold. We packed that bear on the saddle horse. I rode out and the bear rode out and Jerry walked. We were goin' downhill and the cinch slipped on my horse, and I slipped over the front of it and hit my head on a rock and took a little hide off. Jerry, hell, he just took his T-shirt off and wrapped it around my head. He said, "You get back on that horse. You ain't hurt that bad." He was probably the best person to have around in a situation like that. What are you gonna do? You can't do anything. You ain't got no communication. He just wrapped up my head and I got back on the horse and out we went.

JON FOLAND, Missoula crony; former smokejumper

Hog used to really like goin' huntin' on the east side of Montana. It's a different kind of country over there. The west side is mountainous and heavy timber. The east side is open range and sagebrush. We'd be bird huntin' with at least a couple of the Olsens and Oehlerich. Hog loved "shootin' chicken," shootin' birds. I don't know if he really cared if he killed anything or not, but he liked shootin'. He had an old Winchester .22 slide action he kept under the seat of his pickup. If he'd see a grouse in the road, he'd snip its head off with that .22. We'd be out there for hours and hours, walking through the sage.

CHA MOUA, Hmong friend; Hmong funeral organizer

Probably it was September or October when we go with Jerry to the Blackfoot River, just about ten miles from Missoula. Three of us Hmong went: me, Seng Xiong, and Cha Xiong, the two young men that Jerry sent to stay with Louise. That day we shot squirrels and we talked. When we got back to Missoula we stored the squirrels in my refrigerator. I asked Jerry, "How are you going to cook that squirrel?" He said, "Well, I'm going to wrap it in tin foil and put it into the oven." He said, "Maybe you will eat them if I don't." To be honest, I used to eat squirrels in Laos, but I lived in Montana for fourteen years and I didn't even eat one squirrel.

The next day Louise, Jerry's mother, came over and opened the refrigerator. She said, "Honey, what are all those?" I said, "Louise, do you know that Jerry eats squirrels?" And Louise said, "Honey, my Jerry got used to the Hmong way already." Oh, I *laugh* when she says that!

"General" Kurt Olsen, Jon Foland, Jerry Daniels, and Cha Moua near Ryegate in eastern Montana, 1974. This was Cha Moua's first hunting trip in Montana. They hunted sharptail grouse, stayed one night in the field, and went antelope hunting the next day. Daniels family collection. Used with permission.

Conversation between TIM "WEENY MAN" LIEN, LOY "RINGMAN" OLSEN, and RANDALL "PETERBILT" OLSEN, Missoula cronies

PETERBILT: One time we was camped out and Jerry was shootin' squirrels. He had a whole string of squirrels all skinned out there. Those squirrels, he'd put 'em in a pan and fry 'em. Or sometimes he'd stick 'em on a stick and put 'em on the campfire. He tried to get us to eat 'em, but it was tougher than leather and just like eatin' a pine tree. "Squab. This is a delicacy," he'd say. He loved 'em.

WEENY MAN: I know Jerry'd eat pine squirrels and pigeons.

RINGMAN: And porcupines.

PETERBILT: We'd be goin' down those old dirt roads lickety-split chasin' them rabbits, goin' about 100 miles an hour. And every bridge we'd come to, we'd have to stop and Jerry'd go out there and jump up and down on the bridge. The pigeons'd fly out and he'd shoot 'em. He'd be a-laughin' and a-grinnin' and he'd grab up those ol' pigeons and say, "They're mighty fine eatin'!" They had little tiny breasts but he'd cook 'em up out there in the damn prairie and eat 'em. Oh, man! And we'd have twenty or forty empty beer cans layin' around us.

RANDOLPH "TOBY" SCOTT, former smokejumper; former Continental Air Services (CASI) loadmaster, Laos

Jerry and I both hunted and fished all our lives. When we were in Arizona, boy, we just got with the dove huntin'. When we were at Marana in '64, we ate doves almost every day. When you clean 'em you just rip out the breasts and break off the wings. Throw away the head, wings, and feet. You slice the breast into two layers, into two pieces of meat. You roll it in flour, salt and pepper. We had a great big cast iron skillet, and we'd fry 'em. You'd eat them with mashed potatoes and gravy and green beans.

Do you want to know how many Jerry ate? They used to have a place in Tucson that advertised a two-and-a-half-pound sirloin steak that was free to anybody who could eat the whole thing. Well, Jerry went in there and ate the whole thing and drank two beers. They told him, "Don't come back!" After that he wanted to see how many doves he could eat. So we kept track of them. We had to make it an official deal. We counted and made sure that he ate all the meat off of them. He ate four biscuits, drank two beers, and ate forty-two doves. So I was goin' to see how many I could eat. I ate seventeen and I was about to throw up. I don't know how he could eat that many.

KENT "DAN THE ANIMAL MAN" DANIELS, brother of Jerry Daniels

Jerry had a brand-new, blue, '63 Chevy Impala, and when he was going to school at the U of Montana he was putting about a thousand miles on it each week by driving back and forth between Missoula and Helmville to go hunting. He hunted with it all the time. When he'd go out in the woods, if Jerry or I thought it was even *possible* to go somewhere, we'd make the rig go there. We went antelope hunting with it, went cross-country over rocks. It didn't make any difference. Hammer down.

LOY "RINGMAN" OLSEN, Missoula crony; brother of Kurt "General" Olsen

Hunting and fishing is just a lifestyle in Montana, a way of life that we all live. And if you go somewhere else you still do your lifestyle. If there's hunting and fishing, you'll do it. It's not like you're out looking specifically for a desert ram or a bighorn. It's just whatever's local.

Excerpt from an audiotaped letter to LOUISE DANIELS from Jerry Daniels, May 5–10, 1973

Thought I might mention my elephant scuba diving trips down there in Phuket, a two-hour flight by turboprop from Bangkok. . . . It was the first diving that I'd done in an ocean. And it was really mighty pleasin'. Spent about five days there . . . and just got completely out of hand shooting fish. Diving in the ocean—there's so many things to see it's *unbelievable*.

They don't really have elephant fish down there. The groupers get about the biggest. This last time—to tell a big fish story—it was getting dark and I still had some

Daniels scuba diving at Phuket, Thailand, 1973. Daniels family collection. Used with permission.

air left in my tank so I just hunkered around the bottom of the boat, milling around, around thirty feet or so. And I saw an elephant fish, I'd say maybe ten lubs. Grouper. God, I got the quakes lookin' at him because he was bigger than most. I raked at him [with a spear gun] and missed. I couldn't believe it! So then I just had the sads and I restrung 'er. By then I was on my auxiliary air. I no sooner got restrung and I looked up and there was a bigger one yet. It must have been *twice* as big. I know they look elephanty underwater, but I'd say it must have weighed twenty lubs, or close to it. I got up to him and I didn't even waste any time. I raked him right in the midsection, right behind the gills. And [the spear] shot out through the other side and hung up the line on a rock so there was no give. It was just like trying your reel with the drag tightened down to nothing. It was just straight pull right from this rock. Probably I could have got him if I'd just leaped over the rock quick enough and downed him with my knife, but I just kind of hesitated. I didn't know exactly what to do. He looked like such an elephant and I *knew* he was going to get off with big hunks of meat flyin' around and stuff. Needless to say, he darted off.

Conversation between LOY "RINGMAN" OLSEN and KURT "GENERAL" OLSEN, Missoula cronies

RINGMAN: Jerry liked to go coyote huntin' at night. He'd buy a jar of oysters. Then Jerry and General'd go out and park and turn off the lights. Jerry'd get on the roof of the car, callin' coyotes. He'd eat oysters and hot sauce and drink beer, and he'd call coyotes.

GENERAL: One time he was callin' coyotes and he said, "Look at the eyes on that one. That's a big one. They're kinda far apart." Well, that was a *bull* he called. I said, "Get down off there. Let's go!"

JON FOLAND, Missoula crony; former smokejumper

On one expedition Hog was driving and wanting to take a shortcut on an old road that went across the creek, just an old loggin' spur. I said, "I don't know. I'm not sure you can get through there anymore, Hog. That thing's washed out." He said, "Oh, yeah. Yeah, we always used to go this way." Needless to say, we got the rig high-centered, hung up on rocks. We had to get to the chainsaw and winch and cables and stuff, so Hog set out some coolers. I'm in the back gettin' handyman jacks out. I'm gettin' out cables, hookin' 'em up and trying to jack up the pickup to get the wheels to clear, then try to inch it ahead a little bit to get some purchase. I'm back there wrenching around with these cables, cabling it over to a tree. It's twenty or thirty minutes later when I holler, "Okay, Hog, I think I'm ready now. Let's hit it." He's not answering. "Hog, hit it!" He's not answering. I figured he was riggin' the line at the other end and he can't hear me because of the creek. So I walked back down around the pickup and he's got at least three coolers opened, a case of beer, sandwich makin's all spread out, and he's just wadin' into his sandwich, makin' his huge Dagwood sandwich back there. I say, "Hog, what the hell are you doin'?" "Makin' a sandwich, why?" He could care less that we're stuck.

FARRETT DANIELS, nephew of Jerry Daniels; son of Kent Daniels

We were hunting geese up on Flathead River. Geese hunting starts October 2nd and goes until January 1st. It was super cold that day, so it was probably late November, early December. Jerry and I were going to go scare up the geese, and everybody else was going to hide out in a pit and wait. The pit's deep enough you can hunker down in there with your head just above the level of the ground. The one we liked to use was where the river turns a corner and creates a backwater, back eddies. You get set up and wait for the opening minute at dawn. Your decoys are in the backwater and you just wait for someone to scare up the geese. When the geese head for open water they see the decoys and they think, "Oh, there's a safe haven." Then—*Ack! Ack! Ack!* You shoot 'em out of the sky. But I think it's always more fun if you're the guy in the boat, because if you can put the sneak on 'em, then you may get first shot.

So Jerry and I go to scare up the geese. The Flathead's a big river flowing. That day we get up the river and the motor dies. "Oh, well, let's start 'er up." *YEENG*-ga! Well, when Jerry pulls the rope the little plastic handle for the rope breaks and it flies off. *Phewwwww!* "Oh, there it goes!" Into the water. Now the rope's all coiled up inside the top of the motor, just like a lawnmower where the rope goes around inside there, and we have no handle. Well, it's an ice-chunks-floatin'-down-the-river kind of day,

Daniels ponders the cooler and sandwich supplies, October 1976. Photo credit: Jon Foland.

so I say, "Okay, Jerry, what are we going to do now?" He whips out his folding Buck knife, unscrews the top of the engine and gets the rope back out. I'm thinking, *Well, yeah, you've got the string but that doesn't do you any good without a pull handle.* He doesn't think twice before he whips the string through the hole in his knife where a lanyard goes, ties that baby on, and now the motor has his knife handle for a pull. And that pull starts the engine. He was pretty ingenious.

Excerpt from a letter to JON FOLAND, Missoula crony; former smokejumper, from Jerry Daniels, July 18, 1979

I have no great stratedgy for the upcoming game seasons. If, however, there is anyway possible to spread grief and despair in your folk's hunting camps, I'm going to try and oblige. I'm particularly interested in attaining a no hit first two or 3 days of honker slapping, followed shortly thereafter with a devastating blow to anyone's luck at ole yeller. Unfortunately any schedules I've devised most likely would/could not encompass both. Perhaps tho, I could at least track through proposed sites, and freshen past spells of tragedy. So please keep me advised on plans.

Conversation between LOY "RINGMAN" OLSEN and KURT "GENERAL" OLSEN, Missoula cronies

RINGMAN: Thirty-two horses. I remember that trip, for sure. We were on a fishin' trip up on the Hi-Line. The Hi-Line follows the railroad tracks—Glacier Park, Havre, Wolf Point, then Williston, North Dakota. After fishing Nelson Reservoir for walleyes, perch, pike, we were in this bar in Malta having beers and whatnot, and Jerry got to dancin' with a young gal, an Indian gal. Her whole family was in the bar. He was buyin' them all drinks. He even handed out money, I think. He come back and he said, "I'm in love." He says, "I'll offer up thirty-two appaloosas for her."

GENERAL: Actually, the way it went, she was in there and he started buying cigarettes and stuff for her family. Well, he bought 'em all this booze and anything they could drink, and he finally said what Ring said. He said, "I'd give that old man thirty-two appaloosas for her." Me and Ring says, "They're just moochin' off you." It ended with us goin' to the motel drunk, and the Indians goin' home drunk with all the cigarettes.

RINGMAN: Yeah, we had hangovers the next day! But no Indian gal. That was in 1977 when "Lucille" first came out. "You picked a fine time to leave me Lucille . . ." That was sung by Kenny Rogers. It was on the jukebox and Jerry played it a million times. He played that and his other favorite, "Drop Kick Me, Jesus, through the Goalposts of Life."[1]

> *Drop kick me, Jesus, through the goalposts of life*
> *End over end neither left nor to right*
> *Straight through the heart of them righteous uprights*
> *Drop kick me, Jesus, through the goalposts of life.*

Well, anyway, the next morning after the appaloosas party, Jerry was all hung over. At eight o'clock in the morning he showed up with a great, big, two-inch-thick T-bone from a restaurant in town. He'd eaten the steak and just brought the bone back. He was proud of that bone. He was going to take it back overseas and show 'em what a real steak was, I guess. And he's opening a beer for breakfast. General says, "Jeez, Jerry, don't you think you'd better cut back on your drinkin'?" Jerry looks at General and says, "Look at Ringman. Do you think *he* wants to quit?"

Before we left Malta we went to the grocery store. We loaded up the camper with more beer. We'd been on a runner for about four days straight already. And on it went. It went on so bad, we had so much beer in there that somehow during the drive to the river the beer slid back against the handle and we couldn't get the camper door open. Every time we turned the handle, the handle on the inside hit a case of beer. That was a crisis. We tried to slam on the brakes and slide that beer forward. Didn't work. Then we thought about breaking the window. Finally Jerry says, "God, it's just *beer*." And he took the direct approach. Grabbed the handle and went *CRUNCH*. Broke about two beers, but he got it open.

After we rescued our beer we headed down to the Missouri River to go paddlefishing in the Charlie Russell Wildlife Refuge. While we were down there paddlefishing and goofin' around, we saw a goose nest up on a pole. Jerry got this big idea when we come up the river in the boat. He said, "Let me out. I'm gonna get that goose. We'll have wild goose tonight." I said, "I'll go with you." He said, "No, I've been trained to sneak. I'm gonna get that goose." He claimed he had sneakin' abilities and sent us off to not hinder him. So General and I go sit in the truck. We're sittin' up there drinking beer. It's dark. All of a sudden we hear this *HONG-HONG-HONG-Hong-hong!* And we hear this goose flap off. Then a half hour later the same thing, *HONG-HONG-HONG-Hong-hong!* This goes on. Jerry come back about two hours later, and he didn't have any goose. He said, "I could get within about ten feet of that goose. It was always just sittin' on that next branch lookin' at me."

Trying to get the sneak on the goose was one night, and the next day was the firewood. We needed firewood so Jerry got the boat and he took off by himself. There was no plan. General and I were just doing a day-drinkin'-noon-nappin'-then-go-back-and-eat type thing. Jerry came back after about an hour and a half, and I don't know why that boat didn't sink. He had more wood piled on that sucker. And he was drunk. Which is why he fell out of the boat. There was about two inches of boat out of the water. It was just *piled* up with firewood. That's just how Jerry was. He just had fun, you know? To Jerry, when he was doin' that kind of stuff, things didn't run by the watch. It was just however he felt. If he felt like having a beer at four in the morning, well, then that was beer time.

That all took place on a Hi-Line run, May 1977.

DEEDER DANIELS, nephew of Jerry Daniels; son of Kent Daniels

Basically what you grow up doing in Montana is huntin' and fishin' and being out-doors. Then when it gets dark you go down to the pub and you sit around and have a few. I was just a kid, but as far as I could tell, when I'd see Jerry he was doin' his deal. Doin' what he wanted to do. He was out there doin' the hunting, the fishing, the outdoors, havin' some nectars down at the local establishment. Whatever it was that he was up to was like, *Yeah, this is livin' large and lovin' life.* He was enjoyin' his life, as best I could tell.

LOY "RINGMAN" OLSEN, Missoula crony; brother of Kurt "General" Olsen

Yeah, we did a lot of D and D-in'—drinkin' and drivin'—but it was about us getting *out.* It involved fishing trips or rabbit trips. It wasn't just driving down the road drinking beer. We had a *reason!* However weak it might be, there still was a reason there! So the end of the story is this: I miss the guy. I really do. He was a lot of fun. He might have been different if he was a married man, but he was a lot of fun.

Funeral Chant Phase 6:
Sin City and Rodeos

NSTRUCTIONAL section of the funeral for Jerry Daniels continues, wherein his spirit is informed of how to avoid trouble at the Evil Spirit's [*Ntxwj Nyoog*] Sin City, followed by the cowboy rodeo, the marketplace and the bitter pond; stories about whorehouses, rodeos, and bull riding.

Funeral chant phase 6

At the last minute, while they are still on earth, Kia Moua Thao tells Jerry that he can accompany Jerry's spirit only to a certain point. This is the first time that the soul guider mentions that there will be a time when they must part and Jerry must send the soul guider's spirit back home. This is the beginning of the soul guider's separation from the deceased. Here he asks one time to be sent back, then he continues instructing. At the very end of the funeral chant, after Jerry has been guided all the way to the ancestors, the soul guider will again ask Jerry to send his spirit home.

After Jerry puts on his birth shirt, Kia Moua tells Jerry's spirit that he must climb up the sky ladder through twelve gates, twelve levels, to get to Creator-God [*Saub*] who is up-in-the-sky.[1] He tells Jerry what he should say to each gatekeeper in order for that gatekeeper to let Jerry pass. He says, "In one day you go one level. Two days, two levels. Three days, three levels. After twelve days you are up to the twelfth level. After the twelfth level, the twelfth gate, that is up-in-the-sky where you will meet Creator-God. From Creator-God you will get your luck paper [*ntawv noj ntawv haus*], your fate to be reborn."

The luck paper is like a visa for one lifetime.[2] When this life has ended, the spirit of the deceased has to go ask for a new luck paper. Up-in-the-sky, Creator-God assigned Mr. Nhia Vang Toua Teng [*Nyiaj Vaj Tuam Teem*] to be the guard who controls and distributes the luck. The soul guider instructs Jerry's spirit, "When you go to Mr. Nhia Vang Toua Teng, first he will ask you, 'Do you want to be reborn as an animal? If so, what kind of animal do you want to be?' In response, say you don't want to be an animal and tell him this:

You would be reborn a cow but fear people would use you to plow.
You would be born a dog but fear people would beat you.
You would be reborn a pig but fear you would be killed.
You would be born a horse but fear you would be ridden.
You would be born a chicken but fear people would cut you.
You should be reborn a human being so that you will have a good life.[3]

"Next Nhia Vang Toua Teng will ask you, 'What luck paper do you want?'" When you are born as a human being you can make a wish for the luck you bring to your next life.[4] After Jerry's spirit gets his luck paper he will pass on to the Evil Spirit's [Ntxwj Nyoog] area. The Creator is God, but the Evil Spirit is Creator-God's cruel and evil commander. The Evil Spirit creates bad things and drops the seeds of illness and death on earth. The Evil Spirit's area is up-in-the-sky, in Creator-God's Country. In the Evil Spirit's area, Jerry's spirit has four stops to make. The first stop is Sin City. Sin City is like a shopping mall for the spirits with many places to go. There are a lot of adult shows and porno shops. There a spirit can play with women or play with men. The soul guider tells Jerry's spirit, "When you get to Sin City the women and men will ask you to play with them and love them but you must say, 'When I was a human I lived on earth. I've played enough already. I don't want to go play anymore.' That way they don't drag you in there and you can move on."

TED O. "LITTLE O" LYMPUS, high school and college friend

Interstate 90 is a major east-west route that runs through Montana all the way to Seattle. For years it was interstate all the way through except for when you got to Wallace, Idaho. The only stop light was where you had to get off the interstate and drive through downtown Wallace. Which we always thought was kind of appropriate, being that Wallace was infamous for its red light district. [See Map 5 on page 307.]

LEE "TERRIBLE TORGY" TORGRIMSON, grade school friend; Missoula crony

Many times Jerry and I and some others would make a trip to Wallace to visit the hook shops, the whorehouses. There was the Oasis, U. and I., Lux and Luxette. Wallace is one of the oldest mining towns in the northwest, in Silver Valley, Idaho. That's why it had whorehouses. Because of the miners, see? Whorehouses always showed up around mining towns. The Wallace trips started in high school, probably when we were sophomores and juniors, and then they just continued.

I grew up with Wallace. Like I said, we used to go there in high school. Two or three of us would go over on a Saturday and come back on Sunday, sometimes Monday. Sometimes we'd miss school. Ha! That was before the days of the interstate and that old road wasn't easy. I remember some pretty rough trips in the wintertime goin' up there. We just did what we wanted to do. We were independent—Jerry and I and Larrae the Liq.

Later we'd just go to Wallace on a D and D. We'd stop in whorehouses in Wallace and sit and drink with the girls, just shooting the bull for *hours*. Jerry used to love to go there not necessarily to imbibe in the trade but just to go in and drink and shoot the bull with the gals. Good gals. It was really fun. They'd put us in one room and we had a hell of a good time sittin' there and bullshittin' for hours and hours while the gals went in and out doin' their trade. They'd be comin' in, drinkin' with us, then they'd go into the other rooms where the clients were. Just good gals, down-to-earth gals. We'd have a hell of a great time! Then we'd head back to Missoula and drink some more.

Later on there was one particular whore over in Wallace that Jerry especially liked to go visit. On one of his trips home he "fell in love" with that hooker. Ha! He made special trips to go see her, just smitten he was. She probably liked his kinky stuff!

He had some great stories about whorehouses and drinkin' at different places in the Far East, too. Vientiane especially, and Bangkok. Jerry was a whore-man. He loved whorehouses. *Loved* whorehouses! Whether you use their services or not, they are fun just to stop in and drink and shoot the bull with the gals. Some people might think there was a dark side to Jerry. It's not a dark side. Just raunchy. Just being a good ol' Montana boy!

Mrs. PATSY SKELTON LYMPUS, wife of Ted O. "Little O" Lympus

Talk about whores. Jerry, he'd sleep with whores wherever he went. You must know that. Oh, please! It was ridiculous! He even talked about some of the things he *did* with them! He talked about some of those girls over in Southeast Asia. It was like he tried to avoid any permanent relationship with women, any emotional attachment.

RANDOLPH "TOBY" SCOTT, former smokejumper; former Continental Air Services (CASI) loadmaster, Laos

I've got letters from Jerry but you'd better take them with a grain of salt. Boy, he really is a filthy-writin' son of a gun. Unless you knew Jerry, if you saw these out of the clear blue sky, you'd think he was some kind of a pervert. Ha! But that was just Jerry.

Letter to RANDOLPH "TOBY" SCOTT from Jerry Daniels, January 20, 1979

Tobius,

You gizz dribblin asshole, I figured to be pissin on your grave by now—I can't believe your still pushing on, but since you are, I'm sure it is doubtful you can even get a hard on at your age.

Needless to say I'm still lickin these pitutsies chocolate tunnels at random—don't think I could face a round-eye slash anymore. . . .

Believe I'll sign this off & Jack-off for awhile before proceeding to Patpong and gettin a few girls to get their gum for the first time in their life.

SABRD[5]

Hog

HMONG CEREMONY CONTINUED

The soul guider instructs Jerry's spirit that after Sin City he will go to a place for cowboy games and rodeos.[6] There they try to grab a cow and wrestle it to the ground. It is also a place for horse racing. The soul guider says, "Jerry, when they ask you to go see the cowboy games and the horse races you say, 'When I was a human and lived on earth I already saw enough rodeos, cows, and horses. I don't want to see anymore.' Then you can move on."

The next step is to go to the Evil Spirit's marketplace where they peel onions and garlic. The soul guider says, "At the marketplace they will ask you to peel onions and garlic with them. You say, 'I was a human and lived on earth. In my life I've peeled so many onions and garlic that my fingers are bleeding. I don't want to peel anymore.' That way they leave you alone so you can move on." When the soul guider says these words he ties a red string around the middle finger of each hand of the deceased to represent the bleeding fingers. Kia Moua cannot tie any strings on Jerry's fingers, but he verbally introduces the red string to him and instructs him on what to say and how to move on.

The last stop before leaving the Evil Spirit's area is to go to a pond of bitter, salty water guarded by a man and his wife. Kia Moua says, "When they ask you to drink from the Bitter Pond, take three small sips and then you can move on."[7]

Sin City, the cowboy rodeo, the marketplace, and the bitter pond are the four places Jerry's spirit must pass through before he leaves the Evil Spirit's area. The soul guider keeps on singing, still instructing Jerry about what lies ahead. He lets Jerry's spirit know that he will pass through several more challenges before he reaches his ancestors.

Conversation between TED O. "LITTLE O" LYMPUS, high school and college friend; and LEE "TERRIBLE TORGY" TORGRIMSON, grade school friend and Missoula crony

TED: In the early to mid-'60s when we were in college, we'd go to all these rodeos and Jerry would ride. That was just us guys: Jerry, Larrae Rocheleau, me, and Torgy. Every weekend we'd go to these jackpot rodeos all over western Montana—at Arlee at the Pow Wow, or the annual Salish-Kootenai tribal gathering, or wherever. We'd go all over, just drink and have a good time, and Jerry'd ride the bull!

There's an old Montana saying: "Powder River, let 'er buck!"[8] It means something like, "Let 'er all hang out. Let's go for it!" No holds barred. We had a great time at the rodeos. Jerry got into bull riding and *loved* it. He had all the gear. The gloves and the bucking strap that goes around the rear, and the chest strap. Once you're mounted on the bull, you hang onto a strap attached to the bull's chest strap and you put powdered rosin on your glove and strap to keep your hand from slipping. You wrap that strap around your hand and pull on it until the grip is tight. Jerry took it very seriously. He was tough.

TORGY: Tough, but he wasn't very good at it. He talked a better story than he rode.

TED: Jerry didn't come from a ranching family, but he got into bull riding. I think that came with some of the guys he connected with down at Marana. Some of them had that background.

JACK TUPPER DANIELS, brother of Jerry Daniels

I never saw Jerry compete in a rodeo, but I saw him carry a piece of steel around to strengthen his grip. It was a piece of a railroad rail about ten inches long. Where did he find a piece of rail that long? It weighed a lot. He'd grab that piece of rail with his hand and he'd do wrist curls with it. He'd practice gripping it and twisting it around. I asked, "What in the world are you doing with that thing?" He said, "It makes my grip stronger for hanging onto the bull." I said, "Okay, I guess that works."

Conversation between THOMAS C. "SHEP" JOHNSON, former smokejumper; former air delivery specialist, MR2, Laos; and KEN HESSEL, former smokejumper; former Continental Air Services (CASI) Air Operations, MR3, Laos

SHEP: Rodeo ridin' kind of started from the McCall smokejumpers, really. In Mc-Call, Idaho, we rode in different rodeos in the little towns. We'd do it just for the fun of it: Hessel, me, my brother Miles, Paperlegs, John Lewis, a bunch of us. The deal was, every year when the new men came in, they went through jump trainin', see. Back then a big ned class was about twenty.

KEN: We called them "neds," new men, rookies. This was their first year of jump training. They'd train, get their seven training jumps in, and then they're qualified. After jump training was over, the next thing they'd have to take a little fear in was the flip. Because the new men had to be represented in these rodeos. And *nobody* wanted to go ride a damn bronc. So they flipped to see who had to do it. They'd get in a big circle there, and they'd say what the game was. "Okay, heads out, first go-around." Everybody'd flip their coins and look. The ones that had heads'd get out. And of course it would get down to two or three or four guys left, then they'd flip and finally you'd have one guy that *had* to go ride. "Number One, you're *in*." And then the flippin' didn't stop there because if that guy ended up on a fire there had to be Alternate #1 and Alternate #2. There were three guys. Of course, the first guy was prayin' to jump a fire and the next guy was prayin' that he wouldn't!

SHEP: And you was takin' a risk, see, 'cause if you got hurt, and this was our smoke-jumper foreman's policy, he told me, he says, "If you get hurt, Shep, you're *out*." And he meant it.

KEN: That's how it worked for the smokejumpers, and that kind of thing just evolved into rodeo ridin' when we all met up at Marana, the ones of us that went there. Really, Shep and Jerry and Toby were the only ones that really got into it when we were at Marana with Intermountain.

SHEP: Well, none of us were what you'd call professional. We were pretty much amateurs, you could say, but we were in pretty good shape. I wanted to be part of it, so I rode with 'em. We rode in pro rodeos because most of the rodeos are PRC, Professional Rodeo Circuit, but for us it was just a fun deal. We enjoyed it—Toby, Jerry, and me.

RANDOLPH "TOBY" SCOTT, former smokejumper; former Continental Air Services (CASI) loadmaster, Laos

You know, we just went out and started doin' it. We didn't have anybody teach us anything. We got bruised up, beat up. Ha! We rodeoed all summer in '64 before Jerry and I left on our backpacking trip. We rode in a *bunch* of rodeos. Jerry and I rode bulls and bareback and Shep rode saddle broncs. We didn't win any money, but we did okay. Hell, mainly we did it to attract the women! The best picture I've got of Jerry is of me and him with a couple of Mexican whores down there in Sonoita, Mexico. We just rode in a rodeo down on the border, and we still had our cowboy gear on.

Jerry Daniels and Toby Scott enjoying themselves in Sonoita, Mexico, after riding in a rodeo in Arizona, 1964. Toby Scott collection.

See, down at Marana, Gar Thorsrud was our boss. Gar was always jumpin' and talkin' about, "You're gonna get hurt rodeoin'!" He didn't care if we were out testin' parachutes, cheatin' death every day. Just don't get in the rodeo and get hurt! Anyway, we told him, "Gar, the three of us are gonna ride in Tucson next week. Come on down there and you'll see that we're not gonna get hurt. There's nothin' to it." So he and his wife came out to watch the rodeo. And Shep was bucked off and hung his foot up in his stirrup and got drug around there, then the horse stomped on him.

THOMAS C. "SHEP" JOHNSON, former smokejumper; former air delivery specialist, MR2, Laos

I never seen Gar get too excited, but then that horse stepped right in the middle of my back and I thought it ruptured my spleen. Anyway, Gar, he come runnin' out there, you know, and the rodeo clown, he's standin' over me, and I'm hurtin'. My wife had to take me to the hospital.

RANDOLPH "TOBY" SCOTT, former smokejumper; former Continental Air Services (CASI) loadmaster, Laos

After that Gar called us in and said, "Awright boys, make up your minds. Either you're gonna work for me or you're gonna rodeo. If you're gonna work for me, that's

Left to right: Air America helicopter mechanic, Shep Johnson, Jerry Daniels. For Hmong new year at Long Cheng in 1970–71, Shep Johnson and Jerry Daniels showed their skills at bull riding. The two bulls belonged to Colonel Ly Tou Pao. Thomas "Shep" Johnson collection.

Daniels tries bull riding again at Long Cheng during Hmong new year, 1974–75. Larry Woodson on gate; Jerry Daniels on bull named Giap. Larry Woodson collection.

your last rodeo." Ha! So that was the end of our Intermountain rodeoin'. We decided we'd stay and work because we'd already taken our lie detector tests and all that crap for the CIA. I've still got my rodeo gear, my spurs, my ol' bull rope, and my bareback riggin'. But I never rodeoed again. Never did get around to it. You know, we were just kind of fiddlin' around.

TED O. "LITTLE O" LYMPUS, high school and college friend

Jerry had a very adventurous spirit. I heard he'd do rodeos over there in Laos. Rode cattle and water buffaloes.

THOMAS C. "SHEP" JOHNSON, former smokejumper; former air delivery specialist, MR2, Laos

Well, in 1970 in Long Cheng I *rode* my bull. Daniels lasted about one second on his. Those two bulls belonged to Colonel Ly Tou Pao. Those horns come right straight up, not like a water buffaloes' horns that come out more to the side and curve forward. No, these were the *dangerous* horns. I told Jerry, "We've gotta put covers on the bull's horns or we might get impaled on the ends of them." So I got these fire hoses and we cut 'em and stuck 'em on the ends. We taped 'em down but it didn't work. The bull shook his head one time and the fire hoses flew off. See our shirts with the numbers on 'em? We was tryin' to be just as professional as we could be. You notice Daniels' number there is 69? Ha! I think Lulu dubbed that on him. Lulu ran a cathouse down in Vientiane.

After I was gone from Long Cheng, see, Jerry tried it again in '74. He had all the lumber flown up there by a C-130, built his chutes, everything. He wanted to be the king of rodeo. Well, he'd take outta the chutes but he didn't stick. He'd get thrown, get the bull back in the chutes, and ride it again. He rode that same bull seven times.

TED O. "LITTLE O" LYMPUS, high school and college friend

Those Hmong people over there, they just couldn't believe it. Jerry'd go out and get on these bulls and ride them. They'd hoot and holler and they thought that was just the greatest thing! They called him "Mr. Jerry" and they revered him. They truly did.

Funeral Chant Phase 7 and Kheng Performance

USEFUL tools are given to the spirit of Jerry Daniels in the final instructional section of the funeral ceremony; the soul guider separates himself from the spirit of the deceased; crying over the casket. Kheng [*qeej*] instrument performance; introduction to the bamboo kheng and the funeral drum; explanation of the "horse" carrier [*nees*]; the casket is turned; end of day one of the funeral ceremony for Jerry Daniels.

HMONG CEREMONY CONTINUED

Funeral chant phase 7

For the next challenge, Jerry's spirit is going to climb a hot, dry mountain and cross a warm mountain meadow. The soul guider says to him, "When the spirits use their umbrellas to shade themselves, you use your own umbrella. Here is your umbrella."[1] The soul guider already made a small umbrella that he now gives to Jerry's spirit to use to protect him from the sun and heat when he walks. He places the umbrella near the head of the casket.

The soul guider instructs Jerry's spirit that after he climbs the hot, dry mountain, terrible winds will blow. To protect him from the winds, Kia Moua has prepared a fan for Jerry. The fan is a short piece of red cloth that he gives him now.

> *Sho, hey! You have left for good.*
> *You come to the mountain in the burning sky,*
> *The mountain wide open to the winds where the wild wind howls.*
> *All the others have coloured fans to ward off the clouds and the wind.*
> *You have no coloured fan. I put a coloured fan in your hand.*
> *The others will go before, you will follow behind.*
> *They will find their Ancestors, you will find yours too!*[2]

The next challenge for Jerry's spirit is to go to a hill where lots of caterpillars crawl on the ground. Some are hairy caterpillars and some are green caterpillars.

> *Sho, hey! You are leaving for good.*
> *You come to caterpillar mountain, a mountain wriggling with*
>   *caterpillars*
> *It's like a field of grazing sheep. . . . It's like a field of grazing goats.*
> *The others have hemp sandals to wear, you have none.*[3]

The soul guider says to Jerry's spirit, "When they use their sandals to walk on the caterpillars, you put on your own sandals so you can walk, too." Usually the soul guider gives the deceased a pair of funeral sandals he has made.[4] Kia Moua cannot put funeral sandals on Jerry's feet; he can only say the words. Next, Jerry's spirit faces the dragon and tiger:

> *The Dragon and the Tiger of stone open their jaws wide,*
> *Stretch their claws to grab you, come forward to devour you,*
> *Opening wide their jaws they advance to swallow you.*
> *The others have hemp sticks to fling in their jaws and stop them up.*
> *You have no hemp sticks. Your hemp sticks are here in your hand.*
> *The others will throw theirs first, you do likewise.*
> *And the Dragon and the Tiger of stone*
>   *will let you pass through to your Ancestors!*[5]

The soul guider gives Jerry's spirit a small yarn ball[6] to throw into the dragon's mouth to stop it from biting, and a stick to push into the tiger's mouth to stop it from closing. Then he can go on.

After passing the dragon and tiger, the soul guider instructs Jerry's spirit to go to the crossroads: "When you get to the crossroads there are three roads. The top road is very clean; it is a business road. The lower road is also clean; that is where they market cows and pigs. The middle road is a path that is overgrown with weeds and bushes." At the crossroads the soul guider gives a small crossbow and arrow to Jerry's spirit. His spirit will carry that for protection because from this point on he will have to go alone.[7] The soul guider gives these weapons and says to the spirit, "The middle road is where you will go. That's the path you are going to take to reach your ancestors."

> *Houses dot the landscape; their jagged roofs point to the sky.*
> *You dare not enter.*
> *These are the homes of the Chinese and foreigners.*
> *Direct your gaze midway up the slopes*
> *There, you will see simple houses, roofed with just thatch and twigs;*
> *Sitting humbly above the ground, those are the homes of your*
>   *ancestors.*[8]

The soul guider continues: "When you meet your ancestors they may ask, 'Who showed you the way here?' You say to them, 'Somebody that I don't know. His ears are big like fans, and his eyes are as big as cups.' If they ask you, 'When did he get here?' You must tell them, 'He came here this morning but he returned back yesterday.' If they ask, 'How did he get here?' You respond, 'He came here under water way and went back by air storm.' If they ask you, 'Can we catch him?' You say, 'No way! You cannot catch him because he came this year and he returned last year.' And if they ask, 'Can we follow him?' You tell them, 'You should not follow him. He has a crossbow and if you go, he may shoot you.'"

The soul guider tells Jerry's spirit to use tricky words to distract the spirits from finding out who showed the way, or else they will go and look for the soul guider, Kia Moua Thao. The tricky answers make the spirits so confused they cannot question Jerry anymore. That is the only way that Kia Moua's spirit can separate from Jerry's spirit.

> Sho, hey! I have shown you the way up to now,
> the way to the ends of the sky,
> To the edge of the great sky riddle, to the ends of
> the earth, the great earth riddle.[9]

The soul guider has instructed Jerry's spirit how to reach his final destination. Now he tells Jerry's spirit, "You must go alone," and he asks for the second and last time that Jerry's spirit release the soul guider's spirit so that he can return home to the land of the living. The soul guider says,

> You will leap without hesitation into the skirt of your Ancestors.
> Your Ancestors will console you with voices soft as flutes,
> Down here your relatives your brothers will begin to lament you. . . .
> Down here your relatives your brothers will begin to moan.[10]

Finally the soul guider says, "Now that I have told you how to find your ancestors, only look forward, only go forward. In front of you, on the path ahead, everything is bright and shining. At your back, on the path behind you, it is foggy and raining." Raining means that the people left behind on earth are crying. "Don't look back. Otherwise you might not see your path ahead. You might lose your way. Just look forward where everything is bright."

> So, let the gentle rain fall unceasing
> And you will be born again, a new son of your Ancestors,
> And find happiness![11]

Kia Moua uses a big knife to separate Jerry's spirit from his own. He makes three cuts on the floor between the coffin and where he stands. He cuts off their friendship. That is the end of the funeral chant section, "Showing the Way."[12] Now Kia Moua is completely finished with his work as Jerry's soul guider.

When the funeral chant ends, the soul guider is the first person to cry over the coffin. The soul guider cries first because the purpose of his tears is to wash away his footprints up-in-the-sky so the spirits cannot follow him. When Kia Moua cries, the family and friends come and cry with him. They do not cry before this because crying could distract Jerry's spirit during his journey. Now many Hmong people come and join together to cry over Jerry's coffin. Many people wail [*nyiav*][13] and carry on. They cry and talk to Jerry's spirit all at the same time so there is quite a noisy crying babble at the casket.[14]

Mrs. MARY V. YANG, wife of "Lucky" Lue Yang

Have you been to a Hmong funeral? For the crying [*nyiav*], it's a certain sound, like singing, that's used only for the dead. Both men and women sing almost the same way. That day many women come to the coffin and sing about Jerry and how he helped the Hmong people come to the United States and what a wonderful job he did for us. We cry and sing a lot.

For Jerry's funeral I didn't see many men cry. I only saw Moua Cha and Lucky. I know that Moua Cha cried a lot. Lucky cried a lot, too. Cried and cried a lot. He was very, very upset. Cha and Lucky didn't sing; they just cried.

"LUCKY" LUE YANG, former field liaison officer (FLO), MR2, Laos; Hmong funeral organizer

When Jerry died it just totally turned everything around and upside down for me. We had talked about doing business together and we had so many plans for the future. So I was just brokenhearted and I didn't know what to do. It was pretty much a nightmare for me because I was still new to this country. I was not yet self-sufficient and I took a lot of advice from Jerry. Then he died and I did not have any solid future plan about what to do. After that, I started to drink a lot. I got off work and I went to the bar and I drank as much as I could and then I went home. Because I was so frustrated! I was frustrated, *really* frustrated. He died and that just totally turned me into a nightmare. Oh, I cried and cried the day of his funeral!

PAO K. MOUA, younger brother of Chou Moua and Cha Moua

There are lots of people crying at Jerry's coffin. They cry and wail at the same time, "Oh, Mr. Jerry, you were a good person! You helped us for many years. Today will be the last day. From now on we will never see you anywhere on earth!" You express exactly your thoughts and what is in your heart for that person.

For Jerry I see lots of people go cry. At first they cry for Jerry. After that, in our culture, you can also cry and wail for somebody else who has died. Let's say my father died. I can say, "Dad, today I miss you so much." A funeral brings up those feelings of sadness, so you can cry for anybody who's died. That day the people look at the big black-and-white picture of Jerry's face. They rub their hands over his picture and their tears come out. The people feel so sad; they cry on his coffin.

Mrs. JULIE DANIELS MORITZ, sister-in-law of Jerry Daniels

At the funeral home there were the ones laying on the casket crying. I thought, "Gee, these people are Irish Catholics! Not anything else!" I was amazed at the way they laid all over that casket and cried, I'll tell you. Because since I was a child I hadn't seen that.

Mrs. MOE GEARY, wife of Helmville rancher Bill Geary

That kind of crying, wailing, is very traditional for the Irish Catholic background with the banshee women, you know. When I grew up back east in Buffalo, the culture of each neighborhood was still there: the Germans, the Italians, the Irish. There was no melting pot; our Irish neighborhood was still all Irish. There were even two different neighborhoods for the lace curtain Irish and shanty Irish. But at an Irish Catholic funeral, if you didn't have a good banshee in your family, you'd hire one. They were an important part of a funeral. So that kind of wailing and keening over Jerry's coffin seemed normal to me.

Mrs. MARY MAO HEU VANG, wife of Chu Vang; daughter-in-law of General Vang Pao

We go to the coffin but we cannot see Jerry's body. Go to the coffin, cry, come back, sit, go again. People go back and forth but we cannot see the body. People keep saying, "How can we tell if it's Jerry in there? It might not be Jerry." Everybody is crying because the Hmong people are very close to him. Even if you don't talk to him like a close friend, everybody knows him, so you feel like you are close to him.

Conversation between CHARLEY HUGHES and his wife NORMA HUGHES, Ovando ranchers; friends of the Daniels family

CHARLEY: I would imagine somebody's told you about those Hmong people, that wailing? It was really something the wailing that those women did at Jerry's funeral. To me, the thing about it—those women would go into this wailing, and I don't remember how long it would last, but then all of a sudden it would just *stop*. Just cut off like you'd shut a light off. I'll never forget that wailing that they did.

NORMA: Those gals just *wailed* around that coffin. They pounded on that coffin and wailed on that coffin even though most of them didn't believe that Jerry was in there! They wanted that thing opened up. But that would have been drastic! I'm sure he was in there.

CHARLEY: I don't think he was in there. And neither did the Hmong.

NORMA: Don'tcha Charley?!

CHARLEY: I thought about it a lot during that funeral because the Hmong wanted it open. They thought the world of him and they wanted to see if Jerry was really there. They wanted to take a look, the whole bunch of 'em. The authorities wouldn't do that, but I would have been anxious to have them open it, too. I very much wanted to open that casket and see if Jerry was in there.

KHENG PERFORMANCE SECTION (2 PARTS)

After the funeral chant ends and everyone has cried over the casket, the kheng [*qeej*] performance section begins. The kheng performance section has two parts: "kheng song for the end of life" [*qeej tu siav*] and "kheng song for the spirit horse" [*qeej tsa nees*]. The performance section uses only instruments that can communicate with the spirit world—the bamboo kheng [*qeej*] and the funeral drum [*lub nruas*]. People outside of Hmong culture usually think these are only musical instruments, but they are much more than that.

Wang L. Xiong blows the Hmong kheng. Wang L. Xiong collection.

The funeral chant, "Showing the Way," was spoken words chanted by a human being, the soul guider. In Jerry's case the chant was done by Mr. Kia Moua Thao. The chanted words communicate both from human to human and human to spirit. From human to human, the spoken human language is easily understood. But from human to spirit, it can be confusing and the spirits may not understand exactly what's being said. That is why the spoken words of the funeral chant need to be translated into spirit language. Both the kheng instrument and the funeral drum speak the spirit language. For the two parts of the kheng performance section no human language is used, only the blowing of the bamboo kheng[15] and the beating of the funeral drum.[16]

The kheng performance opens with the blowing of the "song for the end of life." The kheng tells Jerry's spirit that he really died and now his spirit is moving onto the next stage. This song is mostly a repetition of the verbal instructions the soul guider gave to Jerry in the funeral chant.[17] To hear the message of the kheng, Jerry's spirit needs to pay close attention. The sound of the drum can be distracting so it remains silent during this song. "Song for the end of life" takes about two hours to complete.[18]

The second part of the kheng performance is "song for the spirit horse" [qeej tsa nees]. "Song for the spirit horse" uses both the kheng and the funeral drum. The drumbeat has a different message and purpose from the kheng. The drum says: Go. Go. Go. It is the sound that sends the spirit forward. From here on, the kheng and the drum will play together almost continuously until the casket leaves the funeral home. During this song a small wood model of the "spirit horse" (which is the litter or "horse" carrier) is placed under Jerry's casket. The "spirit horse" is what will carry his spirit to the land of the ancestors.[19] Usually it takes an hour or less to complete this song.

Until now the casket has been perpendicular to the front wall of the funeral home with the foot of the casket coming straight out into the room. When the small "horse" carrier is brought in, Jerry's casket is turned ninety degrees so it is parallel to the front wall of the funeral home.[20] After the "horse" carrier is in place, the kheng player finishes playing the "song for the spirit horse."

For Jerry, this is the end of the first day of his funeral.

End of funeral day one

Tears in My Beer

S ATURDAY night: A memorial gathering at Big Sky High School; confrontation at a Hmong house; out-of-towners gather at the Holiday Inn; smokejumpers gather at the Oxford Saloon & Cafe; local friends gather at the Flame Lounge; another plan.

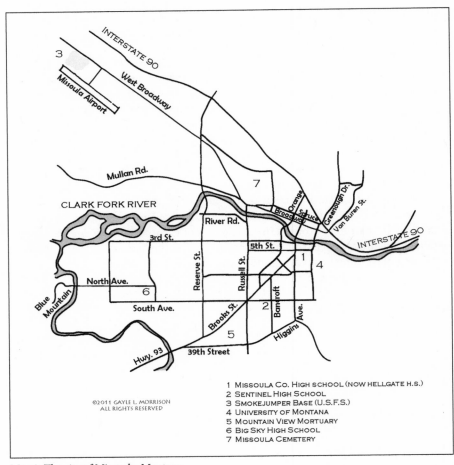

1 MISSOULA CO. HIGH SCHOOL (NOW HELLGATE H.S.)
2 SENTINEL HIGH SCHOOL
3 SMOKEJUMPER BASE (U.S.F.S.)
4 UNIVERSITY OF MONTANA
5 MOUNTAIN VIEW MORTUARY
6 BIG SKY HIGH SCHOOL
7 MISSOULA CEMETERY

Map 3. The city of Missoula, Montana

Big Sky High School

JIM SCHILL, former USAID Laos Refugee Relief Program; former Department of State, Bureau for Refugee Programs

That evening there was a memorial gathering at a school. It was the last roundup, with Hmong and CIA guys, sixty or seventy people. And it was a *wonderful* experience. There was a little movie projector set up. We sat around getting drunk and being treated to Mr. Clean's fantastic home movies of Jerry cavorting around with a bunch of other spooks up in Laos.

Mrs. CAROL LEVITON WETTERHAHN, former Highland Section chief, JVA, Thailand

Louise came to the school that evening; I remember meeting her there. And what do you say to Jerry's mom? What *can* you say? She was in shock. But I remember her telling me, the fact that so many people came to Jerry's funeral, for her that was wonderful. She needed that. That was for her.

CHU VANG, son of General Vang Pao

To be honest with you, it seems like the majority of the American people don't want Jerry to go in a sad way. Jerry was such a happy person. He was never sad and they don't want us to be in that kind of emotion. So we all talk and laugh.

"GLASSMAN" YANG SEE, former liaison between Jerry Daniels/Sky and General Vang Pao/MR2 staff, Laos

When the memorial at Big Sky High School was over, Jim Schill and John Tucker went with us to Moua Chou's house. While we were there, Mac Thompson called from Bangkok to ask John Tucker if Jerry came home okay. After Mac Thompson spoke to John Tucker, I got on the phone and asked Mac did he see Jerry Daniels' body put into the casket? He said no. I asked him did he speak with anyone who witnessed Jerry Daniels' body being put into the casket? He said no. That made me even more suspicious about the whole thing.

CHA MOUA, Hmong friend; Hmong funeral organizer

After Mac Thompson called, the conversation really got going. I stood up in the middle of Moua Chou's living room and I really questioned Jim Schill. I said, "Jim, we don't believe Jerry is in the coffin. It is too *light*. And why is the coffin so short? Maybe it is just a coffin of dirt! We are going to open it up." Jim said, "No, you can't do that." I said, "Well, we have to. We don't believe it. No matter what you say we've got to open it up!" I had a screwdriver and pliers in my hand. We were serious, and

Jim was serious, too. He stood up and he shook his head and his face turned dark and angry. He said, "If you don't believe me, then I will have to call the State Department. I will call DC right now!" He was not really angry at *us*, but escorting Jerry's casket was his responsibility. Jim said, "Absolutely, you can't do that! If you open it, I am going to get in trouble." At that point I threw the screwdriver and pliers under the couch. Forget it! The State Department would not let us open it so we backed off because we didn't want to make trouble for Jim.

NHIA "JUDY" VANG, former field liaison officer (FLO), MR2, Laos

But we still had our doubts that this was Jerry. Me, Glassman, Lucky, Spider, Rainbow, Snowball, Sancho, and Bulldog—we all worked so closely with Jerry in Laos, and we wanted to find out the truth if it was really Jerry, really the *Npuas*,[1] *really* the Hog in there.

Nhia Vang, radio code name "Judy," at Pha Phai, LS 65, 1971–72. Vang was a field liaison officer (FLO) who worked closely with Hog Daniels in MR2, Laos. Nhia Vang collection.

The point was that we remembered back to the old days and how Jerry really helped the Hmong, how he was involved with us in Long Cheng in MR2. And after the evacuation and we moved to Thailand in 1975, he was working to try to get the

Hmong out of Thailand to the U.S. Since he died while he was still on the job, we say he died for us. No matter how good or how bad the body looked, we wanted to know the truth.

"GLASSMAN" YANG SEE, former liaison between Jerry Daniels/Sky and General Vang Pao/MR2 staff, Laos

All the Hmong people at Moua Chou's house are very suspicious that there may not be any Jerry Daniels in the casket. For Hmong people, if we are to believe it, we have to see the body before the funeral ceremony starts, no matter what. If the public health department and the State Department do not allow us to open the casket, maybe that means they know something is wrong. I told the Americans our suspicion that there may not be any Jerry Daniels in the casket. Since nobody saw his body, maybe they put dead pigs in there.

NHIA "JUDY" VANG, former field liaison officer (FLO), MR2, Laos

If Jerry had died in the U.S. then it's another story. But this case happened overseas and we have very small trust in the system over there. There is no autopsy report or DNA report. The cable from Thailand said that when he died the scars on his body and his teeth match the original papers but, hey, they can get a copy of that paperwork and make it so the beginning and end match. That's just paper, not proof! That's why we need to see him for ourselves. If we can check the body with our own eyes, then we can be sure that is really Jerry.

On Saturday night after Jim and John, Yang See, and a few other people leave Moua Chou's house, some of us keep talking. We make a plan to break into the casket secretly. The casket is bolted all around, and we plan to unscrew all the bolts, pop the cover off, and check the body to make sure it is Jerry. That is just our group of field liaison officers: me, Lucky, Spider, Rainbow, and a few others. It is the FLOs who have that idea because who else cares as much about Jerry? We would do this for his family, too, but they didn't say anything to us about breaking into the casket. So we will do it for our own good because this is something we don't trust. We like that plan and everybody agrees. This is a secret mission. We will do what we think is right.

"LUCKY" LUE YANG, former field liaison officer (FLO), MR2, Laos; Hmong funeral organizer

At Moua Chou's house that night we were all so unhappy. We said, "Hey, let's do it anyway; let's open the coffin. We need to see the body." Then Moua Cha said, "Let's ask Louise for permission to see what she thinks." We went that night to talk with Louise. We discussed it with her that night prior and we said we were going to do it early the next morning, Sunday morning. She said she agreed to see that happen.

Holiday Inn

BOB JOHNSON, former Highland Section chief, JVA, Thailand; regional director, International Rescue Committee (IRC), Seattle

After the Saturday night social event with the movies, a group of us went back to our motel, including Burr Smith and T.J. and Schill and Tucker. Actually it was three different groups of people there: refugee program friends, a few locals, and Jerry's buddies from Laos. We sat around in one of the hotel rooms telling Jerry stories with a lot of beer drinking going on, getting to know who was who.

I'd heard a lot of stories from Jerry in 1980 when I worked with him in the refugee program in Thailand. So meeting the guys from Laos was like putting faces to the names. That was interesting. And that group from Laos was a little suspicious of us, the refugee folks, because we hadn't been through the war years with them. There was still some spookiness around about the Laos deal, but that kind of broke down after a while. After a few beers. Quite a few.

THOMAS J. "T. J." THOMPSON, former smokejumper; former air delivery specialist, MR2, Laos

I had never met Jon Randall, but I'd heard of him. In the mid-'60s he was the chief of base at Long Cheng, MR2. Randall had really liked Jerry. Clean and I and Toby and Randall sat down at a table in the motel restaurant. Randall was very stuffy at first because he wasn't sure about us. He didn't know ol' Tobe and me. He asked me something, and I gave him one of those off-colored answers we always talk, you know, and he just *laughed* and said, "Oh, my God, this sounds like the group that Jerry hangs out with!" That broke the ice. Turned out he was a great guy.

Mrs. CAROL LEVITON WETTERHAHN, former Highland Section chief, JVA, Thailand

The motel was kind of the hangout place in the evening. People gathered together, some Americans and some Hmong. A small group, a dozen people or so in somebody's room. Everyone's drinking beer, toasting. People talking and telling stories about Jerry.

The Hmong were questioning if that was Jerry in the coffin. A closed coffin was not typical of their culture, so they had a hard time believing it was really him. There was a lot of denial by the Hmong because they didn't like that closed coffin, but I think it was all based on emotional grieving. For the Hmong, denial was a way of letting out a little bit of hurt and sorrow. People didn't want to believe it so they said it's not him. Wishful thinking, because this was a man who worked for Sky.

I was so affected by Jerry's death. I think it was very emotional for everyone. Everybody brought their own emotions and their own history and their own feelings. And I think everyone had cried a lot. We were all in mourning. Mourning and grieving. So there were tears, anger, and then a lot of humor, because that's how you get through this time—with humor. Finding things to laugh about. Someone in the crowd said, "Well, it was probably some Vietnamese who killed Jerry in Bangkok. I think we ought to go out and get ourselves a Vietnamese!" It was said kind of in jest and another person responded, "All the Vietnamese guys here were on our side!" People were looking for humor to try to cope.

There were a lot of stories told, and they were funny stories. There wasn't anything maudlin that night because that wasn't Jerry's style. It was a kind of humor in which people said some awful things, but it was said humorously because that was a way to cope.

BOB JOHNSON, former Highland Section chief, JVA, Thailand; regional director, International Rescue Committee (IRC), Seattle

I think everybody was trying to whoop it up a little bit at the motel. Inside, everybody was pretty sad, but they were trying to make a little bit of a party in Jerry's honor. That was one thing that people kept saying: "We shouldn't be crying around Jerry's funeral. He wouldn't want that." So we were just sitting around drinking and swapping stories. It certainly wasn't the sort of wailing that the Hmong were doing at the funeral home.

DEEDER DANIELS, nephew of Jerry Daniels; son of Kent Daniels

I know nothing about the Hmong ceremony other than they were doin' their deal and for me it was, "Okay, whatever makes you feel good." The Americans, they were spinnin' yarns in the bars, at the motels, wherever they were. If you were hanging out with anybody, they were spinnin' a yarn. If they were tellin' a Jerry story, I was all over it. But it got to the point where they were talkin' too much theory, about how he died or why he died. I'd be like: "You're comin' up with this theory and you're going to sit on your thumbs and do nothing about it? Then you're all just a bunch of sit-around do-nothin' yack-yack talk-smack you're-pissin'-me-off-gotta-go guys."

The Oxford Saloon & Cafe

KEN HESSEL, former smokejumper; former Continental Air Services (CASI) Air Operations, MR3, Laos

To tell you the truth, a lot of people just stayed kind of comatose through that whole funeral. That's another name for drunk. A lot of beer pullin'. People sat and told Hog stories. A lot of it went on down at the Ox, the old Oxford bar. Have you ever been in that place? The Ox was built in the 1880s. You walk in there, and there's a big old Montana hardwood bar with mirrors on the wall behind the bar. It's kind of a skid-row bar, but it's an institution in Missoula.

At the Ox it was just *people*. You never knew what was going to happen. I mean you'd be sittin' next to some old drunken Indian and he might turn around and puke on you. They had gambling there and always had a keno game and a couple of tables of cards going on in the back room. It's still like that today. And you can still get brains and eggs at the Ox grill.

Aw, hell, I ate at the Ox when I was a student at the U in Missoula in '59. I knew about it because the jumpers all came through there. We knew you could go there to eat at any hour and get the biggest helpings and best food for the least money. That's where we always stopped—at the Ox. "Let's go down to the Ox and have a cool one." Six hours later we're still in there!

The Oxford Saloon & Cafe on Higgins Avenue and Pine Street in Missoula. Photo credit: Tim Eldridge.

RANDOLPH "TOBY" SCOTT, former smokejumper; former Continental Air Services (CASI) loadmaster, Laos

The ol' Ox is kind of a famous place. Nothin' but old men worked there. Ornery old devils! And they had a name for everything you ordered. If you ordered a hamburger the guy would holler over to the grill, "Stretch one!" If you wanted a bowl of beef stew they'd holler, "Under the bridge!" Scrambled eggs and brains for breakfast: "He needs 'em!" Those old men were gnarly! You couldn't hardly say anything to them. "Go somewhere else, by God, if you don't like it!" They'd tell you things like that. *Mean* old rascals. But the food was cheap and good.

There were a lot of old-timers that came to Jerry's funeral. On Saturday night we all met up down at the Ox. Most of us were jumpers that also worked for the Agency in Laos—Shep's brother Miles, "Paperlegs" Peterson, Hessel, T.J., Cahill. We had a few while we swapped lies about *fightin'* fire—that was smokejumpin'. And bein' fired *at*—that was workin' in Laos! Course we all knew Jerry for a long, long time.

KEN HESSEL, former smokejumper; former Continental Air Services (CASI) Air Operations, MR3, Laos

Down there at the Ox, I don't think we knew much about what really happened to Jerry, but at the time I don't think any of us had any reason not to believe that it was Jerry in the sealed casket. The Hmong were the ones that said, "Oh, the box is too short. It can't be him." And you know, that question's been goin' around *ever* since then. What the hell. That rumor, that suspicion, I don't think it's ever gonna be put to rest unless they open that casket and do an autopsy and DNA match or whatever they need to do, which I don't think was ever done, and I don't think they're gonna do. But it's the only way to resolve the mystery. And it *is* a mystery. It's a mystery how Jerry died, and it's a mystery if he's even dead.

Who knows? There were a lot of people after Jerry's butt. From the Russians right on through. Because he was the main man with the Hmong, with VP and his people. And more than the Chinese, the Russians were the power behind the NVA at that time. So maybe they went after Jerry. I know that they would like to have taken him out.

My wife's brother, John S. Lewis, was one of the first three Americans killed in Laos. He and another smokejumper and a third guy died on August 13, 1961, in a C-46 crash a few miles from Long Cheng. They were making resupply drops to Hmong troops. John's body was sent home in a sealed casket. You know, a sealed casket is a sealed casket, and that's the way it goes into the ground unless a member of the family says, "*Open* the damn thing. I want to see."

THOMAS C. "SHEP" JOHNSON, former smokejumper; former air delivery specialist, MR2, Laos

I was there at John's funeral in Texas. What happened with John was that the Agency didn't want anyone to look at him because it was a couple of days before they could get him out of Pha Khao where they crashed, and the body had decomposed some. General Heinie Aderholt had already identified the bodies of John, Yogi [Darrel Eubanks], and Dave Bevan in Thailand, but when John's body was shipped home, his dad, Sylvester, wasn't going to take anyone's word for it. He went to the funeral parlor and had the casket opened, and he positively identified that it was his son, John. He looked at him, and then he hit the wall with his fist. He took his fist and hit the wall out of frustration. But he did look.

BOB WHALEY, former smokejumper; lieutenant colonel, USMC (retired)

The jumpers all talked back and forth about Jerry's sealed casket because it just didn't make sense that in three days, even in an apartment that was not air-conditioned, that a body would decompose to an "unrecognizable" state that quickly. During my medevac days when I was flying helicopters in Vietnam, we took out bodies of Vietnamese and Marines that had been killed. Sometimes we couldn't get to them for three days in the jungle. By the time we got there, some were bloated and some were not, but when we picked them up they were recognizable. There wasn't anybody that you could say you didn't recognize. I could see that they wouldn't want the family to see Jerry's body that way. But he shouldn't have been unrecognizable. That's why I had suspicion.

RANDOLPH "TOBY" SCOTT, former smokejumper; former Continental Air Services (CASI) loadmaster, Laos

Well, something's wrong with the whole thing. Like I told ol' T.J., I said, "You know, I really wouldn't be surprised if it didn't happen pretty much similar to the way they say, but hell, you can't blame anybody for not believin' them!" I mean, Jerry could get about as drunk as anybody I've ever seen in my life. So the gas asphyxiation they said happened might have happened. But the way the CIA handles stuff, hell, they always make theirselves look guilty! My God, even when they try to tell the truth they screw it up. They won't release information. They tell lies and all this crap. I wouldn't believe anything the CIA told me, so I can't blame those guys. No wonder they think that the worst could've happened. That somebody killed him. And that maybe it was the Agency.

The Flame Lounge

LEE "TERRIBLE TORGY" TORGRIMSON, grade school friend; Missoula crony

I don't recall that the cronies spent much time at the funeral home—me, General, Brent, Larrae the Liq, Peterbilt, and Ringman. But when the first day was over, we all went to the Flame and had a hootenanny on Saturday night. We'd all known Jerry for so long, and the Flame is where we always ended up anyway. In 1969 we sat at the Flame and planned Jerry's graduation party. Thirteen years later there we were again, cooking up another plan. 'Cause Brent Russell and I and Ringman got a little hammered the day Jerry's casket came in. We were all pretty pissed about that casket.

At the Flame we talked openly, "Goddamn it, what's going on here? Jerry just didn't die like they say he died. Why in the hell isn't there an autopsy report?" And somewhere in our discussion we said, "Well, maybe we'll just pop him open and see!"

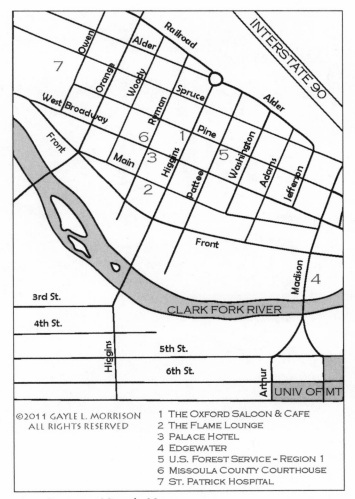

1 THE OXFORD SALOON & CAFE
2 THE FLAME LOUNGE
3 PALACE HOTEL
4 EDGEWATER
5 U.S. FOREST SERVICE – REGION 1
6 MISSOULA COUNTY COURTHOUSE
7 ST. PATRICK HOSPITAL

Map 4. Downtown Missoula, Montana

You know how a bunch of guys that are drinkin' get. And with me having had that last discussion with Jerry being so disturbed with what was going on over there, it became pretty apparent that he ought to be looked at.

RANDALL "PETERBILT" OLSEN, Missoula crony; brother of Kurt "General" Olsen

That was no ordinary wood casket either. That casket was screwed and sealed shut, and they were saying he was so decomposed that there was a container inside that was sealed, too. It just wasn't an ordinary casket situation.

The Flame Lounge on West Main Street as it appeared in the 1960s. [Photo No. 90-269], Stan Healy Photographs, K. Ross Toole Archives, University of Montana–Missoula. Reproduced with permission.

LOY "RINGMAN" OLSEN, Missoula crony; brother of Kurt "General" Olsen

That little wood casket, it looked *very* small to me for a full-grown man. And it was an odd shape. Like a child's casket or like the old-fashioned casket shape that comes on before the *Mystery* show on PBS. So there were reasons why we all wanted to open Jerry's casket. I figured even if it was bad, so what? I still wanted to take a look. In my opinion, I was dead positive he wasn't in there. So over beers we planned a break-in. We talked about what break-in tools we'd need—crowbars and hammers. I do think it was a well-laid plan. I mean, well laid as far as a table of drunks go, it was a good plan.

LEE "TERRIBLE TORGY" TORGRIMSON, grade school friend; Missoula crony

This was an at-the-moment decision. Brent, Peterbilt, and I left the Flame to case the funeral parlor. We got there and we started lookin' around. It was two in the morning and the funeral home was locked, so the three of us were gonna break into the place. We had a truck and we were going to haul the casket to General's garage because we had to use the electric drill. It was screwed shut about every inch. Christ, it'd take a month to unscrew it all with a hand screwdriver! We'd get the casket into the garage and then we'd just *do it*, you know?

We hunkered around there, rooting at every window, every door. After an hour Brent wanted to just bust the goddamn door open, but I thought I could see a security system inside. By then it was almost three in the morning and I said, "No, Brent. I'm not gonna go to goddamn jail for robbing a body out of a mortuary!" I said, "If we can do it quietly I'll do it, but I'm not going to get caught!" Knowing how this government of ours works, they would have claimed the casket as government property and we'd end up in Leavenworth.

RANDALL "PETERBILT" OLSEN, Missoula crony; brother of Kurt "General" Olsen

In the end we chickened out, which I have regretted ever since, because I still don't think Jerry's in that casket.

RICK EVANS, funeral director

Oh, for cryin' out loud. They could have gotten in. The mortuary didn't have an alarm system. It just didn't seem to me like the situation was that desperate at the time. Nothing more than, "We'd sure like to see him to make sure." To be honest, we kind of foo-fooed it off and said, "It's him. We're taking the word of the Embassy and we're trying to protect you. It's sealed, and you can't break the seal."

Silk Stories

SMOKEJUMPING; early fire season in Silver City, New Mexico, including the work, the food, the town, and a parade; Madam Millie Clark; return to home base; a late summer two-manner; flight to Redding, California.[1]

Excerpt from a letter to EARL LOVERIDGE, U.S. Forest Service, Washington, DC, from EVAN KELLEY, regional forester, Forest Service Region One, Missoula, Montana, July 19, 1935

Dear Earl:

. . . You wrote some time ago about [a] scheme of dropping men from airplanes for fire fighting.

. . . I am willing to take a chance on most any kind of a proposition that promises better action on fires, but I hesitate very much to go into [this] kind of thing. In the first place, the best information I can get from experienced fliers is that all parachute jumpers are more or less crazy—just a little bit unbalanced, otherwise they wouldn't be engaged in such a hazardous undertaking; accordingly, I discount materially the practicability of [this] idea.[2]

LARRY NELSEN, former smokejumper

Jerry was one of those guys who got into smokejumping in the late '50s, back when the Forest Service just wanted good kids. It was more word of mouth. If they knew the family, that was all the better, because they knew the quality of the kids that they picked up.

Jerry, you look at his family. Ain't brother Kent a beauty? He is just a joy. A long-haul truck driver, the Montana state heavyweight champion in wrestling, and the Montana state champion single-shot trap shooter. And brother Danny Boone, a great forester. And brother Jack, the Olympian. To come out of Missoula, Montana, and go to two Olympics? That is pretty impressive.

KENT "DAN THE ANIMAL MAN" DANIELS, brother of Jerry Daniels

Jerry was the youngest jumper I know of at barely seventeen. He turned seventeen in June '58, his rookie year. He just lied about his age and doctored up his birth certificate. Jerry was born in '41 and he had to change it to '40. He took an Exacto knife and cut a tiny square out of his birth certificate; he cut the number one out. Where that little square hole was, he cut out another little square with a zero on it and dropped it in, then photocopied it. It was terrible looking when he finished. But he got in!

RANDOLPH "TOBY" SCOTT, former smokejumper; former Continental Air Services (CASI) loadmaster, Laos

Jerry jumped in Missoula, Montana, and Shep and Hessel and I jumped in McCall, Idaho—two different jump bases, but we all jumped at the same time. All of us were pretty good athletes, in good shape. And I'll tell you what about hard work! Smoke-jumpin' and loggin' are the hardest work there is. You get to diggin' fire line and after about twelve hours you're wore out. You're up and down those mountains, and it gets scary. Those snags are fallin' all around you, and the fire burns all the duff under-neath that's holdin' those big rocks and they start rollin' down the mountain at you at about a hundred miles an hour. Oh, God! Our packs weighed about 90 pounds and jumpers couldn't weigh but 180 pounds. That's why there wasn't any great big ol' smokejumpers. We were all 180 or less.

Smokejumpers loading into a DC-3 airplane. [USFS 99-1632] W. E. Steuerwald, Aerial Fire Depot, Missoula, Montana, 1962.

ROBERT H. NICOL, former smokejumper and pilot

I guess one of the first times I ever saw Jerry, I was a smokejumper squad leader and worked in operations. We were runnin' shorthanded, and the rules then weren't as stringent as they are now about rest periods and work-limit time. We were just gettin' guys back out on fires as quick as we could. You'd be ready to go and you'd go.

Anyway, there was a fire call, and I went around the loft to see who was available to go on fire. Jerry was one of the guys that I talked to. He just came off a fire and he *looked* like he just came off a fire. His clothes and what you could see of his skin were black with soot. He probably had a two- or three-day stubble of beard on his face. I said, "Are you up for goin' on another one?" He said, "Sure." He never took a shower or nothing. We suited him up, put him on an airplane, and sent him out on another fire. And that impressed me.

There were a few guys like that, that would volunteer. He didn't have to. Most firefighters don't get much sleep for a couple days if they've been on a fire. If you were tired you were entitled to go take a shower and maybe get some rest and get a good meal in you. You were entitled to do that; that wasn't the *rule* in those days like it is now, but you were entitled to it. So when it's just a regular fire call, not an emergency, and a guy in that condition says, "Sure, I'll go," you bet I'm impressed.

GLENN F. HALE, former smokejumper; former Continental Air Services (CASI) Air Operations, MR3, Laos

Going from the northern smokejumper bases down to Silver City, New Mexico, for early fire season was a very, very coveted assignment because you got two fire seasons in one year. In 1960 we had twenty-four jumpers in Silver from five different bases. We got there about May 25 and we left not long after July 4.

Silver City is about a mile high. It sits at the base of the Gila Wilderness Area. It's an old mining town with a lot of western frontier history, way back to the 1860s. In 1960 the population was about 7,000 people, and the economy was largely copper mining and cattle and lots of ranching. The smokejumpers weren't exactly a big influence on the town, but we did spend all our money there!

ROBERT H. NICOL, former smokejumper and pilot

Jumping in Silver City was good money because if you went down there in May you would have a total of at least five months of fire season. It made a whole lot of difference in how you lived during the winter.

Nobody went down to Silver City their first year of jumping because the conditions are much more severe down there for jumpers—the wind and the altitude. In order to go you had to make a major mark with the overhead your first or second year because they don't want to get down there and have some dud on their hands. The Silver City jumpers were pretty much handpicked by the foreman.

Gila National Forest smokejumpers, pilots, and staff, Silver City, New Mexico, 1960. Back row: fourth from left, Richard "Paperlegs Pete" Peterson. Middle row: fourth from left, Larry Nelsen; second from right, Yogi Eubanks (killed in Laos). Front row, from left: first, Jerry Daniels; fourth, Chris Christensen; fifth, Glenn Hale; last, Roland "Andy" Anderson. LaMonte "Chris" Christensen collection.

LARRY NELSEN, former smokejumper

Silver City, New Mexico, 1960. Jerry was on the crew in Silver City that year. Silver City was Utopia in those days. That was great fire. We'd get ten, fifteen, maybe get twenty fire jumps. You might go on two fires in a day. Great fire! A lot of fun little quick fires that either run you off the hill or you got 'em right away.

MIKE OEHLERICH, former smokejumper; former Air America loadmaster, Laos

Jumping out of Silver City, oh, man, it was wonderful! I ain't shittin' ya. It was a small crew, and the Missoula jumpers that went to Silver City were the older guys that had experience and the foreman knew what they were made out of. Those guys were pretty salty. A kind of unruly bunch, guys that didn't like the discipline or the regimentation of the Missoula base. The stories I heard around campfires that were most colorful were from Silver City. For me it was a more appealing lifestyle—the freedom and independence of Silver City.

And the jumpin'—you got out there in some different kind of country. High-altitude pine with big open areas. The terrain was pretty rocky and with a fair amount of wind. The weather was dry, but the monsoons would start comin' up from the Gulf and then you'd get some good lightning storms. The lightning would hit and you'd get a quick fire and jump it right away. Jump it, put it out, get back, go out again the same day. That's what guys really enjoyed doing.

Silver City was small and nice, and the people there liked jumpers. There was one little restaurant where they'd stake you for grub until you had your paycheck. Chef Grill—absolutely great food! They trusted jumpers and were very friendly to us, and Chef was well respected for that. Silver City was a whole different culture and just wide open. Mexican beer, Mexican food. It was the Southwest. The Southwest has its own flavor, and it was something that was entirely different from Montana.

GLENN F. HALE, former smokejumper; former Continental Air Services (CASI) Air Operations, MR3, Laos

From town it was eighteen miles down to the Grant County airport, which is out in the desert. The temperature'd be somewhere in the neighborhood of 105 and *dry*. Around the airport was just lots of tumbleweed. Twelve jumpers would be working in town, packing parachutes. The other twelve would be at the airport on standby until a fire call came. Sometimes we'd be there for *weeks* at a time, eight hours a day standby. Standby was boring so we dreamed up all kinds of things to do for entertainment, but it was pretty dead out there.

MIKE OEHLERICH, former smokejumper; former Air America loadmaster, Laos

We got a lot of overtime down in Silver because you'd be jumpin' a fire or you were on standby. Standby was boring, but at least there wasn't somebody trying to make sure they got a buck's worth of work out of you. Working you for some damn stupid reason. You had your evenings and that was generally beer drinking down at the Buffalo Bar.

LAMONTE "CHRIS" CHRISTENSEN, former smokejumper

There was a brewing company in El Paso, A-1 Brewing Company. The brewery wanted to do some beer promotional and wanted to use the smokejumpers as a prop for their beer. Of course, the jumpers were well known for drinking beer, so the foreman agreed to have the A-1 representative come to Silver City.

On the day specified, we knew the beer rep was coming to the Branding Iron Bar and Saloon. He came in and there was about a dozen of the guys there. He brought in four or five cases of cold beer, and over the next couple of hours the jumpers very

Smokejumpers Chris Christensen [IDC 55], Jerry Daniels [MSO 58], and Glenn Hale [MYC 57] with A-1 Beer and Mississippi Crooks cigars. Silver City, New Mexico, May 1960. Toby Scott collection.

cordially drank up that four or five cases. We finished it off while he took pictures. We were having a good time drinking his beer and smoking Mississippi River Crooks.

After the beer was all gone, the bartender came around and said that he'd served all the A-1 promo beer, "Would any of you guys like to order another beer?" Some of the jumpers ordered Coors, Budweiser, Millers. None of them ordered A-1. It just wasn't a popular beer. I looked over at that promotional guy and thought, *I guess A-1 didn't win them over.* It was no surprise that brewery didn't last.

If you couldn't find an open bar, Madam Millie Clark had a cathouse in Silver City.[3] She also ran one in Butte, Montana, and another one in Ketchikan, Alaska. Prostitution was always closely related to the mining culture, and Millie's cathouse was adjacent to the smokejumper barracks. Millie's was not one of the places that I went to, but I heard some interesting stories! One thing about Millie's was that she could sell beer there any hour of the day or night, any day of the year because they were not a public bar. She had an arrangement with the mayor and others for "favors," so if the other tanks were closed, guys could go over to Millie's, knock on the door, and drink beer out of the refrigerator. She probably charged five times the price for it.

GLENN F. HALE, former smokejumper; former Continental Air Services (CASI) Air Operations, MR3, Laos

Every Fourth of July there was a parade in Silver with forty or fifty floats, and in '59 and '60 the smokejumpers entered the parade. We borrowed a Forest Service truck for our float and we made a smokejumper display. Then we sat on the back of the truck and drank Coors beer. That was our float. I rode on that float, and Jerry did as well. We were in great physical shape and we thought we were pretty much studs. It was ridiculous, really, because if you had a wagon and put balloons on it, you could get into that parade, you see? But whatever it was, Silver City was happy to have it because it made their parade!

The point is that Silver City was a special place for the jumpers because everybody in the city really liked us. We were young men, we were there for a short time, and we were making and spending good money. We were in the parade and we had guys bull riding in the rodeo. The bad thing about the rodeo was that the jumpers would compete with real cowboys. The cowboys would loan us the rigging to use, then they'd compete against us for the win. Of course there was little risk of one of our guys actually winning, but all the jumpers would go to the rodeo and cheer for our hero. We livened up the town for a few weeks and we had a blast.

KENT "DAN THE ANIMAL MAN" DANIELS, brother of Jerry Daniels

I guess bull riding was the thing to do in Silver City. That was just another deal for chasing women, the Rodeo Queens. Later I ran into one of those women. She said, "Yeah, my girlfriends and I used to go down to see what the new jumpers looked like." They'd go to the bars and to the rodeos to check out the new crop. I guess those gals were groupies or whatever you'd call them.

LAMONTE "CHRIS" CHRISTENSEN, former smokejumper

Every year the smokejumper unit would have a pretty wild farewell or going-home party. It was no different in 1960. Everybody had been to the party that evening, and most had made it back to the barracks there on Hudson Street. In the middle of the night the guys were asleep when we got a knock on the door. It was a couple of policemen. They had a concern. The policeman said they got a call from somebody saying there was a body on the street over on College Avenue. When the police got there they knew that wasn't a local guy, and they figured he was a smokejumper. They told us, "We couldn't wake him up." So they picked him up bodily and put him in the backseat of the police car. They asked if somebody would come out and identify the guy.

A couple of us pulled on our jeans and went out to see. Someone was in the backseat, all curled up in a ball, all tucked in with his knees under his chin. We could see a crew cut and enough of the features to figure it was Jerry. We couldn't wake him up or straighten him out either, so we carried him in and laid him on his bunk, still in a ball until he finally unwound.

The next morning, Jerry didn't remember anything. What he told us was that he was waiting for a ride back to the barracks. That person didn't show up so he just sat down on the curb and went to sleep. He curled up and was having a good summer snooze. Of course that was funny to him.

MIKE OEHLERICH, former smokejumper; former Air America loadmaster, Laos

After you'd been a month or six weeks in Silver City, early fire season was over—and when you came back to Missoula, it was like going from paradise to jail! There was overhead all over the place. Chickenshit this and chickenshit that. Rules up the butt. You had a hard time adjusting when you came back.

LARRY NELSEN, former smokejumper

Mid-September 1960, there was a two-manner fire on Snowboat Creek. Jerry and I flew in the Travelair up the Blackfoot River out of Missoula. We circled, circled. We looked for the fire, looked for the smoke. Finally found smoke. We jumped from

Two smokejumpers descend into tall timber to put out a small lightning-caused fire before it spreads. [USFS 99-1544.1] Photographer unknown, Lolo National Forest, Montana, 1950.

fifteen hundred feet, the plane made one pass at about two hundred feet to drop the fire pack—maybe six C-rations, boxed meals, shovel, pulaski[4]—and another pass to drop the water.

Jerry and I got on the ground. We searched for an hour or two for that fire, but it was small and very difficult to find. Finally Jerry was just like a hound dog. He got in the wind line and used the smoke to smell it out. Followed it right up to it. That fire was just a wimp. Had it out in fifteen, twenty minutes. Next morning we hiked a mile or two down the trail to the road. Got picked up and back to the base we went.

JOHN G. "JACK" BENTON, former smokejumper

In '59 I trained in Missoula as a rookie jumper, and I ran into Jerry in 1960. He was a third-year jumper and a "loft rat." That's what we called them. He was one of the guys who was an ace parachute rigger. I'd see him working in the parachute loft, and then I'd see him in some very intense volleyball games having a great time. The loft rats all came out to play volleyball. And they were very cliquish. You had a difficult time breaking into the team, unless you were a rigger.

Fire equipment and supplies are rigged at the smokejumper base for air delivery to remote, roadless areas in support of wildland firefighters, lookouts, and so on. Because of their expertise in rigging—as well as their equipment, training, and experience—smokejumpers do 90 percent of the rigging and loading, and all of the actual cargo drops. [USFS 99-0852] W. E. Steuerwald, Aerial Fire Depot, Missoula, Montana, 1961.

KEITH "SKID" WOLFERMAN, smokejumper; friend of Deeder and Farrett Daniels

Loft lizard, loft rat. Loft work is the one part of our job as smokejumpers that sets us apart from other firefighters. Not a lot of firefighters have loft skills. It's an exacting place. Smokejumpers manufacture their own jumpsuits and packs, and we make similar rough-terrain jump gear for the military. But the maintenance and repacking of parachutes is the main priority. If you're packing parachutes, even little mistakes are not cool. And you're always trying to improve on your parachute systems through research and development. You're always trying to get the best performance out of your canopies.

JOHN G. "JACK" BENTON, former smokejumper

In the summer of 1960 we had a fairly active fire season in Missoula.[5] On one particular day I was walking a bunch of tourists through the jump base, explaining everything. It's an interesting tour, especially for someone who's interested in parachutes. I noticed Jerry over at a sewing machine in the manufacturing room, working on a project. I saw he was sewing up an article of clothing. When I finished the tour I came back and I watched Jerry for a bit. Then I said, "Jerry, what in the world are you doing?" He said, "I'm sewing a pair of silk shorts." Now you have to understand that they weren't real silk, it was nylon parachute material that he'd gotten from a parachute that had been torn up. He used a panel from that and he was sewing these shorts. I asked, "Why?" And he said, "I always wanted to fart through silk." He said it with a straight face, just as straight as could be, but I got a good laugh out of that. That was vintage Jerry. Daniels was a character with a great sense of humor.

MIKE OEHLERICH, former smokejumper; former Air America loadmaster, Laos

In '60 the jumpers rented a hall downtown for the end-of-the-year party in Missoula. The northern fire season was over, and the next day we were supposed to fly to Redding, California, for a fall deal as fire crew. We had the party, and the next morning Daniels and I got in his car and we went down to the hall to help clean the place up. We went down there and we captured a pony keg of beer that was still good. So we stuck the keg in a gear bag, shoved it in the back of Daniels' car, and went on out to the base. When all the guys and their gear got loaded onto the DC-3, we threw that pony keg on. Back then it wasn't all strict like now. We didn't sit in seats with seat belts and all that kind of stuff. Now the Forest Service has got all these regulations, but in those days it was pretty wild and woolly and loose—no seats, just an open cargo space filled with jumpers and personal gear.

We flew down in the Doug, and we were drinkin' on that pony keg even though we were still drunk from the party the night before. Oh, we were happy as hell that the keg still had beer in it. It was gone long before we got to Redding.

Kickers for the CIA

WHY smokejumpers were recruited to work overseas; chronology of a relationship between the U.S. Forest Service and CIA; admiration for adventurers.

LEE "TERRIBLE TORGY" TORGRIMSON, grade school friend; Missoula crony

Jerry jumped for two or three years before the CIA started recruitin' guys out of the smokejumper base. I remember Oehlerich talking about a bunch of smokejumpers not coming back to Missoula. He said they got "other jobs." And I'm sure that's what it was. They were being recruited by the CIA from their Forest Service jobs so they could train at the airbase in Marana, Arizona, then head overseas.

KEN HESSEL, former smokejumper; former Continental Air Services (CASI) Air Operations, MR2, Laos

I'll tell you why the CIA was interested in smokejumpers. They went after people who knew parachutes, plain and simple. Air drops was the only damn way they could supply those people in Tibet or up there in that rough terrain in Laos. So they came to the jumpers 'cause we had the expertise to rig cargo and not only drop the supplies into timber but jump into timber if we had to.

JACK TUPPER DANIELS, brother of Jerry Daniels

When Jerry was first doing the Air America cargo drops, that's all he was doing, dropping cargo into Laos. He told me he made 300 and some flights in one year and he was shot at almost every time. He said, "But *most* of them didn't reach the plane." Mostly it was rifle fire and you could see tracers coming up and then curve down before they got to you. Once in a while they'd go over a .50-caliber gun. One time he told me he was sitting on a seat and he got up to check on some cargo and a .50-caliber round went right through the chair he'd been sitting on. So he had some close calls, but that didn't seem to bother him at all.

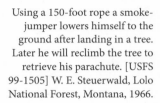

Using a 150-foot rope a smoke-jumper lowers himself to the ground after landing in a tree. Later he will reclimb the tree to retrieve his parachute. [USFS 99-1505] W. E. Steuerwald, Lolo National Forest, Montana, 1966.

MIKE OEHLERICH, former smokejumper; former Air America loadmaster, Laos

I got recruited out of the Missoula smokejumper base after coming back from early fire season in Silver City, New Mexico. Probably that was in the spring of 1961. I got a phone call, and they asked me if I could keep my mouth shut, and did I want to go to work overseas for good money.

Not too many weeks after that I landed at Takhli airbase in Thailand, and right away, to my surprise, I met up with Jerry and Jack Cahill, both Missoula jumpers, along with two other smokejumpers who were already there, Eubanks and Lewis. There were six of us jumpers, two three-man crews, working together as cargo kickers. We were hired when the Agency needed more kickers to resupply General Vang Pao's guerrilla troops. We got up every morning before five-thirty, loaded the airplane, and kicked cargo over Laos: fly in and drop in. Some flights we kicked ammunition and hardware from Takhli; other flights we kicked bags of rice from Vientiane.

I was baptized right away, third or fourth flight. We were in the C-46, and Jerry was giving me an orientation, showing me where we were on the map. He'd say, "This area is okay but watch out over here. Here are the bad guys." We made the drop and are flying away in the empty plane when *ker-WHUMP!* There's a big hole in the wing the size of a saucer. Only three feet from my butt! That's when it hit me that there were people down there who wanted to *kill* me. I was overwhelmed by that thought. After we got back to base, a couple of beers helped to settle me down. Daniels was real philosophical about it: "There's nothing you can do if it's the golden BB that's got your name on it."

I kicked cargo over Laos for about two years off and on. The pilots that we flew with out of Takhli would get at least 250 hours of mountain flying in a month because it was strenuous flying conditions. You'd fly up to Laos and, depending on the season, you were either flying in smoke when they burned the fields or you were flying in rain clouds. You'd cruise on autopilot at 10,000 feet and as you left the plains and headed into the mountains you'd watch the clouds build up below you. By the time you got to the right area you couldn't see the ground or any landmarks. Sometimes you'd be millin' around for ten minutes, lookin' for a hole. You'd try to find a hole that looked safe enough to let down in, but the holes'd be shiftin'. There'd be some inviting-looking holes, and by the time you got down in there, shit, you'd find out it was just tighter than hell. You'd have to get in below the clouds and hope to hell you weren't flying into a mountain at the same time. Then once you got down through the hole it was, *Where in the shit are we?* That was the big deal, and that was why we kickers were good because we were there all the time, flying every day. We knew the country really well, and after a couple of glances we knew where we were from looking at the lay of the land, the lay of the jungle, hills, valleys, size of rivers, landmarks like karsts. And we had some idea where we were because we were supposed to be en route to a certain DZ [drop zone]. So when the pilot let down in a hole we'd say, "*Ho*-ly shit, there's a road and that means this and that. Get the hell over there. We'll get shot over here." You'd make the drop then you'd have to get back up through the clouds. Those holes could close up fast and you can't climb out as fast as you drop in. Sometimes those holes closed up at the same time as the mountains came up in front of you. No choice but to fly blind up through the clouds, knowing that you were only halfway up the mountain with mountains all around you. That was tense. Thirty seconds of flying in the clouds like that, you'd start puckerin'. Sometimes it'd be a minute before you'd come out on top and start to breathe again and could see down through the holes.

I worked with Jerry for about six months or so at Takhli, then they brought in other guys to replace us. Most of us went back to jumping at Missoula and McCall. I went to work at Marana. Jerry went back to school in Missoula, which went on for years and years, part-time. After he was out of school that's when he went to Long Cheng and started to be an advisor to Vang Pao in up-country Laos.

Conversation between KEN HESSEL, former smokejumper; former Continental Air Services (CASI) Air Operations, MR3, Laos, and THOMAS C. "SHEP" JOHNSON, former smokejumper; former air delivery specialist, MR2, Laos

KEN: I suspect a chronological thing is what's needed here. For the jumpers who went with the Company, the early years were '51, '52, '53. That was the first wave: Korea and Taipei, Taiwan. Shep and I started writin' down names of the jumpers that we knew were involved and we could remember clear back to the beginning, '51. That's where it started—with Jack Mathews. Mathews was a smokejumper from Missoula; he was one of the very earliest jumpers who signed on with the CIA. He was jumpin' with General Chiang Kai-Shek's Nationalist paratroops. Worked out of Taiwan during the Korean War.

Then in '52, '53, there was a handful of guys that were recruited from the jumpers.[1] They were in Taiwan when the Matsu-Quemoy Islands thing was goin' on, with Chiang Kai-Shek and the Chinese Nationalists wanting to fight back against the Chinese communists. The Americans were dropping supplies on overflights to infiltrated Nationalist guerrilla forces on the mainland, and working with the Nationalist Chinese paratroopers as guerrilla airborne trainers.

In '53 to '57, after Taiwan, it seems there was a short recruitment gap, I guess. Then about '57 or '58 the Company, the CIA, took more jumpers out of Missoula and out of McCall and sent them to Okinawa for early Laos ops and to Thailand for Laos and Tibetan ops—overflights into Tibet out of Takhli, dropping cargo. That was the second wave.

All the names Shep and I knew about, I wrote them all down. There might be more but it rounded out to about eighty-five. And there aren't that many jumpers anyway, probably five to six thousand total up through today. But about eighty-five jumpers worked for the Company, we figured. The jumpers that worked as kickers for Air America and CASI were not operations people for the CIA. There's a difference. If you go through those eighty-five names, the majority were kickers, not ops people—not Agency per se.

SHEP: Well, I was there in Okinawa. I was doing Lao resupply to support General Vang Pao with airdrops in the fall of 1961. And I made six resupply flights to Tibet in 1960. The CIA used DC-6s and later C-130s. We'd take off from Takhli, Thailand, and fly over the Himalayas at 32,000 feet, then drop down into Tibet to resupply the Tibetans who were on the ground fighting the Chinese communists. I worked for the Agency in the winter months and then went back to smokejumping in McCall during fire season in '60, '61, and '62. After fire season ended in September '62, I went to work at Marana.

Working overseas like that, we'd get our basic salary, maybe $750 a month, and for black ops we got extra pay. It varied, $250 to $1,500 per flight. We never knew what it would be. It depended on how hazardous, the length of the flight, the distance. It was good money, but really we did it for the adventure. When I got a check in the mail after I come back to McCall, it'd be so big that I figured I

Three of the first C-123 Air America cargo kickers were U.S. Forest Service smokejumpers from McCall, Idaho. Left to right: Richard "Paperlegs Pete" Peterson with brothers Miles Johnson and Thomas "Shep" Johnson at Wattay airport, Vientiane, Laos, 1961. Thomas "Shep" Johnson collection.

couldn't cash it in town. It'd raise suspicion. So I went to Cascade to cash the check. Keep it kind of secret that way. Then the bank in Cascade called McCall, so the cat was out of the bag anyways.

In '61 we come back from overseas on a DC-6, a black flight. Nobody knew anything about it. That DC-6, you couldn't see in. Picked up the Tibetans in Guam or Saipan, then flew on and landed in San Francisco. Had a hell of a time there. They wouldn't allow the immigration officers on board because we had those twenty to twenty-five Tibetans. Immigration never did come aboard. The Tibetans was goin' on to Denver, Colorado. When we got there it was night and nobody could see when they unloaded the Tibetans.

KEN: Those Tibetans we trained at Camp Hale[2] in Colorado. Brought 'em into the States black; trained them; sent them back to Takhli, Thailand; put 'em on C-130s; and dropped 'em in Tibet with weapons and food, then resupplied them.

SHEP: Gar Thorsrud knows all about that stuff. He was there in the thick of it, but Gar won't tell you nothin'.

KEN: Tibetan overflights continued up until the time of the U-2 incident when Gary Powers was shot down over Russia. When Powers was shot down in May 1960, Tibetan resupply stopped. Except for one last flight.

SHEP: We made one last resupply flight into Tibet, and Jerry Daniels was on that flight. It was January of 1962. I was with Jerry and Lyle Brown and Fred Barnowsky—all Missoula smokejumpers. They say that was the last Tibetan flight but who really knows, you know?

KEITH "SKID" WOLFERMAN, smokejumper; friend of Deeder and Farret Daniels

Back in the early '60s the smokejumper program was more of a young man's game than now. Physically it was harder on jumpers back then because of the equipment used and the possibility of more pack-outs. Now by the time somebody gets up to the level of being able to do what Jerry and those guys were doing at eighteen or twenty years of age, now a jumper's usually twenty-five, twenty-seven.

I think it's pretty cool that jumpers were recruited to work overseas in Laos and other places. Not just because of the adventure and excitement aspect of it but because to me that was a time in our country's history when the government—yeah, maybe it wasn't entirely on the up and up—but it seemed like that was a time when they could cut through the bureaucratic red-tape BS and get a job done. They stopped and asked, "Where are we gonna find people that can do this kind of job?" And someone said, "Well, there are some guys that are custom fit for what you're looking for. Let's go talk to the smokejumpers."

It was just a neat thing that the government could do. Go to the jumper program and find some young, motivated, fit people with aviation experience that were civilians. And the fact is that a lot of the young jumpers who were quietly approached stepped up and said, "Yeah, there's a need. The pay's good, and I'm unattached. What the hell, let's go!" Thirty grand a year back then was a lot of cash! And the smokejumpers they picked up had all the skills that they were looking for but without the liability, I guess you'd say, of being a member of the United States military.

GLENN F. HALE, former smokejumper; former Continental Air Services (CASI) Air Operations, MR3, Laos

Politically, the Agency is at the whim of the president. Whenever things are going on, like when the U.S. government was having trouble in Vietnam with the Ho Chi Minh trail in "neutral" Laos, that was perfect for the Agency's paramilitary because we could go into Laos and pretend to be whatever our cover was and not have a military uniform on. So the Agency bloomed to I don't know how many thousands of people.

THOMAS C. "SHEP" JOHNSON, former smokejumper; former air delivery specialist, MR2, Laos

The Agency drew from college football players, smokejumpers, some Special Forces. But my analysis of why they used smokejumpers is because smokejumpers are not trained killers. Special Forces are trained to kill, and they do. We smokejumpers were more of an easy-goin'-type people, you know? It doesn't mean you *wouldn't* kill somebody to protect yourself. But it wasn't the way the Special Forces operated. I think that's one of the reasons why the CIA come to the smokejumpers.

The point is that we was there to support, not to kill, and the longer you was overseas and worked with the Thai and the Lao and the Hmong people, you become more sympathetic to them because it's kind of a primitive lifestyle and their losses were great. You felt like you were a part of 'em. You just kind of blended into their way of feelings. Like Daniels did. He just blended right in with the people.

KEITH "SKID" WOLFERMAN, smokejumper; friend of Deeder and Farrett Daniels

It really kind of pisses me off when people in the somewhat liberal university community of Missoula turn their noses up at the smokejumper connection with the CIA and Special Operations. Like there's something unseemly or dirty or underhanded about it. It bothers them, the fact that young men were, and still are, willing to go and do something for their government that might entail not being entirely forthright or open because of the security nature of the operation. They think you're trying to pull the wool over their eyes and hide something because it's wrong, whereas in reality, it's just part of the security measures.

I see it differently from them, so we agree to disagree. But I think I'm justified in feeling the way I do because I've taken the time and made the effort to read up on the people who did these types of operations for governmental agencies. When I was in the service in '85 to '88, before I started jumping, I got interested in "Pop" Buell going to Laos and the whole USAID thing. I'm interested in people like Jerry Daniels, "Pop" Buell, Hmong people, people from Southeast Asia in general, explorers, people with aviation backgrounds in the military who were doing civilian work with Evergreen and Air America. Even when I was a little kid, second grade, I read Lewis and Clark's journals. Those were not techno-wienie-GPS-laptop-computer-type people. They were doing it for *real*.

Then when I was a freshman in college at the University of Montana, I had an anthropology professor, Frank Bessac. I'm listening to this guy say, "When I was attached to the Chinese commando paratroop unit . . ." I'm like, *Whoa!* And then he started telling us that he had been in the hinterlands of western China when the communists took over in 1949. He hooked up with the American vice-consul and they made a seven-month trek over the Himalayas to Tibet to literally flee for their lives. That just blew me away. Now *there's* a guy that's cut from the same cloth as Jerry, as far as I was concerned. Just a little different timeframe. Kids now worship pro sports stars. I say, "Yeah, that guy makes 6 million a year for swingin' a bat. But *this* guy went and did *this*. How can it compare?"

Edgar "Pop" Buell (crouching) was an Indiana farmer who went to Laos and worked for USAID at Sam Thong, LS 20, not far from Long Cheng. Standing: Sergeant Sun (PARU), Captain Decha (PARU), and Jack Cahill (Air Ops, LS 36), 1965. Photo taken just after LS 58 was recaptured from enemy troops. Cahill and Daniels trained together as smokejumpers. Thomas "Shep" Johnson collection.

DEEDER DANIELS, nephew of Jerry Daniels; son of Kent Daniels

I see how Jerry got into it. He was just a guy, just the basic Montana kid lookin' for adventure, you know? "Smokejumpin'? Yeah, let's go!" So he hooks up with smoke-jumpin' and the next thing he hears is, "You're young and you're single and you're lookin' for adventure so. . . ." Don't come with us? No, I don't think so. So he goes over to kick rice in Laos, and the next thing you know here's a kid from a small, rural town in Montana and now he's talking to other people, Hmong people, from small, rural villages who he identifies with. It wasn't like he came from the big city and thought, *Oh, man, how am I going to fit in with these people?* It was, *Yep, I know right what's going on here.* So he just hung, and it was all a good thing for him.

Ms. CECELIA CHRISTENSEN (formerly Mrs. Jack Stratton), friend of Louise Daniels

Louise talked a little bit about how Jerry started working overseas and that she found it satisfying work. He was happy with it. When he realized he could do better there, get promotions and go different places, he came back to school and got his college degree. It was a career he liked. I think he liked somewhat the danger and the intrigue of the whole thing. And he had good friends that he worked with because a lot of smokejumpers from Missoula went to work over there about the same time.

KEITH "SKID" WOLFERMAN, smokejumper; friend of Deeder and Farrett Daniels

I've always felt a connection to the Daniels family. At a younger age there were times when Farrett and Deeder would stay with their Grandma Lou. I'd visit them and *they* were always the ones trying to drag *me* out of Louise's trailer because *I* was the one that wanted to talk to Louise about Jerry.

Just talking to Louise, visiting, you could tell there was something pretty special about the smokejumpers because Jerry had made really good friends, and stayed friends, with some of the jumpers he had jumped with before he went to Laos. The letters that Louise would get from his former jumper buddies, they were always real special to her. She'd show them to us and you could tell that there was something special about the relationship a jumper has with other jumpers. You could tell the friendships ran *way* deeper than just the superficial excitement part of what we do

Two CIA case officers at Long Cheng: Dick "Bamboo" Manns and Hog Daniels, 1973. James Glerum collection.

when we work together. It was a *lot* more than that. They had deep relationships with each other, and I would think even more so after they went overseas.

THOMAS J. "T. J." THOMPSON, former smokejumper; former air delivery specialist, MR2, Laos

We lost a lot of smokejumpers, predominantly in Laos. And there weren't a terrible lot of us anyway. We lost maybe fifteen to twenty of the jumpers. Some were guys that flew as kickers: Billy Hester, John Lewis, Darrell Eubanks. If you tally them up, I think we lost around 25 percent of our guys, so we're pretty well gone, that group of smokejumpers that worked in Laos.

Bag was a smokejumper. Hog was a smokejumper. Clean, Bamboo, and Kayak—those guys were military, Special Forces. They weren't smokejumpers, but once you live together like that in those valleys and you work together like that, under those conditions you become pretty damn close. You're friends for eternity.

The Lingo

T HE unique vocabulary of Jerry Daniels, including "huckleberry" and "ferrit hoag"; some favorite names and expres-
sions.

KEN HESSEL, former smokejumper; former Continental Air Services (CASI) Air Operations, MR3, Laos

Jerry spoke like the old mountain people. He called himself "this huckleberry" or said "this child" is gonna do this or that. He had a name for everybody. He started callin' somebody somethin' and pretty soon that's what everyone was callin' him. It's a language that's still around Missoula among some of the people he knew. That's just the way they talked. But he'd come up with some of the damnedest things you ever heard in your life. Just out of the clear blue. Jerry had a real quick mind.

JON FOLAND, Missoula crony; former smokejumper

I met Jerry when I hung out with General and the cronies in the early '70s. What everybody always noticed right off the bat about Jerry was his jargon. 'Cause he just can't lamp anything without lapsing into his jargon. Lamp means to look at. "Lamp that huckleberry, would ya?" means, "Look at that guy." And all the cronies used that same jargon. We'd get a lot of sideways looks from folks: "What the hell are they talking about?"

LEE "TERRIBLE TORGY" TORGRIMSON, grade school friend; Missoula crony

You'd have to know Jerry to know how he spoke. It made no sense except to a few others. There were only about ten of us who could communicate in the vocabulary and syntax that we used. I have good friends who still live in Missoula and who knew Jerry. They still ask me about certain words that we used and what they meant. So on a continuing basis, year after year, I find myself explaining words used by Jerry and me, General and Ringman, Mike Oehlerich, Brent Russell, Animal Man, and a few others. People still shake their heads about it. Oh, I love it!

Daniels on R and R in New Zealand, where he was joined by his good friend "General" Kurt Olsen, February 1975. Kurt Olsen collection.

KENT "DAN THE ANIMAL MAN" DANIELS, brother of Jerry Daniels

If something was big, it was "elephant." Jerry'd go on an elephant dry. Or if a guy wasn't very smart he had a "shrew wit." Those were Jerryisms. Some of the stuff he came up with was awesome. A word would come out of his mouth and that was it. Why? I don't know. Jerry was just great at naming different things, different people.

Jerry gave me the name "Animal Man." Some people think that means eat raw liver and Rocky Mountain oysters and some pretty animalistic-type things, but it doesn't. One time when we were both teenagers in high school, maybe fifteen and seventeen years old, he and I were rolling rocks down a mountainside. You get up on these hills, and if huntin' isn't any good, rocks are there to roll. There's no purpose to it, you just watch 'em break trees and things, goin' down through the brush.

That day the rock was about a four-feet-by-five-feet boulder. There was a little spot behind it where you could get to push it from behind. There wasn't room for two in that spot, only room for one, so Jerry got behind it and I got around in front of it. I put my arms up over the top of it and pulled it forward while he was pushing it. And when it started to go I had a heck of a time getting out of there. He reached around and grabbed my wrist and held on as the boulder went tumble-bumble down the hill. He kept me from getting ironed out by the big rock. Then Jerry started laughing and said, "God! You looked like an Animal Man peering around the corner clutching that rock!"

Ms. MYRA L. SHULTS, high school friend of Jerry Daniels

Jerry talked the lingo when we were in high school. You couldn't have a normal conversation with him. It was all lingo, all the language that that group of high school boys talked. Developing their language the way they did was a bonding thing for those boys, and it was a way to keep out not only girls but also keep out guys that they didn't want around. That group of guys were the only ones that used the lingo, and one of the best manifestations of it was the names that Jerry gave people. Anybody who was Jerry's friend back then, they still refer to each other by their nicknames. Jimmy Pramenko was Major-Domo. Larrae Rocheleau was the Liq, Liquid Larrae.

That group of boys had names for each other and also they used particular phrases that were different, like "ferrit hoag." I mean, who's ever heard of it before? Little kids were "ruggers." And women were "fair ones." Jerry could carry on a whole conversation and never say one word that you were familiar with. It was fascinating, and it took a great imagination to assign such terms to things and people and whatnot. No way anybody could interpret it unless they'd gone to Missoula County High School in the 1950s!

KENT "DAN THE ANIMAL MAN" DANIELS, brother of Jerry Daniels

In our day there wasn't much swearing. "Huckleberry" was used in place of a swear word because around Missoula we didn't use bad language in public or in mixed company. "Huckleberry" was a word Jerry used *a lot*.

Conversation between MIKE OEHLERICH, former smokejumper; former Air America loadmaster, Laos; and his wife, MRS. DAWN OEHLERICH

MIKE: Jerry had his own language, and it had whatever it was that appealed to people. He would be totally irreverent about things that you just didn't talk about. For example, "skin bubbles." Jerry was on a late fall crew that went to southern California in September 1959. There was a bad brush fire and a southern California fire crew got trapped, and some of them got burned. There was talk about how some of them were so burnt their skin was bubbled. That's how they described the texture of the burned-up crew. They had "skin bubbles."

The Forest Service personnel that were down there and associated with the firefighters took it really seriously. They were all sad and mopin' around this fire camp where Daniels and four or five other jumpers were. People had gotten burned up so they laid a big heavy on safety. There were endless safety talks, and that's probably what ticked off Daniels. He finally got fed up with all this mopin' around and all this dreary talk. He started talking this "skin bubble" talk. "Skin bubble" this and "skin" that. It was, "Pass the skin bubble butter," or "Give me a skin cigarette." Nothing was sacred to Daniels. Everything was held up to ridicule.

In 1960 Jerry and I met because we both ended up on a Forest Service work project in northern Idaho on the St. Joe Forest. Right away I could tell Jerry was a character. Orofino was the nearest town to St. Joe Ranger Station. We went to Orofino on the weekends because we were bored and wanted some excitement. Young and crazy and lookin' for something to do, and we both had that thirst for alcohol. We ended up at the cathouse in Orofino, naturally, and that was when I realized that Daniels and I were soul mates. Ha! I remember coming out of a room, and Daniels is coming out of a room and there's a good-lookin' gal that he'd been with. She's lightin' up this cigarette. She says, "Thanks for the skin cigarette." She was talking Daniels' skin talk! She had no idea.

That skin talk wasn't something that just passed on by in two weeks. The skin talk lasted for *years*. I mean, everywhere that Daniels went the English language changed. There was something about the way he twisted words and made their meaning a humorous sarcasm. There was something so colorful about his language that people immediately latched onto it. It was totally infectious. People picked up on it and started talkin' that way themselves. You could always tell if Daniels had been there because the whole vocabulary changed. Most people had no idea what the hell they were talking about, but it sounded good so they latched onto it. Only the *real* Daniels people knew the background stories of where it came from.

There were only a few of us guys that could talk it well and knew what it meant. Ferrit hoag, black, frog hides and toad skins, slipping on his moccasins. Hand-shoes were gloves. Yellow hands was anybody of Oriental descent. Like the Hmong guys that he worked with. He referred to them as yellow hands this, yellow hands that. I guess you could call that a racial slur in a politically correct world.

DAWN: But Jerry didn't mean that in a derogatory way when he used it. When he had the gold mine at Bayson, the placer claim, he was always talking about getting his crews of yellow hands up there and "slavin' 'em."

LARRY NELSEN, former smokejumper

Jerry had all that humor and charisma. The whole Daniels family had so much of that charisma that you loved every one of them. You wanted to be around them. You wanted to listen, to talk, to hear the stories.

GLENN F. HALE, former smokejumper; former Continental Air Services (CASI) Air Operations, MR3, Laos

Lots and lots of sayings that we all use now were attributed to Jerry. And down the years, whenever we would recite one of those sayings, we would give him credit. One of his favorite ones was: "It's all according to what you say you might say." Then we'd add: "'It's all according to what you say you might say.' Jerry Daniels, '60."

LAMONTE "CHRIS" CHRISTENSEN, former smokejumper

Jerry had an expression for when the guys would do a "rum run" from Silver City down to Las Palomas, a Mexican border town. You could buy alcohol there, and the U.S. Customs Service permitted you to bring back one gallon duty-free per person. So a car full of jumpers'd go the ninety miles down there and would bring back maybe six gallons of rum. We all liked the Cuba Libre, rum and Coke.

One day Jerry came in and said, "Chris, we ought to take your car and go down to Palomas and get some more of that H O." Everybody wondered, "What is H O?" Jerry said, "Oh, you know. On all those labels it says H O in Mexico." *Hecho en Mexico*, Made in Mexico. That's all he needed to remember: "Let's go get some H O."

JON FOLAND, Missoula crony; former smokejumper

One time Jerry and I headed to Fish Creek to go hunting. We wolfmanned up. That means you just go out in the woods and hunker there. We weren't having great success huntin' so I'd recount, "Yeah, up this ridge we got an elk and we got a deer over there." And he'd go, "God, the way you talk I might get my shirt tore just turnin' around here." "Get your shirt tore" was another favorite expression meaning to get injured. And "just turnin' around" is just bein' here. It's kind of hard to explain to somebody who wasn't around his jargon all the time, but if you heard it enough, it all made sense.

BOB JOHNSON, former Highland Section chief, JVA, Thailand; regional director, International Rescue Committee (IRC), Seattle

Jerry called that berry-flavored wine "bowl o' berries." Whiskey was "loudmouth." And it's pretty true. Too much whiskey makes a loudmouth. Beer was "nectar," and a bar was a "nectar parlor." "Pitutsie" was a woman.

DEEDER DANIELS, nephew of Jerry Daniels; son of Kent Daniels

A "nectar"—that was definitely a Jerry word. If you pick up *Webster's*, it's got words about two inches thick, eight and a half inches by eleven inches, full of words. Everybody can use them, but not everybody does. And Jerry'd grab a word and use it. And "nectar" is one that he used for what I call "swill." I go out swillin', and they'd go out and have a few nectars. Maybe the difference is the price! I always liked that one. It lent some class to gettin' drunk.

XUWICHA "NOI" HIRANPRUECK, best Thai friend of Jerry Daniels

Hog and I had a series of code names that we used for people. Mostly the people were important and the name meant something to us. We called Dan Arnold "the Specs" for wearing glasses and for his ability to project power through them. We called Hugh Tovar "the Matador" for his ability to survive the dangers coming at him from "Signora." Lionel Rosenblatt was "Blatman." On and on. Hog's language and vocabulary dominated the Laotian mountains and valleys and, at least for me, was the language of our Sky subculture.

MIKE LYNCH, former provincial advisor, Lima Site 36, Na Khang, Laos

When Jerry and I worked together at Site 36, voice radio communications between fixed bases in Laos and Udorn, Thailand, employed a crude voice code that changed monthly and substituted names of U.S. places and common objects for local locations and things. Once when Jerry was requesting support and supplies from Udorn, he discovered that he was missing a page of that month's code. He just went ahead and improvised. When rifle ammunition was "beans" and Jerry needed 105 howitzer ammo, he requested "a bunch of giant beans. You know, the really big ones." Lacking the code for helicopters he first tried "string beans," which was incorrect. When the guy on the other end asked for clarification Jerry said, "You know, just send me a couple of those whirling death pods." From then on, Jerry referred to helicopters in that fashion.

Excerpt from "Efficiency Report on Jerrold Daniels" by MICHAEL D. EILAND, U.S. Embassy Refugee Coordinator, Bangkok, Thailand, April 17, 1982

Personal Characteristics: Mr. Daniels conveys his thoughts both in speaking and writing in a direct and pithy manner. There are no misunderstandings. His quiet manner of speech rivets the listeners' attention. His writing is a model of brevity.

KENT "DAN THE ANIMAL MAN" DANIELS, brother of Jerry Daniels

In high school Jerry and his cronies came up with the term "fart hog." They didn't want to use that word "fart" in school, so they just rolled "fart hog" into "ferrit hoag." That became the name: ferrit hoag. That was a mythical animal that originated from fart hog. *Anything* could be called a ferrit hoag. If you see some movement in the trees, well, that might be a ferrit hoag out there. If you don't know what it is, if it doesn't have a name, it's a ferrit hoag.

DEEDER DANIELS, nephew of Jerry Daniels; son of Kent Daniels

For pretty much anybody in my family, I can listen to them talk and they'll throw something in there and I could interrupt them and say, "What the hell are you talking about? You just said *that* word for *that* thing?" But I know if I keep my mouth shut and listen, I'll understand *exactly* what they mean.

That name, Hog, is one of those things. In the early '70s, VP's kids plus Mouasu and Moua Cha were living here in Missoula. Jerry'd come along and I'd hear them say, "Hello, Mr. Hog!" So it was, "Okay, Jerry, what's up with *that*? How did you get *that* name?" At the time I asked him I was old enough to shoot a gun but too young to drive a car. In Montana that puts you between twelve and fifteen. So that's about how old I was. So this story is not word for word, but pretty much this is the story that Jerry told me. And everybody in my family knows the same story. It starts out that Jerry wanted to use Ferrit Hoag as his code name in Laos, but the radio operators said, "No, that's too long. You need a radio code name that's shorter. You can't say, 'Supercalifragilisticexpialidotius, over.' No. Ferrit Hoag is too long. Choose something else." He said, "Okay, just call me Hoag." But the Hmong radio operators couldn't pronounce Hoag; they said Hog. Jerry said, "Well, Hog sounds good to me." So after that he was just Hog.

TED O. "LITTLE O" LYMPUS, high school and college friend

Honest to gosh, I never heard Jerry called "Hog" in Montana. I never knew that he had that nickname until his funeral and they were referring to him as "Mr. Hog." All the time I knew him I'd never heard him called that.

"Visiting Day"

SUNDAY: An early-morning meeting at the funeral home; breakfast rituals on "visiting day" [*hnub qhua txws*]; American Sunday morning service with eulogies. Hmong visiting-day ceremony continues, including gifts of food and drink for the spirit of Jerry Daniels; spirit money [*hauv qhua* and *tshua ntawv vam sab*]; stories about gold and gold mining; moral instruction and blessings for prosperity [*foom kom*].

Conversation between "LUCKY" LUE YANG, former field liaison officer (FLO), MR2, Laos; Hmong funeral organizer, and his wife, Mrs. MARY V. YANG

LUCKY: On Sunday morning we met Louise at the funeral home before eight o'clock. It was me and Mary, Moua Cha, and Louise. We were going to open the casket early before the guests arrived. We had a crowbar and a hammer in hand, and we were going to pry it up for sure.

MARY: And Mom agreed with that. Louise agreed to let Lucky and Moua Cha open the casket because they were so upset. Lucky and Moua Cha and Louise agreed that they don't need many people to see that happen. Only the American funeral man was there. He came out of his office and Louise talked to him, but the funeral man disagreed. He said, "You can't do that." And then Mom fought with him, and he still said no.

LUCKY: He said, "No! You can't do it." We keep pushing him, "Well, why can't we?" He said the rules and regulations don't allow us to see that body because it was decomposed so badly.

MARY: Louise was the one that really argued with the funeral man. She said that Jerry was her son, and she wanted Lucky and Moua Cha to open it. Louise was really upset, and that is what she said she wanted. He went back to his office and looked at a note. Then he told Louise, "You stop! If you try to open it I will report it to the public health department." I heard that clearly with my own ears.

CHA MOUA (interjection): Based on the statement that accompanied the coffin, or maybe it was direct communication with the funeral home, someone had told the funeral director not to allow certain things. If we demand to open it, he must defend it and not let us do that.

LUCKY: In those days we were so new to the U.S. We did not know the regulations of this country. If nobody comes out to stop us we would have opened the casket that morning, but he said, "No, no! You can't. Public health will not allow you to do it." That's the final word that stopped us.

After that we said, "If we cannot open it, then let's measure it." I got a tape measure and we measured the casket. We asked Louise how tall Jerry was. The casket looked too short but it was longer than his height so we said, "Well, we have to accept it." That was our solution to make us feel a little bit comfortable.

MARY: It was still early in the morning when we went home. Later we came back and continued with the second day of the funeral ceremony.

KENT "DAN THE ANIMAL MAN" DANIELS, brother of Jerry Daniels

I never heard that Louise agreed to open the box. I know the Big Boys back east were very adamant about not opening it. But I can very much picture her doing that *for the Hmong.*

Mrs. NANCY J. DANIELS, wife of Jack Tupper Daniels; sister-in-law of Jerry Daniels

I remember distinctly being in Kent's house on Sunday morning. Louise was sitting on the couch between her grandsons, Deeder and Farrett. She kind of kept to herself. Then we went to the funeral home for the Sunday service.

JIM SCHILL, former USAID Laos Refugee Relief Program; former Department of State, Bureau for Refugee Programs

On Sunday I found out that some of the Hmong had planned to unseal the casket so they could be sure it was Jerry. Someone had the presence of mind to stop them, but many Hmong still doubted that it was Jerry in the casket and they wanted it opened.

RANDOLPH "TOBY" SCOTT, former smokejumper; former Continental Air Services (CASI) loadmaster, Laos

I know the Hmong really wanted to break into the casket. I was on their side. You betcha, I was. I told Louise, "Well, is anybody gonna open that thing?" "No. We can't do that." "Well, I believe I would, Louise." Then I told Jerry's brother Kent, "Boy, if I was you I'd take a crowbar and tear that damned thing open and check it out. Get an X-ray machine and get some samples of tissue. Make sure it's Jerry." The Hmong wanted to open that box up because, hell, they thought that might not even *be* Jerry.

"Visiting Day" [*Hnub Qhua Txws*], **the day before burial—when relatives and friends bring gifts for the deceased**

Sunday is the second day of the funeral for Jerry Daniels; this is "Visiting Day." All day there will be guests coming to visit him. Because of this, breakfast is fed to Jerry's spirit early in the morning. The breakfast song [*qeej tshais*] is played on the kheng and the matching poem-song [*nkauj*] is sung while the family ritualist [*txiv cuab tsav*], the man who knows the funeral rituals and is in charge of feeding the spirit, pours a drink of beer for Jerry. "Jerry, here is a drink for you. Come and take it!" The family ritualist drops the split bamboo pieces [*txhib ntawg*] on the little table to find out if Jerry's spirit accepts the drink. After three drinks are accepted, the family ritualist gives Jerry's spirit a breakfast of meat and rice.[1] "Jerry, here is your breakfast. Come and eat it!" After Jerry accepts the food and drink, the family ritualist wraps the breakfast meal in plastic and puts it on top of the dead rooster in the cardboard box. Each meal is securely wrapped so nothing will leak out or smell. All of Jerry's meals will go into the box until the funeral is over.

Right after Jerry's spirit is served breakfast, he is served lunch. A kheng player plays the lunch song [*qeej su*], the lunch poem is sung, and the same process is followed using the split bamboo pieces. At the same time the family ritualist feeds Jerry's spirit, the young people do ritual bowing [*xyom*] to show their respect. They bow when the kheng plays the eating songs for breakfast, lunch, and dinner.

At nine o'clock in the morning Jerry's American friends and the U.S. government representatives start to arrive. After they come in, there is a break in the Hmong ceremony to make time for the American Sunday service.

THOMAS J. "T. J." THOMPSON, former smokejumper; former air delivery specialist, MR2, Laos

VP walked into the funeral home and he was talkin', shakin' hands with people all the way to the front. He sat down in an honored place.

JIM SCHILL, former USAID Laos Refugee Relief Program; former Department of State, Bureau for Refugee Programs

Maybe 130 people were present at the mortuary. Many Hmong men and women were there that morning, even children. VP and the other Hmong speakers handled themselves in outstanding fashion, speaking about the help Jerry had always given them and how he would never be forgotten. VP was stoic. He was the general, always the leader of the people. He maintained a composure that he had built up over many years.

CHU VANG, son of General Vang Pao

On Sunday morning people gave speeches at the funeral home. My dad talked. Louise, Jerry's mom, talked. She said thank you to everybody and showed her appreciation for what the Hmong people had done and how her son dedicated himself to the Hmong people. When he was alive he told his mom that he loved the Hmong, that he wanted to be with the Hmong and die with the Hmong. She said, "Jerry would be very proud of what you have done for him here."

Louise Daniels and Tsucheng Vang (Sing Vang). Vang worked with Hog Daniels as a forward air guide (FAG), LS 20A, Laos, 1971–75. Daniels family collection. Used with permission.

JIM SCHILL, former USAID Laos Refugee Relief Program; former Department of State, Bureau for Refugee Programs

That morning I was out of it. Most of us were. I was still drunk when I got up to read the eulogy on behalf of the State Department. And when I looked out at all the Hmong and Americans at the ceremony I simply had trouble saying anything. What

I was thinking was: *Most of the Americans here today just don't get it. They have never seen where we have been and what we have done.* A lot of people there didn't like us. We'd been too closely aligned with the CIA.

I started to read the eulogy but then I began to cry; I couldn't hold it back. Bob Johnson had to finish reading it for me. It was a tough morning.

Excerpts from "EULOGY—JERROLD B. DANIELS," Department of State, Washington, DC

Eulogizing Jerry Daniels is not easy. Not only would Jerry object to hearing himself praised, he would surely take exception to the conventional style because Jerry was one of the great raconteurs—or spinners of yarns—as he would say.

I would like to tell you a little about what Jerry did over there in the refugee camps in Thailand for the last seven years. In the early days in Udorn, Thailand, Jerry operated out of a VW van. He and a colleague used to make rounds through the refugee camps. Their files were in cardboard beer boxes and suitcases. His presence reassured the Hmong and he pleaded their cause with the U.S. and Thai authorities.

Jerry spent most of his time up-country: traveling dusty, bumpy roads, negotiated in taxis without shocks; staying in fleabag hotels, riding overnight trains. Nobody logged more miles, more days up-country in the refugee field than Jerry. Cabdrivers and trainmen, refugees and Thai officials and villagers knew him all along the circuit in North and Northeast Thailand, a country as big and as rugged as his Montana home. To those in the refugee field his exploits were already legendary.

The bottom line in all this was quite simple: the Hmong knew that Jerry stayed with them and took heart from this. Jerry was a one-man symbol to the Hmong of a relationship with the United States going back to the early 1960s.

Jerry leaves us more than his formidable accomplishments. He leaves us with inspiration to journey on. To rededicate ourselves to the task of caring for the Indochinese refugees and keeping faith with the Hmong people who have given us so much.

Excerpts from DEPARTMENT OF STATE cable from U.S. Ambassador John Gunther Dean, Bangkok, Thailand, May 6, 1982, read by John W. Tucker

FM AMEMBASSY BANGKOK
TO SECSTATE WASHDC IMMEDIATE 8124
UNCLAS BANGKOK 24864
DEPT FOR RP
SUBJ: EXPRESSION OF CONDOLENCE
QUOTE. ON BEHALF OF THE MEMBERS OF THE U.S. MISSION IN BANGKOK, I WOULD LIKE TO EXPRESS HEARTFELT CONDOLENCES TO ALL OF THE FAMILY AND FRIENDS OF JERRY DANIELS. HIS UNTIMELY PASSING HAS DEPRIVED US OF POSSIBLY THE SINGLE MOST KNOWLEDGEABLE AND EXPERIENCED PERSON AVAILABLE IN LAO AND HILLTRIBE MATTERS, AND DEPRIVED THE REFUGEES FROM LAOS OF THEIR

MOST HONEST FRIEND AND ADVISOR. IN HIS QUIET BUT DETERMINED WAY HE ACQUIRED A STORE OF EXPERIENCE AND CREDIBILITY UNEXCELLED IN HIS FIELD. HIS VALUE TO THE REFUGEE PROGRAM AND TO THE U.S. GOVERNMENT IN GENERAL WAS INESTIMABLE.

IN HUMAN TERMS, PERHAPS HIS GREATEST CONTRIBUTION WAS TO THE HILLTRIBE PEOPLE WITH WHOM HE SHARED SUCH PROFOUND MUTUAL AFFECTION. HE UNDERSTOOD THEM AS FEW OTHERS EVER HAVE; THEY TRUSTED HIM AS THEY COULD HAVE TRUSTED NO ONE ELSE. IN THE HILLTRIBE REFUGEE CAMPS OF THAILAND THERE HAS LONG BEEN A WELL-USED PHRASE: "JERRY NEVER LIES." THE LOSS OF JERRY DANIELS WILL BE FELT BY US ALL, BUT NOWHERE OUTSIDE HIS FAMILY WILL IT BE FELT MORE PROFOUNDLY THAN AMONG THE REFUGEE PEOPLE FROM LAOS. SIMPLY STATED, HUNDREDS OF PEOPLE FROM LAOS OWE THEIR VERY LIVES TO HIM, AND THOUSANDS OWE THEIR CURRENT AND FUTURE WELL-BEING TO HIM. WE WILL ALL MISS HIM. WE WERE ALL PRIVILEGED THAT HE SERVED WITH US. END QUOTE. [U.S. AMBASSADOR] DEAN

Mrs. JULIE DANIELS MORITZ, sister-in-law of Jerry Daniels

At the funeral, all those speakers from Washington are getting up and having their say, which, being that we *are* Montanans, nobody's going to believe anything they've got to say anyhow. Even if we know it's true.

RANDOLPH "TOBY" SCOTT, former smokejumper; former Continental Air Services (CASI) loadmaster, Laos

Of course the CIA had their speaker, J. R. Randall. He did a pretty good job talkin' about Jerry, but he didn't tell anybody a damned thing. He didn't answer any questions. Just left everything up in the air. You can't blame anybody for wondering what the hell happened, the way they handled it. I'm not workin' for the CIA anymore, so I don't give a damn what they think. I tell it pretty much how I see it. None of them told us a damn thing. Big mystery, you know.

BOB JOHNSON, former Highland Section chief, JVA, Thailand; regional director, International Rescue Committee (IRC), Seattle

There was one guy that flew in from DC as the official representative of the Agency as opposed to "the guys" who were spooks that had worked with Jerry. It was kind of a two-part trip for the Agency guy. He flew in for Jerry's funeral, and also he talked to Vang Pao because all of the Hmong leaders were there. There was a session *during* the events at the funeral home in which the Agency rep said this was not the time to be refueling the Back To Laos movement. Because that was one of the rumors—that Jerry wasn't in the casket, that he was leading the rebellion. The Agency guy wanted to make it clear that Jerry's not leading the rebellion; he's not back in Laos; he's dead.

TOU-FU VANG, former lieutenant colonel, Royal Lao Army (FAR), Laos

I was not at the meeting when Jon Randall told VP to forget about returning to Laos. But even when Jon said that, it was not up to Jon. It was up to the Laotian politicians and leaders in France and the U.S. because the Laotian leadership all over the free world was involved in the resistance movement. As the survivors, they cannot rest because so many people are looking to them for guidance. Even if the Agency or the U.S. government says, "We cannot support you, you need to give it up," General Vang Pao has a higher commander. After we lost Laos in 1975, the acting king in exile was living in France. That was Chao Boun Oum. In his own handwriting, Chao Boun Oum wrote a letter to General Vang Pao and charged him personally with the duty to take back the country of Laos.

General Vang Pao would not say that openly to Jon Randall, but the general's mind was *always* on how to take back the country. Not only because he loves his country, but because he has that *role,* that *honor.* Only once in a lifetime the king gives you such an order.

JIM SCHILL, former USAID Laos Refugee Relief Program; former Department of State, Bureau for Refugee Programs

Just before noon the formal words were finished. The burial would take place the next morning. During the rest of Sunday and into Sunday night, the Hmong would be staying at the mortuary, continuing to perform their traditional rites to make sure that Jerry moved into the spirit world in the proper way. I had a flight to catch back to Washington, DC, that afternoon. I said good-bye, wishing everyone the best. It was the last time I saw most of them.

MOUASU BLIAYA, Hmong friend of the Daniels family

On Sunday afternoon most of the Hmong remained at the funeral home after the Americans left. All but one American CIA that came and stayed with the casket. He didn't say much and he didn't mingle with people, but my impression was that he was making sure the casket was not opened. He was there all the time.

BOB CLIFFORD, funeral director

As one of the funeral directors, I do recall that throughout the whole funeral there was somebody from the U.S. government who stood guard by the casket so it wouldn't be opened. Although there may have been several of them that took turns.

MOUASU BLIAYA, Hmong friend of the Daniels family

Sunday afternoon was a typical noisy Hmong funeral with lots of commotion, pretty much packed with Hmong people. At the funeral home, most of the time I was with

Mrs. Xia Thao Vang, Louise Daniels, Neng Vue, and General Vang Pao at the mortuary during the funeral of Jerry Daniels. "Lucky" Lue Yang collection.

Louise. Just staying by her side, being with her. I told Louise that many people wanted to open the casket: "Why don't we just open it and really find out if there is a body in there or not?" She said, "No, I don't want to see his body in that rotten condition. I just want to remember my Jerry the way he was." To me, it seemed she was not doing too good.

Ms. CECELIA CHRISTENSEN (formerly Mrs. Jack Stratton), friend of Louise Daniels

That Sunday was Mother's Day. Can you imagine having your child's funeral on Mother's Day?

Mrs. JULIE DANIELS MORITZ, sister-in-law of Jerry Daniels

I'll tell ya! The whole funeral was unbelievable to me. There were a lot of local people that came to that Sunday service that had no idea of even what a Hmong was! The Hmong hadn't really been in Missoula all that long. But I think most of the local people who came to Jerry's funeral were fascinated by what the Hmong did that day after the Sunday service was over.

In Montana we're used to everybody doing their own thing at a funeral. And this was *really* somebody's own thing! And because I'm so nosey everybody'd say to me,

"Well, what is that? What are they doing? Why are they playing that pipe thing? What about the drum?" As if I knew. Oh, the locals were interested in that Hmong ceremony! Now in *this* day and age, if it happened *now*, there's enough interested people here in town that somebody would have the story and pictures in the *Missoulian* the next day.

JON FOLAND, Missoula crony; former smokejumper

The cronies and I stopped by at that funeral on all three days. It was a large funeral home and they must have had three hundred Hmong in there. And the drummin'! It was *loud* and it was constant. They were wailin' and bangin' on that drum and blowin' those pipes.

A lot of other cronies blew into town that day. People from all over the country. And a lot of people that Jerry had worked with were *trying* to be there so they were calling constantly. Calling to talk to Toby and T.J. and Hog's Company connections.

Mrs. KATHY G. OLSEN, wife of Loy "Ringman" Olsen

We went for two or three hours each day. I thought Jerry must have gained so much respect from those people for them to do this for him. He helped them so they weren't left dangling.

LOY "RINGMAN" OLSEN, Missoula crony; brother of Kurt "General" Olsen

Yeah, for sending a guy off, he had a lot of friends. He had a good send-off.

HMONG CEREMONY CONTINUED

This is visiting day. For Hmong funerals held in an American funeral home, before the funeral starts a sturdy frame of two-by-fours is built to create two upright posts with a crossbeam. The frame looks similar to the letter "H," about five to six feet tall,[2] with nails pounded in a row across the front of the crossbeam. This kind of frame was built for Jerry in order to hold the long bundles of spirit money.

On visiting day, close family relatives bring gifts of food and drink.[3] For Jerry the food and drink are omitted, but the family ritualist, Kia Moua Thao, brings him a gift of spirit money.[4] Spirit money is made from folded and cut papers that hang down in a long bunch [*tshua ntawv*]. Spirit money will be useful to Jerry when he is up-in-the-sky. He can use it to pay any debts, he can give it away, or he can go shopping with it.[5]

Today the kheng player blows general funeral songs[6] while gifts of spirit money are introduced to Jerry. Because Jerry is not married and does not have a Hmong family, his ceremony is simplified to gifts of money from only his closest Hmong friends and his immediate family. The largest bundle of spirit money [*tshua ntawv*

Bundles of spirit money hang from a wooden frame. These bundles are received on visiting day as gifts for the spirit of the deceased to use on his way to rejoin the ancestors. Photo credit: Gayle L. Morrison.

vam sab] is the gift from Cha Moua because he acts as the immediate family [*xyom cuab*].[7] Tomorrow, the day of burial, all of the spirit money will be taken outside and burned.

Mrs. JULIE DANIELS MORITZ, sister-in-law of Jerry Daniels

I think the main thing for the local people that stayed around on Sunday afternoon, they were *really* fascinated by the fact that the Hmong were going to burn all this paper stuff the next morning. Those papers were like money, and it was all just for this one person, Jerry.

JOHN R. GREENWAY, former Air America pilot, Laos

Money? Ha! If you want to talk about Jerry and money, let me tell you a story about Jerry and *gold*. This was in the spring of '74. Jerry came into the Sky mess hall in Long Cheng. He had a little canvas bag and he said, "John, you're going on leave.

Could you take these rocks and find out what they are? They're awfully heavy and they're sort of strange." Jerry dropped the rocks on the table. He'd picked up quite a bit of it, a good sampling. They were dark green with very miniscule shiny flecks in them. But the extraordinary thing was the considerable weight. I said, "Sure, I'll take them."

I took the rock to Lausch Test Labs in Seattle. They assayed this material, and it assayed out at 1.1 ounces of gold per ton. Oh my, that's a high gold content! More than double anything in Alaska or the rest of the U.S.! Also there was 0.58 ounces of silver, and the rest was iron. When I got that assay report I called Bethlehem Steel and I talked to their exploration department. I said, "Would you guys be interested in something like this?" They said, "My God! Where is it?" I said, "I'm sorry but you won't be able to get to it at this time. Not for at least a quarter of a century."

Conversation between TIM "WEENY MAN" LIEN, RANDALL "PETERBILT" OLSEN, and LOY "RINGMAN" OLSEN, Missoula cronies

WEENY MAN: Jerry talked about gold a lot. He had his gold mine and also he talked about how he had access to a little gold in Southeast Asia. It wasn't ounces or nuggets. It was bars. Ha!

PETERBILT: We always accused him and Vang Pao of loadin' up an airplane and bringin' it back full of gold bars. He'd just grin and say, "Aw, we couldn't get away with that."

RINGMAN: When Jerry talked about gold that's how he mentioned it—gold bars. And he did have gold. I saw a bunch of Krugerrands once. A bunch of 'em.

BOB JOHNSON, former Highland Section chief, JVA, Thailand; regional director, International Rescue Committee (IRC), Seattle

During the years that Jerry spent in Laos, he'd put some of his savings into gold currency. Buying Krugerrands or Canadian Maple Leafs was a pretty convenient way to set money aside. He was saving that for the big rainy day. But he always wanted to get back to being a Montana cowboy and do some gold digging. The gold mine plan, that was his big thing.

Excerpt from a letter to JACK DANIELS from Jerry Daniels, August 23, 1980

Jack,

. . . I am not certain as to where I proceed from here regards the Barker mine. I have ordered five booklets that describe various gold extracting methods. All relatively inexpensive and not a complex operation. First I'll want to review such methods more closely and determine if feasible. I would figure that heavy machinery is a must, specifically something along the lines of a front end loader with backhoe. (Realize must also keep in mind the dreaded environmental impact laws.) I am still on detail here until mid-81 . . . . Depending on the circumstances at that time, I may then "retire" from U.S. Govt., and become a gold baron. . . .

Jerry

BOB JOHNSON, former Highland Section chief, JVA, Thailand; regional director, International Rescue Committee (IRC), Seattle

Jerry had talked about the gold mine deal when we were working together in Thailand. After I got back to Seattle in December 1980, we were in contact by letter. He was looking for some gold-sluicing equipment. I sent him a catalog and got a note back saying he was visualizing how he was going to set it up. Oh, we all had pipe dreams in Thailand! It was probably a big stretch of the imagination. Sitting in 105-degree weather in Bangkok and figuring out what you're going to do with a sluice in the middle of nowhere, Montana.

THOMAS C. "SHEP" JOHNSON, former smokejumper; former air delivery specialist, MR2, Laos

On his last home leave in 1981 Jerry wanted to show me his gold mine, a placer[8] claim up by Butte, so Animal Man and Jerry and I went up there. There was a sluice

Area near gold mine property owned by Jerry Daniels. Daniels family collection. Used with permission.

box set up, and they'd separate out the gold bits, the flakes. I had a backhoe. We figured out a deal where I was goin' to load my backhoe on my hay truck, go up there and we'd start really diggin' for gold. Jerry said he was considerin' leavin the Agency because he had this land and he wanted to get back to it.

The next morning I had to fly back to Boise. Jerry'd given me some rocks from his mine, and I had them in my pocket. When I went through the metal detector the alarm went off so I got ahold of Jerry on the phone. I said, "Get out here, Jerry. I think I've got a pocket full of gold!"

Of course our plan to dig for gold never did materialize. It never come out because Jerry went back with the refugee program.

Excerpt from a letter to THOMAS C. "SHEP" JOHNSON from Jerry Daniels, February 14, 1982

. . . Regards gold mine—in sum looks very good, but have decided to hold further investigation until I can oversee—est. summer of 83.

HMONG CEREMONY CONTINUED

On "visiting day," all afternoon Hmong friends and acquaintances come and cry [*nyiav*] over the coffin.[9] It is a bittersweet day—sad because the Hmong have lost their best friend, Mr. Jerry "Hog" Daniels, but also happy because this is a rare opportunity to meet old friends who have come from other parts of the country. At the funeral home there is a lot of talking going on as family and friends catch up with one another.

All afternoon the kheng and drum play on. There are so many different funeral songs for them to play.[10] In the early evening a kheng player plays the dinner song [*qeej hmo*] and the poem singer repeats it. Jerry's spirit is fed, then the guests eat. For the rest of the evening until closing time, the room is full of Hmong people who sit, talk, speculate about Jerry's death, visit the casket, then sit and talk some more.

For traditional Hmong funerals, there is a standard process of activities that takes place on the last night before a burial. First, a thank-you table[11] is set up. In Jerry's case there is no thank-you table because he is not the member of only one family. He belongs to the entire Hmong community so no helper is thanked individually. After the thank-you table is the discussion table [*hais xim*][12] that is for family business. If Jerry had married a Hmong girl and had a family, the discussion table would be done at his funeral because his wife's family would say, "Jerry passed away. What has he left for my daughter?" But Jerry was a single man when he died, so whatever he gives anyone—his money, his property—that's his business and that is left up to Louise and her sons. After the discussion table is "moral instruction and blessings for prosperity" [*foom kom*].[13] The discussion table and the instruction and blessings include talking, singing, and ritual bowing that often go on all night long.

CHA MOUA, Hmong friend; Hmong funeral organizer

There were some parts of the traditional Hmong funeral that we did not include for Jerry. For him, we did not set up a thank-you table or the discussion table, and we did not do the first three sections of the moral instruction and blessings because Jerry was a single man. But that evening we did perform the fourth section for him. For that section, the moral messenger [*txiv coj xai*] delivered some words from us to Jerry's spirit: "Jerry, you have been helping us for so long and you have been so good to our people. Today we come here to respect you. We wish you to have a better life and to accomplish whatever you want to accomplish."

In the fourth section the messenger sings that we pray for Jerry's spirit and we notify the natural spirits around the world that this is a good man. In Laos when we were serving the CIA, all of Military Region 2 was looking to Jerry. Whatever problem, big or small: "Hey, Jerry! What should we do?" When he could not make a decision he always made calls to find a solution. In the fourth section we Hmong ask his spirit to continue to help the Hmong people, to guide our lives to a better future because we count on him just like a director to run the Hmong future. That is why we make an urgent request to the spirit world for him to become very powerful. We want to promote him to live *better* than how he lived on earth in this life, and we want his spirit to have the power that he deserves in the spiritual world. When Jerry becomes a big shot in the spirit world, he will have the power to come back to earth and help us again, just like he did in Laos. The spirit world does listen to the human voice of the moral messenger. After the messenger delivered our words to Jerry, Jerry gave us a good reply: "My friends, I worked with you for so long. You helped me and were good to me. Wherever you go I will still look back and watch over you. If you need help you can call me, and I will help you."

That fourth section was the communication from both sides that tied together the relationship between the Hmong and Jerry in a spiritual way. During the fourth section a group did the ritual bowing when those words were received. Usually it is just the young people, but for Jerry, many different people wanted to bow and show their respect. Many were officers and soldiers who worked with him in Laos. Others knew him when he interviewed them in Thailand. Those people kneel down and touch their heads to the floor while the messenger sings blessings from Jerry to the people who are bowing.

For Jerry, the instruction and blessings took about one and a half hours to complete. That was the last thing we did on Sunday night because the funeral home said we had to close the program at ten o'clock PM.

End of funeral day two

Marana

SUNDAY evening: smokejumpers gather at the Oxford Saloon. The establishment of Intermountain Aviation at Marana Airpark, Arizona; research and development for CIA's covert air operations overseas; Skyhook and CIA's "Operation Coldfeet"; social outings. Jerry Daniels and Toby Scott leave Intermountain; fifty-eight days of fishing and hunting in Montana.

KEN HESSEL, former smokejumper; former Continental Air Services (CASI) Air Operations, MR3, Laos

The Hmong had a big thing goin' on, a wake. They kind of stayed in their own group over there at the funeral home. We hit that occasionally. We'd go over and visit for a little while and then we'd go back to the Ox. And that's where a lot of it happened. Sittin' around down there at the Ox. That was mostly jumpers, but a select few of those guys from Washington went down there with us. One of the topics we got to talkin' about was Marana.

THOMAS J. "T. J." THOMPSON, former smokejumper; former air delivery specialist, MR2, Laos

I knew Jerry even before Marana. I first met Jerry in '59 smokejumpin' after I got out of the army. We worked together as smokejumpers in '59 and '60. In late '60 the Agency came out to the smokejumper bases in Missoula and McCall to recruit people. Well, we just got damned good recommendations by the smokejumper foremen. There's no way around that. Several of us were hired. The way it worked, we were relieved from the Forest Service to go with the Outfit, the Agency. And in '62 Jerry and I met up again when we went to work for Gar at Marana Airpark. We already knew Gar. He'd been a smokejumper for the Forest Service before he set up Intermountain.

Do you know about Marana? Marana is a small town in Arizona, about thirty miles out of Tucson. At the end of World War II and during the Korean War, Marana Airpark was an air force facility used to train pilots. Then in late '61 it was established as an Agency proprietary under the name Intermountain Aviation. Gar Thorsrud was the president, and it was his child, his son. He developed it, he organized it, he ran it rough, ran it hard, ran it good. Gar's a hard charger and sometimes that got him

Jerry Daniels and T. J. Thompson at Intermountain Aviation, Marana, Arizona, 1962. T. J. Thompson collection.

some bad press, but the end product, he did one hell of a great job. Gar was a kingpin leader, and in those early years he was all over—Laos, Thailand. He had a major role as the chief of air ops in the Bay of Pigs. Intermountain was Gar's child, and it was a great organization. The things we developed at Intermountain we're still using today.

GLENN F. HALE, former smokejumper; former Continental Air Services (CASI) Air Operations, MR3, Laos

The Agency really is an entity that whatever is happening in the world, that's what they're interested in. If you are a whatever-you-are and they have something going in the world and they need someone like that, then they'd be interested in you. Because we were smokejumpers and our training was with airplanes and cargo, they were interested in us. But mostly I think the jumpers were useful because of a can-do attitude. Most of the people in our group at Intermountain were ex-military, airborne or smokejumpers.

Intermountain Aviation was started by the Agency to train pilots and develop cargo systems for different types of airplanes that would have the capability of clandestine missions. As the Vietnam War heated up there was a demand for Intermountain's services in Laos, and Intermountain got into it heavily. The Agency's clandestine side of Intermountain became part of the secret war in Laos; we supported U.S. interests in Laos and Vietnam from the Lao side of the border.

ROBERT H. NICOL, former smokejumper and pilot

I went down to Marana in January '62 to help get the parachute loft set up and licensed by the FAA. I was one of the few people with a master rigger certificate who was available to go. When I got down there, the parachute tower was under construction and the loft was just a big empty building. Jerry and I had to help make the parachute packing tables—four of 'em, forty-five feet long by forty inches wide.

MIKE OEHLERICH, former smokejumper; former Air America loadmaster, Laos

See, there was a legitimate side of the Marana base that hired legitimate employees for Intermountain Aviation. Those guys did base maintenance, were mechanics, rebuilt planes. Intermountain had legitimate commercial aviation projects, like parachute testing for the Forest Service.

And then there were the loft people who worked on the spook side of things. I worked in the loft as a kicker and on development of delivery systems for dropping cargo. We were developing stuff to be used in Southeast Asia. A lot of times we would leave Marana to go work somewhere overseas for a month or two—Africa, Laos, India, Central or South America—then we'd come back and be rehired. We could do that because Intermountain was CIA.

THOMAS C. "SHEP" JOHNSON, former smokejumper; former air delivery specialist, MR2, Laos

Intermountain had both overt employees, and coverts with Intermountain as the cover. On the overt side of it, there were "unwitting"[1] employees that did various things. Maybe fly a C-46 load of chickens down to Mexico or somethin', you know? It was regular contract work, and they thought the parachute loft was regular research and development of aerial delivery. Truth was, the loft was the covert side where we did special R and D for the Agency.

THOMAS J. "T. J." THOMPSON, former smokejumper; former air delivery specialist, MR2, Laos

We were all working for Gar under the proprietary, Intermountain. The local people around Marana didn't care who we were or what we were doing. They didn't even know what "CIA" meant. Maybe some of them did, but this is true: one woman said

286 ll Hog's Exit

to me, "Yeah, I seen in the paper that you all work for Interstate Commerce." I said, "Right." For us, it was always the tune: "Ah, yes, we have no Maranas!"

RANDOLPH "TOBY" SCOTT, former smokejumper; former Continental Air Services (CASI) loadmaster, Laos

In January 1962 it was almost the end of the semester at Texas A&M when I got a call from the smokejumper boss at Idaho City. He asked if I'd be interested in comin' down to Marana and goin' to work for Intermountain Aviation. Well, I was about broke so I said, "Yeah, I probably would." I got down there in February '62 and I hadn't been there but about a month when Jerry showed up. He'd been overseas to Thailand and Laos already.

Back then, we were young and some say we worked for the CIA for the money, but hell, it wasn't just for the money. We didn't make that much money! We figured we were really doin' something for our country, and we worked with a great bunch of people.

GLENN F. HALE, former smokejumper; former Continental Air Services (CASI) Air Operations, MR3, Laos

For me, Marana was all about money. With Intermountain you had a full-time job and they paid well. It paid a *lot* more than smokejumping did. That in and of itself was a draw.

Of 200 or 300 people that worked at Marana, only a few were Agency employees: administrators and their staff, mechanics, pilots, and the rigger-rows. Rigger-rows were the parachute riggers. If you worked in the loft you were a rigger-row. That's a Marana word; it's not part of parachute rigger school terminology. The rigger-row name probably came from the fact that each morning when we reported for work we would sit on a packing table, all in a row, and wait for our work assignments. So we became "rigger-rows," the strange paramilitary group that worked in the loft and the rigging shed. We were a small but important section of that base. At any one time, out of maybe thirty rigger-rows, about fifteen would be manning the loft and fifteen would be working out of the country on TDY [temporary duty].

The way Intermountain was set up, Gar had two or three lieutenants and at least one Agency person in finance in the headquarters. There might be eight people in there who were "witting" and the rest of the staff was "unwitting." It was the same way down on the runway. And the unwitting staff just couldn't understand why we'd just come and go.

What happened was, the Agency would have certain requirements that they would send to us. For example, we would get an airplane and it was up to the rigger-rows to develop the drop system for that airplane. We'd design it, design the pallets and everything, the metal shop would make the roller conveyors, and then we would test all of those things. How much the airplane could hold, the weight balance, and all that. Then we'd develop a manual for that airplane. So every airplane that came in there, our job was to develop the drop system and write manuals on it. Then we'd send the airplane out with the conveyors already in it. It could go anywhere in the world, but in those years probably it would go to Laos. One of us rigger-rows would go along on a TDY assignment for training of this equipment. Then we'd come back to Intermountain until another assignment came in. At Marana we were kind of in a holding pool, waiting for Agency assignments to Laos, India, South America, Alaska, Tibet.

THOMAS C. "SHEP" JOHNSON, former smokejumper; former air delivery specialist, MR2, Laos

After we hired on with the Agency, well, we'd be paid either less or more what the Agency pay scale was. We called it "funny money." Once a month there at Marana, they'd call us out of the parachute loft one at a time by name and we'd go over and get our "funny money." "Awright Jerry, you're wanted over at headquarters." Jerry'd come back. "Awright, T.J. . . ." Then T.J.'d tell the next guy in line, whoever it was, "Go on over and get your 'funny money.'" That was money under the table. Just for the ones that were contract CIA or CIA permanent employees.

TED O. "LITTLE O" LYMPUS, high school and college friend

Jerry and I went to visit Marana in 1964 during spring break when we were both students at the University of Montana. When we got there, what I saw them doing was experimenting with delayed-opening parachutes so they could fly over an area high enough that they weren't so susceptible to small-arms ground fire while they kicked cargo out of the planes—food supplies, medical supplies, armaments. Jerry told stories about how sometimes the people on the ground in Laos were waiting to gather up the supplies, but then they were getting hit by cargo drops when the parachutes didn't open right. It was risky business in Laos.

At Marana they were working, doing their thing. I saw them practicing, doing drops, planes coming and going. I knew they were doing something for Laos. I guessed it was part of the CIA because at that time the official policy of the United States government was that there were no Americans in Laos. Period.

RANDOLPH "TOBY" SCOTT, former smokejumper; former Continental Air Services (CASI) loadmaster, Laos

At Marana we tested all kinds of equipment, parachutes, different things. Most of the time they kind of let us have our head. If someone come up with a good idea we'd work on it. Hell, we used dynamite fuses and everything else to open up the parachutes. We had some of the damnedest things you ever saw.

KEN HESSEL, former smokejumper; former Continental Air Services (CASI) Air Operations, MR3, Laos

You know, all day we rigged and did a lot of testing of parachutes and equipment. Droppin' bundles and pickin' them up. Takin' them up to the loft, re-riggin' 'em, droppin' 'em again. You'd bust your butt all day in 120-degree heat out on that drop zone. You're thinking, *Boy, as soon as this work's over I'm headed for the sack tonight. I'm not goin' to the bar.* It hits five o'clock and everybody, of course, heads for the bars—in particular the Roadrunner Tavern, which was within walking distance because it was on the base.

MIKE OEHLERICH, former smokejumper; former Air America loadmaster, Laos

It got boring hanging out in the bar every night with the same guys, people drinking too much—which we did our fair share of, but it just got tiresome. We needed something else to do. So Kirk Samsel and I started flyin' in the evening after work.

This one particular day, I can't remember who was flying with me in my Air Knocker [7AC Aeronca Champ], but Daniels was with Kirk in his Piper Cub. That day we flew in tandem from Marana to Lordsburg. Then we started flyin' around town more or less at random. There was an ex-smokejumper who lived there, Greg Whipple. We were circling the town to see if we could spot his pickup. By now it was gettin' dark and you couldn't see too well. I don't want Kirk runnin' into me so I'm looking around and I can't find Kirk and Daniels. The next thing I see, there's a grain elevator in town, and Kirk's right above the grain elevator doin' a loop. Him and Daniels are in there together. Those planes just had sixty-five horsepower Continental engines in them. You couldn't pull it all the way around unless you got a hell of a run at it. Anyway, at least I found them, but when he came out of that loop he was below the grain tower. So we're doing a bunch of antics over town and we're only 150 feet off the rooftops. It was dusk when we land at the airstrip at Lordsburg. Greg picked us up, and we spent the night there.

The air was nice and calm in the morning, and we got up really early. We had to get back to Marana to get to work in time. Kirk took off just as the sun was comin' up on the horizon. After about three minutes Kirk gets bored so he turns the controls over to Daniels and says, "Just keep the wings level and keep it at this altitude." Daniels has never flown one of these airplanes before, but Daniels does that and Kirk just goes to sleep. That plane only goes sixty-five miles an hour, so Daniels is cruising along. As it burns off gas, the plane loses weight in the nose 'cause the fuel tank is right in front of the cockpit. Daniels has been flyin' for like ninety minutes. He figures he's gettin' close to Marana so he taps ol' Kirk and wakes him up. Kirk wakes up and says, "Okay, I got the stick." Daniels lets go. Kirk didn't quite have hold of the stick and that plane just went *STRAIGHT UP!* Daniels didn't know how to trim the airplane when it got lighter in the nose. When Daniels told that story later he thought it was funnier than hell.

TED O. "LITTLE O" LYMPUS, high school and college friend

Those guys at Marana, they were crazy! Crazy risk takers! They'd go flying in these small airplanes hunting wild pigs, flying at twenty feet in the air. I mean, they really were a different breed. Jerry could fit that profile, but at the same time he would tell me sometimes, "Those guys are nuts! They're doing stuff that no way I'd do." He was more cautious. He took risks. Obviously he took a lot of risks, but he didn't take risks just for the sake of the risk.

RANDOLPH "TOBY" SCOTT, former smokejumper; former Continental Air Services (CASI) loadmaster, Laos

I'll tell you about one of T.J.'s famous sayings. This was one time when Pete [Richard "Paperlegs Pete" Peterson] was workin' overseas. You know, at Marana they never would get their shit together. They'd pass out different cover stories to different people.

One day ol' Arnold Lindsay, an old rancher that we all liked, he came out to our bar. We had a bar out at the Marana base, and the parachute loft people, which was all the jumpers, we took turns bartending. People from outside could come onto the base to the bar, but almost no one did. It wasn't advertised, so no one knew about it.

Jerry Daniels and Ted O. "Little O" Lympus in Nogales, Mexico, during spring break from the University of Montana, 1964. Toby Scott collection.

Ol' Lindsay, he came out to drink beer with us. He had a lease on a ranch that adjoined the base, so he'd see us flying. He'd be out there on horseback, movin' cows. He'd come in and he'd ask, "Where's Pete?" One would say, "Oh, he's up in Salmon, Idaho, helpin' his dad with hayin.'" Another'd say, "Oh, he's over in India." The security wasn't worth a damn. So Lindsay says, "What the hell, I've got about three stories now! Where in the hell *is* Pete?"

The word got back to the security man. He calls us all in and says, "We gotta be careful about those stories." Security and all that crap. Damn. We walked out of the meeting and T.J. sings: "Tra la la BOOM tee ay, we work for the C-I-A! What have you done for your coun-try today? I worked for the C-I-A." That's the way it went. That was T.J.'s famous saying! After that, we'd be piddlin' around and we'd always sing that.

THOMAS J. "T. J." THOMPSON, former smokejumper; former air delivery specialist, MR2, Laos

You know, security is always such a pain in the ass. You can't say this; you can't say that. Then it comes out in the paper where you've been and who's been there. So the bureaucrats in Washington lived in a phony world. They'd think, *Well, those people in Montana and Idaho probably aren't too swift. We can pull people out of there and tell the locals they went to see their sick grandmother and in spring they'll just show up again.* Well, no one's that stupid! So it caused undue suspicion right off the bat. You can't just disappear. You can do that a few times, but then you're gonna get caught. You've got to have some sort of a plausible story. So it leaked out. A little word here and a little word there. The guys that weren't supposed to talk didn't talk. But just the regular happenings, guys routinely leaving, aroused suspicion. Rumors started surfacing about special operations, and people started putting things together.

KENT "DAN THE ANIMAL MAN" DANIELS, brother of Jerry Daniels

Jerry, Toby, and Mike Oehlerich were at the house one day. They'd been working down in Arizona and they brought jalapeño peppers back from Mexico. They'd just sit and eat them. That's when I found out how to cook jalapeños with eggs. You dice up onions and a pepper or two and sauté that in butter, then put the eggs in. Anyway, here's this gallon can of these things sittin' on the table. They were looking at the side of the can and giggling. The brand name was Garcia—"Gar" plus C-I-A. They covered it up and said, "Oh, we can't tell you about this. Can't talk about it! Otherwise we'll have to kill you." That was the only thing that was said.

I knew that Jerry had been overseas by then. He'd been over there as a cargo kicker, and as far as I knew he was working for Air America, a private enterprise. Same as when they all worked at Marana. I thought that was just a training base with R and D, a research and development place. I didn't know that the CIA backed all of that stuff. I couldn't even tell you what year it was when I finally realized it.

RANDOLPH "TOBY" SCOTT, former smokejumper; former Continental Air Services (CASI) loadmaster, Laos

In '62, me, Miles Johnson, Bob Nicol, and Jerry Daniels were starting to work on the B-17's Skyhook pickup system. It was a secret deal, of course. We were tryin' to figure out how to make aerial pickups of live people. We had a five-hundred-foot nylon rope tied to an ol' dummy, a mannequin that had joints on him. The dummy was on the ground and there was a big ol' dirigible-shaped balloon up in the air that would ride into the wind. We tried a lot of different things, and eventually we figured out a pickup system that worked on the B-17. We used it for Operation Coldfeet in '62. On that deal we dropped two military guys[2] on an abandoned Russian research station out on an ice island in the Arctic Ocean. We were supposed to come back three days later to pick them up with the Skyhook system, but the weather was bad and we couldn't find the damned ice island!

Intermountain Aviation B-17 with Intermountain and navy flight crews, Skyhook team members with maintenance and administrative support personnel. Point Barrow, Alaska, June 3, 1962. Second, third, and fourth from left are Bob Nicol, Jerry Daniels, and Miles Johnson. Original photo was signed by all. Robert H. Nicol collection.

ROBERT H. NICOL, former smokejumper and pilot

That Coldfeet operation was in May and June 1962. Jerry was on that deal. We flew the B-17 from Marana to Point Barrow, Alaska, then went out from Point Barrow to NP8,[3] a Russian station approximately 400 miles south of the North Pole. That B-17 was an old World War II bomber; by 1962 it was an *old* airplane.

That operation was fifteen hours round-trip, and we were *heavy* with fuel. Every fuel tank was full, and on top of that we had every nook and cranny filled with fifty-five-gallon drums of fuel that we pumped by hand into the bomb bay tanks when they started getting low. As heavy as we were, had an engine even belched aloud, we would've gone into the ice. And who's gonna come and get you? If we had trouble, we were on our own.

Jerry Daniels securing the lift line at the Joe Hole with Kirk Samsel. Both are training on Fulton's Skyhook pickup system, Intermountain Aviation, 1962. Robert H. Nicol collection.

RANDOLPH "TOBY" SCOTT, former smokejumper; former Continental Air Services (CASI) loadmaster, Laos

We had our butts hangin' out for three days lookin' for those two guys we dropped. This was during the Cold War, and we were worryin' about Russian MIGs and bad weather and everything else. Finally we found them, but the wind was blowin' like hell and the B-17 was *just* above stallin' speed. It was a touch-and-go situation, but we picked 'em up. We all cheated death. That night me and Jerry and the rest of 'em were sittin' there at the Naval Research Station at Point Barrow drinkin' Russian vodka and smokin' Russian cigarettes. And enjoyin' the hell out of it! Both of those military guys got all kinds of honors and decorations and hell, we never even got a thank-you![4]

KEN HESSEL, former smokejumper; former Continental Air Services (CASI) Air Operations, MR3, Laos

The reason for Marana's existence was to launder planes for Agency operations and to work on research and development of parachute design and cargo dropping techniques. The Laos connection was a well-kept secret until people went and got killed.

There were ten jumpers who died overseas while employed by the Agency: five from Missoula, Montana; three from McCall, Idaho; one from Redmond, Oregon; and one from Cave Junction, Oregon. Ten jumpers. Eight died in Laos, KIAs, and two more were MIAs. They never found them: James DeBruin and Ed Weissenback. Most of them were cargo kickers who worked for Air America. Some of the aircraft were shot down; a couple simply ran into clouds full of rocks. One McCall jumper who worked in Thailand and Laos as an operations case officer, Frank Odom—we called him "the Bag"—he later died in Zambia. And, of course, Jerry died in Thailand.

Between overseas assignments, '63 to '73, all of us would return to Marana and work in the equipment and development section of Intermountain Aviation. We worked on the Fulton Skyhook, beacon jumps, even the James Bond movie *Thunderball*. The Intermountain B-17 with the Skyhook system was featured at the very end of that movie. And of course when not putting in our eight hours, we whiled away the time at the bar or rodeoin' and raisin' hell in general.

RANDOLPH "TOBY" SCOTT, former smokejumper; former Continental Air Services (CASI) loadmaster, Laos

While we were at Marana, probably this was me and Jerry, T.J. and Shep, and maybe Miles was with us. We were at the old Pioneer Hotel in Tucson. God, that was a great bar. We were sittin' in there havin' a beer, and these two pretty gals walk in. I mean real nice lookin'! They walk in and kind of sashay across the room and sit down in the back about fifteen feet from our table. They're by themselves. Jerry looks them over and says, "Watch this fellas." He jumps up and walks over to them, and of course we can hear every word he says. He walks up to the table and says, "Excuse me, ladies, but I'm independently wealthy. Can I buy you a drink?" This gal looks him up and down and says, "Why don't you make an exit?" He comes sneakin' back over to the table all red-faced and sits down. Oh, we were laughing! After that, we'd be workin' in the loft or doin' something and Jerry'd look up and say, "Toby, why don't you make an exit?" Ha! That became his saying for quite awhile after.

JACK TUPPER DANIELS, brother of Jerry Daniels

When I visited Jerry at Marana, he always had friends around. I always got the impression that he had all *kinds* of get-togethers with friends. Certainly that was true later in Bangkok. He talked about going out to dinner, and they'd flip coins to see who'd pay for it. And they'd be two-hundred-dollar dinners. That didn't bother anybody. I'll win it this time and you'll win it next time. Who cares?

GLENN F. HALE, former smokejumper; former Continental Air Services (CASI) Air Operations, MR3, Laos

One time we went down to Nogales and had dinner and drinks and blah, blah, blah. Well, Jerry came up missing. We checked everywhere we could think of and we couldn't find him. We even went to the Mexican jail, and that was hideous. Visualize a cattle corral. Lucky for us he wasn't there.

The car was the center point of our search because the border closed at midnight. By eleven we were getting nervous about getting home that night, and we couldn't go home without him. It was almost midnight when he finally wandered up the side of the street where we were parked. We threw him in the car and took off. We barely made the border in time to get back to Marana.

Guys like that take off, and you don't know whether they find a girlfriend or go lay down in the gutter and go to sleep. You just don't know. He never said where he'd been, and you don't ask.

KEN HESSEL, former smokejumper; former Continental Air Services (CASI) Air Operations, MR3, Laos

Finally Toby and Jerry just got a belly full of it and they both quit Marana. They just left. Hell, they went up to the Bob Marshall Wilderness[5] in Montana. Spent fifty-eight days in the Bob for the big dryin'-out trip. Never had a beer or anything. For fifty-eight days! They were really proud of that. Hell, we were *all* proud of 'em!

RANDOLPH "TOBY" SCOTT, former smokejumper; former Continental Air Services (CASI) loadmaster, Laos

We said we weren't going to drink a beer. No alcohol at all for at least two months. We went on a big dry because everybody got in a rut down at Marana. We'd get off work and every day we'd head for the Roadrunner. That bar was open seven days a week. You'd try to stay out of there but there was always somethin', and you'd be over there and the next day you'd be waking up with bleary eyes again. There really wasn't anywhere else to go. So in the fall of '64, Jerry and I both resigned from Intermountain Aviation. We gave 'em two weeks notice, and we weren't plannin' on going back.

We left Intermountain on the first of September. We kicked the tires and lit the fires, and we headed up to Montana. For fifty-eight days straight we slept without a

Toby Scott shoulders his pack at the start of the Monture Trail into the Bob Marshall Wilderness. Scott and Daniels spent fifty-eight days hunting and fishing, during which time they traveled eighty-nine miles. September 1964. Toby Scott collection.

roof over our heads. Didn't do anything but hunt and fish. Thirty days of that was in the Bob Marshall. [See Map 5 on page 307.]

For two weeks we were on a float trip on the south fork of the Flathead River. We were on the river every day, and every night when we made camp the elk would bugle us to sleep. After the float trip we went on our goat hunt. God, we walked those ridges and looked into snow until our eyes hurt. And wind? My God, that wind would blow up there. After ten days we were lookin' for porcupines or anything else we could eat. We about starved to death before we killed our first goat, a big ol' billy, and the next day we killed a nanny.

After the float trip and the goat hunt we wanted to do some goose huntin' up by Pablo. Well, there was a friend of Jerry's who went with us. He had a wife and a couple of kids. We picked him up in Missoula when it was still dark, something like four o'clock in the morning. We went up there and, God, we sat there all day long. I think we got a few geese. Anyway, we're headin' home and of course we stopped at a little bar to have one for the road. By the time we dropped off Jerry's friend, he was about half shitfaced. We're out in the driveway and he's gettin' out his gear and his shotguns and we're just a-hootin' and a-hollerin' and a-laughin', havin' a great time.

Daniels with his nanny goat in the Bob Marshall Wilderness, 1964. Daniels family collection. Used with permission.

Meanwhile, his wife is standin' up there on the porch with her arms folded. You can tell it's goin' to be bad news for him. He says, "Hi, honey!" or somethin', but she don't hardly want to speak to him. Then Jerry says real loud, "Well, whatd'ya think? You wanna go again next Saturday mornin'?" He says, "Oh, I'll see! I'll give ya a call!" And she's standin' up there and she pipes up and says in this piercing voice, "Well, I guess you know the Joneses are goin' to be here next Saturday." And Jerry looked at me, you know? And you could see that devilish look in his eye.

The guy gets his gear and goes on in and doesn't say another word to me or Daniels. We know it's bad news for him. We drive off and Jerry's laughin' and he says, "Goddamn, doesn't that make you wish you was married?!" So for six months after that, every time something would come up and somebody'd say, "What do you think? Can you make it next week?" Jerry'd fold his arms up and mimic her voice and say, "Well, I guess you know the Joneses are goin' to be here." And, God, we'd laugh.

By the time we finished fishin' and huntin', it was November and there was snow on the ground. We killed elk, antelope, mule deer, two mountain goats, fourteen Canadian honkers, and a bunch of mallard ducks and pheasants. Caught two bull trout one day—one weighed eleven pounds and one weighed fifteen pounds. When we'd get something we'd gut it and skin it and chop it up and haul it to a freezer in

Jerry Daniels and Toby Scott with Canada geese, fall 1964. Daniels family collection. Used with permission.

Missoula, then go right back out again. When we finished our fifty-eight-day trip, we had two meat lockers plumb full. I doubt we'd spent $300 between us, and we had about 500 pounds of meat in the freezers.

Reluctantly, I went to work in the woods for a logging company and Jerry went back to school at the University of Montana.

JACK TUPPER DANIELS, brother of Jerry Daniels

Off and on Jerry went to the School of Business at the University of Montana in Missoula. I got the impression that it was a degree of convenience. He told me on occasion that he was being encouraged to *finish* his degree, but he never told me he was encouraged to get it in any certain area. Finishing a college degree probably had to do with his status in the Company. I know it took him nine years. He would come back and do a semester or a year. Spend all the money he had saved. Then go back to work overseas again.

A Man's Man

MEMORABLE traits of the character of Jerry Daniels, including dedication, intelligence, and humor; why he never married; "drinkin' and drivin'"; Sunday circles; Clark Canyon Dam 1978; thoughts about his sexual preference; commitment and risk; coming to a crossroads.

JACK TUPPER DANIELS, brother of Jerry Daniels

Was there anything unusual about Jerry? Yes, there were some things about him that you would notice. For one thing he was left-handed. But more importantly, I'd say he was very, very trustworthy. If he said he'd do something, he'd do it. And Jerry was dedicated to whatever he was doing. Dedication. Whether it was working or hunting or fishing or playing. I think he was absolutely dedicated to the U.S. Right or wrong, he used to get upset that we were going to leave Vietnam and Southeast Asia. He thought we needed to stay and clean the commies out.

Excerpt from a letter to RANDOLPH "TOBY" SCOTT, former smokejumper; former Continental Air Services (CASI) loadmaster, Laos, from Jerry Daniels, January 20, 1979

With Carter in and all of the U.S. turning in their nuts for mustard seeds they don't need any real men here. I still wished we had napalmed those students at Kent State "U", H bombed Hanoi, and that Nixon was digging up divots on the white house lawn with his wheelbarrow that carries his nuts.

KENT "DAN THE ANIMAL MAN" DANIELS, brother of Jerry Daniels

Dogged. Tough. "Fearless" is another word I've heard used. And very knowledgeable about what he did. I don't know that you'd say he was overly book-smart, but when he worked like he did, he could put things together.

KEN HESSEL, former smokejumper; former Continental Air Services (CASI) Air Operations, MR3, Laos

You know, Jerry had an I.Q. of probably 160. I'm not kiddin' you! When he went up there to Long Cheng, he could probably speak the Hmong language in two weeks. He'd just pick it up. And he could probably read and write it if he was there six weeks. He was sharp.

"LUCKY" LUE YANG, former field liaison officer (FLO), MR2, Laos; Hmong funeral organizer

Jerry was a hard worker. And friendly. He could adjust himself into the high class and the low class. He could go to the top and talk to the Big Boss and he could play with kids. A very intelligent man, a real smart guy. *Very* smart.

JON FOLAND, Missoula crony; former smokejumper

He was probably one of the most intelligent people I've ever met in my whole life. That's what really impressed me. He wasn't some hick that fell off the turnip truck. This guy was *really* sharp, incredibly intelligent. I can't imagine anybody who didn't admire Jerry, whether they knew him very well or not. A lot of the women were quite offended, oft times by his jargon, but they were still pretty mesmerized by him.

Mrs. DAWN OEHLERICH, wife of Mike Oehlerich

Jerry was so handsome when he was in his late 20s and 30s. It wasn't just women that were drawn to him. He was so charismatic and handsome on top of it that if you were even across the street he was somebody that would immediately draw your eye.

MIKE OEHLERICH, former smokejumper; former Air America loadmaster, Laos

Daniels had this magnetic personality that just drew people to him. He could say things to people and address, confront your innermost fear, your secret thoughts or anxieties. He'd just blurt 'em out, spit 'em out in your face, stomp on 'em, and laugh about it. If you hid your dirty laundry in the back recesses of your closet, he'd drag it out and hang it out in the sunshine for everybody to look at and hold you up to some kind of ridicule that turned out to be funny. Pretty soon you'd be laughing about things that you thought were totally important. All of a sudden those fears and anxieties just didn't have any power.

He was just an exceptional person. He had some kind of talent about reading people, a special insight into what made them tick. There was just something that he connected with in everybody. And I don't give a shit if you were the best pilot in the

Passport photo of Jerry Daniels, 1970s. Daniels family collection. Used with permission.

country or some kind of big dog; there was just something about Daniels that totally appealed to you unless you were a total stuffed-shirt horse's ass.

You know how young kids talk with such irreverence or just dirty talk, filthy talk? Jerry was *full* of that. And he would talk like that to people who were totally respectable, like the captains of the airplanes. Daniels would talk about somebody being a scum-suckin' pig. Right in their faces. God, they'd look at him like, "What the hell?" But those pilots just *loved* him. They'd see him comin' and they'd start laughin' and start talkin' the Daniels talk, jivin' back and forth with this kind of rotten, totally irreverent talk. He was such an achiever and accomplished so much, but he was still "low ball," still one of the guys. He never changed, no matter how much authority or power he had.

LEE "TERRIBLE TORGY" TORGRIMSON, grade school friend; Missoula crony

Three or four of us were out at Blue Mountain one day, drinkin'. Jerry parked his truck in the meadow and there was another rig parked there, too. And along the river the riparian zone was probably sixty to a hundred feet of bushes and cottonwood trees. Jerry'd only been home a couple of days. He still had diarrhea, coming from overseas. He pulls his pants down and says, "Watch this." Poof! He shoots crap and it went to the other side of the road. He just laughed. You needed to hear him laugh because he had a *wild* laugh. He says, "I can do that again!" "Oh, bullshit, Daniels! You can't do that again." Boom! He hits it.

About then two girls, strangers, came around the bushes. They were walking along the river and they just came out of the bushes and there's Jerry doin his shittin' trick! He dove into the front seat of his pickup with his pants still down. He had crap all over the back of his butt. Dove into his truck and made himself a mess. And laughed every goddamn minute of it! He rolled around in the front of his truck laughing and got it all over his seat covers and everything. Then he was pissed because he had to drive his truck with his own crap all over it. But he thought that was funny, being able to shoot it about thirty-five or forty feet. Of course we did too. We damn near fell down laughin' about it! Oh, God. He was unreal!

RANDOLPH "TOBY" SCOTT, former smokejumper; former Continental Air Services (CASI) loadmaster, Laos

I think the only people who probably wouldn't have liked Jerry would be the Big Fat Businessmen, as he used to call them, that worked for the CIA in the Vientiane office or somewhere. None of them would go out and live with the Hmong like Jerry did. Then they acted like it was a big mystery: "How in the hell does Jerry get along so well with those people?" My God, not one of those guys would spend one night up there at Site 36, much less stay there for weeks or months on end. They'd go up there for a few hours then get on a plane and get the hell out. So much for the big dogs.

MIKE LYNCH, former provincial advisor, Lima Site 36, Na Khang, Laos

One day during a month of heavy action at Site 36 we got a radio call from Vientiane asking if we were going to send down a "sitrep," the Situation Report on the day's activities. Jerry grabbed the microphone and said: "If I *sit* here on my ass and write a sitrep, there will be no 'sit' to report. If I go out and make something happen, I won't be sitting here to write the damn sitrep. Take your choice." Vientiane wisely did not pursue the matter further that day.

DEEDER DANIELS, nephew of Jerry Daniels; son of Kent Daniels

As far as I could tell, Jerry was enjoying his life. Toby tells stories about when they were jumpers. They'd pull up alongside a carload of girls and Jerry'd shout, "Pull over, girls! We're smokejumpers!" After that it was: "Where can I go from here? I can go be a spook in a far-off land? Okay, I'm there! I am *so* there!" So the guy was doin' what he wanted to do to enjoy his life, and that's all good. That's the way I perceive it, you know?

When I was a little older Jerry'd come back from overseas and he'd be talking about things. Like how the government was treating the Hmong, that they're getting the short end of this deal. He never actually *said* it, but you could tell by the way he talked that he was there with the feeling that he was doing something good. And it was pissin' him off that it was out of his control. From what I can remember, he was tellin' the Hmong that this was what was going to be done for them because he had been given the authority to say that, and now they were yankin' that authority away from him—and he's left hangin' out there, just like the Hmong were.

I don't know how he felt about his job at the end. Whether or not he was frustrated because he couldn't do what he wanted to do or whether he was happy that he was doin' something and gettin' the last ounce out of it that could be got out of it instead of just turnin' his back. I don't know about that.

The way I perceive it, this country's still the best thing goin', but at the same time there's a *lot* of shit that we could be doin' better. You've got the *people* of the country who are basically good individuals, but people are sheep. When the people adapt to government herding and control, the only thing that the government has a problem with are individuals. And there aren't a lot of them out there. And Jerry was one.

Daniels game hunting in the Gravelly Range southeast of Dillon, Montana, fall 1969. Daniels family collection. Used with permission.

KEITH "SKID" WOLFERMAN, smokejumper; friend of Deeder and Farrett Daniels

Psychologists always used to try to pigeonhole people into Type A or Type B personalities. Type B is passive and Type A is aggressive. Now there's this Type T personality, the "thrill seeker." Type T seeks out intensity. They're quite assertive, but they're not necessarily driven for success within society. They might eschew all of that in order to pursue something that *they* feel is important. Type Ts hear about something that intrigues them and they go after it. And they like to be creative in the face of uncertain and unpredictable situations. Type T people go after what they want and they're willing to take risks. They understand the payoffs of taking risks. There are a lot of people like that in mountaineering, skiing, whitewater kayaking. And I think there's a lot of that Type T aspect in the smokejumper group. Certainly there was in Jerry.

JACK TUPPER DANIELS, brother of Jerry Daniels

You know, for quite a few years Jerry had a very close girlfriend in Missoula. But anytime I talked to him about a wife or family he said, "Until I finish what I'm doing, I'm not in a position to have a family. It wouldn't be fair." That was sad because she spent many years waiting to see if he would give it all up and come home. Jerry was just so dedicated to his work.

Conversation between MIKE OEHLERICH, former smokejumper; former Air America loadmaster, Laos, and his wife, Mrs. DAWN OEHLERICH

DAWN: Sometimes Jerry'd come home on leave and he would just disappear for a few days and we knew he was holed up with Sharon, the Maid. He went with her for a long time. The Maid always wanted Jerry to do something more straight with her. Have a life together. I think she got to the point where she could see that she was never going to be first. Because he was so involved with the Hmong; they took precedence over everything. In the end she left.

MIKE: Yeah, Jerry ran with the Maid for quite awhile, but I just never knew him to commit to any woman. He never did. Jerry was terrible as a womanizer. He was crude and clumsy. He just wasn't a lover. He was too direct and didn't have any finesse. Everything was left brain with Daniels. There was no romanticism in him. If there was any romanticism it was calculated to get him from point A to point B. It wasn't because it was supposed to be an enjoyable thing. It was just so much trash to get out of the way to get to the real deal.

He was a very, very good-looking guy. Definitely liked women. But he didn't like any strings attached. He liked the straight thing, you know? Go to a whorehouse, lay down the money, you get what you paid for and that was it. Then back out on the street. He wasn't looking for anything emotional.

Ms. MYRA L. SHULTS, high school friend of Jerry Daniels

Jerry never married. That was not necessarily a natural outcome of the Jerry I knew in high school, but a natural outcome of the life that he chose for himself. If Jerry had come home and gotten his degree in business and gone to work in a company, he may have gotten married. But what would it have been like to have been married to Jerry Daniels? Jerry wasn't your touchy-feely, sensitive, let-me-bring-you-a-bouquet-of-flowers kind of guy.

Women need people to talk to them. I'm not sure that other than over a glass of beer Jerry was very communicative with a woman. And I don't know that a relationship would have lasted because it would have been all one way; it would have been all Jerry's way.

Jerry Daniels and his girlfriend Sharon, "the Maid." Daniels family collection. Used with permission.

Mrs. BAO V. BLIAYA, wife of Mouasu Bliaya

Mouasu and I met Jerry's girlfriend. In '72 when Jerry came to Montana with VP and his group, Sharon came to visit Jerry. Later Louise told me that Jerry and Sharon had broken up. When I saw Jerry I asked him and he said, "Oh, I don't want any woman like that. She followed me and I don't like that." Jerry said he was on home leave and he and his cronies were up at Tupper Lake doing man-things. Maybe they were swimming naked in the lake. Probably they were drinking. Jerry said he asked Sharon specifically not to join that group and she showed up anyway. When he told me that, he waggled his index finger and said, "I can't stand possessiveness! Don't ever be possessive!" That's what he thought Sharon was doing when she showed up at the lake. "Sharon showed up and she didn't butt out." Those were his exact words! And I kind of teased him: "You asked her to butt out?" And Jerry said, "Yes!" And that was the end of it. He did not like possessiveness. Soon after that he broke off with her.

Mrs. JULIE DANIELS MORITZ, sister-in-law of Jerry Daniels

Jerry was somewhere overseas talking with an American man who had sunglasses on. The guy was talking about his wife and kids, and then he got shot right in front of Jerry. It was the reflection off the glasses that got him shot. Well, see, when something like that happens right in front of you, then you *know*. You *know*. It's a hard reality. It was after that that Jerry had to make up his mind about whether he was going to have the life he was living or was he going to get out like others did and have a regular life.

Maybe Jerry was smarter than most of us, not to marry. Because Jerry, *he had a life!* He had a *big* life.

Conversation between TED O. "LITTLE O" LYMPUS, high school and college friend, and his wife, Mrs. PATSY SKELTON LYMPUS

PATSY: One time Jerry spent three days sitting at our house playing with our infant daughter. She was born in the spring of 1971 and was probably six months old. He was there for three days, drunk the whole time and fascinated with this little baby. He'd never been around children much, as far as I knew. From watching him, I was pretty sure that he'd never held a baby. He'd just sit and hold her. I remember that being so sad because it was like he wanted a life that he knew he was never going to get.

I don't know how long he'd been drunk, but I think it was for a long time. And those three days were just part of this drunk that he was on. He wouldn't talk much. He didn't want to do much. He would just sit and hold the baby and he'd mumble all the time. I'd try to understand him, but I never did figure out what he was saying. He seemed very sad, very sad.

TED: I think Jerry always knew he would never be a family man. He never said it, but that was my strong impression. He always knew he would not have a family.

PATSY: Maybe it's just because I'm such a homebody, but I got the sense that he really enjoyed being with a normal family, doing normal things: living in a house, raising children, eating home-cooked meals, having normal conversations. At the same time, it was always like Jerry to go back. He was always off in the distance, always thinking about somewhere else.

TED: The other day I found in my den a poem by Robert Service called "The Men That Don't Fit In."

> *There's a race of men that don't fit in,*
> *A race that can't stay still;*
> *So they break the hearts of kith and kin,*
> *And they roam the world at will.*

That always reminded me of Jerry. But he always wanted to come back to Montana. And when he was here, he loved just being here. We'd go on those two- and three-day fishing trips up the Blackfoot.

PATSY: He loved Montana. He wanted to be here. Fishing, hunting. I always had a sense that he yearned for a simpler life, but he got caught up in something that was vitally important. I think he became very deeply involved with, very empathetic about what was going on over there in Southeast Asia. He was important, he knew he could do it, and he did it with zeal. He gave it all he had. But I have always believed that he yearned for a simpler life. I think what he really longed for was Montana.

Daniels with two "Mack" trout, Flathead Lake, Montana, 1974. Mackinaw is a nonnative lake trout that endangers native trout and other species of fish in Montana, Wyoming, and Idaho. Kurt Olsen collection.

LEE "TERRIBLE TORGY" TORGRIMSON, grade school friend; Missoula crony

Western Montana was a great place to grow up. It's part of Jerry's character and mine too. When Jerry'd come home one of his favorite things to do was just D and D, go "drinkin' and drivin.'" A D and D was an all-day thing and full of nectar. It was just great times! It's not like these days when they'll throw you in jail just for sniffin' a beer in the car. In those days, D and D-in' was an acceptable, and preferable, Montana pastime. It was wonderful!

A real good D and D was to go northwest out of Missoula to the Bison Range in the Mission Valley. Many times it was me, General, and Jerry, the three of us in a pickup. We'd grab a burger at Brownie's Stop & Go in Missoula, then we'd head on out

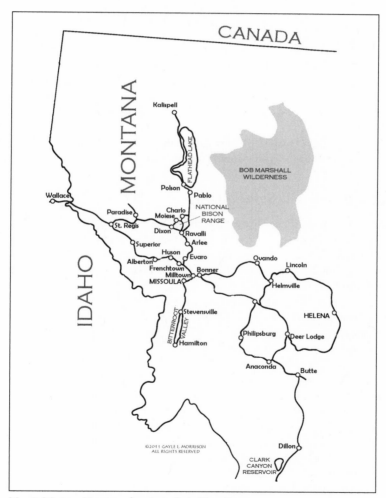

Map 5. Western Montana showing selected locations

about twelve noon, come west out of Missoula and stop at the "Y" and hit Johnny LaFlesch's place, Marvin's Tavern. That's nine miles out of town. We'd have a cooler full of beer, too, but we'd stop there just to get going. Then we'd stop for another beer at the Evaro bar, right up at the top of Evaro hill. Probably another nine miles. Although General, the way he drank, he'd probably get two beers in at every stop. Jerry and I'd just be short hitters. Then after Evaro we might stop in Arlee. That was another nine or ten miles. Arlee's on the Flathead Indian Reservation. Sometimes there were guys that we would sit and bullshit with in the bars up on the Rez. It's Arlee, then Ravalli, then Dixon to Moiese and the Bison Range.

The National Bison Range has a little road that winds through it and you can drive down through the valleys and over the hills and see herds of buffalo and elk and eagles and rattlesnakes and pronghorns and geese. Then we'd continue on to Paradise and have a few at the Paradise Bar, then west to St. Regis. From St. Regis we'd head southeast, and in Superior we'd stop at Honest Tom's Montana Bar then go on to a bar in Alberton—I don't recall the name—then to No-Neck Larry's bar in Huson, on to Frenchtown and a stop at the strip joint out at the "Y" and back to Marvin's Tavern. We'd get back to Missoula at seven or eight o'clock in the evening and go to Trail's End. Then we'd go on into the Flame where we'd finish the night, then to the Turf just across the street for food—noodles and curdled clam chowder on Fridays.

A good D and D was a fifteen-to-twenty-miles-per-hour-on-the-back-roads thing, just cruisin' along. It was wonderful. Just really enjoying Montana.

Mrs. MOE GEARY, wife of Helmville rancher Bill Geary

Montana's famous for those big driving circles. You'd get in a car on Sunday and you'd make these circles. It seems every road went around and met somewhere else and always came back. Sometimes you'd make the great circle from Helmville up to Lincoln then over Stemple or Flesher Pass to Helena then west to Deer Lodge then back to Helmville. That would be one circle. Another circle would be south from Helmville to Drummond to Philipsburg, southeast to Anaconda and around and back up through Deer Lodge and Helmville again. People did that all the time because Sunday was the one day of the week we'd have off from ranch work. We'd stop at all the bars to socialize and visit with neighbors.

Back then, every man, woman, and child in the whole community was in the bar on Sunday! That's where we sold our cows. Cattle buyers would come through, buy a beer, and ask what's for sale, go take a look at the stock, come back to the bar and make an offer. Politicians came out and bought drinks for folks when they were running for office. So much was done there because you could visit with everybody. We'd start a game of penny-ante poker and play all day long, with people constantly coming and going. I've often heard of people missing those days. They were very sociable, but there was a lot of drinking and a lot of driving, which was normal then but would just be appalling now.

JON FOLAND, Missoula crony; former smokejumper

It was April 1978 when we went on the CC adventure—Clark Canyon. My wife and I heard that some of the cronies were going to be at Clark Canyon and we'd better get over there and darken the water. Mike Oehlerich, General, and the Hog would be there.

It was dark by the time my wife and I rolled in. We had no idea where anybody was camped, so we drove around looking for smoke, fire, and beer cans. Eventually I spotted General's truck, and there was General propped up on the tailgate. He was having a heavy discussion mostly with himself because nobody else was standing up, but General was still vertical with a beer in his hand. Oehlerich, that was in his drinkin' days and he definitely had his moccasins on. He wasn't moving; he was crumped face down in the sagebrush doing dirt angels. Hog was still mobile but not vertical, and I'm not sure he even recognized us. I tried to introduce him to my wife, but I don't think he could focus too well and he just came out with some string of profanity. My wife said, "Boy, oh boy, Hog, I've seen your act." He was fiddle-crabbed up there crawling around in the fire 'cause apparently he'd lost his sunglasses in the fire. He wore his sunglasses virtually all the time. It seemed like *apparel de rigueur* for him. My wife said, "Shouldn't you drag him out of there?" I said, "Well, he'll crawl out eventually." He kept crawling, kicking the fire all around, because he was pretty well blottoed. But he kept pushing on. I never saw him vertical but he was moving at least.

Hog just didn't want to go to sleep. General was kind of swearing at him, and Hog was kind of swearing at the world and at General. Drunk-man babble since neither one of them knew what the hell they were arguing about. They weren't much fun to talk to, just layin' there with big kerosene breath comin' out of 'em. They all pretty much crumped so we went to sleep in the back of my truck.

At daylight my wife and I got up. We were ready to go fishing. We figured there wouldn't be a sign of life because there was just a sea of beer cans over there where everybody else had hunkered the night before. General's boat was already in the water. I tried to get General up, but all you could get out of him was a couple of roars and grumbles. He was workin' on a *good* hangover. Hog was nowhere in sight. Oehlerich wasn't to be seen either. Usually when Oehlerich passed out he just got the complete nonremembers for a half day afterwards.

Well, the hell with them. My wife and I headed to the boat, threw some poles in, and wonder of all wonders, here came Hog stumbling out of the bushes with a hat pulled over his head because he didn't have his sunglasses. He was fightin' the bright rays of the morning sun, but he was up and ready to go fishin'! We were just amazed. Hog climbed into the boat, and our mistake was letting him operate the motor. Because he was still fairly drunk.

There's a certain way you have to troll and fish Clark Canyon. We fish it with leaded line and fly rods, but you troll at a real slow pace and try to find a certain depth. It takes kind of a soft touch, and there are certain lines that you troll to get over the best ground in the lake. And Hog wasn't doing any of that. He didn't know *what* he was doing, because we'd just roar around the lake and then we'd be at a standstill. Then he'd gun the motor again and we'd just roostertail and our lures'd be springin' off the tops of the waves behind us. I'd say, "Hog, you'd better get fishing. Let me operate that motor. You're screwing it all up." "No! I've done this before. I'm the captain!" Then we'd roar off again. We went through several hours of that, not doing any productive fishing. I just couldn't get him away from the motor.

Finally it occurred to him to head in for some reason. Maybe he wanted to get something to drink. Usually on the day after, he'd have a mean cottonmouth and would consume vast quantities of water. Or maybe he thought it was time to pull his moccasins on and pop a couple of nectars because the sun had been up for a couple of hours by then. Well, anyway, the next thing I knew we were headed to shore. My wife was thinking, *Oh good, we can get him away from that motor and get back out and do some real fishin'.* But the closer he got to shore the more he gunned the motor. Hell, we were just *roaring* towards shore! We plowed in. *Rrrrrrrr-klunk-klunk-klunk-klunk*, right up on shore.

Granny Peters was sittin' in a lawn chair with crawler and mallow.[1] She's fishin', kids are runnin' around, and they are all kind of horrified to watch us rush ashore. They were runnin' for cover, actually, but they were even more horrified after Daniels stood up and fell out of the boat onto dry land. That's how far we'd run up. Granny started to grab the kids and get them out of his path. One little kid was saying, "What's the matter with him?" Granny said disapprovingly, "That man is *drunk.*" Hog says, "Fuck you, you old cunt!" Oh boy, that scattered them just like popcorn.

Daniels made a beeline for the nearest outhouse. I don't think he quite got to it before he did a face plant in the doorway. We drug him off into the shade. We sure weren't gettin' help from any of the bystanders because they scattered pretty heavy after he lit into 'em. We jumped back in the boat and went fishin' for the rest of the day. We wanted to make sure we were gone before Hog came to life again because he was an awful resilient guy.

Surprisingly, even with all that, Hog wasn't really a drunk. When he was working overseas he'd go long stretches without ever touching a nectar. That's why when he got out he *liked* to go on a long binge. He'd say, "Yep, I'm a binge man." He made no excuses for it whatsoever. He could care less what you thought about it. He liked to go on a binge!

By clinical standards he probably would be an alcoholic, but he wasn't alone. *All* of the cronies were at the time. We *all* did a lot of drinking. Some that took the cure aren't drinkin' anymore. Some are still drinkin', but none of us can do what we did twenty years ago. Everybody thought they were indestructible then!

Conversation between LOY "RINGMAN" OLSEN, TIM "WEENY MAN" LIEN, and RANDALL "PETERBILT" OLSEN, Missoula cronies

RINGMAN: Jerry'd come back and we'd go out and have a good time. Jerry's idea of a good time was a ten-pound ham, a loaf of bread, and ten cases of beer. And you could never have enough beer. Because it won't spoil. And that's the way he

Daniels gathering wood for the campsite.   Kurt Olsen collection.
Kurt Olsen collection.

lived life when he was here. He wanted to get with the boys and hunt moon-faces [bobcats] or drink beer 'til three days later.

WEENY MAN: And we could do that here in Montana. In Missoula in the '60s and '70s you never had to worry about traffic. It was all open space. There were so fewer people, and we weren't causing any trouble. As long as you didn't get in trouble, drinkin' and drivin' wasn't an issue.

PETERBILT: Now we can't do what we did back then. You'd end up in jail all the time.[2]

WEENY MAN: There was definitely a Montana culture in those days. It was the way we all were. We never thought about it. It seemed normal. Maybe it doesn't seem normal now, but now we're gettin' older than dirt!

Conversation between NORMA and CHARLEY HUGHES, Ovando ranchers; friends of the Daniels family

NORMA: Jerry definitely would be a proud one to call a Montanan. Independent, that's what Montanans are. He grew up here, and this was the life he knew.

CHARLEY: See, Jerry was strictly like us. Whatever we did he fit in. When he was with the Hmong, he probably fit into the Hmong way of life, too. He was person enough that it didn't matter what was goin' on. He chimed right in and fit in with whatever it was.

JON FOLAND, Missoula crony; former smokejumper

When Jerry came home he didn't talk much Company business. And people didn't bother asking him. But he'd still maintain a phony front that he was actually working for the State Department. It was a pretty loose cover because all the cronies in Missoula knew what he was doin' and all the commies over there knew him by name and where he was from: Jerry Daniels from Missoula, Montana. With a price on his head.

DOUG VINCENT, former JVA caseworker, Thailand

There were so many rumors after he died and I have forgotten a few, but the rumor about being gay was that supposedly the Agency wouldn't let any gays stay in and Jerry was refusing to leave. So sexual preference was one of the rumors behind his death, that an Agency case officer couldn't be gay so he was offed.

I was with Jerry on different occasions where I would have only believed that he was straight. For example, he took me to the short-time hotel called the Coconut in Udorn. He went there because he liked to get high school girls who would come over still dressed in uniform.

Then in 1980 Jerry and Prok went to Manila for a week, and Jerry invited me to go with them. Prok was pissed because he didn't want to be around any namby-pamby JVA type like he thought I was, but Jerry assured him that I was okay. Anyhow, we went to a place called the Eagle's Nest. You sat at the bar downstairs and ordered a drink, and a girl would come over and talk to you. After a bit she would ask if you wanted to go upstairs. Upstairs was a room that was kept pretty dark with a couple of small red lights on, and it had several high-backed upholstered sofas strewn about. The girl would arrange the sofa so others couldn't see, and then she went to work on you. Jerry and I went up there, and when I got done I saw Jerry was getting worked on. I said, "I'm done, I'll see you downstairs," and he said, "Okay, see you in a bit."

The point is he definitely was into women. Or maybe he went both ways, who knows? And if he was straight or gay was not important to me. Jerry seemed to me to be more of a hedonist when it came to sex, meaning if it felt good, do it, no matter what sex you did it with.

LEE "TERRIBLE TORGY" TORGRIMSON, grade school friend; Missoula crony

Oh, he was a raunchy character! Jerry was a doozy. Apparently he was pretty famous overseas for his whorehouse escapades. Those escapades were self-reported by Jerry when he came home, but I didn't have any reason to doubt his veracity because I'd been with him in Wallace, Idaho, so I knew *exactly* what he was doing.

Jerry told me this story about Vientiane. There was a whorehouse he called "House of a Thousand Assholes." That was his whorehouse of choice. He said you could get anything done to you and you could do anything you wanted to them. Whatever you wanted. He used to describe the procedures. He would go to the

House of a Thousand Assholes for what he called a basket job. There was a basket hanging from a rope with a hole in the bottom. A gal sat in the basket and Jerry laid on the floor. They twisted the basket so the rope got a real good twist in it, then they let the basket spin. Ha! Another favorite was a rug job. He always mentioned the basket job and the rug job. He and a gal would be rolled up in a rug. I guess if you didn't have claustrophobia you could get by with it. Oh, he loved the rug job! Among other tricks with pitutsies. They had a good time over there, I'm sure. Oh, that brings back so many good memories of that meathead! Every time I think of him I giggle. He was so bad!

Letter to THOMAS C. "SHEP" JOHNSON from Jerry Daniels, February 14, 1982

Dear Sheep Shit,

. . . Louise (mother) is coming out for a visit in a few days. She has another think coming if she figures her presence will gear me down any regards pussy and nectors.—I recall last visit in (or about) "71." I kept her awake most of the night at some motel-hotel joint near Ubon with the pitutsie's head hitting a separating wall at every stroke.—Mighty pleasin.

Well old timer—All is well & good here.

Hog

GLENN F. HALE, former smokejumper; former Continental Air Services (CASI) Air Operations, MR3, Laos

Jerry could have had any kind of a girlfriend that he wanted because he was a good-looking guy and muscular, but he was more of an I'm-cutting-my-own-swath-here-and-that's-the-way-it-goes type guy. He was very much his own person. It was my impression that his attitude about women was that he didn't want a relationship with a woman to interfere with his other ambitions.

BARRY REED, former smokejumper; former Air America loadmaster, Laos

When I got to Laos, Jerry's reputation already was larger than life—the way he accepted and blended in with the Hmong. He was one of the first people I ever heard about who learned their language, other than missionaries. I didn't have that much contact with the Hmong because I only met them if I was loading or off-loading cargo up-country. Whereas Jerry, he lived with them, he ate and drank with them, and he fought with them. He accepted the dangers with them and was on the firing line with them. Literally! I mean he was in the trenches within twenty-five yards of the bad guys, poppin' up and down, shootin' at the enemy *with* them. He accepted their risks. He accepted their culture. He didn't judge. And because of that, they accepted him. They were equals.

That's very unusual for an American to go to those lengths. The typical American does not do things like that. Put it this way: Jerry was not an American emperor in Laos. He did not set himself up. What he did was more than just a job to him. It was 100 percent commitment. It was a way of life.

JACK TUPPER DANIELS, brother of Jerry Daniels

The last time that my wife, Nancy, and I saw Jerry was in 1979 in Thailand. It seemed that anything that was dangerous or presented a challenge was funny to him. Anything. I can't imagine him ever thinking anything was seriously bad. But the impression I got was that he felt he was living on borrowed time. It was like every day he had a new thing he had to do, something he had to take care of. "I've gotta go here to do this. I've gotta go there to do that." Like he felt obligated. Every day he lived he felt was one more than he expected, for all the things he had to deal with.

MIKE OEHLERICH, former smokejumper; former Air America loadmaster, Laos

Daniels admired guys like Art Wilson, an Air America pilot. Art always showed up with a baseball cap on, a Hawaiian shirt, shorts, a pair of flip-flops, and five days of beard on his face. Wilson would be flyin' a DC-3, hauling rice all over Laos. Big Andy[3] was his crew, and he'd be in the back end, sittin' in the doorway cross-legged, reading a newspaper with nothing but space out there in front of him. Art Wilson and Big Andy flew in a style that Daniels really admired.

BOB WHALEY, former smokejumper; lieutenant colonel, USMC (retired)

Jerry's lifestyle was always one that was on the edge. And the edge that he was living on, it seems to me that he was coming to a crossroads: "The war is over. What am I going to do next? Is Africa looming for me? Is there something I can do there?" There were a lot of things going on in the world at that time that he could get involved with. But his life was in Southeast Asia. He immersed himself in the culture, the people. I don't know that he would have found as much of an edge again after that kind of a life.

Jerry's Last Visit

SUNDAY night: Missoula friends meet in the Edgewater Lounge; disturbing memories of the last home leave for Jerry Daniels in spring 1981; trip to Washington, DC; drinking habits; a call from "mystery man"; late-night calls to friends; Daniels in Bangkok, December 1981.

TED O. "LITTLE O" LYMPUS, high school and college friend

That last evening of Jerry's funeral, Sunday evening, several of us got together over at the Edgewater. It was Rocheleau, Pramenko, and I. Torgy was there, and General and his brothers probably. We were sitting in the lounge, looking out at the river, having a beer, talking, speculating about what might have happened and whether or not Jerry was in the box. That the box couldn't be opened caused all kinds of suspicion because there were people, probably from DC, who couldn't leave town until the box was buried. So we had some real doubts about it. And there was a troubling amount of concern among us about Jerry's last home visit to Montana a year earlier.

CHA MOUA, Hmong friend; Hmong funeral organizer

The last time I saw Jerry was in the spring of 1981. One whole night we were in my office at Lao Family Community. It took us all night to type out short resumes for each of twenty-seven former Hmong employees who had worked for Jerry in the Sky office in Long Cheng. Mostly it was the forward air guides and the field liaison officers, the FAGs and the FLOs. Jerry said the State Department needed that list. He said he would take the short resumes to the State Department in Washington, DC, so they would know exactly who and where those people were. All twenty-seven were in the U.S., but scattered around in different places. Jerry said, "If something happens in Laos and the U.S. government has the opportunity to go back there, then we can call these people back to work." The U.S. government can re-recruit the Hmong for work regarding Laos. I thought that was wonderful information, and I said, "Well, I hope that happens!"

We worked there all night long. About five o'clock in the morning I told Jerry that we have lots of Hmong who came to Missoula and they have no jobs. I said, "Jerry, you should quit your job and not go back to Thailand. You said you made a mining claim so let's take twenty Hmong out to your property and we will look for gold. If you are lucky, we may find a big chunk of gold then you can become a millionaire." Jerry said, "Charlie, you have a good idea! Let me call DC and ask." Jerry was so excited and serious about the gold mining. He would not go back to work in Thailand if the State Department would release him.

He called from my office to Washington, DC, at six o'clock in the morning Montana time. After he talked to the people in DC, Jerry told me they said, "Not now. You must go back for one more year until we can find someone else for the job." Jerry was very disappointed and his face color dropped. He sat back on the couch quiet for a while and was not happy. Then he said to me, "I knew they would not let me quit my job because there is nobody to replace me." Two days later he took the twenty-seven resumes with him and went to Washington, DC. I still wonder about those resumes. Who did he give them to? Nobody will tell us now!

"LUCKY" LUE YANG, former field liaison officer (FLO), MR2, Laos; Hmong funeral organizer

On his last visit, I was the one who took Jerry to the Missoula airport to fly to DC. It was April, a beautiful day. We sat at the airport for at least half an hour before the airplane departed, and we planned for the future. Jerry told me, "The State Department asked me to help them for twelve more months so I'm going back to Thailand. Then I will come back to Montana." He said, "When I come back we're not going to work for someone else. We have to work for ourselves and make a business together." He mentioned two ideas: concrete construction and gold mining. He said if we cannot set up a concrete construction business we might just set up and open a gold mine, because his land has some gold in it. He said, "Lucky, you keep working at the mill for now. Wait until I come back. When we do business you'll have your own land." So we had quite a plan that we were going to do. Then he departed to DC.

JIM SCHILL, former USAID Laos Refugee Relief Program; former Department of State, Bureau for Refugee Programs

Jerry came to Washington, DC, in the spring of 1981 to check in with his agency, then came over to the Department of State and checked in with us in the Refugee Bureau. I escorted Jerry to most of the State appointments. While we waited, Jerry and I spoke about his future plans, which included some thought of leaving his agency and finding something else to do. Possibly the State Department could pick up Jerry to work directly for State in the refugee program rather than being "on loan" from his agency. He liked the idea and promised to get back to us if he was interested in moving over.

"GLASSMAN" YANG SEE, former liaison between Jerry Daniels/Sky and General Vang Pao/MR2 staff, Laos

That 1981 trip, Jerry wrote a final report on the Hmong people in this country. I was living in DC and I worked on that report with him, which he submitted to the State Department. The day before he left DC he had dinner at my house. He said after this trip to Thailand he will not go back again as a contractor to the State Department. He said it would be about a year. So my wife and I encouraged him to get married to a Hmong girl from the refugee camp and settle down when he comes back. Then he said, "Oh, I don't know. At forty-one years old, maybe I will die." That is something that shocked my wife and me to hear. He was not making a joke, he just stated that. I think he was just talking, but he did say forty-one. So when I heard he died at forty-one years old, I had a very complex feeling that if he was not murdered, he may have committed suicide. I don't think he would do that, but it could be. I just don't know.

CHA MOUA, Hmong friend; Hmong funeral organizer

Jerry came back to Missoula after he went to Washington, DC, but we didn't talk any more about the list of twenty-seven Sky employees or the gold mining. When he came back he showed me he bought a 200-proof bottle of liquor there. A big bottle of clear liquor. I said, "Two hundred proof?!" He said, "Charlie, I'm gonna take this and scare General." I said, "Jerry, don't kill yourself with that!"

MIKE OEHLERICH, former smokejumper; former Air America loadmaster, Laos

Every time Jerry came home he had a routine he went through. He had a pattern. He'd go see the people he needed to see, like his mom and Vang Pao and anybody else he needed to be responsible to. He'd take care of his responsibilities for two or three days or whatever it took. Then he'd go with the boys and he'd cut loose. Party with the boys, binge drink, go fishin', huntin'. He'd turn himself loose with his drinkin' buddies. And once he was with his drinkin' buddies and on a roll, then that just went bang until two or three days before he had to report back to work.

When home leave was over and he had to go back to work, he'd just disappear. He'd be done drinkin'. A lot of times he'd go to the Palace Hotel downtown and hole up—get a room and sleep for twenty-four hours. Often it would be under an assumed name so we couldn't bother him. He'd hole up for two or three days, not drink at all, sober up and get himself straight. He'd get on the plane sober, fly to Seattle, and go overseas from there.

Conversation between RANDALL "PETERBILT" OLSEN and his brother LOY "RINGMAN" OLSEN, Missoula cronies

PETERBILT: Yeah, he'd drink every day until it was time to make his move. Then he'd come staggerin' up out of that drunk man's bed down in the basement. He'd shut right off and start trainin'. He'd start runnin' every morning, like ten or twelve miles, cleanin' up his system. It was amazing how he could be partyin' and hootin' and hollerin' and then he just shut it down and got right to business. Started gettin' on the phone, doin' paperwork, doin' this and talkin' that, and that was it. He'd just dry right up.

RINGMAN: He never whined about it. Like the week before he's leaving you'd never hear him say, "Aw, shit, I've gotta go back." Never. It was just, "That was a good time. See you guys later."

PETERBILT: Then he was gone. A year or so would go by, and he'd show up again with that old duffel bag he used to carry and that old briefcase he had. He'd store them down by the drunk man's bed where he stayed, and we'd start it up again.

MIKE OEHLERICH, former smokejumper; former Air America loadmaster, Laos

Well, that routine worked for a while; then his drinkin' progressed. During the last few years his standards slacked off to the point that he was drinkin' right up until the time he left town. It got so he couldn't stay in Missoula and sober up. He had to go to Seattle a day early where he didn't know anybody and nobody could find him. He'd hole up in Seattle and sleep for twenty-four hours or two days before he took his flight. Get his health back and his mind back. And then after a while that didn't work either. One of the hard-and-fast rules he always had was he never drank overseas when he got back to work. And then that quit, you know. To me, it looked like he was losing ground.

If a guy gets strung out on alcohol and it's not doing what it's supposed to be doing, it starts turning on you. It's been your lover and your best friend for twenty-five years, and all of a sudden it starts betrayin' you. You can't trust it anymore. That's what I'm saying about his patterns changing. At first he could just quit and go to the Palace and stay there for a couple of days. He had control. Later he had to get the hell out of town to have control. I just think his chop-off point to say, *I'm going to quit tomorrow, then go back to work for the next six months*, that got more and more difficult to do and he had a harder time getting away from it.

Excerpt from a letter to JON FOLAND, Missoula crony; former smokejumper, from Jerry Daniels, March 27, 1981

. . . Well-founded fears prevail that talent scouts will take note of my greyhound features and mistakenly apprehend for the race circuits. Pursuant to this I plan a body swelling sortie on skids of Manila, with follow-up fiddler activities in the whimpering zone of the U.S. Latter visit to take place circa early April-May 81. I feel confident that after several weeks into foregoing plans that my putrid whiskey breath will easily draw the likes of Ogelthorpes [Oehlerichs] to save me.

LEE "TERRIBLE TORGY" TORGRIMSON, grade school friend; Missoula crony

I remember Elmer, the Old Man, and I kind of talking about Jerry's condition on that last trip. Not why he was the way he was but what he was doing. Because when he used to come home it was just a good ol' boy drinkin' session. But that last trip, it was almost a drunken suicide mission that he was on. Elmer may have been the only person in the house when Jerry was goin' through that because General was up working in Alaska. I'd stop over every day or so. Jerry'd either be crashed or if it was evening he'd be trompin' around the house with his Sorel boots on, unlaced. One time he came out with his shirt on, no goddamn skivvies and his boots on with his bare ass showin'. He'd kind of roam around Elmer's house and he was just out of it.

On that last trip he was drunk, totally. There might be half an hour where something he said made sense. Just drunk. He'd be drinkin' mostly all night, sleep all day. He'd get up about six or seven in the evening. I'd get there after work and we'd have

Daniels fishing at Clark Canyon Dam, Montana, April/May 1981. Daniels family collection. Used with permission.

something to eat, and I'd shoot the bull with him while he was drinkin' his beers. Then I'd go home. After I left he'd walk to the Am-Vets bar, probably five or six blocks from Elmer's house. He'd get a good buzz on, then he'd go back to Elmer's house and shoot the bull with the Old Man until Elmer went to bed, probably about ten or ten-thirty, then he'd just sit there and drink beer by himself until he passed out. Then he'd wake up and he'd sit there and drink more. He'd drink all night by himself until three or four in the morning, then he'd crash.

Elmer said he'd wander around the house, talkin' to himself, drunk, rootin'. He never did that before. He'd get drunk and pass out, but he pretty much had regular hours like the rest of us. But this last time he was disturbed. And that was when I got this understanding about him wanting to quit his job. We didn't do much fishing or hunting on that trip. And there weren't many D and Ds either. He was hunkered in at Elmer's house, and he was disturbed. He said, "I'm gonna quit," in the context of the government doing something over there which he didn't delineate, but there was stuff goin' on over there with our government that wasn't right and he knew it. He was a mess. He was disturbed like I've never seen him before. He said, "I don't like what they're gonna do over there." He never disclosed what was going on, but he wanted to quit. And they wouldn't let him quit. And I think that's why he was so despondent and was drinkin' himself into a stupor every day. I assumed it was the Agency, the U.S. government, that wouldn't let him quit. Rhetorically, they "wouldn't let him quit," and that's why he ended up dead. That's my feeling.

THOMAS C. "SHEP" JOHNSON, former smokejumper; former air delivery specialist, MR2, Laos

I was workin' in Missoula for about a week in April or May '81. And that happened to be when Daniels was on home leave. We got together, and I went with him down to General's house where he was stayin'. While we were there the phone rang. Jerry answered it, and when I looked at him he had a funny look on his face. Afterwards I said, "Well, Jerry, who's that?" "Mystery man." I said, "Mystery man? Who's that?" He said, "Oh, some Hmong down in Las Vegas." Jerry said that. He said, "I think it's a Hmong that is unhappy with me." That's the way Jerry put it. That is all that was said. But Jerry did say, "He's called me before." And that the call was a death threat. Mystery man was gonna kill him. He knew where Jerry was. All the time. I guess Jerry got calls from him in Bangkok and all over. That's what was strange about that mystery man.

I think Jerry did have some suspicion as to who it was. I think Jerry did, yes, but he didn't tell me. All he said was that the call was from Las Vegas. Maybe mystery man wasn't in Las Vegas; maybe mystery man just said he was. For all I knew, mystery man might have been right there in Missoula.

"LUCKY" LUE YANG, former field liaison officer (FLO), MR2, Laos; Hmong funeral organizer

We joked about that! When he came home the last time he came to my house, and we talked and laughed about the "mystery man" because Jerry and I worked together in Thailand. He said, "You know the way we work over there, some people get ticked off. Every day some people come out smiling and some people come out with a mad face. The threats are not serious." I know what he's talking about, because when I worked with him in the refugee camps in Thailand, I had people poke my tires and do all kinds of things. But what can you do? We tried to do the best and most honest job we could. So we said, "Well, that's okay. Some people like us, some people don't like us." We already got used to that.

Jerry told me he got phone calls from the mystery man both in Thailand and in the U.S. He never mentioned to me if it was a Hmong or a Thai or an American caller. He just said "someone" called, but it should be someone who knows him very well, really well, whether Lao people or Hmong people or Thai people. It was someone unhappy with him and someone who knew him well. Otherwise, who has his phone number? Who knows he's here? That is not a stalker. It's someone who knows Jerry, who listens and knows that he is coming to Montana. Then that person asks somebody who knows his telephone number here and he calls. Jerry can be called from anywhere in America, anywhere in the world. We didn't take it seriously. We just laughed. I didn't think it was a real death threat, just bad words.

RANDOLPH "TOBY" SCOTT, former smokejumper; former Continental Air Services (CASI) loadmaster, Laos

The last time I talked to Jerry was on the phone. I was in Texas, and he was in Missoula. I called to General's house, and when we talked, Jerry brought up the call from the "mystery man." He said, "Well, if the mystery man doesn't get me." I said, "What's the mystery man? Whatd'ya mean?" He said, "Oh this crazy goddamn guy. He keeps callin' me sayin', 'I'm gonna get you. I'm gonna kill you.'" He said he thought he was a Thai, but could have been a Hmong or a Lao. I said, "You're kidding!" He said, "No, but I think it's just a bunch of baloney." He figured the "mystery man" was probably one of those he turned down for a refugee visa to the U.S. Well, that worried me. I told Jerry, "Jerry, you ought to get the hell out of there." He laughed, but it seemed it was fresh on his mind. I could tell. It didn't seem to worry Jerry, but he brought it up so I think he kind of wanted somebody to know.

CHU VANG, son of General Vang Pao

The last time Jerry came home he did not show any bad feelings, but I started to feel that he knew something could happen to him. He talked to VP about his apartment in Thailand. He mentioned that he would move to a place that only a few people would know about. It seemed like he was worried about something.

Louise Daniels and Jerry Daniels leave General Vang Pao's house in Missoula, April 1981. Daniels family collection. Used with permission.

That time he also talked to his family and told them what property he will leave for them in his will. His mom was there, VP was there, and I was there, too, so I heard part of that conversation. He mentioned to his mom that he wasn't sure of his own security. He said, "If something happens to me, I want you to have this and that." Louise acted normal, and she seemed to understand what situation he would be facing. It seemed there was no surprise in her mind about what could happen to her son. She didn't ask him any questions. Just accepted it. That was the last trip that Jerry made to America. But he still laughed and he still joked. CIA style.

TED O. "LITTLE O" LYMPUS, high school and college friend

The last call we had from Jerry was at a strange hour. Patsy and I were already in bed. Jerry called, and he was unhappy. He talked about how many enemies he was making and he was in a no-win situation. Several of us were trying to talk him into getting out of there. Jimmy Pramenko talked to him quite a bit: "Get the hell out of there, Jerry. You don't need to be over there. Come home."

He wasn't happy with what was going on. There was a lot of turmoil over there. I don't remember anger, just him being disturbed about what a mess things were. There was confusion and a lot of animosity in the refugee program. He was in a situation where he was calling the shots as to who got to come to the U.S. and who didn't. He was so close with the people. And I remember him saying, "I'm pissing off thousands of people a day. Big time." Jerry was in a dangerous situation. He knew that he was making enemies because of his decisions. I think he was kind of disenchanted with what was going on and the way the Hmong were being treated.

But anyway, when Jerry called me that last time he wanted to make sure his will was okay. He had a holographic will. It was several pages handwritten on a legal pad. A self-done will dated December 9, 1980. He'd been thinking about it for several years, and finally he finalized it a few months earlier. Not long after that call he went back to Bangkok. That last call raised all the more suspicions in our minds when we were told that he was dead.

Conversation between MIKE OEHLERICH, former smokejumper; former Air America loadmaster, Laos, and his wife, Mrs. DAWN OEHLERICH

DAWN: The last time Jerry visited, the Old Man [Elmer Olsen] called and talked to me. He was concerned. Elmer said he wanted Mike to come down to Missoula and talk to Jerry. And the Old Man didn't mess around. If he had something to say, you knew what he was thinking.

The Old Man called because Jerry'd been crashing around the living room at night and had what's called the "blind staggers," knocking over furniture and stuff. Somehow, Jerry had graduated from the basement bedroom to the upstairs bedroom. You had to be really goin' some to get out of the basement bedroom. Like with Elmer's kids, you always knew who was on the shit list because you'd walk into his house and he had graduation pictures of all of them on three shelves by the fireplace. If you were on the bottom shelf, you were really in the doghouse. If you were on the top shelf, you were high in the Old Man's esteem. So to be in the upstairs bedroom was like getting to be on the top shelf. And if I was going to speculate on that, I'd say that Elmer was worried about Jerry and wanted him upstairs where he could see what was going on or could hear him because Elmer's bedroom was upstairs, too.

The Old Man said Jerry was supposed to be making calls and he was supposed to be getting back to Moua Cha and doing some business, but he'd been drinking way too much. Elmer was really worried that Jerry was not going to be able to finish his business. That's what he said on that call.

MIKE: When Dawn told me about the call from Elmer, I didn't pick up on how much concern there really was. I just thought it was one of those deals where they expected me to come down to Missoula to talk to Daniels because I'd quit drinkin' and I'd been to treatment and I was still in A.A. I had this spiel about alcoholism symptoms, and I guess they thought as an ex-drunk myself, I might get through to him. Would he have listened to me? Probably not. Generally if somebody's drunk, you're just talking to the alcohol, not the person. But you just never know when you're going to say the right thing that does get through.

Anyway, I didn't think that call was serious. The Old Man told Dawn I should "come down and 'save' Daniels" because "we're worried about him." "Saving" was a common phrase that was part of the Jerry lingo, and being "worried" about somebody was something we said as a jokey thing. So I thought it was just an invitation to come down and visit. Talking to Daniels was something I wanted to do and thought maybe I could get it arranged, but I was working as a painter, supporting a family on lousy wages, so I kind of put it off. Anyway, I didn't make it down there.

It wasn't until after Jerry left that I talked to Elmer myself. He said, "I'm kind of sad you didn't make it down to Missoula." Then he started telling me how serious it was and that they were actually very concerned, worried. It wasn't a joke. The Old Man said Jerry never went to sleep at night and they couldn't get him to eat. They'd put a plate of food down in front of him and they'd all eat, jabberin' and stuff, and his plate would sit there and get cold because he'd still be drinkin'. He was drunk all the time. He would sit down and fall asleep for a while and then start babbling without making any sense, like he was not in control. It was serious. And they were worried about his drinkin'. Then he was gone.

Did I have regrets after I heard that? Sure. I wish I'd have gone down. Turned out to be one of those things in life that was a lot more important than I thought it was at the time. I mean, I loved that guy more than anybody.

THOMAS C. "SHEP" JOHNSON, former smokejumper; former air delivery specialist, MR2, Laos

Jerry was always in good spirits. I never did know him or see him to be down. But on that last trip I think he was troubled by the resettlement problems, trying to get the Hmong out of Thailand and to the U.S. He had quite a bit on his mind about what he had to do when he went back out. He had quite a bit of responsibility. There just wasn't anybody else who could do that job. There just wasn't anybody.

CHA MOUA, Hmong friend; Hmong funeral organizer

On the last day when he's ready to go overseas, Louise and I drove Jerry to Spokane, Washington, about a three-and-a-half-hour drive. That day Jerry's mood was not good. Mostly Louise talks to Jerry. Louise says, "I'm getting old and maybe I will retire soon. I don't have much savings. Maybe I'll have to get food stamps." Jerry said, "You do what you want to do, but you'd better save your money." Louise just looked down and didn't respond. Even now, I still don't understand why Jerry's response to Louise was so negative and harsh. That was the first and only time I ever heard him talk to Louise that way.

At the airport I said, "Jerry, remember our plan about your gold mine." Jerry said, "Indeed, I will. The plan is solid in my heart." Louise and I watched Jerry get on the airplane to fly from Spokane to Seattle. Then we headed back to Missoula.

Conversation between MOUASU BLIAYA and his wife, Mrs. BAO V. BLIAYA, friends of the Daniels family

BAO: In late May 1981 Jerry called us one night. This was the first time he called us really late after we were already asleep. It was late, late, late. Mouasu ran and answered the call. He was gone the longest time.

MOUASU: It was Jerry calling and he was kind of drunk. He said he was very unhappy and disappointed in me. He thought that I would stay behind and help him work in the refugee program, processing all those people in Thailand.

BAO: Which was very unreasonable! From 1975 to 1981 Jerry never mentioned anything about wanting Mouasu to stay behind, so it was very strange.

MOUASU: Mostly he was complaining that he was unhappy working over there, unhappy with the refugee program. He talked about how this would be his last trip to work in Thailand. I had the feeling that he couldn't get much done the way he wanted to get it done. He was frustrated by people trying to stop him from bringing as many Hmong to the U.S. as he legitimately could. He didn't come out and say that, but that was the feeling I got. We talked for quite awhile, and he went on and on and on about that.

BAO: I'm an early riser, and the next morning was a Saturday. I was up doing my chores. Mouasu was up, too, and he said, "You know something? When Jerry called last night he sounded upset." Mouasu was recounting the conversation to me when the phone rang. Who is calling so early in the morning? It's six or seven o'clock. I answered the phone and it was Jerry again. Usually when Jerry called he said, "Hi Bao!" and asked how were we doing. This time he didn't say, "Hi Bao!" He just kind of attacked me right away. His exact words were, "Why did you let me talk to your husband last night when I was *khee-mao*?" He didn't say in English, "when I was drunk." He said in Lao, "when I was *khee-mao*." He said, "Why? Why? Why?" It wasn't like him at all. He was very serious and irritated. That's when I said, "Wait a minute, Jerry. I wasn't the one who answered the phone last night! How can I stop you from talking to my husband when I wasn't there?"

For thirty minutes he went on and on, going over the whole scenario of him talking to Mouasu when he was drunk. He probably remembered what he had said to Mouasu. He was so upset, and that was very unusual for Jerry. And he sounded kind of bitter, I think. Jerry did most of the talking and I just listened. I tried to change the subject and ask about Louise, but he was still upset and we didn't get anywhere. Finally I said, "Do you wish to talk to Mouasu?" And he said yes.

MOUASU: We talked quite a bit that morning, and at the end he said, "I'm going back to Thailand soon. I have a layover in L.A. for a couple of hours. Why don't you drop by and see me? We can talk."

BAO: After those two telephone calls Mouasu and I had a long discussion. I said, "Jerry was so strange on the phone." Mouasu said, "Yeah, last night when he talked to me he wasn't himself. He was raving and ranting about how this was going to be his last year with the Firm," let's put it that way. We concluded that he wasn't happy about something, but we didn't know exactly what it was.

MOUASU: About two weeks later I went to LAX in the afternoon. My brother, Colonel Moua Sue, went with me, because Colonel Moua Sue spent a lot of time working with Jerry in Laos and then in Thailand, processing the refugee applications in Ban Vinai. He worked with Jerry until 1980 and was very close to him.

Colonel Moua Sue and Jerry Daniels at Moua Sue's house in Ban Vinai refugee camp, Thailand. Carol Leviton Wetterhahn collection.

We met Jerry at the domestic terminal. When he got off the airplane and was coming down the walkway I could see that Jerry was not happy. No, not at all. Right away his face looked like he was in a temper. That was very unusual. We walked from the domestic terminal to the international terminal and sat down at the bar. Mostly we listened to him complain! He was sober but he was very down, very unhappy. Bitter and angry, both. He talked again about the refugee program and said he was thinking about retiring. For two hours he did most of the talking and pretty much he was talking to himself. I had never seen him in that kind of a mood before. There were no jokes from him that day. He was unhappy, complaining, bitter. After two hours we left the bar and he flew on to Bangkok.

Excerpt from a letter to KENT "DAN THE ANIMAL MAN" DANIELS, brother of Jerry Daniels, from Jerry Daniels, June 20, 1981

Bud,

Needless to say I cheated death and made her "back here." Met a round eye pitutsie on the plane. When we got to Bangkok it got to be a real mess, with gizz and pussy hairs flying at random. Of all things, come to here and get tied up with one of them. Anyway she was only here for a night, so as soon as she got gone I turned my self sideways and began to darken the real thing. After a few days though, Mac (the boss) began to peer down at my feet, seems my moccasins interested him, so I pulled them off and stacked em for a few months anyhow.

J. Bud

THOMAS J. "T. J." THOMPSON, former smokejumper; former air delivery specialist, MR2, Laos

In December '81 I left India and went to Bangkok. That's where I stopped to see Jerry. I spent three and a half days there and we visited. He was on a health kick. He was running a lot and was workin' out and was in really good shape. He wasn't drinkin' hardly at all. He'd come down for lunch and never have a beer. In the evening we'd get together and he might have one beer, maybe two, and that'd be it. I think he drank maybe, *maybe*, six beers in three days.

Excerpt from an audiotaped letter to LOUISE DANIELS from Jerry Daniels, November 1 and 2, 1981

I stayed up on lubs a little bit for a while but now I seem to be back down. Have been running fairly steadily lately. . . . And I've switched to running in the mornings even though I don't like 'er. Five o'clock, five-fifteen, get up and shave first. By then she's gettin' to be daylight and I flail off. Needless to say the weight's kind of gone down again. I'm starting to have the definite appearance of a greyhound. I like that better than that puffy feeling, even though some people say it looks hideous. . . .

It's six-thirty on Monday the 2nd. I just got through making the big five mile run. Under forty minutes. Everything went well.

THOMAS J. "T. J." THOMPSON, former smokejumper; former air delivery specialist, MR2, Laos

Jerry looked real good in December. His weight was down, he was doing a lot of refugee resettlement work, a lot of hours. He was pretty much a workaholic. At that time the refugee program was moving along, and he was trying to get as many refugees in as he could. He was really pleased with the results with the Hmong. One of my deals was, I said, "Well, are you gonna come home pretty soon?" And he said, "Yeah, I have about another year of work, and I think that's about all I can do here. Then I'm coming home."

Jerry wanted to come home. Not necessarily quit the Outfit, but at least take some time off. He was going to "shut down for a while." That's the term. Take some leave time and sort of regroup. Drink and think and whatever. We talked about what he planned on doing when he got home. Mainly he was just going to go gold mining for a while. Because he had a real good feeling and fixation about doing some gold mining, and he'd have probably made it pay. He had bought 460 acres out of Butte, Montana. He would go up and do some prospecting for gold on that property. And he wanted to work with the Hmong there in Missoula and make sure that they got started right and were able to get off welfare. So he had a mission in his own mind. Jerry had done very well. He was very wealthy in a lot of ways—money-wise, land-wise. And of course job-wise. He was very well respected.

Our friendship went for many years, and we talked about a lot of things during those three and a half days. Each evening I would go to his apartment and we'd talk. We had so much to talk about. After he died I heard rumors about Jerry supposedly crossing the Mekong River into Laos in November '81 to find American POWs. Well, I don't believe that. I'm sure that when I visited him in Bangkok in December he had not gone back across that river. If Jerry had crossed the Mekong a few weeks before I saw him, he would have told me. We would have talked about it. He didn't bring it up, so I thoroughly believe he didn't do it.

That last night we talked until around ten o'clock PM. We finished a long evening of talking, and I was returning to the States the next day. As we walked to the door I remember very well he kept saying, "Well, what is this fixation you have on India?" I said, "Like you haven't spent twenty years in Laos? What the hell's wrong with you?" We shook hands and said good-bye as we had done many times before. When I said good-bye to him, I stood there and looked at him for a second. We stopped and I turned around and looked at him and the thought just flashed through my mind: *I wonder if I will ever see Jerry again.* Nothing triggered it, and I can't say it was anything mystical. I just remember looking at him and thinking that. And as it turned out, that was an omen. A bad omen. Because I never did. That was December 12, '81, and he died in the spring.

Final Gathering

MONDAY morning: Hmong ceremony continues at the funeral home on the day of burial [*sam sab*]; spirit money gifts are burned; friends and relatives arrive for the third and final day of the funeral for Jerry Daniels; observations about the presence of government representatives.

> **TRADITIONAL HMONG FUNERAL CEREMONY—DAY THREE**
> **MONDAY, MAY 10, 1982**
> **"BURIAL DAY" [*SAM SAB*]**

Early in the morning, before eight o'clock, Hmong people arrive for the final day of Jerry's funeral. The kheng player blows the breakfast song [*tshuab qeej tshais*], the matching poem-song [*nkauj tshais*] is sung, and the family ritualist offers three drinks to Jerry's spirit. Jerry accepts each of them using the split bamboo pieces [*txhib ntawg*], then the family ritualist offers him a breakfast meal of rice, meat, and a drink. Jerry accepts that also. Today's schedule is tight, with less than two hours in which to complete the Hmong rituals. As a consequence, right after Jerry's spirit is fed breakfast, he is fed lunch.[1] That lunch is the last meal for Jerry's spirit.

After the last meal, the hanging bundles of spirit money are presented to Jerry as one big gift. The family ritualist pours three drinks and says, "Jerry, this money is from your close relatives and friends. It is for you to use in the spirit world. You accept it, then you get it."[2] After the spirit money gifts have been introduced and accepted, the funeral drum beats while the kheng player blows the burn-paper song [*tshuab qeej hlawv ntawv*].[3] During the song, quite a few people kneel down and bow [*xyom*] to show respect to Jerry for the last time. Then all of the spirit money is taken out of the funeral home to be burned. The money from the close relatives and friends is burned in a large metal trash can. As the money burns it turns to smoke and floats into the sky to be received by Jerry in the spirit world. The money gift from the immediate family is burned separately. Cha Moua burns it because he acts as the host family.[4] Then everyone returns inside the funeral home.

For the past two days there has been very little American participation in the Hmong ceremony, except for Jerry's mother, Louise, and sometimes Jerry's brothers and a few of Jerry's friends stop by. This morning many new American guests begin to arrive, and soon the funeral home is full of Hmong and Americans. Quite a few people have to stand outside in the hallway. While the Hmong rituals continue, many Hmong notice that the American guests are very attentive to what is going on, even though they do not understand it.

BARRY REED, former smokejumper; former Air America loadmaster, Laos

I read Jerry's obituary notice in the local paper. I probably hadn't seen him since 1972 in Laos, but I wanted to go to his funeral because he was a living legend. And they're rare. He was a living legend among those Americans who were living and working in Southeast Asia. And among the smokejumpers. And among the Hmong. And at the Agency. He touched a lot of lives. Plus, I was interested in seeing what other old friends I would run into.

On Monday I took some time off work for the scheduled funeral. I saw lots of familiar faces there, some of which were ex-smokejumpers like me that had worked for the Agency. Also there were a few people I knew who had retired from the Agency and were living in western Montana. And there were a lot of others there that I hadn't seen since when they were "Customers," either working in the "White House" [CIA management] at Udorn or at Long Cheng, Site 20-Alternate. Those people lived in Texas, California, Washington, DC, and elsewhere. So I was pleasantly surprised to see many of the people who came for that funeral.

Mrs. DAWN OEHLERICH, wife of Mike Oehlerich

Mike and I came into Missoula for the last day of Jerry's funeral and the burial. There were people there that we were not familiar with but we knew who they were: CIA people, Agency guys. It didn't surprise any of us locals that the guys with the shiny black shoes were there. I mean, it was pretty obvious they were not Jerry's close friends, just CIA people and they were making notes! They were checking it out.

HMONG CEREMONY CONTINUED

The family ritualist performs a rite [haws plig] that protects the souls of each guest from the influence of any spirits that may have been stirred up or drawn to the funeral ceremony.[5] Then he pours nine drinks for Jerry's spirit, one after another, saying, "Now I'm going to give you nine drinks,[6] then you are going to leave [sawv kev]. Even if you are not thirsty, you keep the drinks. You can give them to your grandparents, use them to hire someone to help you build your new house, or do whatever you want to do. We give you nine drinks, you take them all with you, and please take all illness and bad things with you also. Put them somewhere else. Leave behind only good things. Now go!" After the nine drinks are poured, the split bamboo pieces are tossed and this time the family ritualist wants to see that both faces of the bamboo are closed. Both faces closed means Jerry's spirit accepts that he must go.

Mrs. PAT DONTIGNY, former Missoula County public health nurse

I started working with the Hmong when they first came to Missoula in '76. As the only public health nurse working with refugees, I was continually going from house to house to help deal with their health issues. So I was with the Hmong in Missoula and the Bitterroot a lot. I had grown up in little ol' Billings, Montana, with a traditional American way of life. You went to school, you got an education, you got a job. On Sunday you spent the day at church and then you had a fried chicken dinner at home. The *Hmong* opened up another world to me! Being in touch with people who were actually *in* a war and what they went through to survive and get here and then all of their problems after they got here, the difficulty in adjusting. I learned a lot from them, but had not had time to get involved with them beyond work.

When I heard from the Hmong that Jerry Daniels had died, it didn't mean a lot to me. I'd never met the man. But I knew Louise, so I did go to the last day of the funeral. That funeral was an eye-opener to me. I figured it would be a regular American funeral, but it was not. The Hmong were just thick in there. That funeral was bigger than I thought it would be, and it was not a Christian funeral. That did not bother me. If you're going to work with foreign-born you have to accept them for who they are. You can't work with them unless you try to understand where they're coming from.

Mrs. MOE GEARY, wife of Helmville rancher Bill Geary

My husband, Bill, and I did go to the last day of Jerry's funeral. I was impressed that there were entire Hmong families there, all generations, with a lot of children playing in the aisles, just enjoying each other. Seeing so many children at a funeral, that impressed me.

The other thing that impressed me about that funeral was that they had pictures of Jerry there. I'd never seen pictures at a funeral before. I was brought up a pretty strict Catholic, and in the Catholic Church, funerals were such mournful ceremonies that it was a *delight* for me to see and enjoy this funeral celebration.

BARRY REED, former smokejumper; former Air America loadmaster, Laos

The newspaper obituary notice said that Jerry had died from an overdose of propane. So when I got to the funeral home I talked to one of the Agency case officers who had worked with Jerry quite often. He'd been a smokejumper, too. I said, "What the heck is this about the propane? That's not right, and you know that's not right.

What *really* happened?" And he said, "What difference does it make? The guy's dead. Let's just let it go at that." His attitude was just acceptance and that's it.

I knew through rumors that I heard when I left Southeast Asia in '74 that the communists had a price on Jerry's head. So I was just curious. I was convinced he was dead, but the story about the propane never added up.

Mrs. PAT DONTIGNY, former Missoula County public health nurse

Like I said, the funeral itself was an eye-opener. It fit with all those spy stories I had read. But they were *stories*. I really enjoyed *reading* them, but I never thought that in a sense I'd get involved in something like that, you know?

During the final ceremony when we were all sitting in the audience, three American men were sitting in front of me. They stood out because they were speaking quietly among themselves *in a foreign language*. That's what kind of triggered my thinking that maybe they were CIA. I assumed they were talking about things that they didn't want other white people to know about. They wouldn't want to speak English if they thought there was something going on with Jerry's death. Other than a few of the Hmong, no one else talked to the CIA guys that I saw. And they were kind of looking around, observing. Later I got to talking to Hmong people who said, "Oh, yeah, they were CIA. They worked in Laos with Jerry." They said it was Thai that those men were speaking. So the atmosphere of his death was not like a typical funeral. It seemed like there was this atmosphere of hush-hush and shadowy. Things weren't really clear.

Mrs. NANCY J. DANIELS, wife of Jack Tupper Daniels; sister-in-law of Jerry Daniels

At the funeral there were CIA guys there the whole time. They just stood there, very unemotional and said nothing. It was like they were watching over everything, like they were guarding. I don't know what they were doing, but they weren't friendly. They didn't come up to us, the family, and say, "We knew Jerry." It was like they were totally detached from the situation.

JACK TUPPER DANIELS, brother of Jerry Daniels

The CIA were at the funeral that morning and later that day at the burial, too. My feeling was that they were there just to make sure Jerry was put into the ground. Nobody *said* that's why they were there. And it's easy for the government to say, "We're sending these people as representatives." Like escorts that had to be there. I don't even know if they all knew Jerry.

Mrs. MOE GEARY, wife of Helmville rancher Bill Geary

It didn't bother my husband and me like it did some of the others that there were quite a few people from the Company at Jerry's funeral. For many years we'd been around Missoula smokejumpers who went with the Company in the early '60s. And since I was working for the Forest Service I knew the connection between the Forest Service and the Company was very strong, because of the smokejumpers that were recruited and also because of the airplanes. There were cargo planes that had been bought by the Forest Service for firefighting but they were never picked up. Instead, they were picked up by Air America or some other Company airline and were used in covert operations. When one of the planes went down on foreign soil it became a real issue because that plane belonged to the Forest Service on paper. So we grew up knowing there were people, even people in our family, who were willing to do covert things for their government. We always knew it existed. That's something that we considered to be part of our family heritage.

Regarding Jerry's funeral, anything that is different is a learning experience for me. It doesn't scare or frighten me or seem strange to me. I didn't know what was going on, but I didn't feel like I was left out either. The overall respect for Jerry was there, so you just respected what the Hmong were doing. You knew it was something deep within them and you were there, just following along, like being on the same river but in a different boat. I thought it was an extremely respectful way of taking care of someone you loved.

Louise

LOUISE Giblette Daniels as a mother; the relationship between Louise Daniels and Jerry Daniels; her attitude toward women; Hmong friends; last trip to Thailand; old age and death.

JACK TUPPER DANIELS, brother of Jerry Daniels

My parents weren't well educated, but my mother was *brilliant*. I mean, gosh, she graduated from high school when she was *fourteen*. And she *married* Bob when she was fourteen. And her mother—we called her Kakaw—was a clinical psychologist. Kakaw's specialty was interviewing kids who either had or were thinking about killing their parents. Louise's father left when Louise was born so she never knew her father. She had no sisters or brothers.

Louise Daniels with her mother, Mrs. Catherine Tupper Giblette ("Kakaw"), after they climbed the Statue of Liberty, New York, May 1931. Daniels family collection. Used with permission.

KENT "DAN THE ANIMAL MAN" DANIELS, brother of Jerry Daniels

The only thing that I'd like to know about Louise's dad is who he was. Because he left, supposedly, when Louise was born a girl. He was a coach, and a girl was no good. When he didn't have a boy he fled. So I'd like to call him up and say, "Jerry was a superman over there in Southeast Asia, Danny was the top forester here, I was the state champion wrestler and trap shooter, and Jack medaled at two different Olympics. How do you like that, asshole?"

JACK TUPPER DANIELS, brother of Jerry Daniels

My father grew up in an orphanage. I don't remember a lot about him. He was gone a lot; during World War II he installed switchboards at different military bases. What I *do* remember is that my mother was very, very into her children. Everybody else would say, "I can hardly wait for school to start so the kids will go back to school!" She was the one mother who would say, "I hate to see school start in the fall because my boys will go to school. I want them home." I can remember her saying that when I was a kid. She enjoyed us.

Mrs. NORMA HUGHES, Ovando rancher; friend of the Daniels family

Louise did *not* care for girls. She said that to *everybody*. When she was little and growing up she wanted to have nine boys after she was married, and no girls whatsoever. As the years unfolded, she got her nine boys because she had five sons and four grandsons: Boone and Tupper, Deeder and Farrett. So that equaled her nine boys. She was very happy about it.

Ms. CECELIA CHRISTENSEN (formerly Mrs. Jack Stratton), friend of Louise Daniels

Louise liked outdoorsy-type stuff, and she didn't mind being dirty. She liked guns, camping, hunting. She *really* liked to fish. And she enjoyed the things her boys did. She sent Jerry's bull riding gear to him in Laos when he asked for it. She didn't worry about him riding a bull. She thought it was interesting!

Ms. MYRA L. SHULTS, high school friend of Jerry Daniels

In that family you could characterize the boys as being mountain men. They hunted, they fished, they lived off the land. They all were smart, but there was something almost feral about them. And Louise was like the leader of the pack. Louise was a beautiful woman, but she wasn't a feminine woman. I think if she had her druthers she would have been a man.

Louise Daniels downs an antelope. Daniels family collection. Used with permission.

I was in Louise's house when she lived behind Kent and Julie, and also I was in her trailer. Louise's home was bare existence. That's all it was. It was just utilitarian. There were no touches that you would expect to see in a home.

Excerpt from a letter to the DANIELS FAMILY from JOHN BARKER,[1] January 24, 1948

Louise, my father's idea of cleaning a house was to sprinkle sand on the floor, sweep it out, and go hunting while the dust settled. He had no pride in ownership of a house as such—only if it looked like nature had created it as a part of the land. He could never see any thing remarkable about any public building. They were all just piles of material to him. You are so very much like him in that respect.

Ms. MYRA L. SHULTS, high school friend of Jerry Daniels

Louise was factual. Factual is the only way that I can describe her relationship with her own mother, Mrs. Giblette; her relationship with her boys; her relationship with her grandchildren. I don't want to use the word "nonemotional," but gushy emotions were just not her at all. Nor any of her boys. Louise was very proud of her sons but more like admiration of an equal. When she talked about her sons it was matter of fact. She didn't fuss over them. And she never voiced any concern about what Jerry was doing or that he was so far away.

Jerry was really good to Louise. He wasn't married, and I think he sort of made her his priority. People say, "Look at how a son treats his mother, and you can tell how the son will treat a wife." So you might ask, "Why did Jerry have such a good relationship with his mother?" I think it was because older women were revered in the Hmong culture. He must have picked up some of that. He took Louise overseas, and I know she liked going over there to visit him. He gave a dimension to her life that she had never had. And the Hmong loved her. She had this status among the Hmong because older people are revered anyway, and she was "Jerry's mom." And then she took care of the Hmong when they came here, so she had a purpose. It was something to do. And by then the Hmong were family. They were Jerry's people. If they were Jerry's people, they were Louise's people. She was supportive of them. The Hmong were family.

Excerpt from an audiotaped letter to LOUISE DANIELS from Jerry Daniels, May 5–10, 1973. This recording was made in Long Cheng, Laos, and seems to be the first audiotaped letter that Jerry Daniels made.

I received your tape and have decided to try to push on with this type of communication since yours was pretty pleasin' and a guy can just kind of ramble on. I will give it a try.

This year the Meo [Hmong] new year wasn't a pretty sight. You might say that she was whiskey flyin' around at random. The Animal Man would be proud to be here. Just loading people on airplanes, including myself, and we just yicked[2] around from place to place. It lasts a couple of weeks or so. This year I think it started some time in middle of December. In the old days, when there was numerous people right in the valley here, it was all around here. But this time everybody lives in different places to the south, so we have to take a chopper and flap around and try to hit two or three parties at a time. One night we ended up spending at Lucky's house downing white lightning at random. Like I said, it wasn't a pretty sight.

Tell everyone hello, Sharon and the Animal Man along with General and any other whiskey-soaked rumbuckets that you might see around the area.

Mrs. NORMA HUGHES, Ovando rancher; friend of the Daniels family

Sharon and Louise were real close. Louise thought a lot of her, and she was a nice girl. It was Sharon that told Louise that Jerry said it wouldn't be fair to her for them to be married with the lifestyle that he lived. And I never heard Louise say she thought Jerry should come home and settle down. Years would go by and Jerry was still in it. That was his life, doing what he was doing with the Hmong. Louise was dedicated in her belief of what Jerry believed in, and she came to love the Hmong, too.

Excerpt from a letter to Jerry Daniels from LOUISE DANIELS, December 16–25, 1980

Moua Cha closed his office for Christmas Eve and he called and said Mailee should bring me home to dinner which he had ready. We had boiled pork and roast pork and rice which is fine with me. [Then] Mailee's mother called and asked me to come to her house as she had some food for me. I thought she meant a dish of something to take home. She prepared the table and we sat down to boiled pork and roast pork and rice (and peas from her garden. She says she has "many, many" in her locker.) I finally realized that the boiled pork was a pig's head. She gave me an ear and she ate an eye with gusto. Things like that are fine with me, but 2 meals of fat pork on top of each other! I always think of you when I eat with the Hmong.

Ms. CECELIA CHRISTENSEN (formerly Mrs. Jack Stratton), friend of Louise Daniels

Before 1975 there were just a few special Hmong people here in Missoula—Mouasu and Bao, VP's boys and Saykham, then Moua Cha. Moua Cha *really* connected with Louise. Then after 1976 all of a sudden there was a glut of Hmong people coming here as refugees because their country fell. It was neat how they all revered Louise because of her age and because of her connection as "Jerry's mom." She was really driven to help them. She became a big part of their lives and vice versa. It was a good thing for her. A good thing.

Excerpt from an audiotaped letter to Jerry Daniels from LOUISE DANIELS, August 26, 1981

Lucky's wife came over the other night when she heard I'd been sick with my head. She cooked a dinner and brought me over about four dishes. It was really nice. . . .

FARRETT DANIELS, grandson of Louise Daniels

To me, over the years Louise became paranoid and pretty shaky. I think it was because she had worked with a lot of chemicals when she had the janitorial business. I remember in one of the bathrooms there was a weird stucco-type floor. The only way you could clean it was to scrub it with bleach. One day she was out of bleach or maybe she mixed bleach and ammonia or something. You go in there and she's on the floor scrubbin' away, and the floor, it's just *smokin'*. It's like, "Hey, get outta here, Grandma Lou!" As she got older that could have even brought on her Parkinson's disease. Who knows how long ago that started before they knew what it was? Because I saw a difference in her during her life.

Excerpt from an audiotaped letter to Jerry Daniels from LOUISE DANIELS, August/September 1981

I'm having so many, many headaches. They're constant. . . . I plan to go tomorrow over to your [gold mine] and just sit by the sluice box for about a week. I liked it so much there. . . . I can just sit out in the wilds and know that no human being is around. . . . Sorry to be such an "ish."[3] . . .

Lots of love, little Jerry.

Good bye. Be careful.

FARRETT DANIELS, grandson of Louise Daniels

Louise was still sharp mentally, but she got pretty paranoid. She'd burn stuff in her kitchen sink at night. That was when Jerry was still alive. I'd see her do that and then she'd throw the ashes away the next day. I don't want to get cloak-and-dagger about it, but it was almost like a middle-of-the-night thing. Probably it was done that way just for the sheer reason of her not having to say anything about it to anybody. "If I burn this in front of someone they're going to ask, 'What's that?'" I never talked to her about it. It wasn't *my* business, but I think she was burning letters and stuff from Jerry.

Excerpt from an audiotaped letter to LOUISE DANIELS from Jerry Daniels, November 1 and 2, 1981

Right now I'm hunkered here in my apartment. She's evening time, Sunday evening. I have a brace of pork chops hunkered under the water thawing, so off and on I'll be milling out to peer at them. . . .

One thing off the bat, I was walking home this evening and a nice gentleman dapper on a motorcycle pulls up and asks, "Are you Jerry Daniels?" There was no way to deny it. Some freelance journalist from Washington, DC, who had me pinpointed and wanted to talk to me. I spun a nice yarn and said I had to snarl off to Vinai tonight on a bus. I guess he'll continue to gadfly me. He wants to know about when men were men and threw their beer cans out of the window up in dreaded Laos. . . .

I just got through with the consumption function of the pork chops and eggs. They were mightily pleasin' and I topped it off with about half of over-a-lub cherry cheesecake that I had thawed out. A big Sandra Dee deal. I poured a little chocolate on it. So now I'm puff-addered up, layin' here on the bed.

Mrs. MARY V. YANG, wife of "Lucky" Lue Yang

Louise took a trip to Thailand to visit Jerry in late February and early March '82. She had a good time on that trip. She didn't walk very well by then, but she was doing okay. That was the last time that Louise was with Jerry. That was only six weeks before Jerry died.

Excerpt from a letter drafted by Louise Daniels to TONI BARILLA and JIM THOMPSON, 1982. Ms. Barilla had been a JVA caseworker in the refugee program in Thailand.

I had a wonderful trip to Bangkok. Jerry and I traveled 3,800 miles visiting the refugee camps. I had such a happy time and have so many happy memories. Since I had been in Thailand before this time I asked to just see the camps as I have so many refugee friends and have been so interested in them for a long time. We also did things like going on the working elephant tour and the orchid nursery tour. Jerry had made so many special happy plans.

Mrs. MARY V. YANG, wife of "Lucky" Lue Yang

After Louise came back from Thailand she said, "Honey, Jerry told me to go visit before something happened to him." She didn't like that. Then after he died, Mom got very mad. She said Jerry *knew* that Jerry would die. That something was going to happen to him. That's what she kept saying, many times, over and over again.

I don't know if Jerry really knew, but Louise *believes* that Jerry knew that he would die because he kept saying to her, "Come on over before something happens to me!" She was very, very mad, very, very upset, very sad after Jerry died. She never laughed. She never smiled anymore. She was so heartbroken.

Ms. MYRA L. SHULTS, high school friend of Jerry Daniels

Louise was *devastated* when Jerry died. I never saw her cry, but I know she was depressed for a long time after that. And she had *horrible* migraine headaches. It was a terrible thing to have her oldest son, Danny, die, but it was a whole different thing for Jerry to die. There was a relationship between Louise and Jerry that was unlike what she had with any of the rest of her sons.

Excerpt from a letter to MOUASU BLIAYA and his wife, Mrs. BAO V. BLIAYA, from Louise Daniels, August 20, 1982

Dear Mouasu and Bao,

I have thought of you many, many times. I can never find the words to thank you for all you did at the time of Jerry's funeral. . . .

I have received so many letters saying such wonderful things about Jerry, and every one is a treasure to me. He had a wonderful life because of the Hmong people he loved so much, and we are very proud of the life he had.

With very much love and many, many thank yous

Louise

P.S—Sunday nite,

Mouasu, we spoke of Jerry's suitcases. They are sending his things in 2 sections—

one by air and one by sea which they say may take several <u>months</u>. Yesterday the things sent by air arrived. His camera, wristwatch, tape recorder and cassette player and several other things are <u>missing</u>. The stuff went thru customs in <u>Chicago</u> at O'Hare Airport; I wonder!? This makes me very sad. There were 5 big boxes of stuff. We were going to give away his clothes—and they sent them. They sent over 50 clothes <u>hangers</u>, and a bunch of cleaning junk—like 3 mopheads. Even sent 2 cans of whole milk!—a couple of old pans—and a box of old white crackers and shoe polish—unbelievable! We'll see what the luggage situation is if they ever arrive.

L.

Mrs. MARY V. YANG, wife of "Lucky" Lue Yang

In August 1982 they sent a lot of boxes from Thailand. Louise called us one morning and said there were a lot of boxes from Jerry in front of her trailer. She wanted to look for the embroidered Hmong blanket that Jerry bought for her when she was in Thailand. And she wanted to look for her silver necklace from Jerry. We went through *every* single thing. Oh, so many things. That took many days. Jerry's passports, a lot of letters that were stamped from the United States. We found her silver necklace but not the Hmong blanket. After we went through everything she didn't feel happy.

The next day when I came back it was raining. I asked her where she wanted to put the rest of the boxes. She said she burned two of them already. She had four or five big metal garbage barrels outside where she burned the boxes. She wanted me to check at the bottom of the barrels and see if everything was burned down. We went and dug in the barrels. Some of it didn't burn down all the way so she said, "Let's burn it more." I didn't know what she was throwing away and I didn't care. I just said, "Okay, Mom, let's do it. Let's do it." Then we burned more. We burned everything down. We burned a lot of pictures, Lao money, we burned *everything*. Mom was very sad. She was sad the whole time we burned those things.

KEITH "SKID" WOLFERMAN, smokejumper; friend of Deeder and Farrett Daniels

After Jerry died the State Department went through some sort of processing and put all of his personal effects in one big, giant shipping crate. Farrett and Deeder were really excited when this big wood crate of personal effects came. It was six feet high and two and a half to three feet wide and probably six feet deep with big black two-inch block letters stenciled on the diagonal right across it: THAILAND. I mean it looked like a prop off an old cargo ship in a Hollywood movie. That crate just barely fit through the front door of Grandma Lou's trailer. Inside the crate they had clothing, papers, even canned food. There were wall maps of the Everest region, Hmong embroidered tapestries, pots and pans. It wasn't depressing. There wasn't anything in there that was macabre, and there was nothing in there that was so personal that it made you feel ashamed to be seeing it. It was just a bunch of stuff. And here it was. The summation of his existence, all in one spot.

Excerpt from a letter drafted in 1983 by LOUISE DANIELS to HOWARD FREEMAN, former provincial advisor, Lima Site 36, Na Khang, Laos

It took me many months to go thru Jerry's things. Boxes of stuff—you wouldn't believe. Almost everything but not his VP ring which he had requested I take out to him when I visited him a few weeks before he died. I think someone turned his desk upside down into a huge box. I sorted and sorted. Finally Lionel [Rosenblatt, Washington, DC] came here and also sorted and packed up a number of boxes of papers which he said some day could be historically valuable. I think he was just getting things out of my sight.

KENT "DAN THE ANIMAL MAN" DANIELS, brother of Jerry Daniels

Danny went, then after Jerry went, Louise never really got perkied. She never perkied up after Jerry died. Just "woe is me." Do you remember Nancy Reagan at Ronald Reagan's funeral? She'd talk to one of her boys and the way she looked up to the side like that, a slow head turn with that woebegone look. Louise had that same expression of "Oh, my."

RANDOLPH "TOBY" SCOTT, former smokejumper; former Continental Air Services (CASI) loadmaster, Laos

Louise and I stayed in touch. I'd call her regularly, and I visited her when she lived in that damned ol' trailer house with the steps about to fall off. A few months after Jerry died, the CIA invited Louise to go back east to Langley and they gave Jerry posthumously the Distinguished Intelligence Medal.[4] They gave her this medal, and then said, "Don't show this to anybody." Shit! Well, Louise showed it to me. That medal was in a box, real fancy lookin'. She said, "Don't tell anybody."

Central Intelligence Agency Medal for Distinguished Service. Daniels family collection. Used with permission.

Central Intelligence Agency Medal
for Merit. Daniels family collection.
Used with permission.

Central Intelligence Agency Medal
for Valor. Daniels family collection.
Used with permission.

What the hell's goin' on? That's a hell of a deal to give him a damned medal and
say don't tell anybody. Like the CIA can't give any recognition. That's bullshit. They
should have put her picture on the front page of the *Missoulian* and said, "Mother of
Jerrold B. Daniels Receives Posthumously This Famous Medal."[5]

Mrs. SUSIE LINDBERGH MILLER, co-curator of *Hmong Voices in Montana* exhibition

Louise was in declining health when I first went to visit with her in 1990. At the time,
I was gathering information for the Montana Hmong cultural exploration that cul-
minated in an exhibition at the Missoula Museum of the Arts. I met Louise because
her son, Jerry Daniels, was beloved by the Montana Hmong for the role he had
played in their lives.

Louise was helpful with the exhibition. She found old letters, photos, and slides sent by Jerry while he was in Laos and Thailand. She would call me from time to time to let me know she had uncovered something more. Sometimes she would show me the Hmong embroideries that had been gifted to her over the years. I would sit and visit with her about how she was feeling that day, and she would share her recollections of Jerry and his love of hunting and fishing, and how she would take me one day to the family property in Ovando, Montana. She treasured her memories of Jerry.

Excerpt from a letter drafted in 1983 by LOUISE DANIELS to HOWARD FREEMAN, former provincial advisor, Lima Site 36, Na Khang, Laos

Jerry left me the gift of a whole new world full of his wonderful friends. To the Hmongs I will always be "Jerry's *niam* [mother]," and I will always be proud of the look that comes into the eyes of a Hmong I have never met before when I am introduced. They often throw their arms around me—men and women alike—and say "I love you. I love Jerry!"

As I sit here thinking about him I am indeed proud to have had him for my son.

Louise Daniels on the balcony of "Colonel Moua Sue's house" in Ban Vinai refugee camp, northern Thailand, March 1982. Daniels family collection. Used with permission.

Mrs. SUSIE LINDBERGH MILLER, co-curator of *Hmong Voices in Montana* exhibition

Our conversations about Jerry were at the beginning of the time that I knew her. In the early months she spoke of Jerry's steadfast friends who continued to call her and visit from time to time when they would swing through Missoula.

The exhibition, *Hmong Voices in Montana*, took about three years to complete. As the months and years went on, Louise's health and memory declined considerably. By 1992 we didn't talk about Jerry often. I moved away from Missoula in the spring of 1993 and didn't see Louise again. I often wondered how her remaining days were.

THOMAS J. "T. J." THOMPSON, former smokejumper; former air delivery specialist, MR2, Laos

I used to go back to Missoula, and I always stopped to see Louise. My God, she was a hell of a woman. When you went to the house there was fresh fish in the sink that she had just caught and cleaned. Later she was in the convalescent home, which was really dreary. To see her diminished like that was terrible.

Ms. CECELIA CHRISTENSEN (formerly Mrs. Jack Stratton), friend of Louise Daniels

Louise never wanted to end up in a nursing home. She always said to me, "Promise that if I end up in a nursing home you'll come and kill me." She felt very strongly about that. Her mother was in a nursing home for about two years before she died. Louise spent a lot of time with her and did not want to end up that way. And I'd say, "Oh, yeah, Louise," thinking, *Oh, this'll never happen.* Then she ended up in the nursing home, and it was devastating for me to go see her because she didn't even know who I was.

Mrs. MARY V. YANG, wife of "Lucky" Lue Vang

By the time she was in the second nursing home, she was tired and she didn't talk anymore. I still went there and took care of her. Sometimes I reminded her about when we had our English classes together and I made many mistakes with my English. But I never mentioned anything about Jerry or anyone in the past because I didn't want to upset her.

Mom died in January. It was cold. Dry cold, no snow. She always told me that when she died she wanted to be burned up, cremated. And she wanted her ashes to be buried in the same cemetery with Jerry and Danny and the uncle that gave her the property at Tupper Lake. One time when we went together to put flowers on Jerry's grave she pointed to a spot right at the toe of Jerry's grave and said, "When I die I want my ashes right here." She said that was her spot.

Mrs. JULIE DANIELS MORITZ, daughter-in-law of Louise Daniels

I don't think anything ever eased her sorrow. Jerry did for her what none of the rest of her sons did. If she needed something, he saw that she had it. He did for her, he took care of her. It was never the same again. I think she died feeling the way she did when she found out he was dead.

Excerpt from the LAST WILL AND TESTAMENT of Jerry Daniels, dated December 9, 1980

It is my instructions to Jack T. Daniels that to the extent possible, even if immediate liquidations of assets is required, that best efforts be made to assure my mother, Louise G. Daniels, is provided sufficient cash support to maintain a reasonable life style as she may so desire until her death or incapacity, whichever may come first. My definition of a "reasonable life style" for Louise would include all creature comforts (housing, clothing, food, medical care) also entertainment such as traveling, all with no work required.

Until Horse Grows Horns

SUNDAY midday and afternoon: The Hmong ceremony at the funeral home concludes with the "leaving song" [*qeej sawv kev*]; a group photo; pallbearers; the drive to the Missoula Cemetery; Higgins Avenue bridge remembered. Hmong burial rituals at the Missoula Cemetery; a blessing on the Daniels family; final gifts; Lao dirt; comments after the burial service. [See Map 3 on page 230.]

HMONG CEREMONY CONTINUED

The kheng and drum play the "leaving song" [*qeej sawv kev*][1] as the kheng player leads the pallbearers and the casket out the door of the funeral home. Though a short song with a strong quick tempo, the message is still sad: "This is your last day on earth. All rituals have been done. Close your eyes and don't miss the friends you left behind. Now you go on your own. You will see your ancestors, so go." All the guests, Hmong and American, stand in two lines as Jerry's casket passes between them on its way out.

Now all is done at the funeral home. The drum is dismantled while everyone prepares to leave and go to the cemetery for the burial. Jerry's tools need to go with him: the split bamboo pieces, the crossbow and arrow, the umbrella and the small horse carrier. The family ritualist gathers them up and carries them in a bag.

KEN HESSEL, former smokejumper; former Continental Air Services (CASI) Air Operations, MR3, Laos

There was a *crowd* of people in that chapel. When it was over we all filed outside. Probably ten or fifteen of us were former jumpers who had worked overseas with Jerry. Someone took a picture of just about all the jumpers that were there. Some local friends got into the picture too, but mostly it was just a select bunch of guys that Jerry jumped with and worked with for years. After that picture was taken, one of the jumpers turned around to me and said, "I'm gonna go get a beer at the Ox. You comin'?" I said, "That sounds good to me."

Group photo of smokejumpers, government representatives, and Missoula friends of Jerry Daniels. Left to right in order: Kirk Samsel, Ken Hessel, Mike Oehlerich, Jon Randall, T. J. Thompson, Kent "Dan the Animal Man" Daniels, Burr "Mr. Clean" Smith, Bill Demmons, Joe Glasgow, Kurt "General" Olsen (with beard), Elmer Olsen, Ted O. "Little O" Lympus, Randall "Peterbilt" Olsen (with beard), Leonard Krout; three in back at right: Lee "Terrible Torgy" Torgrimson, Roger Savage, Brent Russell; one in front at far right: Loy "Ringman" Olsen (with beard). Photo taken outside the Mountain View Mortuary, Missoula, May 1982. Toby Scott collection.

CHARLEY HUGHES, Ovando rancher; friend of the Daniels family

Without any question all the pallbearers were there on the third day. We moved that casket from the funeral home to the hearse, then from the hearse to the gravesite— and I'll never forget the weight of it. Because I've been a pallbearer to a lot of different people, including all three of the Daniels that have passed away. And I'm telling you, I've never run acrost a casket that weighed like that one did. They said it was lined with lead. There was six of us pallbearers, and if there wasn't five other fellas there that was pretty danged husky we could never've packed that thing! It was that heavy.

JON FOLAND, Missoula crony; former smokejumper

I was a pallbearer along with some of Hog's other local cronies: General, Ringman, Peterbilt, and Terrible. My wife was all concerned because all we had with us was our fishing clothes from Clark Canyon, no decent clothes to go to a funeral. I said, "I don't need funeral clothes. I just need my Whites." It was Jerry's mother that requested I wear my Whites. Those are jump boots, and she thought that would be good.

There's always enough people to tote a friend's box. We toted that box to the hearse, and I'm telling you it was hugely heavy. And I'm pretty good sized—six foot two inches, and my jumpin' weight was 200 pounds.

CHA MOUA, Hmong friend; Hmong funeral organizer

I will never understand why the Americans say the casket was heavy. Only three or four of us Hmong lifted that casket from the airport to the funeral home and it's not that heavy. In fact, we think it is too light! So I don't know. Maybe Jerry rode on their shoulders!

BOB JOHNSON, former Highland Section chief, JVA, Thailand; regional director, International Rescue Committee (IRC), Seattle

Worm, Lucky, Sancho, Judy, Spiderman, and Glassman were listed on the memorial card as the Hmong honorary pallbearers. Those were the radio code names that Jerry had bestowed upon them in Laos. They were the field liaison officers who were fifteen- or sixteen-year-old kids that spoke some English when they started working as translators between Jerry and the Hmong troops. They came from all over the U.S., and all of them were there.

We emptied the funeral home and formed a big procession out to the cemetery. It was one of those fire drills with trying to get everybody into a car. As we're going down the street, there's water dripping out of the trunk of my rental car from the beer we're hauling around. I thought we might have a problem if we got pulled over because we had a full police escort from the funeral home to the graveyard, and there were more than a few weaving cars. I said, "We ought to be a little careful because most of the people here are drinking." Whoever was riding with me sort of laughed and said, "Yeah, but the cops are leading the procession. This is not unacceptable behavior for a funeral in Missoula."

RANDOLPH "TOBY" SCOTT, former smokejumper; former Continental Air Services (CASI) loadmaster, Laos

Well, ol' Jerry and I, we always would say, "God Almighty, that guy must be forty years old!" That started when we were down at Marana, and of course we weren't even twenty-five back then. "Damn, he's over the hill." Forty years old was just *it*. So we always said, "Well, if we ever hit forty years old we're gonna jump off the Higgins Avenue bridge." That old bridge in Missoula crosses the Clark Fork River. Boy, you go off that thing, you're done. Right through there the water's only about two feet deep and it's rocks. Solid rock, no survivors. Back then we figured we'd live forever, you know?

View of the Clark Fork River and part of downtown Missoula as seen from the Higgins Avenue bridge. Photo credit: Gayle L. Morrison.

I was thinking about that pact we made on the way out to the cemetery. That story about jumpin' off the bridge was just something that went on and on, for years and years. Jerry would always bring it up, "Well, the old Higgins Avenue bridge is gettin' closer and closer." I still got a letter from Jerry and he says, "Welp, ol' timer," he says, "the closer I get to forty the more I think that we ought to push this thing up to about fifty-five." Ha! That letter was only about a year before he got killed, because he was forty-one when he died.

BOB JOHNSON, former Highland Section chief, JVA, Thailand; regional director, International Rescue Committee (IRC), Seattle

It was a long cross-town drive. The Mountain View Mortuary was on the south side of town, so you had to go straight through part of town, then over the railroad tracks, and Boot Hill was out at the edge of town at the north end. It was a long drive, and everybody was still basically hung over. And sort of fired up again, too, to a certain extent. Because we'd had all morning to kind of get going.

I remember Burr Smith, that's Mr. Clean. Burr had good Jerry stories, and he was a real character, an interesting guy to talk to. Burr had a bottle of cognac that got passed around at the gravesite because, well, it was kind of cold and a little breezy out there.[2] So it was something to take the nip off. I stood pretty near Burr because he had that bottle of cognac! Burr had on his green beret, his actual combat beret, from his military days before he was with the Agency. He must have been an Army Special Forces type. It looked pretty dog-eared, but he put it on for Jerry's burial.

"BURIAL" [FAUS]

It is a chilly day at the Missoula Cemetery. Jerry's family members sit in front, and a large crowd of friends stand around the gravesite. After the casket arrives, again the Hmong are unable to complete their rituals for Jerry in the traditional way, but they adapt and do the best they can.[3]

In Hmong tradition the first burial ritual is "cut clothes" [txiav ris tsho].[4] Usually the family ritualist cuts slits into the burial clothing, then he opens and closes the casket three times. He will say to the deceased: "You will see the sun then we close the coffin and all will be darkness. You will see the sun again then we close the coffin and all will be darkness. The third time, when darkness comes, that will be the end of this life on earth for you." For Jerry, the family ritualist says the words, but he cannot cut the clothes or open and close the coffin.

Kia Moua Thao has acted as the family ritualist; now he represents the important position of "sister" [muam phauj] and gives a special blessing. The Daniels family already suffered one death when Jerry's oldest brother, Danny, died in a car accident just outside of Missoula. The U.S. government is saying that Jerry also died in an accident. For Hmong, if that is true, two tragic accidents in one family could be related to bad luck or to a curse. To be on the safe side and to prevent it from happening again, a special blessing is given to Louise and her family:

> Now that you have passed, Jerry, you have carried away these bad things. From this point on the Daniels family will never again suffer like this. Not until the horse grows horns, the cow grows canine teeth and the river runs uphill.

After the blessing, Jerry's casket is prepared to be lowered into the cement box that is in the ground.

CHA MOUA, Hmong friend; Hmong funeral organizer

When the Hmong rituals are spoken, Louise asks me, "Honey, what did he say?" I sit close to Louise and I translate for her. I tell her what is said about cutting the clothes and about the blessing, but to translate and talk about things between the living and the dead is complicated.

BOB JOHNSON, former Highland Section chief, JVA, Thailand; regional director, International Rescue Committee (IRC), Seattle

There was a large spray of evergreen boughs across the top of Jerry's casket. I watched Animal Man work something out of his pocket. He had a Louis L'Amour book with him and he said, "Well, Jerry's going to need something to read." I said, "Well, then he'd better have a beer too." I gave Animal Man the beer can I was holding, and he slipped the novel and the Oly Gold under the pine boughs on top of the casket.

CHA MOUA, Hmong friend; Hmong funeral organizer

They prepare to lower the wood coffin into the cement box in the ground. The flowers that Louise ordered and the evergreen wreath from Norma and Charley will go down with the coffin. That's the time when I see Mr. Clean [Burr Smith] standing on the other side of the grave. When the coffin is ready to be lowered he looks back and forth, back and forth, but he cannot say *anything* because he is too emotional. And what can he say? Jerry's gone. Burr looks back and forth with his tears falling down. He looks at that coffin and he pulls off his wristwatch without saying a word. The way he did that, in my mind I knew that there was a special relationship between Burr and Jerry that was very tight, very close.

Kent "Animal Man" Daniels bids farewell to his brother, Jerry Daniels. Front row of onlookers: Dr. Bruce Bliatout (Portland), Yang See (Chicago), Hang Sao (Seattle), Chou Moua (Missoula), Long Yang (Michigan), Chu Vang (Santa Ana, CA). Mouasu Bliaya collection.

JACK TUPPER DANIELS, brother of Jerry Daniels

There's a bar on both sides of the casket that the pallbearers use. Mr. Clean took his watch off and I saw him buckle it to the bar on the side of the casket. The leather strap probably has rotted away by now, but his watch should still be lying there outside the casket.

RANDOLPH "TOBY" SCOTT, former smokejumper; former Continental Air Services (CASI) loadmaster, Laos

When Jerry was up at Site 36 and I was in Vientiane I'd get on the horn and tell him, "Damn, I'm about out of snoose." He'd send me two cans. Then he'd call me when he was out, and I'd send him a couple of cans. So I dropped a can of snoose into Jerry's grave. Just kind of spur of the moment. Just for the hell of it.

THOMAS J. "T. J." THOMPSON, former smokejumper; former air delivery specialist, MR2, Laos

Toby put in a can of snoose and I dropped in an empty Golden Oly. The thing I regret is that I crushed the empty can. For what reason I did that I don't know. And when I did, I spilled some beer on Jon Foland's Whites.

JON FOLAND, Missoula crony; former smokejumper

My snoose can went in the grave with him. It was just kind of a tribute to Hog, a can of Copenhagen for Hog. And several of us drained an Oly and tossed the cans in. Somebody was concerned that Louise might be offended, but she wasn't at all.

CHU VANG, son of General Vang Pao

One guy drank a beer before he put the can in there. I think it was empty because he kind of squeezed it a little bit and he said, "Well, this is for you," and dropped it in there. And we wondered, "Why?" Because the Hmong people want to remove the can. According to Hmong culture, we don't want any metal to go into a grave. No metal in or on the body, no metal in the casket and no metal in the grave. But then we kind of have a feeling that maybe that is the way Jerry's life is, and his family and friends want him to have some beer along when he goes to heaven.

LEE "TERRIBLE TORGY" TORGRIMSON, grade school friend; Missoula crony

I'd never thrown anything into a grave at other burials. This was the first time. I guess I just wanted to leave something of mine with Jerry, you know? So I threw my pocketknife in there. I figured he needed a knife because many times when we went on a D and D, Jerry would buy a chunk of that stinky limburger cheese and would put it up on the dashboard. He'd cut chunks of cheese with his Buck knife. So I kind of figured he needed to have a knife with him for his stinky cheese because he loved it so much. He needed it for his D and Ds in the sky.

That pocketknife was one I'd carried for a long time, a Schrade. I put my pocketknife in there and I started tearing up, so I walked away and stood by myself. It was not only missing him. I was going to *miss* him, but also I had some anger. 'Cause I had that gut feeling after his last visit that this goddamn government of ours would do that to our own people. I remember feeling that at that time, and I'm totally convinced of it still. It was a waste of a helluva good man.

LOY "RINGMAN" OLSEN, Missoula crony; brother of Kurt "General" Olsen

There were people puttin' in watches, lighters, beer cans, everything. I put in elk teeth. Elk teeth was something I had with me on my key chain. They're not real ivory but they're a trophy for gettin' an elk. They're kind of special and we all keep them. So that was something that might mean a little bit to throw in there. Elk teeth are better than just pickin' up rocks and throwin' them in!

Mrs. JULIE DANIELS MORITZ, sister-in-law of Jerry Daniels

I was interested in all the stuff the different people put in the grave. That was a surprise to me! Somebody put a watch in. And somebody put a bottle of Jack Daniels in. I thought, *Well, some day somebody's gonna dig this grave up like they do to the Indian graves and they'll say, "Oh, boy, look at this!"* The jewelry things, like the watch, I was astonished at that.

CHA MOUA, Hmong friend; Hmong funeral organizer

At the funeral home, I wrapped up all the ashes from the burned part of the family money gift [*tshuab ntawv vam sab*] and put them in a paper bag. After the coffin is lowered into the cement box I say, "Jerry, here's your spirit money that I give to you," and I drop it down next to the coffin. Then the cement lid is closed.

Mrs. JULIE DANIELS MORITZ, sister-in-law of Jerry Daniels

After that I said, "Hey, enough." I left because I wasn't going to stay like the Hmongs. It was cold and the wind was blowing and it was miserable. But the Hmongs stayed to the very end, until they pounded in all the dirt. And some of the Americans stayed, too. You have to know people in this part of the country. They hadn't seen anything like this before. They didn't know what the Hmong were doing staying behind at the cemetery for so long, so *they* would stay, too. There's always that group that's going to stay until the last drink is poured and the dogs go home.

May 10, 1982, at the Missoula Cemetery: Joe Glasgow, "Rainbow" Chou Moua, Toby Scott, Miles Johnson, T. J. Thompson, and "Snowball" Chou Thao. Photo credit: Bob Johnson.

CHA MOUA, Hmong friend; Hmong funeral organizer

At the cemetery when they closed the cement box, one American man carried a bag of dirt and put it under a tree. I don't know who he was. That bag weighed about five pounds, and the dirt filled one corner of the bag, not the whole bottom. The American man said, "*This* is dirt from Laos. Maybe it's a good idea for everybody to grab a handful of dirt and throw it into Jerry's grave." He said "everybody" but mostly he means the Hmong. "Maybe you *Hmong* might want to use this dirt from Laos." And that was encouragement for all of us. I said, "Okay! That's good!"

I was the one who opened the bag and called to the Hmong people, "Come here! This is real dirt from Laos! This is the last gift to Jerry." Everybody was so excited! They said, "Where? Where is it?" Probably I was the one who reached in with the first hand to grab it. Then everybody in the whole Hmong group came, at least fifty Hmong. Each one grabbed a small handful of that dirt and threw it on the lid of the cement box. That dirt was very dry and it was kind of red. It really did feel like dirt from Laos! We don't know who brought it, but every Hmong who was there that day grabbed it until it was gone.

SHUR V. VANGYI, former Ministry of Economy, Royal Lao Government; former executive director, Lao Family Community Inc., Santa Ana, California

In February 1976 when we were in Thailand, Jerry had said, "I'll take care of it for you. Don't worry about it," so I had not thought about the Lao dirt for many years. *Only* after Jerry died and I was at his funeral, then I remembered the last time I saw him, and in my mind over and over I thought: *Where did Jerry put the Lao dirt? Where did he put the dirt?*

Then Moua Cha made the announcement at the cemetery that someone had a bag of dirt from Laos. Oh, I was so surprised when Moua Cha announced that! It had been so many years, and I thought the dirt went to VP, to the main post. Because the purpose of the dirt was for VP to hold the souls of all Hmong who followed VP to America. When VP says only one word, both the Hmong in America and the Hmong in Laos will come to him and work together. We hoped that the people who still fought for freedom back in Laos would keep the fire alive. That fire would be the door for us to go back. But VP never mentioned receiving the Lao dirt.

Six years later the Lao dirt was there at Jerry's burial. I said nothing about the dirt to anyone because all that mattered was that now the Lao dirt was given to Jerry to carry. It didn't go to VP as planned, but I was happy because I knew that Jerry's spirit carried the Hmong soul back to Laos. He loved Laos, and the excellent service that he did there was so great for the Hmong people.

The way it turned out, *Jerry* carries the dirt that holds the soul of all the Hmong and Lao refugees who fled from the communists and came to America. Part of my soul and part of Jerry's soul is in that dirt, too. And when that dirt was buried with Jerry, everything changed. All the Hmong and Lao souls that were brought to the U.S. were planted here and won't be able to go back. That is the final point of the dirt—that the souls who came here are here to stay. We may not go back to Laos as we had hoped, but we can survive and succeed here because our soul is here. And that is what Jerry always wanted for the Hmong in this country.

HMONG CEREMONY CONTINUED

According to Hmong custom, the Hmong will stay at the cemetery until the grave is filled in, all the dirt is tamped down and the grass is replaced. When the ground is level, the family ritualist completes his work. First he picks up the crossbow and shoots the small arrow into the sky. The purpose is to kill any bad spirit that is lurking nearby. He says, "We shoot you because you caused this death!" Then he uses his big knife to cut the small carrier, the spirit horse, right down the middle. When he cuts it, he kills it. He kills the horse so it cannot return to earth to pick up someone else to take to the spirit world. Then he puts the split bamboo pieces, crossbow, parasol, and broken carrier on top of the grave. All of Jerry's tools are left there for him along with the flower arrangements. By two or three o'clock in the afternoon, everything is finished. The box with the rooster and all of Jerry's meals goes into the trash barrel as everyone goes home.[5]

End of Hmong Funeral and Burial Ceremony

Mrs. MOE GEARY, wife of Helmville rancher Bill Geary

I think it would have pleased Jerry to have that ceremony. Oh, for sure! I mean *anybody* would be pleased. It was wonderful. And in the conversations afterwards at his mom's house no one questioned what went on as being strange. But I did hear a rumble that some still wanted to find out if it was really him in the coffin. I didn't have that concern, and I believe a lot of families would have suffered greatly if he wasn't in that coffin—his Hmong family, his smokejumper family, and of course, the Daniels family.

Conversation between TED O. "LITTLE O" LYMPUS, high school and college friend, and his wife, Mrs. PATSY SKELTON LYMPUS

PATSY: On the way home after the burial Ted was so quiet. He felt real empty. He was pensive. We talked about it off and on all the way back to Kalispell, just how weird the whole funeral experience was. We still had a lot of questions, and there wasn't any conclusion for us.

TED: We had a lot of suspicions. That service wasn't comforting at all because I was far from satisfied that I knew why or how Jerry Daniels was dead.

Four

AFTER THE BURIAL

May 11, 1982–2012

Question Remains

TUESDAY morning: Cha Moua returns to the cemetery to perform the Hmong ritual of feeding the spirit [*tawm tshais*]; questions about the autopsy report, Thai boy, and investigation in Thailand; suspicions and conspiracy theories; the question of exhumation.

"OFFER BREAKFAST" [*TAWM TSHAIS*], A RITUAL THAT TAKES PLACE FOR THE FIRST THREE DAYS AFTER THE BURIAL DAY

CHA MOUA, Hmong friend; Hmong funeral organizer

In the Hmong tradition, for the first three mornings after the burial I take food to the cemetery to feed Jerry's spirit. I do this because I represented Jerry's family at his funeral. On the first morning after the burial I carry a lunch sack to Jerry's grave. In the sack is a piece of cooked meat and a serving spoon of rice, all wrapped in tin foil, and a can of beer to drink. I tell Jerry's spirit, "Jerry, I come this morning to bring you breakfast. Here's your food. Come and eat." That's it. On the first day I hang the meal on a tree branch at the grave. That meal is supposed to hang in the air, not sit on the ground, because spirits don't walk on the earth like humans, they travel by air. Like a humming-bird! They come and suck it up then *GO!* That meal will hang where I leave it until it falls down by itself. After I deliver the meal I come more than halfway from Jerry's grave to the cemetery gates and I put a stick there as a marker. I put the stick down and I say, "You wait here, Jerry. Tomorrow I will come again and bring you breakfast here."

The second morning I go to the marker, not all the way to the grave, because I already led his spirit to where the stick is. I come to the stick and bring him the breakfast food: meat, rice, and a drink. I hang the sack lunch on a bush and say, "Jerry, here is your second breakfast. Come and eat." Then I pick up the stick again and take it to the gates of the cemetery. When I stop and put the stick down I tell him, "You wait here. Tomorrow I will come again."

Usually you are leading the spirit back to your home. If Jerry were part of my family, that day I would take the stick all the way to the corner of my house. But I didn't lead Jerry to any house. Not to my house and not to Louise's house either. I cannot take him to his mom's house because how is she going to do the rest of the rituals when Jerry's spirit returns to her house? Special words need to be said and daily feedings for thirteen days [*puv tsug kaum peb hnub*]. How can Louise do that?

On the third morning, I know that Jerry loved fishing so I take the stick and put it near the Orange Street bridge on the bank of the Clark Fork River. I put his breakfast where the stick is, and I call him: "Jerry, this is the third morning. I bring you breakfast here. Come eat!" I leave the stick there and I say, "Jerry, after you eat you can stay here and fish for as long as you want!"

Mrs. PAT DONTIGNY, former Missoula County public health nurse

It wasn't until after the funeral was over that I started to ask the Hmong questions. Then their attitude about how they believed Jerry was killed started coming out. If you talk to our government, it was a gas leak. If you talk to the Hmong, he was killed.

So the big question about this funeral was why was there such a fight to keep this casket closed? There should not have been any public health concern since there was no communicable disease. If there was some embalming done and there were no concerns other than disfigurement, they could have opened that casket. Even if he looked bad, I don't think you could have shocked the Hmong whatsoever. I was a public health nurse, and to me the excuses for not opening the casket were inadequate. Why was there such a fight to keep the casket closed?

Ms. MYRA L. SHULTS, high school friend of Jerry Daniels

Louise told me that the State Department or the CIA or whoever was giving the orders, told her she *could not* open the casket when it came home. I remember that *very* clearly. *Very* clearly. Jerry's friends were asking her to open it: "Let's make sure." But our government told her not to do it. She had orders.

Ms. CECELIA CHRISTENSEN (formerly Mrs. Jack Stratton), friend of Louise Daniels

Louise said to me that somebody had advised her not to open the casket. So in Louise's mind there was always a question: *Was it an accident or did somebody do something to him?* And I don't think that was ever resolved in her mind. Never.

Years later Louise did say that she wished the casket had been opened. She talked about Lucky saying that he wished he had been able to look in the casket. I think she was regretting that he didn't because she would have trusted what he said. So she did talk about it much later. Not a lot. It was a really hard thing for her.

KEN HESSEL, former smokejumper; former Continental Air Services (CASI) Air Operations, MR3, Laos

You know, I asked Lucky, "Lucky, what do you think happened to Jerry, and who was responsible?" Shep was sitting right there, too. And Lucky said, "There are three possibilities: the United States government, the mystery man, or the communists." Well, you know, I looked at Shep when Lucky said the U.S. government. That surprised the heck out of me. I thought, *What do you mean by that?* I didn't ask him, but if that's the thinking among the Hmong, what the hell's goin' on here?

"LUCKY" LUE YANG, former field liaison officer (FLO), MR2, Laos; Hmong funeral organizer

No one is comfortable with that story about the gas water heater. Some of us think there is some political question about Jerry's death. I don't want to say this, but my personal feeling is that it's not good when you know too much. It's dangerous. I don't want to say anything further. This is just my personal feeling.

We still have no proof that Jerry was in that casket, or figured out what really happened to him. No proof. No answers. Until somebody proves something, *this* question will stay with me and it will be a mystery for me until I die.

NENG VANG, former lieutenant colonel, SGU Army, MR2, Laos; former Hmong chief of Ban Vinai refugee camp, Thailand

When we fled Laos in 1975 we knew that genocide would happen to the Hmong left behind because almost all of the Hmong in Laos were American-influenced, no matter what. The North Vietnamese came into Laos, and they were going to force the Hmong to become communist even if we wanted only democracy.

Jerry and I had worked together in Laos. After I became chief of the Ban Vinai refugee camp in Thailand in 1979, I asked Jerry if there was a way to help support the Hmong in Laos. Jerry was the only one that we trusted and approached for help. We believed Jerry was still CIA so he might know something that we didn't know. But Jerry said, "No, there is no way. America is not going to help. Just go to America." Jerry said America had washed its hands and had no more interest in Laos or in getting Laos back as a democratic nation. I asked him periodically, not just one time, but Jerry never changed his story.

TOU-FU VANG, former lieutenant colonel, Royal Lao Army (FAR), Laos

In 1981 to '82 *big* things were happening in Thailand. General Vang Pao, the surviving Lao leaders overseas, and the military leaders who stayed in Thailand had the mission to try all they could to retake the country. There were thirty or forty thousand resistance troops along with civilian people inside Laos who were ready to launch a full military resistance against the communist Lao government. The resistance was expanding and going quite well, with troops on the ground and troops being trained. Neo Hom [United Lao National Liberation Front] was getting help from the Thai military, and there is no doubt that General Vang Pao was talking with the U.S. government about support.

NENG VANG, former lieutenant colonel, SGU Army, MR2, Laos; former Hmong chief of Ban Vinai refugee camp, Thailand

About one month before he died, Jerry came to Ban Vinai and talked to me privately. He said the position of the United States government was changing. He said since I didn't want to go to the United States there might be something else possible. Jerry said to me, "Neng, maybe it will be possible for you to stay here instead of me asking you to go. There might be work for you to do." Because at that time the United States was secretly funding aid to the Thai government to support the Cambodians to find out what was going on in Cambodia. After Jerry told me that, I got my hopes up. Then he went back to Bangkok. When I heard he died I was so shocked. Maybe somebody knew that Jerry had said something. After Jerry was gone, nobody ever said anything more about that.

TOU-FU VANG, former lieutenant colonel, Royal Lao Army (FAR), Laos

In '81 to '82 Neo Hom was ready to launch the resistance. That didn't happen because our people in Washington, DC, were competing for policy. Nothing happens until policy is decided and signed; then you are sure you can implement it. The U.S. government did not commit to a policy to support the resistance in Laos, so our politicians in Washington, DC, turned their attention and activities elsewhere.

Mrs. PAT DONTIGNY, former Missoula County public health nurse

I always understood the Hmong attitude to be that he was killed by the U.S. government, the CIA, because he was too interested in the Hmong. He was becoming too powerful and demanding certain things for them, trying to get the people to the U.S. and helping them once they got here. And once the Vietnam War shut down, I would say that the Hmong were not a priority for the U.S. anymore. So the stories about his death continue to fly over the years.

RANDOLPH "TOBY" SCOTT, former smokejumper; former Continental Air Services (CASI) loadmaster, Laos

The way it all happened, you can't blame anybody for bein' suspicious, the way the CIA handles everything. They may even do it on purpose just to make everybody wonder what in the hell's goin' on. They could have been a lot more forthright. Hell, you could find out more reading the Bangkok newspaper than you could from the damn CIA.

Conversation between TIM "WEENY MAN" LIEN, Mrs. KATHY G. OLSEN, LOY "RINGMAN" OLSEN, and RANDALL "PETERBILT" OLSEN, Missoula cronies

WEENY MAN: Is that him in there? Is that how he died? Well, the government should have had a better story. Shoulda said Charlie came in and shot him. Or

Pol Pot did. Somebody could have come in and fragged him. He could have got hit with a .155 round and it just "mistified" him. The list is endless. But to die under these circumstances? Being gassed? Come on!

RINGMAN: They should have just opened the casket. It would have been a simple thing. But all the cloak-and-dagger stuff by the government just made it worse.

KATHY: And where's the Thai boy that survived? Was he ever questioned?

WEENY MAN: The conspiracy theories ran rampant from the very first second we learned that Hog was dead. Under those circumstances, there were just too many questions to be common sense.

PETERBILT: The Hog's too sharp for that. Maybe they slipped a rubber hose with gas under the door. Maybe they killed him off that way.

WEENY MAN: Or maybe they bound his hands, tortured him, and stuck his head in a propane can.

Mrs. DAWN OEHLERICH, wife of Mike Oehlerich

After Jerry's death it seemed to me that all of our friends, especially the Animal Man and his family, were so concerned that it had been a conspiracy and that there had been foul play and that's why the casket was sealed and nobody ever saw Jerry's actual body. There was so much concern and so much hullabaloo going on about that whole thing. The official government story didn't really stack up, that's true. But *our* take on it, Mike and I thought that probably he died from alcoholism. We've seen it. We've seen those kinds of situations where maybe something is coughed back into your lungs, like an aspiration. *We* thought it probably was alcoholism.

MIKE OEHLERICH, former smokejumper; former Air America loadmaster, Laos

That was Dawn's theory. This might be a real stretch, but I think maybe if he wanted to sleep, and he's already got too much alcohol in him, he might take something to give him some rest, some sleep, and that may be enough to shut you down. The muscles are going to relax and your brain that tells you to breathe may stop talking to you. I mean, there were a lot of drugs around in Thailand. I was there. I know. Jerry was a big anti-drugger. He had no use for drugs. But if he had something to help him get some sleep or get some relief, to get away from that craziness, I think he would have used it. And maybe the Thai kid would have helped out with this. Maybe it had worked before. This time it didn't. So that's *my* theory. It may offend people, but it's still possible.

TED O. "LITTLE O" LYMPUS, high school and college friend

At the time of Jerry's death in 1982 I was Flathead County attorney, a prosecutor, so I had contact with the state medical examiner in Missoula, Dr. Ron Rivers. I had

Jerry's original death certificate in Thai, along with an English translation of it; the affidavit of the mortician at the Institute of Forensic, Police Department in Bangkok, along with a translation of it; and the mortuary certificate that accompanied the body to Missoula. I told Dr. Rivers what the U.S. Embassy told us, and he said it was not consistent. He said if Jerry was on the bed passed out drunk, asleep, or whatever—if there had been either LP gas or CO leaking into the room, both are heavier than air and would have flowed down to the floor. It would not have reached him up on the bed.

Louise was in Jerry's apartment six weeks before his death, and she had described a substantial gap under the door. So the gas would have flowed across the floor, under the door, and down the stairs. Dr. Rivers said Jerry's death didn't seem physically possible under the circumstances as we were led to believe they occurred. That came straight from the state medical examiner, a forensic scientist. So the death certificate stating "carbon monoxide intoxication" just didn't wash. And we never got an autopsy report. We never got *any* proof that there *was* an autopsy.

JACK TUPPER DANIELS, brother of Jerry Daniels

We never received any autopsy report on Jerry. The postmortem examination report done by the Thai police department was sent to us completely sanitized, *all pages were blank*. We never received any toxicology report. No information about his blood alcohol level or anything else. And certainly no comparison of lab results from Jerry's body with lab results from the Thai kid who was taken to the hospital by the police. What was *his* blood saturation level of carbon monoxide? Why weren't we given that information?

KENT "DAN THE ANIMAL MAN" DANIELS, brother of Jerry Daniels

The autopsy—that's always been one of my favorite thorns in the ass because apparently no American attended any part of it. I would *suppose* there's an Embassy doctor, an Embassy medical man who investigates American deaths. Even if you or I died in a foreign country, as U.S. citizens, the Embassy would be responsible for investigating the circumstances of death. But it appears from the signatures on the postmortem exam that it wasn't up to any American official to do Jerry's autopsy. Why was there never an American doctor involved? Why only the Thai police department? Jerry was a U.S. citizen and a U.S. government employee. His death should have been handled by somebody within the U.S. government structure.

THOMAS J. "T. J." THOMPSON, former smokejumper; former air delivery specialist, MR2, Laos

There was a lot of stuff that came from the Embassy that was all blacked out. Hell, I saw it. There was so much blacked out that it meant nothing. You'd read about three or four words in a sentence and the rest was blacked out. And who authorized the blackout? I guess it was the Embassy. Security plays a big role in it, but it was just a poor setup that led to mumbling. I mean, there's no reason for it to end like that! He was an honorable guy who did an honorable job and he's been covered in mystery.

RANDOLPH "TOBY" SCOTT, former smokejumper; former Continental Air Services (CASI) loadmaster, Laos

They've got the casket sealed and they won't tell anybody what their autopsy results were. I mean, what kind of an autopsy could the Thai police have done anyway? No, the suspicion will *never* be done the way the U.S. government handled it.

Excerpt from cable 147316, SECRETARY OF STATE, Washington, DC, to American Embassies in Bangkok, Manila, Kuala Lumpur, Singapore, and Hong Kong, May 28, 1982

SUBJECT: REFUGEES: POSSIBLE PRESS INQUIRIES ON DEATH OF REFUGEE OFFICER JERRY DANIELS—GUIDANCE

Q. IS THE DEPARTMENT SATISFIED WITH THE INVESTIGATION INTO THE MATTER?

A. YES. AS PART OF THEIR CONSULAR FUNCTIONS, AMERICAN EMBASSIES IN ALL FOREIGN COUNTRIES VERIFY THE CIRCUMSTANCES OF DEATHS OF AMERICAN CITIZENS WHO DIE WITHIN THEIR JURISDICTIONS. IN THIS CASE, AS USUAL, THE THAI AUTHORITIES WERE EXTREMELY HELPFUL AND COOPERATIVE AND THE EMBASSY IN BANGKOK IS COMPLETELY SATISFIED WITH THE THOROUGHNESS AND COMPETENCE OF THE INVESTIGATION.

"GLASSMAN" YANG SEE, former liaison between Jerry Daniels/Sky and General Vang Pao/MR2 staff, Laos

I hoped the State Department or whoever conducted the investigation would have done more with this case, but they closed it so soon, so early. It is unbelievable that they did that, but what can I say? To be frank, if the Thai boy survived, and apparently he did survive and then he just disappeared after that, then I believe that probably Jerry was murdered by that boy opening the gas. And he must have had somebody else behind him. That was my suspicion, but I did not take it to the authorities because the U.S. Embassy certified Jerry's death and quickly closed the case. To me, I believe it was a very lousy government investigation into this matter.

TED O. "LITTLE O" LYMPUS, high school and college friend

None of us were satisfied. The Montana state medical examiner, Dr. Ron Rivers, and I were disturbed that the coffin was sealed. We had some real strong feelings that the cause of death wasn't as we had been told. And wasn't as was represented on the death certificate. Dr. Rivers said, "We can always exhume the body and conduct our own postmortem examination."

KENT "DAN THE ANIMAL MAN" DANIELS, brother of Jerry Daniels

Little O was at Jerry's funeral. Now he's a district court judge and he has always been interested in digging up Jerry. What would I hope for if we dig him up? That he's in there, dead. Without a bullet hole or a crushed body.

JACK TUPPER DANIELS, brother of Jerry Daniels

Do you want to know what my greatest hope would be if we opened the casket? My greatest hope would be that he's not in there, that he's alive some place and we could actually find him. What could be better than that?

KENT "DAN THE ANIMAL MAN" DANIELS, brother of Jerry Daniels

If Jerry's still alive I would think that he was taken prisoner and is still a prisoner over there and *that* would really get me irritable. Every now and then I wonder if maybe he was captured and some day he'll show up and be pissed off that the insurance money is all gone and that his property has been sold. I think about this in the middle of the night sometimes. It's always just a wonder. But I suspect that if he was captured he'd be dead by now. Jerry said that he and VP had a reward on their heads. I wouldn't think that he would still be alive if they had a reward out for him.

"LUCKY" LUE YANG, former field liaison officer (FLO), MR2, Laos; Hmong funeral organizer

Would we *still* like to open the casket? If we can, yes! Yeah, and if he's in there or he's not in there, both are bad. If he really died and we know he died—that's bad, but at least we know the truth. But if we open it and it's not him, or there's no body in there or he died some other way, then what would you think?

BOB WHALEY, former smokejumper; lieutenant colonel, USMC (retired)

If the family wanted to put this thing to bed once and for all, couldn't they get a court order to open the casket? But then the drama rises over whether the government would permit that. And that's what continues to fuel this whole issue. All hell breaks loose if it isn't Jerry in there!

MIKE OEHLERICH, former smokejumper; former Air America loadmaster, Laos

Is Jerry in that box? My bet? I'd say yes. I don't care who gets shot or who gets killed, there's always conspiracy theory. People *like* conspiracies. They *want* some secret shit. It's all bullshit. The simplest thing you can think of is probably what happened.

Mrs. DAWN OEHLERICH, wife of Mike Oehlerich

Yes, he's in there. I know people like to talk about it. Like Jerry's somewhere in Nepal on a secret deal. That's something I could imagine a person like Jerry being capable of because he had so much charisma. But the way he was operating on the last visit, he was too self-destructive to have kept it together to pull something like that off.

Conversation between RANDALL "PETERBILT" OLSEN, LOY "RINGMAN" OLSEN, Mrs. KATHY G. OLSEN, and TIM "WEENY MAN" LIEN, Missoula cronies

PETERBILT: My vote's nay. He's not in the box. In fact, I saw a picture of him down there at Sportsman's Warehouse the other day. It looks just like him, in Russia hunting polar bears. Looks just like him!

RINGMAN: I took my wife to see it because it really does look just like him.

KATHY: It really does! There's no date and there's no name on the back of the picture.

PETERBILT: You never know. Maybe he's softened up in his older age and he thought, *Well, I could slip this in and I'm sure the Olsen boys and some other cronies will stagger in there and see it in the Sportsman's store and say, "There's Hog! He is alive!"* Hunkered over a big polar bear, which is just what he'd be doin'.

RINGMAN: The cloak-and-dagger's got some appeal to it, and everybody can make up their own mind, I guess, but it probably ended like it should. Jerry was there at the right time. It was kind of a wild time and he'd done a lot of things. And he treated everybody right. To me, he lived in a better time than now.

WEENY MAN: I think Ring's right. It worked out right because I just can't picture Hog here now. What the hell would he do here?

RINGMAN: I guess he could sit around and get fat like the rest of us, but I don't think so.

KATHY: He'd be in Russia.

PETERBILT: Yeah, that picture has me convinced. I think he's in Russia somewhere, huntin' polar bears.

RINGMAN: Yeah, I really hope that's Jerry there with that polar bear. And I hope someday I'll be sittin' in my chair and there's a knock at the door and it's Jerry saying, "What's goin' on, huckleberry?" I really hope that happens.

An Echo of Death

ORGANIZERS and guests describe the Hmong spirit-release ceremony [*tso plig*] performed for Jerry "Hog" Daniels in September 1982 at Tupper Lake on the Daniels family property near Ovando, Montana. [See Map 5 on page 307.]

CHA MOUA, Hmong friend; Hmong funeral organizer

A couple weeks after the funeral I told Louise, "I know Jerry keeps working toward his future, his new life. We don't want to hold him back. According to Hmong tradition, after thirteen days we want to release his spirit in a final ceremony [*tso plig*] so he will be free to reincarnate or do whatever he wants to do." I said, "We don't have to do that at the funeral home. We can do that on Jerry's property. We can take Jerry back to his own land at Tupper Lake. He will be happy about that." And Louise said, "I like that idea, honey. I like that."

Conversation between NORMA and CHARLEY HUGHES, Ovando ranchers; friends of the Daniels family

NORMA: See, Jerry never made it to heaven as far as the Hmong were concerned. By the end of the funeral in Missoula he never made it there. How they knew this I don't know, but that's what they said. That's why they had a party up here at the lake.

CHARLEY: Now that's one that if you didn't see it, that's one you missed.

TRADITIONAL HMONG SPIRIT-RELEASE CEREMONY [*TSO PLIG*] SATURDAY, SEPTEMBER 25, 1982

Traditional Hmong believe that each person has three spirit-souls [*plig*]. When somebody passes away, one spirit is reborn to be an animal or a human. Another spirit returns to the ancestors during the funeral ceremony so that it can be reborn into the same family. The last spirit stays with the body of the deceased. That spirit still suffers the pain, the hurt, and the hunger that was in this life. That spirit must be released so that it can be reborn.

After a traditional Hmong funeral there are thirteen days of waiting [*puv tsug kaum peb hnub*]. When the thirteen days have passed, there is a final ceremony [*tso plig*] that fully releases the spirit that stays with the body. A spirit-release ceremony can be done anytime after the thirteen days, even years later. Cha Moua and Lucky Yang, their wives and four or five other helpers organize a spirit-release ceremony that takes place four months after the funeral.

Excerpt from a 1983 draft letter from LOUISE DANIELS to HOWARD FREEMAN, former provincial advisor, Lima Site 36, Na Khang, Laos

I'm so glad we had the Hmong [funeral] ceremony. It means so much to the Hmongs. I think how Pop [Buell] would've loved a ceremony like that, but his family is very religious and I'm sure would've been disapproving.

We also [will do] the required 2nd ceremony in which a cow is killed. It [will be] held on our property up in Deer Park. To prove the Hmongs will never change—one of the men with a Ph.D. called me from Portland offering to have the necessary 2nd ceremony there—if we couldn't do it here. He thought we might have a problem with reporters, which we indeed had had. As these things went on, I could just hear Jerry say, "This is a dandy!"

CHA MOUA, Hmong friend; Hmong funeral organizer

The day before the spirit-release ceremony, Louise and I went to the cattle auction to buy a live cow. We choose which cow we want, then Louise asked a friend who was there, "Can you bid this for us? Whatever you think is fair." We got that cow for four hundred dollars. Louise paid for the cow.

I asked the people at the auction to help me load it onto my blue truck. I had an open pickup, so they tied the cow's feet together so it couldn't kick or get out. Then I took off to Ovando. Oh, I shouldn't have taken that chance! When I drove on the highway the cow almost jumped out of my truck a couple of times. I was so scared! After I went close to forty miles I pulled off the road and I retied the cow. Maybe Jerry held the cow for me while I drove the rest of the way!

Conversation between FARRETT DANIELS, nephew of Jerry Daniels, and KEITH "SKID" WOLFERMAN, smokejumper

FARRETT: Keith and I'd gone fishing up at Tupper Lake the day before this deal for Jerry was going to happen. We were driving out to go home, and there's a couple miles of flatland right off Highway 200, Kleinschmidt Flats. We dropped down onto the flats and from a distance we saw Moua Cha's rig coming at us, kicking up dust. "Oh! Here comes Moua Cha with the cow." I knew he was bringing up the cow the day before the ceremony. His pickup truck was coming at us, and it looked empty. I was thinkin', *Wow! No side rails. Where can the cow be?* Keith and I stopped and flagged him down. "Hey, Moua Cha, where's the cow?" "It's in the back." We didn't see any cow, so we hopped out of the rig to take a look. He had this cow hog-tied, layin' on its side in the back of his pickup.

SKID: We peeked over the side of this truck bed and there's this cow lying on its side all trussed up and tied down to the back of this truck, one big ol' wild eye staring up at us. We were like, "Oh! Never seen a cow hauled this way unless it was already dead!"

FARRETT: Its eyes were as big as saucers. It didn't know what was going on, but it can't be a good ride from Missoula to Ovando for a cow lyin' on its side. It knew that its life was in peril.

Keith and I drove on home to Missoula. We talked about going back up to Tupper Lake the next day. We figured this would be a pretty good deal because the Hmong were going to cook the cow and we were pretty much poor and hungry. So, wow, a barbecue! That's what I was picturing—a barbecue. *Hoooo*, that sounds like a good time!

CHA MOUA, Hmong friend; Hmong funeral organizer

I got to Jerry's lake, and I left the cow tied to a pine tree. Then I came home. Early the next day, Saturday, I picked up Louise, and we went to the cemetery. Louise stayed in the truck while I went to Jerry's grave to call his spirit [*plig*]. Now he's no longer a

Kent and Jerry Daniels fishing from a homemade raft at Tupper Lake, 1950. Daniels family collection. Used with permission.

human friend. Now he's a spirit and I have to make contact at the grave. I carried a small Hmong crossbow [*rab hneev*] and arrow with me. The crossbow I made just for today's ceremony. It will *never* be used except for this ceremony.

That morning, this is what I did. I laid the crossbow on his grave. Then I picked up the crossbow and I spoke to Jerry in Hmong while I moved the crossbow in a circle over the grave to call his spirit. I said, "Jerry, today I come here to get you. . . ." At the cemetery that morning I felt quite emotional. It was hard for me to speak, *very* hard to talk. The hurting I had in my heart was because I called him by name but I didn't see his face. I said, "Jerry, I come here to pick you up to take you to your lake at Ovando. In the Hmong way, we will do the ceremony to release your spirit forever. Release you from any pressures or problems. After that, you will be free to do whatever you want, no strings on your back." I explained that to him. I said, "Jerry, I have a cow that is waiting for you at your property. I come here to get you so we can drive there together. Let's get into the truck. We go now." Then I felt warm in my heart, like I made a connection to him. I carried the crossbow and arrow and led Jerry's spirit to the truck.

Louise was waiting there, and I knew she was very sad. Her face was so red. She didn't ask me any question because she felt too emotional. In her eyes there were no tears, but I knew she cried in her heart. I said, "Mother, we go now. I got Jerry with us." Then we drove sixty-five miles to Ovando.

KEITH "SKID" WOLFERMAN, smokejumper; friend of Deeder and Farrett Daniels

Farrett and I went back to the lake on Saturday. After seeing Moua Cha with a cow tied down in the back of his truck it was, "Well, that was worth it! Let's see what else happens!" Because I knew there'd be a procession of interesting people cruising up there that day. And there was.

Mrs. NORMA HUGHES, Ovando rancher; friend of the Daniels family

That day the Hmong came through here, *carloads* of them. There must have been ten piled into every rig. I'm sure there was a hundred at least that came for this party. They all knew their way up here to the lake. They'd been here so many times before for picnics or to fish.

FARRETT DANIELS, nephew of Jerry Daniels; son of Kent Daniels

We could always tell when the Hmong'd been up at the lake fishing. If they'd been there we'd find these rudimentary fish traps with many lines on one little string. We'd see all the lines and the remains of really small heads and tails from fish that normally we'd throw back. Americans will do two or three fishing lines but these guys that lived in the jungle, they were fishing to *eat*. Of course the Hmong were always welcome up at the lake. But it was kind of like haulin' the cow, you know? The way they fish just wasn't the way Americans do it. It's different.

Mrs. NORMA HUGHES, Ovando rancher; friend of the Daniels family

I know it was the 25th of September because that was the birthday of Hazel McGuiness. I had baked a cake, and Charley and I were going to go down there for supper. Charley and I and my mom and Louise all went together over to the Daniels' property. Louise was doing great that day. She had an inner strength.

Louise Daniels and "Lucky" Lue Yang at the spirit-release ceremony for Jerry Daniels on the family property at Tupper Lake, September 25, 1982. "Lucky" Lue Yang collection.

HMONG SPIRIT-RELEASE CEREMONY CONTINUED

In 1982 almost all of the Montana Hmong live in Missoula. On a Saturday morning in late September, over sixty Hmong adults get together and go up to Jerry's property. Husbands, wives, and children go. Most of the men had been soldiers in Laos and knew Jerry. Louise Daniels and a few of her American friends are there. Everybody is there all day long for Jerry's final ceremony, his spirit release.

When the Hmong get to Tupper Lake, the first thing they do is cut some small trees to make a shelter or "house" [*lub tsev*] for the ceremony. The "house" is a temporary structure made from rough posts, rope, and sticks. Black plastic sheeting is used for the roof.[1]

Next they make a small "bed" [*lub txaj*] that is the size of a small table, about twenty-four inches square and thirty inches high. It is made from sticks and is very simple. It only needs to be sturdy enough to hold a large basket. The "bed" is placed in the middle of the "house," near the fireplace [*lub qhov-cub*] that they build with rocks.

Next, about fifteen feet from the house, they build a simple spirit gate [*rooj vag*]—two vertical wood posts with a crosspiece on top. In Hmong belief, when a soul is led away from the cemetery, some bad spirits may tag along. The spirit gate acts as a screen so only the chosen spirit is allowed to enter.

To hold Jerry's spirit, someone brings a large flat basket [*lub vab*] woven from bamboo. Usually that flat basket is used for winnowing rice. Today it will be used as a spirit basket [*kauj vab*]. The organizers use sticks to make a frame that arches over the flat bamboo basket. Louise has given them one of Jerry's shirts to use, a long-sleeved white shirt, which they put over the frame. With the shirt on, now the frame looks like the shoulders of a sitting man. They put a pine branch stick into each of the two shirtsleeves to make arms for the man.[2] Now the man looks like an eagle with his arms spread out wide. Finally they roll a length of black cloth into a ball. Usually that cloth is used to make a woman's head turban [*hauv phaum*], but today they put it on top of the shirt frame for a head. After they make the figure of a man's head and shoulders, they place three rice cakes [*ncuav*] and a new pair of split bamboo pieces [*txhib ntawg*] inside the shirt frame on the bamboo basket. A new bottle of wine and a small cup are set outside of the basket.

Kia Moua Thao was the family ritualist [*txiv cuab tsav*] for Jerry's funeral ceremony in Missoula, and he is the family ritualist for Jerry's spirit-release ceremony as well. There are two kheng players and two drummers. Khoua Ker Xiong and Nhia Koua Vang will beat the funeral drum.[3] Now the Hmong are ready to begin the ceremony.

First, Cha Moua goes to his truck to get the crossbow that brings Jerry's spirit from the cemetery. He returns with the crossbow and stops outside the spirit gate to wait for the people inside the house to bring the basket with the frame of a man's head and shoulders. Inside the house, the kheng player starts to blow his instrument[4] and Khoua Ker Xiong beats the drum that hangs chest high in front of him. The family ritualist and the person who carries the basket with the frame follow the kheng player out of the house to meet Cha Moua outside the spirit gate.[5] All the people are standing and watching. Louise is in front so that she can see everything clearly. One of the Hmong women explains to her what is going on, and Louise pays close attention.

When the three men get outside the gate, the basket with the frame of a man is placed on the ground. Cha Moua puts the crossbow and arrow on the ground next to the basket, and at that point Jerry's spirit moves to the basket, to inside his shirt. Jerry's spirit has returned to his family and friends and is sitting there waiting for his ceremony. This is an emotional moment, and there are tears from the people standing there who loved him.

Kheng player greets Jerry's spirit. Behind him on the path is the spirit basket; behind him on the right is Chialong Moua holding a cup for drinks. "Lucky" Lue Yang collection.

CHA MOUA, Hmong friend; Hmong funeral organizer

Chue Pao Moua's wife and Lucky's mother-in-law cry a lot. Later on Louise said, "Honey, I like the way the Hmong ladies sang that song." I told her, "Louise! You thought they sang a song? No, they were really crying hard!" Louise said, "Oh, honey, I didn't know that. I thought they sang a song to Jerry."

HMONG SPIRIT-RELEASE CEREMONY CONTINUED

The family ritualist opens the bottle of wine and pours a drink for Jerry's spirit, to welcome him to his ceremony. He says, "Jerry, this is your first drink. You accept it, then you get it."[6] After Jerry accepts three drinks, the family ritualist "washes his face" and feeds him a snack.[7] Then the kheng player blows a song that says,

"Now that you have finished drinking and eating, we will take you to see the house for the last time."

The man who carries the spirit basket follows the kheng player back through the spirit gate. Going through the gate means that Jerry is entering the world of the living. The kheng player plays a "follow me" song while leading Jerry's spirit to the house where they will have his ceremony.[8]

The kheng player, the family ritualist, and the man carrying the spirit basket enter the house. Jerry's spirit is taken on a tour of the house before they set the basket on the small table, the "bed."[9] The kheng's song tells Jerry's spirit, "Now we have brought you back to the house. We bring you here to release any bad luck, all negative pressure and any bad spirits that continue to bother you. We send those things away so you can be free forever." This ceremony performance goes on for about an hour until the time when they give the cow to Jerry.

Mrs. NORMA HUGHES, Ovando rancher; friend of the Daniels family

That fellow with the long flute instrument, he played on that and danced around. It was an older man and he was up in front, doing this music. It was the same music both at the funeral and up here at the lake. Dancing around and playing. And those trinkets on that instrument, they were a-jingling as he was playing. It had spangles and decorations on it that jiggled and jingled. He'd go up and down with that and then dance over it and under it and around it. That was really impressive!

HMONG SPIRIT-RELEASE CEREMONY CONTINUED

Accompanied by the drum, a kheng song introduces then gives the live cow to Jerry's spirit while the family ritualist pours three drinks for him to accept. The cow is for Jerry to take with him to help with whatever he needs.[10] After he accepts the cow, the cow is told, "Cow, you will be slaughtered and cooked, and Jerry's spirit will eat the first meal." The ceremony breaks for at least two hours while the cow is killed, butchered, and cooked. During this time Jerry's spirit can relax while everyone helps to prepare the meal.

Conversation between NORMA and CHARLEY HUGHES, Ovando ranchers; friends of the Daniels family

NORMA: It was September twenty-fifth and the grass was tall and dry, and the Hmong had a fire going. The little kids had small birch sticks that they'd cut and they were sticking them in the fire and running around with them.

CHARLEY: Oh boy, that dry grass there could catch fire instantly. Well, I asked the kids to stop but they didn't pay any more attention to me than if I'd been talking to the moon, or if the dog had barked at 'em. So I got Moua Cha and I said, "You'd better stop those kids or they're gonna set fire and we'll be fightin' fire here because it's so dry." Fires can happen so quick and can spread so dang fast that a lot of times there's not much you can do about it. Moua Cha said something to them in their language and that was it—*snap!*—right now! There was no argument, no nothin'. Just one bark came out of him, and I'm telling you those sticks were put away. Not after a while, *now*. Which I was real thankful for.

KEITH "SKID" WOLFERMAN, smokejumper; friend of Deeder and Farrett Daniels

Usually in the fall in the Helmville-Ovando area you get that Indian summer weather. Warm and lazy afternoons, but crisp, hard, cold frosts in the night. The vegetation matures and cures out and becomes more of an underbrush. The leaves are your reds and yellows and the grass is brown and kind of brittle. 'Eighty-two was a slower fire season in Montana, but the twenty-fifth of September would probably be the peak of fire danger in a normal year.[11]

That day Farrett and I were fishing long enough to know the fish weren't biting. So Farrett said, "I'm gonna go check out what's goin' on over there." We were at some distance from the Hmong deal so it was the lure of the unknown. He didn't know what to expect after seeing how the cow was tied down in the truck, so he put down his fishing pole and went on over.

FARRETT DANIELS, nephew of Jerry Daniels; son of Kent Daniels

The Hmong had built several fires. They weren't fire pits, just fires out in the field. That's probably why Charley was freakin'. They had several different fires going, and all of them were cooking.

HMONG SPIRIT-RELEASE CEREMONY CONTINUED

Before the meal can be cooked the cow must be killed. The back of an ax is used to hit the cow's head. *Pung!* When the cow is dead, some people go into the forest to find leafy branches to put on the ground to hold the meat as the cow is butchered.[12] Everyone helps with the work, so a chunk of meat is given to each family to take home. Some people hang their meat in a tree to keep it clean since they will take the meat home raw, not cooked.

Conversation between NORMA and CHARLEY HUGHES, Ovando ranchers; friends of the Daniels family

NORMA: The Hmong were a-butchering this cow. It was primitive butchering. They just hacked chunks off, you know, and had chunks of that cow hanging in the trees, and they threw more chunks into a big pot over an open fire to boil. And there was blood all over the ground. When you cut a cow open there's lots of blood, but they were a-cooking that meat. Oh, you could smell that fresh-meat-butchered-kill smell. You could smell it.

CHARLEY: It just about gagged you, the smell.

NORMA: Meat should be left to hang and cool off for a while or it spoils in nothing flat. Charley and I age our meat for at least a week before we cut it up.

HMONG SPIRIT-RELEASE CEREMONY CONTINUED

As the cow is butchered, the meat is piled on top of the leafy branches so that it won't get dirty. Then it is boiled in large cooking pots or barbecued. Today the men do most of the cooking. The women help, but today it is the men's job to cut and cook the meat because most of the men were soldiers in Laos. This is their way to honor Mr. Jerry because the cow is a special gift for his spirit.

Hmong men and Jack Stratton gather for a group photo at the spirit-release ceremony for Jerry Daniels at Tupper Lake, September 25, 1982. "Lucky" Lue Yang collection.

FARRETT DANIELS, nephew of Jerry Daniels; son of Kent Daniels

What I couldn't understand was that they just lit the fires and threw hunks of meat on there. You know how you slice meat with the grain so it's the most optimum flavor and tenderness? If you cut it the wrong way every bite's going to be tough. Well, they just hacked at it. It was just *hack-hack-hack*. It didn't matter—*whack, hack*, with the grain, against the grain. There was no slicing of nice steaks. They took off chunks and threw 'em right on the fire, right on the burnin' logs. No racks, no sticks to hold it, just throw it on there so parts of the cow were burnt like charcoal and some of the wood and ashes were stuck on the meat. Throw it right on the fire instead of making a spit or a grill or sticking it on a stick and roasting it. It was not succulent, roasted food at all. Skid and I were thinking we're gonna eat fat on barbecued cow all day and we get there and it's inedible! If it was happening now I'd say, "Hey! Hey! Hey! Whoa! This is no good. There's no sense ruining this meat. Let's just slice it up nice. If you want to burn yours you can, but I'm cookin' mine like this."

HMONG SPIRIT-RELEASE CEREMONY CONTINUED

For a spirit-release ceremony only one real meal is prepared, one lunch with plenty of rice and meat. The food is not prepared for the purpose of making it as delicious as possible. It is cooked in a very simple way and served as part of the ceremony. After the meat is cooked, the family ritualist takes the first plate of food to Jerry's spirit. That cow was killed for Jerry, so his spirit must eat before everyone else eats.[13]

Mrs. NORMA HUGHES, Ovando rancher; friend of the Daniels family

We had no idea they were cooking the whole cow that morning, but they did. And here it was noontime or a little after and they're *eating* it. We didn't eat any of that cow because of the smell, so we took mostly out of our own food. I had made baked beans, and my mother fixed a salad of green vegetables. And probably the Hmong were just as skeptical about our type of food as we were of theirs!

CHA MOUA, Hmong friend; Hmong funeral organizer

That day I had the feeling the American guests didn't want to eat with us. For preparing meat, between the Hmong way and the American way, the American way is much better. But for the Hmong and the Laotians and people in all other countries that lack meat lockers or a cool place to hang meat, the faster you eat it the better. We just get the job done.

HMONG SPIRIT-RELEASE CEREMONY CONTINUED

After everyone finishes eating, the family ritualist introduces a bundle of paper spirit money [tshua ntawv vam sab] to Jerry. He says, "This is the last time we will bring you here, Jerry. Cha and Lucky give this bunch of money to you. If you have any debt, you pay your debt. If you don't have any debt, just take it with you and spend it on whatever you want." Jerry must accept the bundle, then the kheng player plays the burn-paper song [qeej hlawv ntawv] and the young people bow.

Cha and Lucky lay the bundle of spirit money on the ground in an open area where the grass has been cleared away. The bottom end of the bundle is lit, and no one touches it while it burns. When the fire goes out, whatever is left un-burned, that is the luck Jerry leaves behind. Jerry was very generous. He left a lot unburned, a piece maybe five inches long. Cha and Lucky cut that piece in half to split it between them. Everybody is happy and laughing, "Oh! Mr. Jerry loved you guys! He left a lot of money for you!" The ashes from the money bundle are not collected, but the part that is not burned will be kept by Cha and Lucky for good luck. That is the last gift from Jerry.

Mrs. NORMA HUGHES, Ovando rancher; friend of the Daniels family

They were going on quite awhile with this singsong chanting. And it runs in my mind that there were pieces of paper? There was something there that was supposed to be Jerry's and they set it a-fire. Just a little fire. But like I said, we didn't know the whole ritual of what was going on.

HMONG SPIRIT-RELEASE CEREMONY CONTINUED

After the bundle of spirit money is burned, people are happily shouting, "Now we are going to send you home, Mr. Jerry!" Everyone goes back into the house where the kheng player plays the leaving song [qeej sawv kev]. Nine drinks are poured and accepted by Jerry's spirit, then the family ritualist says, "Jerry, don't take any-body with you who came here today for your ceremony." The man picks up the spirit basket from the little bed and follows the kheng player, carrying the basket out of the house, then out through the spirit gate while the rest of the people watch. When Jerry's spirit basket is outside the gate, the kheng player finishes playing the leaving song. The arrow is shot from the crossbow; then the family ritualist takes the rice pastries out of the basket. He removes Jerry's shirt, undoes the cloth ball that served as the head, and pulls apart the arch frame.

The family ritualist offers a drink to Jerry's spirit. Jerry accepts his drink with the split bamboo pieces. Then the family ritualist pours the drink straight onto the ground because there's no longer a spirit basket to pour it into. He pours two more drinks and with the last one says, "Jerry, here's the third drink before we send you home. You have been here too long already. Accept this last drink and then go home!" Jerry's spirit accepts his drink, then the man who carried the spirit basket says, "Okay, it's time he leaves!"

It is time for Jerry's spirit to go. The man stands the empty basket on edge and pushes it so it rolls like a car tire. The basket rolls across the ground and falls face up, open. "No, he's not gone!" Jerry's spirit does not want to go. The family ritualist pours Jerry another three drinks and says, "You go home, Mr. Hog! Accept the drink, close your eyes, and go!" They roll the basket again. It rolls and falls face up a second time. He still won't go. Jerry's spirit is given three more drinks while the people watch and laugh. The family ritualist says, "Hurry up, Mr. Jerry! Close your eyes and go! If you don't go home, the ants will take over your house!" They roll again and this time the basket falls face down. Jerry's spirit accepts it, and he responds, "Okay, now I am gone." Everyone gives a big shout, and with that, all is finished. The ceremony is done for Mr. Jerry B. Daniels. His spirit is released forever.

End of Hmong spirit-release ceremony

Mrs. NORMA HUGHES, Ovando rancher; friend of the Daniels family

At the end they kicked or threw something, and if it landed a certain way that meant Jerry was happy and was going to heaven. What deciphered that he wasn't in heaven in the first place, how they knew that he hadn't gone, and then how they knew by the way this thing landed that he *had* gone, we don't know. And if that thing didn't land right, I don't know what would happen. I said to Charley, "I sure hope it lands right. Because if we've got to go through this again . . ." They wanted to get Jerry to heaven, and we were *all* hoping that thing landed right. And it did. And they just started hugging each other, laughing, shouting, jumping up and down. Jerry had gone to heaven! They were happy and, boy, were we glad that he made it!

KEITH "SKID" WOLFERMAN, smokejumper; friend of Deeder and Farrett Daniels

I couldn't see anything from where I was fishing, but I heard drumbeats and shouting. Farrett came back and said that the Hmong were really happy because everything turned out good. They told Farrett that this was the only time they'd ever had that type of ceremony for someone who was not their own culture. I thought that was cool.

Conversation between NORMA and CHARLEY HUGHES, Ovando ranchers; friends of the Daniels family

NORMA: We were there all day from the time it started. That party was different. Interesting! All the things we ever did with the Hmong were very interesting.

CHARLEY: I learned a lot, you know, as far as their doings. It was all really something. Jerry went to heaven, which we're all thankful for. And that was the end of that.

CHA MOUA, Hmong friend; Hmong funeral organizer

The whole funeral ceremony system was done for Jerry, and all the funeral performances met the customary standards. That responsibility was in my heart, and I wanted to do everything possible to make him pleased and satisfied with the way we performed the ceremony for him. I feel proud that Louise gave me the chance to do this for Jerry on behalf of his family. That makes me feel warm in my heart.

After the spirit release was over, did I feel better about the whole situation? Actually, not at all! We were not happy about doing this for Jerry and saying that he died. We still don't accept he's dead without seeing the actual body. And that's the whole thing. We did it because the American Embassy in Bangkok and the State Department insisted that he died and that the coffin represented his body. They completed his death certificate, so the ceremony had to go along with that. Whether it was true that he was dead, or only an echo of death, we *had* to do it. That is our responsibility and we did that from our heart, even if we still do not know how or even if he died.

Sometimes people feel very sad when we say the word "dead," but without seeing the actual body we also think, *What are we doing here?!* I talked to myself that way. Ha! Hmmmm.

HMONG SPIRIT-RELEASE CEREMONY, POSTSCRIPT

The spirit-release ceremony began at Tupper Lake about ten o'clock in the morning. By the time the ceremony is finished it is almost four o'clock in the afternoon. The Hmong quickly tear down the house, bed, and gate. The sticks that were used to make the arched form on the bamboo basket are thrown into the woods. The guts and bones of the cow are buried in a hole in the ground, although everyone suspects that bears probably will come and dig it up later. The crossbow is left hanging on a tree. Everyone finishes cleaning up and packing the food into the cars. By the time they get home to Missoula it is almost dark.

Central Intelligence Agency

Washington, D.C. 20505

18 August 2003

Jack T. Daniels, Ph.D.
948 Walden Pond Lane
Cortland, NY 13045

Reference: F-2003-00944

Dear Dr. Daniels:

  This acknowledges receipt of your letter dated 14 July 2003 concerning your 22 May 2003 Freedom of Information Act (FOIA) request for records pertaining to your late brother, **Jerrold Barker Daniels.**

  I regret that we are unable to assist you, but trust that you can appreciate the fact that this agency, which is responsible for the clandestine collection of foreign intelligence and the clandestine conduct of foreign intelligence operations, cannot confirm the existence or extent of information that would divulge the identity of an unacknowledged employee.

  Therefore, we must be consistent in our response to neither confirm nor deny the past or present affiliation of individuals with the CIA--unless their CIA affiliation already has been officially acknowledged. Section 6 of the CIA Act of 1949 exempts from disclosure "the organization, functions, names, official titles, salaries, or numbers of personnel employed by the Agency," and Section 103 (c)(6) of the National Security Act of 1947 requires the Director of Central Intelligence to protect information pertaining to intelligence sources from unauthorized disclosure.

  We regret that we could not be of greater assistance in this matter.

        Sincerely,

        Robert T. Herman
     Information and Privacy Coordinator

Interviewees

Daniel C. Arnold: former CIA chief of station, Laos. Mr. Arnold is now retired.

Jack Benton: former smokejumper [MSO 59]. After smokejumping, Jack served twenty-six years in the U.S. Army. He now spends winters in Florida fishing the backwaters and summers in Montana visiting friends, hiking, and enjoying the outdoors.

Mrs. Bao V. Bliaya: wife of Mouasu Bliaya. In 1971 Bao was the second Hmong girl to come to the United States and the first Hmong girl to graduate from an American high school. In October 1972 Mouasu and Bao's first son was the first Hmong born in the United States. Currently Bao is very happy being a grandmother.

Mouasu Bliaya: Hmong friend of Jerry Daniels. High school exchange student from Laos to the United States, 1967–74. Mouasu graduated from Hellgate High School in Missoula. In 1974 he graduated with a B.S. from the University of Montana. He and his wife were very close friends with Jerry's mother, Louise Daniels. Mouasu is a successful businessman in California.

Ms. Cecelia Christensen (formerly Mrs. Jack Stratton): friend of Louise Daniels. Cecelia works for the University of Montana in Missoula.

LaMonte "Chris" Christensen: former smokejumper [IDC '55]. After five years of smokejumping, Chris worked for the U.S. Forest Service as an administrative officer until transferring in July 1967 to the U.S. Public Health Service, Indian Health Service. He retired in November 1985 and lives in Silver City, New Mexico.

Bob Clifford: former funeral director at Mountain View Mortuary, Missoula. Now living in Santa Fe, New Mexico.

Deeder Daniels: nephew of Jerry Daniels; first son of Kent Daniels. Deeder calls himself a "saler and a logger," enjoying yard sales and logging onto the Internet. He lives near Missoula, is married, and has two sons.

Farrett Daniels: nephew of Jerry Daniels; second son of Kent Daniels. Farrett works in construction, installing underground utilities. He has one son, Talon, who is majoring in computer science at Montana State University, Bozeman. Farrett lives in Helena, Montana.

Jack Tupper Daniels: brother of Jerry Daniels; former smokejumper [MSO '54]; second son of Bob and Louise Daniels. Jack earned two Olympic medals and one world championship medal in modern pentathlon. He holds a Ph.D. in exercise physiology from the University of Wisconsin–Madison, has taught and coached extensively, and was the NCAA Division III Women's Cross-Country Coach of the Century. He has five books and over fifty scientific articles published. Jack and his wife live in Arizona.

Kent "Dan the Animal Man" Daniels: brother of Jerry Daniels; third son of Bob and Louise Daniels. Dan was the Montana state high school heavyweight wrestling champion in 1957 and Montana's sixteen-yard trapshooting champion in 1990. A former bartender and long-haul trucker, Dan and his wife are now teaching people to live healthier lives; they live south of Missoula in the Bitterroot Valley. Dan is the father of Deeder and Farrett Daniels.

Mrs. Nancy J. Daniels: wife of Jack Tupper Daniels; sister-in-law of Jerry Daniels. Nancy qualified for the 1988 U.S. Olympic marathon trials and won eight New England champion-
ships in track, 1981–83.

Mrs. Pat Dontigny: former Missoula County public health nurse. Missoula was the first town
to receive Hmong refugees for resettlement, and Pat was the first nurse to work extensively with Hmong new arrivals in the United States. She retired in 2001. She lives in
Missoula.

Gregg Elovich: legal aid to seniors coordinator, Central California Legal Services, Fresno,
California. Gregg has worked with the Southeast Asian community in Fresno for more
than twenty years as a disability rights advocate.

Rick Evans: former funeral director at Mountain View Mortuary, Missoula. Currently Rick is
the funeral director at Garden City Funeral Home in Missoula, Montana.

Jon Foland: Missoula crony; former smokejumper [MSO '68]. Known to many people as Jon
Jack, Jon was a smokejumper for twenty years. He is now retired from the U.S. Forest
Service and lives in Grangeville, Idaho.

Mrs. Moe Geary: wife of Helmville rancher Bill Geary. The Gearys are longtime friends of the
Daniels family. Bill is a fifth-generation rancher in Helmville, Montana.

Lee Gossett: former smokejumper [RDD '57]; former Air America kicker, 1964–65; former
Air America and Continental Air Services (CASI) fixed-wing pilot in Laos, 1966–72. Lee
lives in Oregon.

John R. Greenway: former Air America pilot, 1965–75. John was in Vietnam flying helicopters
and C-47s for six years; he was in Laos flying helicopters and Porters for four years. During his ten years of flying for Air America he carried 2,700 wounded and 270 dead. He
lives on Bainbridge Island, Washington.

Glenn F. Hale: former smokejumper [MYC '57]; former Continental Air Services (CASI) air
operations, MR3, Laos. Glenn worked for Intermountain Aviation in Marana, Arizona,
before he was the Continental Air Services (CASI) air operations "customer" in Savannakhet, Laos, 1966–68. Glenn returned to work for Intermountain at Marana until 1972.
He was a successful businessman in Arizona until he passed away in August 2010.

Ken Hessel: former smokejumper [MYC '58]. Ken was a smokejumper for five years and
worked at Intermountain Aviation in Marana, Arizona. In Laos he was the Continental
Air Services (CASI) air operations "Customer" in MR3 for five years, 1968–73. Ken returned to work at Marana until June 1975, then returned to work for the U.S. Forest
Service. He and his wife live in Oregon.

Xuwicha "Noi" Hiranprueck: best Thai friend of Jerry Daniels; organizer of the memorial
service in Bangkok for Jerry Daniels. Khun Xuwicha is a successful international businessman living in Bangkok, Thailand.

Charley Hughes: Ovando rancher and longtime friend of the Daniels family. Charley was a
pallbearer for Bob Daniels, Ronald "Danny" Daniels, and Jerry Daniels. Charley passed
away in June 2009.

Mrs. Norma Hughes: wife of Charley Hughes; Ovando rancher and longtime friend of the
Daniels family. Norma made the evergreen spray for the top of Jerry's casket. She continues to live on the family ranch in the log cabin house that her husband, Charley, built
with his father. *Author's note: If the state of Montana named "Living Treasures," Norma and
Charley Hughes should have been at the top of the list.*

Garry R. Jenkin: former communications officer, MR2, Laos. Garry was the last communications officer out of Long Cheng in 1974. He retired from the CIA after twenty years. After
more than ten years as a research analyst at Perot Systems, Garry now is a marketing

consultant working in marketing communications, computer graphics, and data visualization. His hobbies include photography, tennis, and yoga. He lives in Carrollton, Texas.

Bob Johnson: former Highland Lao Section chief, JVA, Thailand. In 1980 Bob worked with Jerry Daniels in the refugee program in Thailand. Currently he is the regional director of International Rescue Committee (IRC), Seattle, Washington.

Jeff Johnson: former Air America "runway guy"; Jeff's radio code name was "Yellow Hat." He was supervisor of facility development, opening and maintaining runway strips all over Laos, 1971–73. Jeff passed away in Bangkok, Thailand, in January 2005.

Thomas C. "Shep" Johnson: former smokejumper [MYC '56]; former aerial delivery specialist, MR2, Laos. Shep worked at Intermountain Aviation in Marana, Arizona, and for the CIA for fifteen years in Thailand, Laos, and elsewhere. From 1976 to 1982 he worked for the Bureau of Land Management (BLM) Interagency Fire Center helicopter operations in Boise. He retired from the BLM in 1990 and lives in Idaho.

Jack Knotts: former Air America and Bird Air helicopter pilot in Laos, 1969–75. Captain Knotts was the Jet Ranger helicopter pilot for the evacuation of General Vang Pao and Jerry Daniels from Long Cheng, Laos, in May 1975. He is retired and lives in Florida.

James W. "Bill" Lair: eventually became the CIA's deputy branch chief for Southeast Asia (Laos and Thailand). Mr. Lair was the key to forging a covert joint war venture in Laos between the CIA and General Vang Pao. Working simultaneously as a covert CIA paramilitary officer and as a legitimate officer in the Thai police force, Lair is acknowledged as the mastermind who created the Thai Police Aerial Resupply Unit (PARU). Bill lives in Texas.

Bill Le Count: former U.S. Air Force pilot until 1964; former Air America and Continental Air Services (CASI) pilot in Laos, 1964–69. Bill was a pilot for PSA for ten years, after which he was a nonscheduled pilot until retirement in 1998. He lives in Billings, Montana, and enjoys fishing.

Tim "Weeny Man" Lien: Missoula crony. Tim served in the 101st Army Airborne in Danang, Vietnam, 1969–71. In Missoula he worked for BFI as a dedicated "G-man," a garbage collector. At BFI he worked with "Ringman" and "Peterbuilt" Olsen. Tim is retired and now runs horse clinics and breaks horses in his spare time. Otherwise he can be found hunting and fishing. He lives in Missoula, Montana.

Ly Tou Pao: former colonel and chief of staff for SGU Army, Military Region 2, Laos, 1962–73; former commander of Xiengkhouang Subdivision, Laos, 1973–75. He lives in California.

Mrs. Patsy Skelton Lympus: wife of Ted O. Lympus; friend of Jerry Daniels. Patsy was born and raised in Missoula and attended the University of Montana. She and her husband, Ted, have two children and five grandchildren.

Ted O. "Little O" Lympus: friend of Jerry Daniels in high school and at the University of Montana in Missoula. Currently he is a district court judge in the Eleventh Judicial District, Flathead County, Montana.

Mike Lynch: provincial advisor in Laos, 1963–67. He worked with Jerry Daniels at Lima Site 36, Na Khang, Laos, 1965–67. He currently resides in Virginia and remains involved as an independent consultant assisting the U.S. government in assuring the security of overseas diplomatic installations. By coincidence, Mike is married to the former spouse of an RF-4 Phantom pilot who once prowled the skies over northern Laos.

Ms. Deirdre McNamer: former newspaper reporter for the *Missoulian*. Dee now teaches creative writing in the Department of English, University of Montana in Missoula. She has published four novels. Her most recent novel, *Red Rover*, won the 2007 Montana Book Award.

Mrs. Susie Lindbergh Miller: co-curator of the *Hmong Voices in Montana* exhibition at the Missoula Museum of the Arts, October 1992 to February 1993. Susie and her co-curators, Bounthavy Kiatoukaysy and Tou Yang, strove to present the material from the Hmong perspective, using Hmong voices. Susie lives in Arlee, Montana.

Mrs. Julie Daniels Moritz: sister-in-law of Jerry Daniels; first wife of Kent Daniels; mother of Deeder and Farrett Daniels. Julie passed away in Missoula in June 2003.

Cha Moua (also known as Moua Cha, Charlie Moua, and Chercha K. Moua): Hmong friend of Jerry Daniels. In Laos, Cha's radio code name was "Spider." He was one of the earliest Hmong to live in Missoula and became a very close friend of Louise Daniels. Cha was one of the organizers for Jerry's traditional Hmong funeral. He lives in Sacramento, California.

Chou Moua (also known as Moua Chou): older brother of Cha Moua and Pao K. Moua. In 1961 he joined the Special Guerrilla Unit in Vang Pao's army. He was an SGU army captain and later became chief of the forward air guides (FAGs) at Long Cheng, MR2, Laos. His radio code name was "Rainbow." Mr. Moua and his family have lived in Missoula since March 1976. In the summer he is a popular vendor of fresh flowers, fruits, and vegetables at the Missoula Farmers' Market.

Pao K. Moua: younger brother of Chou Moua and Cha Moua. Pao lives in Missoula where he and his family own and operate the popular Thai Spicy Restaurant. In the summer he also operates a mobile unit, cooking Asian food at special events throughout Montana. Pao enjoys fishing, hunting, camping, and horseback riding in the woods.

Larry Nelsen: former smokejumper [MSO '56]. Larry was a smokejumper for thirty years with more than 400 jumps. He lives in Missoula, loves retirement, and spends as much time as possible hunting, fishing, and going to the woods.

Robert H. Nicol: former smokejumper [MSO '52] and pilot. Bob served two and a half years in the Marine Corps. He started flying for a living in 1962 with Johnson Flying Service. He also has flown for Intermountain Aviation, Southern Air Transport, Interior Airways, Evergreen International, U.S. Forest Service, Empire Airways, and Leading Edge Aviation. While employed by the Forest Service he flew for many years as a lead plane pilot in the air tanker program. Bob retired from commercial flying in 2005. He lives in the Bitterroot Valley near Hamilton, Montana, where his family settled in 1862, twenty-seven years before Montana gained statehood.

Mrs. Dawn Oehlerich: wife of Mike Oehlerich; friend of Jerry Daniels. Dawn has been a Registered Investment Advisor for more than twenty years. She is an active conservationist.

Mike Oehlerich: former smokejumper [MSO '60]. Mike worked at Intermountain Aviation in Marana, Arizona, and as an Air America loadmaster in Thailand and Laos. Mike and his wife, Dawn, live in an energy-efficient straw bale house that Mike built in Whitefish, Montana. Mike continues to have an adventurous spirit and enjoys physical challenges.

Mrs. Kathy G. Olsen: wife of Loy "Ringman" Olsen. Kathy graduated from nursing school at Montana State University in Bozeman. She is an R.N. at St. Patrick Hospital in Missoula. Kathy is a quilter, a reader, a hunter, and a fisher who loves to go camping with family and friends.

Kurt "General" Olsen: Missoula crony. "General" was the oldest of the three Olsen brothers. He was a heavy equipment truck driver who lived for hunting and fishing. General passed away in Missoula in November 2007.

Loy "Ringman" Olsen: Missoula crony; brother of Kurt "General" Olsen. Like his brother Pete, "Ring" was a BFI sanitation engineer truck driver until retirement. "Ringman" and "Peterbilt" continue to enjoy their lifelong pleasures of hunting, fishing, and camping with family and friends. "Ringman," also known as "Butch," and his wife, Kathy, live in Missoula next door to "Peterbilt."

Randall "Peterbilt" Olsen: Missoula crony; brother of Kurt "General" Olsen. Pete served in the army in Vietnam, Forty-Seventh Combat Engineers, 1969–70. He was a BFI sanitation engineer truck driver until retirement. He lives in Missoula.

Barry Reed: former smokejumper [MSO '60]; former Air America loadmaster in Laos and Thailand, 1966–74. Barry worked for Missoula Job Service until retirement. He lives in Missoula and is an active volunteer in the community.

Ms. Berta J. Romero: caseworker/manager for Joint Voluntary Agency (JVA), Thailand; she was the founder of the first refugee women's project in Thailand. In the United States, Ms. Romero has continued her strong commitment to refugee protection. She serves on the board of directors for the Southeast Asian Resource Action Center (SEARAC). She lives in Maryland.

Mrs. Maosay Ly Saykao: mother of eleven children, many of whom are well known in the Hmong community and beyond. Mrs. Saykao lives in Fresno, California.

Jim Schill: former USAID Laos, Area Development Advisor, 1972–75; Jim was posted to and resided in Long Cheng, 1973–74. He was the U.S. Department of State Refugee Coordinator for Malaysia, Singapore, and Indonesia, 1978–84. He worked for the Bureau for Refugee Programs, Department of State, 1980–82. Jim retired from foreign service in 1995 but continues to serve in many posts overseas on short-term assignments. Between assignments he lives in California.

Randolph "Toby" Scott: former smokejumper [MYC '57]. Toby spent fifty-eight days with Jerry Daniels in the Bob Marshall Wilderness in western Montana. He worked as a loadmaster for Continental Air Services (CASI) in Vientiane, Laos, and later worked in communications in South Vietnam. After leaving Southeast Asia he ran a fishing camp convenience store for fifteen years at Inks Lake, Texas. Toby and his wife, Nancy, split their time between Texas and Montana.

Ms. Myra L. Shults: a "fair one" friend of Jerry Daniels from Missoula County High School. Myra was "in awe" of the entire Daniels clan at wrestling matches. Later she became especially close to Louise Daniels. In her past, Myra skied, flew airplanes, golfed, and gardened, but now prefers to buy her produce from the Hmong at the Missoula Farmers' Market. Myra has degrees in pharmacy and law. She is currently a land use attorney in Missoula.

Mrs. Mary Ellen Stubb: sexton, Missoula Cemetery. Mary Ellen has a degree in accounting; she has worked in county and city governments. She became the sexton at the Missoula Cemetery in 2003. Under her direction the historical tours and retelling of life stories have become an integral part of the cemetery and are highly anticipated events within the community. Mary Ellen devotes her personal time to her family.

Roger Waxeng Thao: electronics engineer and Hmong culture intellectual. After graduating from California State Polytechnic University–Pomona, Roger studied Hmong culture in depth. Since then he has served the Hmong community with great respect. He travels throughout California to participate in Hmong funeral rituals as *txiv xaiv* and in Hmong marriage rituals as *meej koob*. Roger lives with his family in Sacramento.

MacAlan Thompson: worked for IVS and USAID in Laos, 1966–75, including four years at different places in the north. He was deputy refugee coordinator in the U.S. Embassy, Bangkok, Thailand, for most of 1975–83. He retired from USAID in 1992 and lives just outside of Bangkok.

Thomas J. "T. J." Thompson: former smokejumper [MSO '55]; paratrooper with the 82nd and 101st Airborne Divisions; air delivery specialist, MR2, Laos; director, Air Delivery Operations, Airborne, Research and Development, and remote area training and training sites until retirement. T.J. worked extensively in India, Asia, Central America, Africa, and Europe. He lives in Texas, where he owns and operates Precision Parachute Recovery Systems, which develops, tests, and manufactures recovery systems for UAVs (unmanned aerial vehicles). He is acknowledged as a world-renowned parachute designer.

Lee "Terrible Torgy" Torgrimson: Missoula crony. Torgy was a good friend of Jerry Daniels since seventh grade. For many years he was a railroad engineer with the Burlington Northern Railroad, as well as an entrepreneur. Torgy had strong opinions, especially about politics. He passed away in Missoula in October 2007; his ashes were scattered throughout western Montana.

John W. Tucker: former U.S. Peace Corps volunteer, Thailand; former USAID Refugee Relief in Pakse and Savannakhet, Laos. In 1975–80 John was the ethnic affairs officer (EAO) for lowland Lao in the refugee program in Thailand. Later he worked in the Bureau for Refugee Programs, Department of State, Washington, DC, until 1983.

Bee Vang (also known as Vang Bee): former Hmong T-28 and Baron pilot in Laos; his radio code name was "Fackee." Vang Bee was one of the Hmong leaders at the Ban Vinai refugee camp in Thailand. After many years of living in North Carolina, he now lives in Minnesota.

Chu Vang: son of General Vang Pao; high school student in Hawaii, 1972–74. He and his wife lived in Missoula, 1978–83. Chu was a popular singer and entertainer at many Hmong events. He is now retired and a full-time grandfather. He and his wife currently live in Arizona.

Geu Vang (also known as Colonel Vang Geu): joined the Special Guerrilla Unit (SGU) army, MR2, Laos, in 1968 and rose to the rank of colonel. He is now retired and lives in North Carolina.

Mrs. Mary Mao Heu Vang: wife of Chu Vang; daughter-in-law of General Vang Pao. Mary has worked in the insurance industry for twenty years as a customer services / claims specialist.

Neng Vang (also known as Colonel Vang Neng): joined the Special Guerrilla Unit (SGU) army, MR2, Laos, and rose to the rank of lieutenant colonel. He fled to Thailand during the air evacuation of Long Cheng in May 1975. He was the Hmong camp leader in Ban Vinai refugee camp from September 1979 through December 1982. Neng Vang lives with five of his brothers and their families in North Carolina.

Nhia "Judy" Vang (also known as Vang Nhia and Nhiasu Vang): worked for Jerry Daniels as a field liaison officer (FLO), MR2, Laos; his radio code name was "Judy." Nhia was a telecommunications operator for USAID and for Jerry Daniels/Sky in Long Cheng. After coming to the United States, Nhia worked for twelve years as an insurance agent for New York Life, then as a computer technician until retirement in 2003. He lives in southern California and enjoys playing golf with friends.

Nhia Yang Vang: soldier with the French military in Laos beginning in 1953. Later he joined General Vang Pao's Special Guerrilla Unit army and became a first lieutenant. Nhia Yang escaped from Laos in 1980 and resettled in the United States in 1987. He lives in Fresno, California.

Thomas Tong Vang: Lycée student in Luang Prabang, Laos, when communist forces took over the country in May 1975. His family fled to Thailand a month later. In the refugee camps he worked as a Hmong interpreter for JVA caseworkers, Jerry Daniels, and INS officers. Thomas now lives in Sacramento, California, and works as a Hmong Health Project coordinator with the Southeast Asian Assistance Center.

Tou-Fu Vang: high school exchange student from Laos to the United States in 1963. Mr. Vang attended the University of Southern California from 1964 to 1966, and Iowa State University from 1966 to 1968, graduating with a B.S. in government and history. He returned to Laos as a bilingual teacher at Dong Dok University. In 1969 he was integrated into the Royal Lao Armed Forces (FAR), initially as a captain, and rose to the rank of lieutenant colonel in 1973. He returned to the United States in July 1975. Mr. Vang worked for the Department of Health and Human Services at the federal regional level for over twenty-nine years.

Shur V. Vangyi: high school exchange student from Laos to the United States, 1964–66; graduated in 1971 with a degree in marketing from the University of Hawaii. He returned to Laos and became deputy director for trade in the Ministry of Economy, Royal Lao Government, 1972–75. Mr. Vangyi was the national executive director, Lao Family Community Inc., Santa Ana, California, 1978–84. Currently he works in the Planning and Development Department, City of Fresno, California.

Doug Vincent: former U.S. Peace Corps volunteer in Thailand, 1975–78. Former caseworker for Joint Voluntary Agency (JVA), Thailand, from September 1979 to September 1990. Doug has an M.A. from Ohio University in Southeast Asian Area Studies. He has worked for the U.S. Immigration and Naturalization Service (INS) and is currently an intelligence analyst for the Department of Homeland Security, U.S. Citizenship and Immigration Services. He lives in southern California.

Mrs. Carol Leviton Wetterhahn: worked for the Intergovernmental Committee on European Migration (ICEM) as administrative officer for the U.S. Embassy Refugee Program, Bangkok office. Under contract with the International Rescue Committee (IRC) / Joint Voluntary Agency (JVA), she served as Highland Lao Section chief from 1979–80, and immigration caseworker / team leader from 1989 to 1993. Currently she is a substitute teacher in the Long Beach Unified School District in southern California.

Bob Whaley: former smokejumper [MSO '56]; lieutenant colonel, USMC (retired). Bob had three tours in Vietnam flying helicopters from 1962 to 1969, and the OV-10A reconnaissance/light attack aircraft in 1968–69. He is on the national board of directors of the USMC Combat Helicopter Association. He lives in Missoula, Montana.

Keith "Skid" Wolferman: smokejumper [MSO '91]; close friend of Deeder and Farrett Daniels, nephews of Jerry Daniels. Currently Keith is the parachute loft foreman at the Aerial Fire Depot smokejumper program in Missoula. In 2008 he participated in the U.S. Forest Service evaluation of RAM AIR parachutes for use in fire suppression. He is married with four children.

Chao Yang: former student in Moung Cha, Laos. Chao escaped from Laos to Thailand in March 1979. He came to the United States as a refugee in February 1980. For many years he was a field supervisor for Lao-Hmong Security Agency Inc. in California. Chao and his family now live in Alaska.

Koua Yang: former SGU soldier for General Vang Pao, MR2, Laos. Koua lives in Sacramento, California.

"Lucky" Lue Yang: worked for Jerry Daniels as a field liaison officer (FLO), MR2, Laos. Lucky was one of the organizers for Jerry's traditional Hmong funeral ceremony. He worked for over thirty years at Smurfit Stone Container Corp., a pulp mill, in the utility and recovery department control room. He is an avid outdoorsman who enjoys fishing and hunting. Lucky and his wife live in Missoula, Montana.

Mrs. Mary V. Yang (also known as Mayjoua V. Yang): wife of "Lucky" Lue Yang. Mary was a very close friend of Louise Daniels, mother of Jerry Daniels. Mary worked with the Refugee Assistance Corporation in Missoula for twenty years, 1980–2001.

Yang See: former liaison between Jerry Daniels/Sky and General Vang Pao/MR2 staff, Laos; his radio code name was "Glassman." Yang See was sponsored by Henry Kissinger and the U.S. Department of State as the first Hmong to come to the United States as a refugee. He and his family live in North St. Paul, Minnesota.

Prachuap Yangsa-ngobsuk: Thai-Hmong interpreter for JVA, Thailand, from January 1980 to April 1984. Khun Prachuap is a Thai citizen. For several years he worked as a programme officer for the United Nations High Commissioner for Refugees (UNHCR) Sub-Office Dadaab, in northeast Kenya near the Somalia border. He now works for UNHCR in Sri Lanka.

Notes

CHAPTER 1—DISCOVERY

1. NIACT means "night action," in that the duty officer must telephone the action officer regarding receipt of a telegram. If it is classified, the action officer needs to pick it up in person and take any action necessary.

2. The North Vietnamese had taken over South Vietnam and Cambodia and effectively controlled Laos since 1975. Thailand is bordered by Cambodia and Laos.

CHAPTER 2—SHOCK AND DISMAY

1. Sky was an informal name used for CIA personnel and operations during the war years in Laos.

2. "Expat," short for "expatriate," refers to all foreigners residing in a country not of their own nationality. In Thailand it usually meant Western residents; during the Vietnam War era it most often referred to Americans.

CHAPTER 3—LAOS, PART I: NA KHANG

1. Lima Site 36, Na Khang, was a vitally important outpost during the secret war in Laos. Located 60 miles south of the border with North Vietnam and 150 miles west of Hanoi, Na Khang was the most forward staging base for General Vang Pao and his SGU troops. LS 36 was the departure point for northern troop movements and for search-and-rescue teams trying to find downed U.S. air crews before they could be captured by enemy troops. It also functioned as a much-needed fuel depot for smaller aircraft and an operational base for protection of the top secret U.S. TACAN and TSQ-81 radar facility on Phou Pha Thi, LS 85, located approximately 35 air miles north of LS 36.

2. Ammunition and weapons clandestinely supplied by the CIA to General Vang Pao's Special Guerrilla Unit (SGU) troops.

3. "Sheepdipped" refers to USAF pilots who flew as forward air controllers (FACs) in Laos, a highly classified operation. Usually they were second-tour captains with considerable flight experience. Their call sign was "Raven." When their tour ended in Laos, they reentered the USAF.

4. By 1966 the three political/military factions in Laos were the U.S.-backed royalists/rightists, the communist Pathet Lao, and the neutralists. The neutralist troops based at Moung Hiem had come to a nonagression understanding with nearby communist forces. Consequently, the royalist soldiers and Thai PARU from Na Khang were not welcome at Moung Hiem since their presence could, and eventually did, draw a brutal communist attack. Moung Hiem was located nine miles northwest of Na Khang.

5. Moung Son is listed on the "Air Facilities Data—Laos" as Lima 59; Lima *Site* 59 is Phou Kouk, a completely different site. Moung Son was twenty-eight miles north of Moung Hiem and twenty-three miles south of the Lao border with North Vietnam.

6. Don Sjostrom was twenty-six years old when he died. His name is on the Wall of Honor in the lobby of the State Department in Washington, DC.

7. According to the CIA, there were 100,000 Pathet Lao and North Vietnamese troops in Laos in 1968. The loss of Na Khang on March 1, 1969, led to a substantial increase in dry season fighting for control of the Plain of Jars. In spite of massive air support by USAF air strikes and bombing runs made by modified T-28s flown by Hmong, Lao, and Raven pilots, Vang Pao's troops, already thinned

by losses, suffered 25 percent casualties in 1969. See Thomas L. Ahern, Jr., *Undercover Armies: CIA and Surrogate Warfare in Laos 1961–1973* (Washington, DC: Central Intelligence Agency, 2006).

CHAPTER 4—HOMETOWN FRIENDS

1. In 1977 Nan Borton was the Joint Voluntary Agency (JVA) representative in Thailand. In 1982 she was the executive director of International Voluntary Services (IVS). Hank Cushing had worked for USAID Vietnam. In 1982 he worked for the Department of State, Bureau for Refugee Programs, Washington, DC.

CHAPTER 5—MISSOULA HMONG

1. A cow ensures that there will be enough meat to feed all the visitors. In the United States, usually it is killed off-site and the meat is brought to the funeral home to be cooked. When all the fresh meat is delivered, one hind leg is given to the family ritualist [*txiv cuab tsav*], and three whole ribs are cut from the backbone and given to each kheng player [*txiv qeej*]. The kheng players are not paid any money for their services, but each of them gets three ribs of meat to take home.

CHAPTER 6—LAOS, PART II: LONG CHENG (1968–73)

1. In 1953 James W. "Bill" Lair, American CIA paramilitary officer in Thailand and also a Thai police officer, set up the recruitment and training program for the Police Aerial Resupply Unit (PARU) along the northern Thai-Lao border. The Thai PARU were well-trained five-man teams. In 1961 Lair armed 5,000 to 6,000 Hmong fighters in Laos in less than thirty days. He believes this feat was possible because the Thai PARU were able to access and blend into isolated villages in Laos for the purpose of recruiting and arming village men as an indigenous anticommunist force. In later years the Thai PARU directly supported Vang Pao's troops in Laos.

2. In September 1966 a TACAN navigational aid was installed on Phou Pha Thi, LS 85, a 5,800 foot mountain top in northern Laos. A TSQ-81 ground-directed radar bombing facility was operational on November 1, 1967. Located fifteen miles from the border between Laos and North Vietnam, it electronically guided USAF all-weather bombing attacks on North Vietnam and northern Laos. This remote site was protected on three sides by steep cliffs and hundreds of Vang Pao's SGU soldiers and Thai soldiers. On March 11, 1968, Lima Site 85 was lost in a fierce attack by NVA soldiers. Twelve Americans were killed or declared missing, along with many Hmong casualties. For a detailed and insightful account read Timothy N. Castle, *One Day Too Long* (New York: Columbia University Press, 1999).

3. According to the CIA's online document *Undercover Armies*, in mid-1968 there were approximately 100,000 NVA and Pathet Lao troops compared to 110,000 Royal Lao Army and Irregular (SGU) troops in Laos.

4. Richard Helms was director of Central Intelligence, 1966–73.

5. Lao Theung (Kmhmu) is a large ethnic minority group that lives at midslope elevations in Laos.

6. In 1969 there was intense fighting for the Plain of Jars. According to the CIA's online document *Undercover Armies*, General Vang Pao's troops had 25 percent casualties that year. NVA and Pathet Lao troops made steady gains.

7. G. McMurtrie Godley was U.S. ambassador to Laos from July 1969 until April 1973.

8. William H. Sullivan was U.S. ambassador to Laos from December 1964 until March 1969.

9. Burr Smith, code name "Mr. Clean." Clean was General Vang Pao's CIA case officer, 1966–68.

10. Three regiments of seasoned North Vietnamese Army troops with 130mm guns heavily attacked Long Cheng in January 1972. For several months enemy troops remained on Skyline Ridge above Long Cheng until they finally withdrew.

11. According to author Roger Warner, who has done extensive interviews with Bill Lair, "they" refers to "the entire U.S. policy apparatus in Laos—Shackley as CIA station chief, of course, but also the military attaches and the Vientiane embassy staff, which together in a loose gaggle were calling the shots" (personal correspondence with author).

12. When the rainy season started in late May or June 1972, General Vang Pao planned to retake the Plain of Jars in order to secure a buffer between Long Cheng and the communist troops. While some progress was made to regain the Plain, by the end of the rainy season the SGU troops had suffered very heavy losses from which they never recovered.

13. Colonel Moua Cher Pao was the tough commander at Bouamlong, LS 32. Bouamlong was a bowl-shaped valley located northeast of the Plain of Jars. The airstrip was inside the bowl, and defensive positions were sited on the surrounding hilltops. As government territory was lost, Bouamlong became an isolated military stronghold that was never overrun by enemy troops.

14. Jerry Daniels, General Vang Pao, and VP's party had arrived from Washington, DC, where Vang Pao met with Secretary of State Henry A. Kissinger to discuss U.S. support of Laos operations. In Washington Daniels attended a luncheon at the Pentagon; it was held in honor of General Vang Pao and given by the chairman of the Joint Chiefs of Staff.

CHAPTER 8—LAOS, PART III: THE FALL (1973–75)

1. After bitter negotiations, the Paris peace agreement was signed on January 27, 1973, by the North Vietnamese, the U.S. government, the Saigon government, and Viet Cong's National Liberation Front. The agreement did not include Laos. A separate ceasefire agreement was signed in Laos on February 22, 1973.

2. The chief of the Powatan tribe in the early 1600s was a major leader of the Indians in Virginia. His daughter, Pocahontas, saved the life of Captain James Smith from execution in 1607. There are alternative spellings of the name Chief Powatan.

3. In his book *Shooting at the Moon: The Story of America's Clandestine War in Laos* (Hanover, NH: Steerforth Press, 1998), Roger Warner wrote that in early April 1974 there was a huge parade and rally held when the Pathet Lao's Prince Souphanouvong entered Vientiane for the first time in a decade. Although enemies at war for the previous two decades, the procommunist Pathet Lao now were coming to Vientiane to help rule Laos as part of the new coalition government.

4. This gain included the important Sala Phou Khoun road junction approximately 100 miles northeast of Vientiane.

5. A C-130 piloted by Air America captain Matt Hoff, copiloted by Joe Burch.

CHAPTER 9—LAOS, PART IV: UPROOTED

1. Lyteck Lynhiavue was a young Hmong man who graduated in political science from a French university in the early 1970s. He returned to Laos with high hopes for a political office, and was a strong advocate for cooperation with the Pathet Lao in the new coalition government.

2. Susan Lindbergh Miller, Bounthavy Kiatoukaysy, and Tou Yang, eds., *Hmong Voices in Montana* (Missoula, MT: Missoula Museum of the Arts Foundation, 1992), 18. Reprinted with permission.

CHAPTER 10—COMING TOGETHER

1. Edgar "Pop" Buell was a retired Indiana farmer who went to work in Laos for International Voluntary Services (IVS) and USAID refugee relief from 1960 until 1974. Buell's main base was at Sam Thong, LS20. Blunt and caring, he was enormously popular with the hilltribe people. "Pop" Buell died from a heart attack in the Philippines on December 30, 1980.

2. Elder clothes [*tsoos laus*] are burial clothes that look like traditional Hmong clothing, but have never been worn. Generally, each married son prepares and gives one set of elder clothes to

each of his parents. A long funeral coat covers the elder clothes. The funeral coat is made from natural hemp cloth [*ntaub maj*] handwoven in Laos.

3. Hmong say a drum-keeping family "feeds the drum" [*nruas yug*]; they raise and take care of the drum spirit. In reality, to "feed" a drum means that they make and keep a drum. For those families, before they become drum keepers, someone in the family gets very sick. A shaman is called in and determines that they need to raise a drum in order for that person to get well and to protect the family in the future. That family then has to go and find a tree of the kind of wood recommended by the shaman. They cut down the tree to make the drum, then they raise the drum, generation after generation. If they do not continue to feed the drum, someone in the family will get sick again. Only those families have drums because drum keeping is a calling. A person or family cannot decide on its own to be a drum keeper. Hmong bring their belief in the drum spirit from China where they lived over 2,000 years ago.

4. The family ritualist [*txiv cuab tsav*] ties a narrow strip of red cloth around the wrist of each of the main participants: the funeral coordinator [*kav xwm*], kheng player [*txiv qeej*], and the food preparers [*tshwj kab* and *niam ua mov*]. In Laos the casket maker [*txiv txiag*] would also be included. After the family ritualist ties the strips of cloth, the funeral coordinator or some other elder ties a strip of red cloth around the wrist of the family ritualist.

5. Under normal circumstances when a body is present, the body is carried in on a litter of some sort and placed on the floor with feet facing into the room. Later in the ceremony the body is lifted up and placed into a casket. At that time the casket is turned to be parallel to the front wall.

CHAPTER 12—CONDOLENCES AND RUMORS

1. The man assigned to be in charge of the cash contributions [*thawj xyom cuab*] is the main person in the immediate family who can be trusted to oversee the money. In turn, he assigns two family members, usually young men, to sit at a table where one person counts the money and the other one writes down who gives how much of a contribution. When money is given in any amount, other family members will be called upon to say thank you [*ua tsaug*] to the giver. A typical thank-you would be, "Your coming to visit is already greatly appreciated. You also think of the close family relationship we have and give us a cash contribution to help with the funeral expenses. In the future, if my family members earn a good living, then one day your contribution will be returned to you. If my family members can't earn a good living, your contribution will disappear like a rain drop on the path. However, we will remember your contribution forever. Thank you for your contribution." While the thank-you words are said, a group of younger men from the family of the deceased gather in front of the giver, bow, kneel, touch their heads to the floor, then stand up again. The thank-you ritual is repeated for each money gift received.

Cash contributions usually are received before the burial but can be made on any day of the funeral, especially from guests who come from far away and arrive late.

2. Kue Chaw, radio code name "Bison," was a field liaison officer (FLO) who worked with Hog Daniels in Long Cheng, Military Region 2, Laos.

CHAPTER 13—FUNERAL CHANT PHASES 1, 2, 3, 4, 5: "SHOWING THE WAY"

1. Traditional Hmong believe each person has three spirits or souls [*plig*]. When someone passes away, that person's spirits stay near the deceased. For one spirit, the deceased passes away because a child, an animal or some other living thing is born at the same time. This belief is supported by the occasional occurrence in which one might see a pregnant woman in a village grow larger and larger, while at the same time another villager becomes sick and gets worse. If this situation is recognized in advance, a soul-calling [*hu plig*] ceremony may be held to call the soul back to the sick person. If the

soul returns, the sick person improves and the woman may miscarry. A second spirit will stay with the body and remain at the cemetery until there is a spirit-release ceremony [tso plig]. A third spirit will return to the ancestors and be born again into the same family. The job of the soul guider [txiv qhuab ke] is to communicate with the spirit that will return to the ancestors to be reborn.

2. The bamboo divining pieces [txhib ntawg] are made from one three- to four-inch segment of bamboo stalk split lengthwise. The curved side of the bamboo is the "back," and the flat side is the "face." The bamboo divining pieces are used only for funerals. They are a communication tool, like a telephone to the dead. To use them, the soul guider drops the two bamboo pieces onto a small table. The way the bamboo lands communicates yes and no answers from the spirit of the deceased. If the two faces are "closed," face down, that is a "no" communication. It means the spirit is sad or his eyes are shut or he doesn't understand. If the two faces are "open," face up, that means he is happy or willing to do a favor, but that is not the same as a "yes" communication. If both sides are closed or both sides are open, the soul guider tosses the bamboo pieces again. He will repeat his question until one face is closed and the other face is open, signifying acceptance. When the living and the dead communicate in this way, they are in harmony.

3. Roger Waxeng Thao, personal communication.

4. For the second drink the soul guider says, "This is still yours. Accept it, then you get it." The soul guider again drops the split bamboo pieces onto the table until the spirit of the deceased accepts the second drink. The soul guider repeats the same instructional poem, then pours another little bit of the second drink from the cup into the receiving bottle. When the second drink is done, the third drink is offered and accepted in the same way. The soul guider repeats the poem and pours the rest of the drink from the cup into the receiving bottle.

5. Roger Waxeng Thao, personal communication.

6. Jacques Lemoine, Kr'ua Ke, Showing the Way: A Hmong Initiation of the Dead, trans. Kenneth White (Bangkok: Pandora Press, 1983), 11–12.

7. In the Hmong creation story, Creator-God sent a flood to earth. When the flood came a brother and sister crawled into a big drum. The drum floated on muddy water and saved them. After the flood was over and the water went down, those two crawled out of the drum. They looked around, but they saw no other people. All the humans and animals were dead. Only the brother and sister were left. The brother's name was Nraug Oo and the sister's name was Nkauj Iab.

Seven years went by, and the brother and sister still could not find any people. They were lonely, so they decided to go up-in-the-sky [saum ntuj] to talk to Creator-God-Mother and Creator-God-Father [Puj Saub thiab Yawm Saub]. Up-in-the-sky is both heaven and hell. The brother and sister told Creator-God, "The earth was flooded and all humans and animals are dead. We are the only two left. We have been living alone for seven years. How are we going to create more people?" Creator-God told them, "Go back down to earth and each of you carry a rock up two different sides of a mountain, then let them roll down. If the two rocks roll down on two different sides of the mountain and land on top of each other, then you two have to marry so you can produce humans." The brother and sister went down to earth and each of them carried a rock up two different sides of a mountain. When the two rocks rolled down, they landed on top of each other, so the brother and sister married as Creator-God had told them to do.

The next poem says that the brother and sister plant crops so they can eat. They plant, but nothing grows because each day has nine suns and each night has nine moons. During the day the earth is very hot and dry. During the night it is dark and very cold. The brother and sister can barely survive, so again they go to see Creator-God. Creator-God tells them, "Go and ask Ya Yee [Yaj Yig] to bring his metal bow to shoot the suns. Go and ask Ya Youa [Yaj Yuam] to bring his brass bow to shoot the moons." The brother and sister do as they are told.

> *Ya Yee shoots the sun eight times.*
> *The sun goes down in eight pieces, only one sun left.*
> *Ya Youa shoots the moon eight times.*
> *The moon goes down in eight pieces, only one moon left.*
> *Sun is scared, it doesn't come out.*
> *Moon is afraid, it doesn't show up.*
> *The sky is dark and the earth is cold for seven years.*
>   (Roger Waxeng Thao, personal communication)

Now earth is all dark so the brother and sister ask Bull Cow to call the sun. Bull Cow bellows three times but the sun is afraid and it doesn't come out. Then they ask Stallion Horse to call the moon. Horse neighs three times but the moon is scared and it doesn't show up. The sister and brother again go to see Creator-God. They ask, "Who can call the sun and the moon to come up?" Creator-God says, "Go back to earth and find an animal with legs the size of a spoon's handle. That animal knows the life of the sky. Ask that animal to call the sun and the moon because that one knows how to communicate with them."

The sister and brother return to earth and search until they see Rooster. Rooster has legs the size of a spoon's handle. They ask Rooster to call the sun. Rooster crows three times and the sun comes up. Rooster crows three times and the moon comes up, shining at the horizon. The sky is bright again. In thanks, the brother and sister give Rooster a silver and gold comb for his feathers. Rooster doesn't know how to use the comb. He puts the back of the comb to his head with the teeth facing up toward the sun. That's why to this day Rooster wears a comb on his head.

The next poem says that the sister and brother have been married for seven years. Now they have two boy children. The younger boy's name is *Tub Ci Tuj* and the older boy's name is *Tub Tuj Nplug*. But the world still is not populated. When the boys are full grown with knowledge and skills, they want to survey the earth to see if it is wide enough to hold more humans. The boys see Miss Toad. They ask Miss Toad to survey the earth. Miss Toad has short legs and arms. She jumps three times and falls into the footprint of a cow, where she stays. Three days later the boys go back and ask Miss Toad, "You went to survey the sky and the earth. How wide is it?" Miss Toad says, "The sky is as narrow as the palm of your hand. The earth is as narrow as a cow's hoof. If you produce more humans and animals and they do not die, there will not be enough room on earth to hold them."

The boys are unhappy with Miss Toad's answer so they ask Black Eagle to survey the sky. Black Eagle flies out for three days and three nights, then returns. They ask Black Eagle, "How wide is the sky?"

Eagle says with a sigh:

> *The sky is huge.*
> *If men go there they will be able to build houses for miles on end.*
> *If spirits go there, they will find endless room to move about in.*
>   (Lemoine, *Kr'ua Ke*, 16.)

When the boys hear that from Black Eagle, they are very angry at Miss Toad. They hit Miss Toad with a cow-poop paddle and mortally wound her. Miss Toad cries out, "The sky and earth were created by me! I blew a bubble to create them. While I am alive, humans get old, but then they are young again. They get sick, but then they get well. They are born, but they do not die." Just before she dies she curses, "From today on, when humans and animals get old, they will not be young again. When they get sick, they will not get well. They will be born and they will die and follow the path of me, Miss Toad. From now on, humans, you will die and leave behind your parents, spouse, children, and cousins *forever!*"

8. Lemoine, *Kr'ua Ke*, 21–22.

9. In Hmong custom, a coffin is never built before someone dies. When a person dies in Laos, four or six people are appointed to go and find a special tree [*thwj suab*] to build the coffin. The wood from that tree will last a very long time and will not rot or be eaten by insects. The coffin makers chop down the tree and split the wood to make thick heavy boards to build the coffin.

10. Lemoine, *Kr'ua Ke*, 22.

11. After the rooster is presented, it's taken outside and killed, and its liver is cooked.

12. In Laos a Hmong funeral ceremony is held inside the family's house. The soul guider continues to sit next to the deceased while he talks about going to visit each house spirit. In the United States, the soul guider says all the same words even though the ceremony is held in a funeral home, not in the family's home.

13. Vincent K. Her, "Hmong Cosmology: Proposed Model, Preliminary Insights," *Hmong Studies Journal* 6 (2005): 12, http://www.hmongstudies.org/HmongStudiesJournal.

14. Ibid., 12–13.

15. In Laos a Hmong house has a small fireplace [*qhov-cub*] where the rice and the daily food for the family are cooked. Also there is a larger fireplace [*qhov-txo*] that is built up with earth so a large pan can be set on it. The large fireplace is used to cook the feed mash for the animals. It is also used to cook large amounts of food for people at large events.

16. Before the ceremony started, the soul guider cut paper to make the spirit money he will give to the spirit of the deceased. Each paper is the size of a Lao *kip* note, a little smaller than a dollar bill. This money can be used by the spirit of the deceased to pay for travel visas, entry permits, airplane tickets, gate fees, taxes, or any debts or other expenses the spirit encounters along the way.

17. If the soul guider doesn't have everything he needs, the dead person's spirit may get stuck somewhere. Other spirits will say, "Go back and complain to the person who sent you here." Then the spirit comes back and makes the soul guider sick. That's what a spirit does to get someone's attention—makes him sick and sicker. If the soul guider gets sick, he will call a shaman and the shaman will travel into the spirit world to find out what's wrong. "Oh! The reason you got sick is because so-and-so's spirit could not get to his ancestors. He came back to bother you to let you know." Then the soul guider has to send more spirit money to the deceased so he can pay for whatever he needs to free himself. When the spirit reaches the ancestors, the soul guider will get well. This is why the soul guider is well prepared with everything he needs to give to the spirit.

18. In Laos most Hmong houses have dirt floors that can be dug into. The birth shirt [*lub tsho menyuam*] for a boy is buried at the main post of the house. For a girl it is buried under the parents' bed.

19. Lemoine, *Kr'ua Ke*, 28–29.

CHAPTER 14—A WAY OF LIFE

1. "Drop Kick Me, Jesus, through the Goalposts of Life," *Bobby Bare Greatest Hits*, Bareworks Inc. Words and music by Paul Craft. This song made number seventeen on the U.S. country charts in 1976.

CHAPTER 15—FUNERAL CHANT PHASE 6: SIN CITY AND RODEOS

1. The soul guider instructs the spirit of the deceased, but the soul guider's own spirit [*plig*] will never go through the gates with the spirit of the deceased. In Hmong belief, if the soul guider walks through the gate, he will die.

2. When a person dies, Hmong say, "Eat paper, drink paper, finished" [*ntawv noj ntawv haus tas*]. It means that person's luck in this life has ended.

3. Patricia V. Symonds, *Calling in the Soul: Gender and the Cycle of Life in a Hmong Village* (Seattle: University of Washington Press, 2004), 230.

4. You may wish to be whatever you want—a rich person, a leader, an educated person. Some people are educated but still poor. Some can barely read or write but they are rich or have leadership qualities that people respect and follow. Some die young, so they ask for a paper to live longer in the next life. Those are examples of the different luck that each person brings with him or her when they are born.

5. Suck A Big Red Dick.

6. *Chaw qhau nyuj qhau nees.*

7. The instructional details for drinking from the bitter, salty pond [*pas dej iab pas dej daw*] vary depending on who trained the soul guider. Some soul guiders instruct the deceased to cup both hands together, only pretending to drink the water. Others instruct the deceased to say his/her mouth is bleeding so drinking is impossible. Some soul guiders believe that a deceased who drinks the water will not remember anything from the past life; if the deceased does not drink, perhaps something will be remembered.

8. The Powder River runs through southeast Montana and into Wyoming. "Powder River, Let 'er Buck!" is believed to have been coined on a cattle drive somewhere near Casper, Wyoming, in the 1890s. Later it was picked up as the battle cry of the 361st Infantry Regiment of the 91st Infantry Division.

CHAPTER 16—FUNERAL CHANT PHASE 7 AND KHENG PERFORMANCE

1. The umbrella is about twelve inches tall. The handle is wood and the skirt [*lub kaus ntawv*] is made from pleated bamboo paper. The soul guider makes this parasol ahead of time because he knows when he gets to this point in the ceremony he will need to have it.

2. Jacques Lemoine, *Kr'ua Ke, Showing the Way: A Hmong Initiation of the Dead*, trans. Kenneth White (Bangkok: Pandora Press, 1983), 31.

3. Ibid., 33.

4. The hemp-cloth sandals [*khau maj khau ntuag*] are only for the dead to wear.

5. Lemoine, *Kr'ua Ke*, 32.

6. In Laos the ball is made from hemp yarn. In the United States, hemp yarn is not readily available, so twine is used.

7. The crossbow [*rab hneev*] is a weapon the spirit can use if it is frightened. Sometimes the soul guider also gives a length of bamboo that can be used as a pipe to blow a warning. The crossbow and pipe are tools used for "fighting Chinese [*ntaus suav*]." When a spirit has to "fight Chinese," a black cloth is tied to the crossbow as a flag because the spirit needs to have its own flag. For Jerry Daniels, the soul guider gives the crossbow and arrow but not the bamboo pipe, which is optional.

8. Vincent K. Her, "Hmong Cosmology: Proposed Model, Preliminary Insights," *Hmong Studies Journal* 6 (2005): 19–20, http://www.hmongstudies.org/HmongStudiesJournal.

At this point the soul guider says, "When you come to the village, your rooster will crow. If their rooster answers, that is not your ancestors. If their rooster crows and your rooster answers, that is your ancestors. That is the home of your grandma and grandpa."

9. Lemoine, *Kr'ua Ke*, 35.

10. Ibid., 37.

11. Ibid., 40.

12. After the soul guider finishes showing the spirit of the deceased the way to his ancestors, his own soul has to return to earth. This is a dangerous time for him. In order to avoid any problems,

the family of the deceased gives the soul guider one live rooster, one cup of uncooked rice in a bowl with one boiled egg sitting on top of the rice, and one stick of incense stuck in the rice. The soul guider is told, "This rooster and egg is to call your spirit back. You take them." The soul guider will take the live rooster home and someone in his family will do a soul-calling ceremony [*hu plig*] for him. That is always done after the funeral chant is finished because if it isn't done, the soul guider may get sick. For the egg, the soul guider asks the senior family members of the deceased, "Do you want me to break the egg or not?" If they do not want to break the egg, then the deceased will still be able to see and communicate and remember all the people left behind. But if nobody objects, the soul guider breaks the egg so the spirit of the deceased is cut off from remembering his past life. Now he will totally forget everything and not remember who or what he left behind.

13. In Hmong culture, *quaj* is to cry in the normal way—for example, when a person is hurt or angry or very frustated and starts to cry. When a person cries the normal way, he or she cries but not with words. *Nyiav* is a different kind of crying. *Nyiav* expresses one's grief in words. It is a wailing sound, a keening, that's made only for the dead, and only on three occasions. The most common is when someone has died and people go to wail over the body. The second is when people go to the cemetery and wail at the grave. Third is when they wail at the spirit-release ceremony [*tso plig*]. They wail only on those three occasions because the emotional words used can be very disturbing to others when they hear them.

14. For Hmong funerals, the casket is always open and at least one family member stands at the casket to guard the body. Hmong believe that most people who come to the casket to visit the deceased are good people. However, there may be someone who wants to bring trouble to the grieving family. They may carry small bones or pieces of metal with them. When they come to show their love and cry over the body, they may secretly hide something in the clothing of the deceased. If there is anything in the casket that will not decompose (foreign matter, e.g., bone not from the deceased, metal), this will cause problems for the family in the future. The children left behind, and perhaps the following generation as well, will have sickness, won't heal properly, or will have some other problem. That is why the men in the family inspect the casket and check the clothing many times during the funeral ceremony.

15. During the kheng performance section, the order of songs played by the kheng may change from one funeral to the next. Once a kheng player learns the songs from his teacher, a master player, he can juggle the songs around and it doesn't matter much what order they are in.

16. The drummer is also a kheng player because he must be able to understand the language of the kheng in order to do the correct drumming. The style in which the funeral drum is played depends on what part of Laos the drummer is from and who his teacher was. In some parts of Laos, such as Sam Neua, the kheng and drum are played together for almost every song.

17. In spirit language the kheng "speaks" the words of the funeral chant, repeating almost everything said by the soul guider from beginning to end. Only a few things are left out: introducing the rooster, the food and drinks, and the travel from town to town. Otherwise, it repeats the same process, leading the spirit of the deceased to the ancestors.

18. Toward the end of "song for the end of life," ritual bowing [*xyom*] is done just before the kheng instructs the spirit of the deceased to go up-in-the-sky. Ritual bowing is done in order to receive good wishes from the deceased. A group of young people kneels or sits on the floor to listen to the kheng. When "good words" are played, the young people bow in acknowledgment. After that, the kheng sends on the spirit of the deceased.

19. In Laos two people who are not family members of the deceased go into the forest to cut down a tree to make the full-size "horse" carrier [*nees*]. In reality the "horse" carrier is wood boards tied together by strips of bamboo to form a litter on which to carry the body. In the spirit world the boards are perceived as a "horse" that carries the body. The "horse" carrier is brought to the house

where the funeral is being held. It is laid on the floor, and the kheng player steps on it to show the deceased that there's nothing to be afraid of.

In the United States there is a casket to hold and carry the body, so there is no physical need for the "horse" carrier. However, there still needs to be a "horse" to carry the spirit to the ancestors. To accomplish this, a small wood model of the "horse" carrier is made, twelve to fifteen inches long. Two people bring the model of the "horse" carrier into the funeral home where it is placed under the casket that holds the body, just as the full-size carrier would be placed under the body in Laos. For the spirit of the deceased, it is much better to have a "horse" to ride when he or she goes up-in-the-sky.

20. In Laos when the spirit of the deceased is invited to ride the "horse," the body of the deceased is moved onto the carrier. The carrier is raised up off the ground and turned ninety degrees to be parallel to the front wall of the house. This is when the family ritualist [*txiv cuab tsav*] pours drinks for the journey. Nine drinks for a man or seven drinks for a woman. There are only two times during the funeral ceremony when nine or seven drinks are poured. All other drinks are poured three times.

CHAPTER 17—TEARS IN MY BEER

1. *Npuas* means "hog" in the Hmong language.

CHAPTER 18—SILK STORIES

1. "Silk stories" are told whenever smokejumpers get together. Smokejumpers are experienced wildland firefighters who parachute from airplanes to remote, inaccessible areas where fires are burning. They are a tough, well-trained, and self-confident group. Of approximately 20,000 wildland firefighters in the United States, there are only 400 smokejumpers, almost all working in the western states and Alaska.

Designators for smokejumper bases are: Missoula, MT [MSO]; West Yellowstone, MT [WYS]; McCall, ID [MYC]; Grangeville, ID [GAC]; Idaho City, ID [IDC]; Boise, ID [BOI or NIFC]; Winthrop, WA [NCSB]; Redding, CA [RDD]; Redmond, OR [RAC]; Cave Junction, OR [CJ]; La Grande, OR [LGD]; Fairbanks, AK [FBX]; and Anchorage, AK [ANC].

2. A few years after this letter was written, parachuting to fight fire in remote areas was proven to be practical. Though still experimental, the first operational fire jump was made in 1940 out of Missoula, Montana.

3. Prostitution was legal in Silver City until Madam Millie's houses were shut down in 1968.

4. A pulaski is the wildland firefighter's main work tool, a combination of an axe and hoe. It was invented by Edward Pulaski, a Forest Service ranger.

5. During the 1960 fire season, Jerry Daniels made two refresher jumps and eighteen fire jumps: nine fire jumps in Region 3, Silver City, New Mexico; eight fire jumps in Region 1, Missoula, Montana; and one fire jump in Region 5, Shasta, California.

CHAPTER 19—KICKERS FOR THE CIA

1. Gar Thorsrud [MSO '46], Jack Wall [MSO '48], Lyle Grenager [MSO '48], Herman Ball [MSO '50], Wally Dobbins [MSO '47], Les Grenlin [MSO '46], Jonathan "LaVon" Scott [MYC '48], Glenn "Smitty" Smith [NCSB '40], and perhaps a few more.

2. Camp Hale was a training site located above 10,000 feet in an isolated area of the Colorado Rockies. Covert training of Tibetan guerrillas started there in 1957.

CHAPTER 21—"VISITING DAY"

1. According to the Hmong ritual system, the rooster liver that was cooked and fed to the spirit of the deceased on the first day of the funeral is not considered a meal. The rooster liver was fed to the spirit so his mind could understand the rooster's spirit language. Today the spirit of the deceased is served real meals [*laig dab*] taken from the food that has been prepared for the guests. Before the guests eat breakfast, lunch, or dinner, the family ritualist will take out one piece of well-cooked meat and one scoop of freshly cooked rice and put that on a plate to feed the spirit. For each meal the family ritualist will bring the food and pour three drinks of beer. He will toss the split bamboo pieces and ask the spirit, "Do you accept this?" The family ritualist will keep asking until one of the bamboo pieces is face up and one is face down, meaning, "Okay! I accept it." As long as the casket is in the funeral home, the spirit will be fed three meals per day, just like all the people attending the funeral.

2. In Laos the Hmong do not build this frame because funeral ceremonies are held inside a Hmong house. There they poke the branches that hold the spirit money into cracks between the top of the house wall and the slope of the roof.

3. A food gift for the spirit of the deceased is a small piece of cooked chicken liver and a small scoop of cooked rice. The visitor wraps the small meal and brings it along with one bottle of wine. In the United States, beer is often substituted for wine. Each visiting family group also brings a large basket of food: two boiled chickens, a large packet of cooked rice, and a bottle of wine. Again, in the United States, beer may be substituted for wine. The small meal is for the spirit of the deceased, and the big basket of food is for the family and their visitors.

4. The bundle of spirit money from the family ritualist is always the first gift and is considered to be the main gift. The family ritualist's bunch of spirit money hangs in the first position at the far left on the crossbeam; it is the starting point on the frame. While the family ritualist hangs his bundle of spirit money, someone else who knows the correct words informs the deceased that the family ritualist has brought him/her two boiled chickens, rice, and drink, which the spirit must accept using the split bamboo pieces. After the family ritualist, if the person who passed away was a man, the sister [*muam phauj*] who will later participate at the discussion table will give two boiled chickens, rice, and drink along with the second bundle of spirit money. The sister's bundle hangs just to the right of the family ritualist's bundle. These are the two most important gifts from the close relatives. In the third position will hang spirit money gifts from all married sisters-/brothers-in-law. Fourth will be the parents of daughters-in-law and sons-in-law [*cuas nyab cuas ntxhais*]. No more positions are assigned. Bundles of spirit money from everyone else can be added to any of the four main gifts.

5. According to Hmong custom, close family relatives prepare a special gift [*hauv qhua*] to bring to the funeral. Each special gift includes a small meal for the spirit of the deceased, a basket of two boiled chickens, rice and wine or beer for the family and visitors, and a bundle of spirit money. Close family relatives give spirit money to ensure that the spirit of the deceased will not be waylaid by other spirits when he/she travels up-in-the-sky. Family and friends on earth have spirit relatives up-in-the-sky that know the spirit of the newly deceased is coming. As the new spirit travels to the ancestors, the spirit relatives of family and friends will come to meet the new spirit along the way. They will ask, "Eh, you come here! Did anyone send something to me?" The spirit relatives already know if their human relatives gave money to the new arrival spirit. If the new arrival spirit says, "I don't have anything for you," and that is true, the spirit relatives know that already and they say, "Okay, never mind." If the new arrival says he has nothing for them but really he has it, the spirit relatives will know that, too, and will accuse him, saying, "No? Only lies! *Dag xwb!* I know you have something for me!" The spirit relatives will keep accusing him until he says, "Oh, yes! Here it is!" Their pestering stops only when he gives them the spirit money that was given to him on visiting

day by their relatives on earth. When the spirit relatives are satisfied, the new arrival spirit is free to go on.

Close family relatives prepare spirit money at home, then bring it with them to the funeral home on visiting day. To make the spirit money, several pieces of a special paper are folded together then punched to make round paper coins, or cut to make paper bills. To make the coins, two metal punches are used. One punch [*txheej txham*] is curved to make the round coin, and the other punch [*txheej xeeb*] has a sharp point that puts a hole in the center of the coin. That paper coin looks like the old Chinese copper coin that has a hole in the middle of it. A string runs through the holes in the coins to hang them. One piece of folded paper can make ten coins in one punch.

For the bills, the paper is folded and cut in long strips from the bottom almost to the top, but not all the way through the top. When all the long pieces of paper are unfolded and separated, the bundle becomes a large bunch of hanging paper. It looks like a white paper octopus that hangs down several feet. Sometimes folded silver and gold papers [*ntawv nyiaj ntawv kub*] are added to make it even more valuable.

Most visitors cut a sturdy tree branch and tie the bundle of spirit money to it so it is easier to carry. The branch with the hanging paper money and three sticks of incense are carried into the funeral home along with the gifts of food and drink. At the funeral home, each gift must be individually introduced to the spirit of the deceased. To introduce each visitor, the family ritualist uses that person's name and relationship title, such as, "Today your brother, Mr. So and So, really loves and cares for you. He and his family are here to see you and visit you. He brings you food and drink. Now I give you a drink from his bottle. You have to accept it, otherwise you won't get it." After the spirit accepts three drinks using the split bamboo pieces, the family ritualist says, "Since you accept the three drinks, next I will give you the food." If there are many close relatives, it can take a long time to individually introduce each of the visitors and their gifts. While the family ritualist makes the introductions, the bundles of spirit money are received by the funeral coordinator [*kav xwm*] and hung on the frame.

The family ritualist is the only one who communicates with the spirit using the split bamboo pieces. However, in the United States, some Hmong people also bring flowers, which is not a traditional Hmong custom. Flower gifts started after Hmong came to the United States as refugees. Visitors who bring flowers may say directly to the spirit, "In the past we never gave flowers, but now we are in America. Here we bring flowers to you so you can take them up-in-the-sky to decorate your new home." But for communication with the split bamboo pieces, only the family ritualist can do that.

6. These kheng songs are about how it is when parents die—the children will suffer, they will be orphans, there will be hardship. Each of the main visitors [*hauv qhua txooj*] may have their own kheng player come in and blow a particular song when they give their gifts [*hauv qhua*]. Sometimes instead of having their own kheng player, a main visitor asks a kheng player already there to play a certain song. If the kheng player is unsure of the song, he will ask the person, "Can you speak the words of the song first so I will know what words you want played?" After the person speaks the words, the kheng player, accompanied by the funeral drum, can blow the same tones so the kheng repeats the song to the spirits. For the rest of the visitors [*hauv qhua tab*], just general funeral songs are played on the kheng and drum.

7. The money gift from the immediate family [*tshua ntawv vam sab*] to the spirit of the deceased looks similar to the other bundles of spirit money except it is bigger and longer. Larger pieces of paper are used, and more pieces of paper are folded together. For the immediate family's bundle, the family ritualist uses the same procedure as with the other gifts of spirit money: three drinks are poured and accepted before the gift is introduced, the spirit of the deceased accepts the gift through the split bamboo pieces, then three more drinks are poured and accepted.

The money gift from the immediate family is for the spirit to start his new life. No other spirit will ask him for it; this is his personal capital. As long as he has paid all debts owed, he can use this money to do whatever he wants. For example, he can go shopping in the spirit world. Just as on Earth, there are all kinds of things for sale there.

The immediate family gift doesn't have to arrive at any particular time. When there is enough room, the funeral coordinator hangs the money gift from the immediate family separately from the other money gifts, either in front or in back of them.

8. A placer mine has gold in the surface dirt; it is not a mine where one digs a shaft.

9. On visiting day, often members of the family kneel down near the door. When the visitors come in, they lift up the family members and lead them to the casket so all of them can see the body and cry together: "Today our loved one has passed. . . ." If the family does not go to the casket and cry loudly that means they do not really love the one who died.

10. Poem-songs [*nkauj*] are optional. They can be completely skipped depending on the funeral schedule and whether a poem singer [*txiv nkauj*] is available or not. If poem-songs are included, the first one is *nkauj tu siav*, which is sung after the kheng plays the "song for the end of life [*qeej tu siav*]." Other poem-songs that may be included are: *nkauj tsa nees, nkauj tshais, nkauj su, nkauj hmo, nkauj hlawv ntawv,* and *nkauj sawv kev.*

11. On the last night before the burial day, a long table and chairs are set up in a different room of the funeral home. The purpose of this table is for the family to say thank you to all the helpers at the funeral, from the soul guider [*txiv qhuab ke*] who opened the funeral to all the visitors who brought gifts of food, drink, and bundles of spirit money.

12. After the thank-you table is finished there is a short break while another long table and chairs are set up right in front of the casket. This is the discussion table [*hais xim*] where there will be singing and discussion and remembrance speeches. Sometimes this takes all night long, depending on the family and on the rules of the funeral home.

The purpose of the discussion table is different from the thank-you table. Now it is to come and talk about the life of the person who passed away, and what he is leaving behind for his family. The discussion table is full of representatives [*kis*] of the main positions for that funeral. Each person who holds one of the main positions already has chosen someone knowledgeable to be their representative and do the necessary work. A person is chosen to be a representative because he knows how the traditional Hmong funeral system works, knows how to sing the proper songs, and knows how to speak correctly at the discussion table. After the discussion is done, everything is cleared off the table. Then a song is sung to the important elder asking him to flip the table over. The representative of the elder kicks the table *hard* and it falls over. Then the table and chairs are taken away.

13. Instructions and blessings has four sections. The first section is the general introduction about the man, how he lived, what he has done, where he was living. The second section talks about whatever he left behind for the family when he died. The third section teaches the children how to be good. For the third section, the representatives who sat at the discussion table now have the opportunity to lecture to the children that are left behind. This is their chance to instruct them on how to be a disciplined person, a good person, now that their close relative has passed away.

The rest of the evening is for the fourth section, when the moral messenger represents the deceased. Now he sings words that come from the deceased back to the family, especially to the young people. First he faces the deceased and says something like, "Leave your luck to me and I will pass it along to your family." Then he turns to the family and says, "[Your father, your mother] passed by and gave me these words that I give to you. This is what he or she said: 'All of you people live longer than me. You have to stay together as a group and help each other. Be hard working and behave right. Go to school, go to work. Don't steal, don't lie, don't be an adulterer, don't do bad things. Be open-minded. Keep your doors open so your family and friends can come visit. If any of you become leaders, don't squabble with each other. Help each other. Don't be jealous or you will fight among yourselves and will lose very quickly. I teach you correctly. If you don't listen, you will have bad luck for life.'" This is a lecture [*qhuab qhia*] with the deceased as the teacher.

The children and young people kneel or sit on the floor and listen to the instruction. They hold sticks of burning incense [*xyab*] between the palms of their hands in prayer position. The burning incense is the symbol that they pay attention and respect the deceased. For both blessings and admonitions, they acknowledge the message by ritual bowing [*xyom*], which is done by holding the incense and bowing their heads to the floor. After the moral messenger gives the blessings and warnings from the deceased he sings, "Now you have to go do business to make money. Go get an education so you can learn and succeed." Last he sings about the environment of the gravesite and how to look for a good place to bury the dead. Grave siting for Chinese is called *yin feng shui*; for Hmong it is called *looj meem*.

CHAPTER 22—MARANA

1. An employee was hired as "unwitting" and remained so until an extensive background check gave a positive security clearance, at which time he would either be let go or become a "witting" employee.

2. Leonard A. LeSchack, navy lieutenant, and James F. Smith, air force major. For a detailed account of this mission, see William M. Leary and Leonard A. LeSchack, *Project Coldfeet: Secret Mission to a Soviet Ice Station* (Annapolis, MD: Naval Institute Press, 1996).

3. NP8, North Pole 8, was a Soviet drifting research station.

4. On April 21, 2008, after more than forty-five years of silence, a ceremony was held at CIA headquarters in Langley, Virginia, at which members of the Coldfeet crew were awarded a Citation, Agency Seal Medal, and a signed copy of a painting titled "Seven Days in the Arctic: Project Coldfeet." The original painting by artist Keith Woodcock hangs in the CIA museum at Langley. Jack and Kent Daniels, Jerry's brothers, accepted his award. A 1962 report to the CIA stated that Operation Coldfeet produced intelligence "of very great value." See William M. Leary, "Robert Fulton's Skyhook and Operation Coldfeet," *Studies in Intelligence* (Central Intelligence Agency) 38, no. 5 (1995): 67–77.

Although not labeled as such, and with the Skyhook apparatus removed, the former Intermountain B-17 used in Project Coldfeet is on display at the Evergreen Aviation Museum near Portland, Oregon.

5. The Bob Marshall is 1.5 million acres of wilderness located in western Montana. It is named after Bob Marshall, a legendary forest ranger.

CHAPTER 23—A MAN'S MAN

1. Crawler and mallow is a method of fishing. A night crawler is put on a hook with a marshmallow, then the line is cast out. The marshmallow floats the hook off the bottom and also keeps the crawler on the hook. This is a relatively passive method of fishing that is looked at with disdain by "real" fishermen.

2. On October 1, 2005, a law banning open containers of alcohol while driving went into effect in Montana. This brought the state into compliance with federal regulations while causing a major cultural change for residents.

3. Roland "Big Andy" Anderson [MSO '51] was a former Missoula smokejumper. Jerry Daniels worked with Big Andy as a smokejumper, then at Intermountain Aviation in Marana, Arizona, and later in Thailand and Laos.

CHAPTER 25—FINAL GATHERING

1. The kheng player blows the lunch song [*qeej su*], the matching poem-song [*nkauj su*] is sung, then the spirit of the deceased is poured three more drinks, each of which he accepts through the split bamboo pieces. After he accepts his drinks his spirit is fed lunch.

2. The family ritualist uses the split bamboo pieces to ask the spirit to accept the *hauv qhua* money gifts. After the spirit accepts them, three more drinks are poured and accepted.

3. The burn-paper song [*nkauj hlawv ntawv*] is performed inside the funeral home. For this song the kheng and the poem singer [*txiv nkauj*] alternate. The singer sings a short poem, then stops while the kheng and drum repeat the same poem. Then the kheng and drum stop while the poem singer sings another short poem.

For Jerry Daniels, Kia Moua Thao takes on the role of the poem singer and sings the burn-paper song: "Your family and loved ones are giving you this spirit money. As humans we see it only as paper, but in the spirit world it is money. You take this money and use it to buy a good place to live, a good house in a good town. Whatever you need, you can use this money to buy it."

4. To burn the money gift from the immediate family [*tshua ntawv vam sab*], the bundle of papers is laid out on the ground and the bottom of the bundle, the tail end, is lit. It burns from the bottom up to the top, to the head of the bundle where all of the strings of paper are tied together. Many Hmong believe that if the whole bundle burns, then the person who died takes all the luck with him or her. Nobody says that out loud, but many people believe it in their minds and hearts. On the other hand, if the bundle burns and the fire goes out before it burns the head, that means there is some luck and good fortune that the spirit of the deceased is leaving behind for the family.

When the burning is finished, the ashes of the family money gift are gathered and put into a piece of paper that is then folded up. Usually the ashes are gathered by the sons; if there are no sons, they are gathered by the daughters. The folded paper is put into the casket and the deceased is informed, "Here is the money from your family." The part of the family money gift that does not burn is the luck that is divided and kept by the sons or daughters. In the case of Jerry Daniels, Cha Moua keeps the luck. All of the money gifts [*hauv qhua* and *vam sab*] must be burned before the casket can be moved out of the funeral home.

5. For the *haws plig* ritual, the family ritualist takes a pinch of a mixture that is in a small cup. The mixture is hemp string and a little piece of meat finely chopped together. As he passes a pinch over the head of each guest, he says a few words such as, "Soul come back! Do not follow the soul of the deceased!"

6. Nine drinks are poured for a man, seven drinks for a woman.

CHAPTER 26—LOUISE

1. John Barker was first cousin to the mother of Louise Daniels. John Barker and Louise Daniels were first cousins once removed.

2. According to Kent Daniels, "yick" was a term coined by Jerry Daniels in 1950 at Tupper Lake. It referred to the jerky darting motion of the dragonflies they saw there.

3. According to Kent Daniels, Louise Daniels never used any "bad words." Anything negative was put into a euphemism. "Ish" was used in place of a negative word.

4. Jerrold B. Daniels received (posthumously) the Distinguished Intelligence Medal on July 9, 1982. The citation that accompanies the medal reads: "In recognition of his outstanding service with the Central Intelligence Agency for more than seventeen years. His exceptional career was distinguished by professional excellence, true devotion to duty, and a unique ability to gain the respect and confidence of all with whom he came in contact. Mr. Daniels' calm and forceful leadership, often in the face of grave personal danger, reflected the highest standards of the Operations

Directorate and left a legacy for younger officers to emulate. He excelled in a career of accomplishment and dedication, becoming a true friend to a nation of people, and justly earned the respect and admiration of all those with whom he was associated. Mr. Daniels' superb performance upholds the finest traditions of the Federal service, reflecting the highest credit on himself and the Central Intelligence Agency."

5. In addition to the Distinguished Intelligence Medal, Jerrold B. Daniels was awarded by the CIA the Intelligence Medal of Merit for "meritorious service" and the Intelligence Star Medal for "courageous action." The Intelligence Star Medal is the second-highest medal awarded by the CIA for valor, and is considered to be the Agency equivalent to the military Silver Star.

CHAPTER 27—UNTIL HORSE GROWS HORNS

1. In Laos large stalks of bamboo would be cut to make torches for the daughters-in-law [*cuas nyab*] to carry when the "leaving song" is played on the kheng. The bamboo torches are about eighteen inches tall. To make the torches, the ends of two or three sticks of bamboo are pounded. When the shredded end is lit, the torch burns. The torch is a light that goes ahead of the spirit so the deceased can see the way to go. The daughters-in-law would carry torches and follow the kheng player out the door of the house, while pallbearers would follow carrying the body. For Hmong funerals in the United States, bamboo torches cannot be lit. Here each daughter-in-law carries two sticks of incense, lit or unlit.

2. Data from the National Weather Service in Missoula, Montana, shows May 10, 1982, was a cloudy day, cooler than normal. The local recorded high was 53 degrees and the average temperature was 46 degrees. A breeze blew from the southeast, which was unusual.

3. In Hmong custom, at the gravesite before any of the burial rituals take place, the men in the family would reopen the casket to check the body, the clothing, and the inside of the casket to make sure nothing (metal, bone, or anything that doesn't readily decompose) was dropped in there that would bring misfortune to the spirit of the deceased or to that person's family.

4. For the cut-clothes ritual, the family ritualist opens the casket and cuts slits all over the burial clothes and the hemp shoes of the deceased. Since the coffin holding Jerry Daniels cannot be opened, the family ritualist holds a big knife in his hand and says the words of the cut-clothes ritual while he pretends he is cutting the burial clothes and shoes.

The cut-clothes ritual goes back to when the Hmong lived in China. It originated in the days when the Hmong were fighting with the Chinese. Many Hmong soldiers died, and their families dressed the dead in good clothes to bury them. After the Hmong left the burial site, Chinese people who were very poor came at night to dig up the graves. They stole the good clothes and left the bodies to rot. The purpose for cutting the clothes is to disfigure the clothes in order to stop the grave robbers. When the family ritualist cuts the clothes he says, "Now you are going to go. If the Chinese want to steal your shirt, you say your shirt is torn. If the Chinese want to steal your pants, you say your pants are torn. If they are going to steal your shoes, you say your shoes are torn." Those are ancient words that have never changed. Hmong still refer to the Chinese people from long ago.

Over time, the cut-clothes ritual became a Hmong spiritual necessity as well. When the spirit of the deceased goes up-in-the-sky there may be some spirits there who are very poor and who may try to steal the burial clothes. So generation after generation the Hmong continue to cut the burial clothes so everyone will leave their dead alone.

5. In Hmong tradition, usually after someone is buried the guests go back to the family's house. Outside of the house a small fire is lit in some kind of container. In Laos sometimes the small fire is set on the path coming into the village; in the U.S. it is set a few feet from the front door. In front of the fire there is a large basin or bucket of fresh water. The idea is that each guest washes their hands

in the water, then dries their hands over the fire before going inside the house. This ritual washing, called "dry hands, dry feet" [*sub teg sub taws*], gets rid of anything negative coming from the cemetery before the guests enter the house.

After the guests come in and say a few words to the family, those who have other things they need to do may leave. For those who can stay with the family for awhile, a small dinner will be prepared. Everyone will eat and then go home.

CHAPTER 29—AN ECHO OF DEATH

1. To make the "house," the men put up two tall posts and string a rope between them. Then they put up four shorter sturdy sticks at the four corners and string ropes between the side sticks, marking a space about twenty feet by twenty feet. In Laos they would cover the frame of the roof with thatch. Since they don't have any thatch in Montana, they pull a roll of black plastic sheeting over the top to cover the "house." As soldiers in Laos, the Hmong men had made many of these simple shelters.

2. In Laos bamboo would be used to form the frame of a man's shoulders and arms because it is flexible. Bamboo can be bent into a curve to make it appear that the hands are clasped in front.

3. The drum is made from a white plastic bucket with heavy black plastic stretched across the top and secured. This is not the same drum that was used at the funeral. Every time a makeshift drum is made and used for a funeral or a spirit-release ceremony, the drum is dismantled immediately after the ceremony is over.

4. The kheng song says in spirit language, "Today we bring your spirit back to release all bad luck, all disease, anything obstructive that surrounds you. Today we bring you back to wash those obstructions away so you will be free to go wherever you want to go." In other words, be free to reincarnate and start a new life.

5. Before leaving the house, the family ritualist and the person carrying the flat basket follow the kheng player around the extended leg [*nceg nruas*] of the drum tripod. The family ritualist carries a bottle of wine and a cup because he will pour the drinks and talk to the spirit of the deceased. The three men make nine rounds, then walk from the house to the spirit gate.

6. For the funeral and the spirit release it is the same procedure: the family ritualist pours a drink, then tosses down the split bamboo pieces until the spirit of the deceased accepts it. For the spirit-release ceremony, after the drink is accepted the family ritualist pours the small cup of wine right into the basket next to the rice pastries. Since the basket is made from woven bamboo, the wine goes through the basket into the dirt.

7. The kheng player blows a song about washing the face [*rau dej ntxuav muag*]. There is a bowl of warm water and a new white washcloth. The family ritualist says, "Today we call you here. We wash your face, wash your hands and feet." He rinses the cloth in warm water, then wipes the cloth across the "face" of the turban ball that is used for the head. His actions always match his spoken words.

After washing the face, the kheng player plays a song about feeding the spirit. The family ritualist gives the spirit of the deceased one boiled egg with boiled rice soup. This snack is called a "hungry meal" [*noj kob tshaib*]. It is a quick bite eaten when someone has been away and arrives back very hungry. It is not considered to be a real meal. The family ritualist tells the spirit, "You have been gone for so long. Take this snack before we start the ceremony."

8. Outside the door of the "house" there is a little table with some liquor [*cawv*] and a cup. The kheng player and the person who carries the spirit basket must drink the liquor before entering the house, but before they drink they will say, "We are not sure if this liquor is good or bad. Maybe there is poison in this drink. You are the person inside. You taste it first!" For the ceremony for Jerry

Daniels, inside the house is Grandpa Chialong Moua. Chialong Moua drinks first, finishes his cup, then pours liquor for the two persons outside to drink. After that they start to talk.

The kheng player and the person carrying the spirit basket ask to come inside the house. The person inside, Chialong Moua, says, "Where are you from? We don't allow guests to come into our house because today we release the spirit of Jerry Daniels. *Peb tso plig Jerry hnub no.*" The two persons outside ask again. The inside person says, "You came in the long way. Did you see Jerry Daniels?" The kheng player answers, "Oh yes, we traveled all over the world. The way we came we saw Jerry Daniels on the trail. He has one cow and he's coming." Then the person inside says, "Oh, that's good. We gave one cow to him." But the person inside still does not allow them to come in. First the kheng player must sing a poem. Then the person inside sings a poem in response. They sing back and forth three or four times. Only then does the person inside ask the two men to come in.

When the kheng player and the man carrying the spirit basket come inside the house, the person inside says, "I see you carry the soul of Jerry Daniels. Did he ask you to say something to the family?" The kheng player says, "Yes, he said the family gave him a cow and he received it. And the paper money you gave to him, he got that, too. Jerry said whatever you gave to him, he will leave the same for the family—money or a cow or whatever. You will get the same as he got. You will have a good life, have good wishes, have good health!"

Inside the house, the man who carries the spirit basket hands it to Cha Moua and Lucky Yang because they represent the family. The spirit basket is carried to the little fireplace where the kheng informs the spirit that the three men will go around the fireplace nine times. The family ritualist and the man who carries the spirit basket follow the kheng player around the fireplace four times in one direction, then turn around and go back five times. They go around the fireplace nine times for a man, seven times for a woman. It is the same principle as nine drinks for a man and seven drinks for a woman during the "leaving" at the end of the funeral. When they go around the fireplace the words of the kheng are, "You have been gone too long. Now that you come to the house, you go around the fireplace to let the house spirit know that you have come back." As the three men go around the fireplace, the young people do ritual bowing [*xyom*] and many people cry.

9. In Hmong tradition, a special "bed" is made for this ceremony because the Hmong will kill a cow for the spirit of the deceased. When a cow is killed, the spirit basket cannot sit directly on the ground. Killing a cow gives great honor to the spirit, so the spirit basket has to be raised up and placed on the bed where the spirit will have more respect. The bed is located on the south side of the fireplace at the center of the house.

10. When they give the live cow to the spirit, one end of a piece of rope is tied around the neck of the cow and the other end is tied to a shirt sleeve, which acts as a hand. This way the end of the rope is held securely. Then the family ritualist introduces the spirit to the cow: "Today we bring you back to visit your home, your family, your loved ones. We love you and care for you and today we give you one cow [*tus nyuj*]. Now that your spirit is released from anything unlucky or unhappy, you can use your animal for whatever purpose you want. Please accept it." The family ritualist tosses down the two pieces of split bamboo. When the two pieces of bamboo land with one face up and one face down, that means the spirit accepts the cow. If the spirit doesn't accept it, the family ritualist will toss the bamboo pieces again and keep asking until it is accepted.

11. The weather report from the National Weather Service in Missoula, Montana, states that on September 25, 1982, Ovando had a high of seventy-six degrees, a low of thirty degrees, no precipitation.

12. The dead cow is laid on the grass. The hide is removed, and a hind leg is cut off. For Jerry's spirit release, the ceremony coordinator and the family ritualist agree that the meat belongs to everybody because all the people came to work that day. The leg meat is cut into enough pieces so that every family can take a piece home.

13. The family ritualist sits on a little stool in front of the spirit basket and introduces the meal: a well-done piece of meat, a big scoop of cooked rice, and beer. He talks to the spirit and drops the split bamboo pieces until the meal is accepted. When the family ritualist finishes feeding the spirit, he offers a cup of liquor to the kheng player and says, "I'm done feeding. Now you may play the breakfast and lunch songs [*qeej tshais, qeej su*]." The kheng player uses the spirit language of the kheng to repeat the action of introducing the meal to the spirit. When he finishes playing, all the guests may eat.

Terms, Places, People

HMONG words are *italicized* and marked [Hm]; Lao words are *italicized* and marked [L]; Thai words are *italicized* and marked [Th]; French words are *italicized* and marked [Fr]; English words are unmarked.

Agency: U.S. Central Intelligence Agency. See CIA.

Air America: CIA's proprietary airline that operated in Laos as the major supply vehicle for both military and civilian needs.

Alternate: name commonly used for Long Cheng air base by American pilots because of its designation as Lima Site 20-Alternate. See Long Cheng.

baci [L]: a well-wishing ceremony in which strings are tied on the recipient's wrist to give good wishes, blessings, and protection.

black or black ops: clandestine missions run by the CIA.

Bouamlong: Lima Site 32 (LS 32); Colonel Moua Cher Pao was the tough commander of this isolated base in northeast Laos.

C-130: Four-engine transport plane; largest transport plane that could land and take off at Long Cheng air base.

CASI: Continental Air Services Inc. CASI operated aircraft in Laos on a contractual basis hauling cargo and people, mostly for the CIA and USAID.

CIA: U.S. Central Intelligence Agency. Other terms referring to the CIA are the Agency, the Company, the Outfit, the Customer, and OGA (Other Governmental Agency); CIA case officers sometimes are referred to as operatives, advisors, handlers, or spooks.

Customer: CIA personnel on the ground who worked closely with American aircrews in Laos during the war years.

D and D: "drinkin' and drivin'," a term used by Jerry Daniels and his cronies.

Dean, John Gunther: U.S. ambassador to Thailand, 1981–85; U.S. ambassador to Cambodia, 1974–75; deputy chief of mission, Vientiane, Laos, 1972–74.

EAO: ethnic affairs officer, Department of State Refugee Program; a person with an extensive background and relationship with a particular ethnic group.

FAC: forward air controller. All Raven pilots were considered FACs and often called "Raven FAC." An English-speaking Hmong or Lao "backseater" would accompany the Raven FAC as a radio translator between the pilot and indigenous ground force commanders for the purpose of directing air strikes onto targets. The primary aircraft flown was the O-1 Birddog. In MR2 Laos all "backseaters" had the call sign "Robin."

FAG: forward air guide. Hmong radio operators on the ground who directed airplanes to targets.

FAR: *Forces Armées Royale* [Fr]; Royal Lao Army.

FLO: field liaison officer. English-speaking Hmong who worked directly for Jerry Daniels/Sky in MR2 Laos.

GM: *Groupement Mobile* [Fr]; Mobile Group. Three or four battalions of soldiers made one GM.

Helms, Richard: director of Central Intelligence, 1966–73.

Hmong: the largest of many highland hilltribe groups living in Laos. Hmong people also live in the mountains of China, northern Vietnam, and northern Thailand. After 1975, thousands of Hmong who had fought against communist troops in Laos came to the United States as political refugees.

Hog: radio code name used by Jerry Daniels during the war years in Laos.

Intermountain Aviation: a CIA proprietary set up for research and development of air delivery systems to be used in covert paramilitary air operations, primarily in Laos. Intermountain was located at Marana air base, thirty minutes northwest of Tucson, Arizona.

IRC: International Rescue Committee; an agency involved in refugee resettlement.

IVS: International Voluntary Service.

JVA: Joint Voluntary Agency. JVA contracted with the State Department to do in-country screening of refugee applicants.

karst: irregular limestone outcroppings common to northern Laos.

kheng: *qeej* [Hm]; Hmong multiple-reed bamboo musical instrument that can communicate with the spirit world through tonal "speaking."

kicker: loadmaster or air freight specialist, the term preferred by Air America. Kickers load and unload cargo on aircraft, "kicking" cargo out when air delivery is required. They spot drop zones, drop loads on target, and are flight radio operators.

L: Lima airfield; designation for airstrips generally large enough to accommodate a C-47.

LS: Lima Site; designation for aircraft landing sites used by smaller aircraft, often dirt strips in isolated areas.

loft: a parachute loft is a facility, usually a large building, used for the inspection, repair, and rigging (packing) of parachutes.

Long Cheng (Long Tieng): classified CIA air base and military town in northeast Laos; Military Region 2 headquarters of General Vang Pao; elevation at 3,120 feet with approximately a 4,000-foot all-weather airstrip. Also known as Alternate, 20-Alternate, LS 20A, and LS 98.

Marana: air base near Tucson, Arizona. See Intermountain Aviation.

Meo: generally considered to be a derogatory name for Hmong people. See Hmong.

MR: military region. There were five military regions in Laos; MR2 was located in northeast Laos (Xiengkhouang and Houa Phan Provinces) and was commanded by General Vang Pao. [See map of Laos (Map 1 on page 33).]

Neo Hom: United Lao National Liberation Front; a worldwide organization formed after 1975 by former Royal Lao Government political and military leaders for the purpose of launching a military resistance to overthrow the communist government in Laos.

NVA: North Vietnamese Army; Vietnamese communist troops.

nyiav [Hm]: a crying lament from a Hmong person or group used only for the dead; an eerie wailing sound to unaccustomed Western ears.

Ovando: small ranching town sixty-five miles northeast of Missoula, Montana. The Daniels family property at Tupper Lake is in the Ovando area.

PARU: Police Aerial Resupply Unit. Thai mobile military units that worked inside Laos in support of anticommunist troops; PARU training was designed and implemented in the 1950s by Bill Lair, CIA paramilitary officer.

PDJ: *Plaine des Jarres* [Fr]. The Plain of Jars is named for the large, prehistoric stone urns found there. The PDJ was a heavily contested area during the secret war in Laos.

Phou Pha Thi: Lima Site 85 (LS 85); 5,800-foot mountain in northeast Laos less than fifteen miles from North Vietnam; site of a top secret U.S. TACAN and TSQ-81 radar station.

While operational, many of the air strikes in North Vietnam were directed from Lima Site 85. LS 85 was lost in March 1968, along with twelve Americans working there, after a fierce and unanticipated attack by North Vietnamese commandos.

pitutsie: woman, in the terminology of Jerry Daniels.

PL: Pathet Lao; communist Lao forces.

qhuab ke [Hm]: central part of the Hmong funeral ceremony; a guided journey to the ancestors for the purpose of eventual reincarnation.

rigger: a person who repacks cargo parachutes, makes sure that the cargo is bundled together correctly, attaches packed parachutes to the prepared bundles, and confirms that the weight of the load is appropriate for the carrying capacity of the parachute.

RLG: Royal Lao Government; also referred to as Vientiane government, royalists, or right-side government.

Sam Thong: Lima Site 20 (LS 20); site of "Pop" Buell and his medical clinic/hospital as well as a USAID supply warehouse; located twelve miles north of Long Cheng.

SGU: Special Guerrilla Unit. Hmong soldiers loyal to General Vang Pao and the Royal Lao Government were the bulk of the SGU army during the war years in Laos, 1961–75. SGU troops were supported entirely by the CIA.

Sky: name coined by Jerry Daniels referring to CIA and all covert U.S. military advisors, intelligence officers, operations, buildings, and compounds in Laos, in particular the "Sky Compound" at Long Cheng. Sky referred to Jerry's home state of Montana, "Big Sky Country."

Smith, Burr: radio code name "Mr. Clean"; the bald-headed CIA paramilitary officer who was case officer to General Vang Pao prior to Jerry Daniels.

smokejumper: experienced and specially trained wildland firefighters who parachute from airplanes to remote, inaccessible areas where fires are burning.

snoose: chewing tobacco; a name borrowed from Norwegian loggers living in Montana and Idaho.

STOL: fixed-wing aircraft with the capability of short take-off and landing.

TACAN: Tactical Air Control And Navigation system. See Phou Pha Thi.

Takhli: a joint U.S.-Thai air base in west-central Thailand. During the Vietnam War, the USAF was the primary tenant on the base, utilizing most of the facilities.

tso plig [Hm]: Hmong spirit release ceremony.

T-28: single-engine two-seater airplane modified to become a fighter-bomber; effectively used by Hmong and Lao pilots during the secret war in Laos.

txhib ntawg [Hm]: a pair of split bamboo pieces used only by the family ritualist [*txiv cuab tsav*] to communicate with the spirit world at a traditional Hmong funeral or spirit release ceremony.

Udorn: large American air base in northeast Thailand; CIA headquarters for clandestine operations in Laos.

USAID: United States Agency for International Development; major supplier of food and basic household goods to refugees forced to move due to the circumstances of war.

VC: Viet Cong; Vietnamese communist troops.

Vientiane: administrative capital city of Laos. Vientiane is located on the Mekong River across from Sri Chiangmai, Nongkhai Province, Thailand.

volag: volunteer agency. After an individual or family is approved by Immigration (INS) for resettlement to the United States, a volag finds a sponsor and provides some funding to assist the sponsor with resettlement.

VP: initials referring to General Vang Pao, commander of Military Region 2 in Laos.

wat [Th]: Buddhist temple.

Ahern, Thomas L., Jr. "Undercover Armies: CIA and Surrogate Warfare in Laos, 1961–73." Center for the Study of Intelligence (Central Intelligence Agency). Washington, DC, 2006.

Bertrais, Yves, ed. *Kab Ke Pam Tuag: Cov Zaj.* Javouhey, French Guiana: Association Communauté Hmong, 1986.

Briggeman, Kim. "Too Many Secrets: Family Wants Answers to CIA Agent's Mysterious 1982 Death." *Missoulian* (MT), February 10, 2008, sec. A.

Castle, Timothy N. *At War in the Shadow of Vietnam: U.S. Military Aid to the Royal Lao Government, 1955–1975.* New York: Columbia University Press, 1993.

———. *One Day Too Long: Top Secret Site 85 and the Bombing of North Vietnam.* New York: Columbia University Press, 1999.

Cohen, Stan. *A Pictorial History of Smokejumping.* Missoula, MT: Pictorial Histories Publishing Co., 1983.

Conboy, Kenneth. *Shadow War: The CIA's Secret War in Laos.* Boulder, CO: Paladin Press, 1995.

Courtney, Don. ". . . And If You Find Out, I'll Have to Kill You." *Smokejumper Magazine* 26 (January 2000): 16–18.

———. "Quota of Luck." *Smithsonian Air and Space Magazine,* October/November 2002, 18, 20.

Crosby, Jackie. "To Speed the Journey Home." *Minneapolis* (MN) *Star Tribune,* November 8, 2004, A1.

Donner, Fred. "A Missoula Smokejumper Won the Second, Third, and Fourth Highest Medals of the Central Intelligence Agency: Jerry Daniels (Missoula 58–60) Remembered." *Smokejumper Magazine* 40 (July 2003): 24–27.

———. "Overland from China." *Foreign Service Journal* 62, no. 4 (April 1985): 38–40.

———. "Smokejumpers and the CIA: A Bibliography." *Smokejumper Magazine* 37 (October 2002): 32.

———. "These We Remember: Smokejumpers Who Died in Laos." *Smokejumper Magazine* 42 (January 2004): 30–31.

Evans, Max. *Madam Millie: Bordellos from Silver City to Ketchikan.* Albuquerque: University of New Mexico, 2002.

Falk, Catherine. "Upon Meeting the Ancestors: The Hmong Funeral Ritual in Asia and Australia." *Hmong Studies Journal* 1, no. 1 (1996), http://www.hmongstudies.org/HmongStudiesJournal.

Gup, Ted. *The Book of Honor: The Secret Lives and Deaths of CIA Operatives.* New York: Anchor Books, 2000.

Hamilton-Merritt, Jane. *Tragic Mountains: The Hmong, the Americans, and the Secret Wars for Laos, 1942–1992.* Bloomington: Indiana University Press, 1993.

Heimbach, Ernest E., comp. *White Hmong-English Dictionary.* Data Paper: Number 75. Linguistics Series IV, published by Cornell University Southeast Asia Program, Ithaca, NY, August 1969.

Her, Vincent K. "Hmong Cosmology: Proposed Model, Preliminary Insights." *Hmong Studies Journal* 6 (2005), http://www.hmongstudies.org/HmongStudiesJournal.

Hessel, Ken. "Smokejumping/Forest Fire Fighting." Interview by Troy Reeves. Transcript OH #1465. Idaho Oral History Center, Idaho State Historical Society. Boise, Idaho, 2001.

Holober, Frank. *Raiders of the China Coast: CIA Covert Operations during the Korean War.* Naval Institute Special Warfare Series. Annapolis, MD: Naval Institute Press, 1999.

Hurst, Randle. *The Smokejumper.* Caldwell, ID: Caxton Printers, 1966.

Kuhn, Ernest C. Interview by Arthur J. Dommen, March 25, 1995. The Foreign Affairs Oral History Collection of the Association for Diplomatic Studies and Training, 1998.

Laird, Thomas. *Into Tibet: The CIA's First Atomic Spy and His Secret Expedition to Lhasa.* New York: Grove Press, 2002.

Leary, William M. "Robert Fulton's Skyhook and Operation Coldfeet." *Studies in Intelligence* (Central Intelligence Agency) 38, no. 5 (1995): 67–77; https://www.cia.gov/library/center-for-the-study-of-intelligence/kent-csi/vol38no5/html/v38i5a11p.htm.

———, and Leonard A. LeSchack. *Project Coldfeet: Secret Mission to a Soviet Ice Station.* Naval Institute Special Warfare Series. Annapolis, MD: Naval Institute Press, 1996.

Lemoine, Jacques. *Kr'ua Ke, Showing the Way: A Hmong Initiation of the Dead.* Translated by Kenneth White. Bangkok: Pandora Press, 1983.

Long, James, and Lauren Cowen. "CIA Recruited Smokejumpers for Duty in Laos." *Oregonian,* August 15, 1988, sec. A.

Maclean, Norman. *A River Runs through It.* Chicago: University of Chicago Press, 1976.

———. *Young Men and Fire.* Chicago: University of Chicago Press, 1992.

McKibben, Brian. *English-White Hmong Dictionary, Phau Txhais Lus Askiv-Hmoob Dawb.* Provo, UT: n.p., 1993.

McNamer, M. Megan. "Musical Change and Change in Music: Implications for Hmong Identity." In *The Hmong World 1.* Edited by Brenda Johns and David Strecker, 137–63. New Haven, CT: Yale Southeast Asia Studies, 1986.

Miller, Susan Lindbergh. "Traditional Costumes of the Lao Hmong Refugees in Montana: A Study of Cultural Continuity and Change." MA thesis, University of Montana, 1988.

———, Bounthavy Kiatoukaysy, and Tou Yang, eds. *Hmong Voices in Montana.* Missoula, MT: Missoula Museum of the Arts Foundation, 1993.

Morrison, Gayle L. "The Hmong Qeej: Speaking to the Spirit World." *Hmong Studies Journal* 2, no. 1 (1997), http://www.hmongstudies.org/HmongStudiesJournal.

———. "'Poor Old George' (An Interview with Bob Nicol)." *Smokejumper Magazine* 71 (January 2011): 24–25.

———. *Sky Is Falling: An Oral History of the CIA's Evacuation of the Hmong from Laos.* Jefferson, NC: McFarland & Co., 1999.

Murray, John Q. "Members of Missoula Elite Unit Recruited for CIA Mission to Taiwan." *Smokejumper Magazine* 49 (October 2005): 9–11.

Parker, James E., Jr. *Codename Mule: Fighting the Secret War in Laos for the CIA.* Naval Institute Special Warfare Series. Annapolis, MD: Naval Institute Press, 1995.

Ray, Ellen. "Mystery in Bangkok: Yellow Rain Skeptic Found Dead." *Covert Action Information Bulletin* 17 (Summer 1982): 43–46.

Ronk, Don. "The Legend of Long Cheng: War's End Unveils a Forbidden Valley." *Asia Magazine* (*Bangkok Post*), April 21, 1974.

Scott, Toby. "Project Coldfeet." *Smokejumper Magazine* 67 (January 2010): 13–15.

Smith, Steve. *The Ox: Profile of a Legendary Montana Saloon.* Missoula, MT: Pictorial Histories Publishing Co., 1983.

Symonds, Patricia V. *Calling in the Soul: Gender and the Cycle of Life in a Hmong Village.* Seattle: University of Washington Press, 2004.

Tapp, Nicholas. "Qha Ke (Guiding the Way) from the Hmong Ntsu of China, 1943." *Hmong Studies Journal* 9 (2008), http://www.hmongstudies.org/HmongStudiesJournal.

Thao, Roger Waxeng. Hmong funeral system notes, personal communication, 2005–11.

Warner, Roger. *Shooting at the Moon: The Story of America's Clandestine War in Laos.* Hanover, NH: Steerforth Press, 1998.

Yang, Kao Kalia. *The Latehomecomer: A Hmong Family Memoir.* Minneapolis, MN: Coffee House Press, 2008.

Page numbers in *italic* indicate diagrams or photographs.

Gayle L. Morrison has worked with the Hmong community since 1977 in education, refugee services, private enterprise, and as an oral historian, researcher and writer. Her first book was *Sky Is Falling: An Oral History of the CIA's Evacuation of the Hmong from Laos (1999)*. Based on the quality of her oral history research, she received a fellowship from the National Endowment for the Humanities (NEH) in 2003–2004. She lives in Santa Ana, California, and Missoula, Montana.